ACTA UNIVERSITATIS UP...
Studia Historica Upsalie...
213

Utgivna av
Historiska institutionen vid Uppsala universitet
genom Torkel Jansson, Jan Lindegren och Maria Ågren

Leos Müller

Consuls, Corsairs, and Commerce

The Swedish Consular Service and Long-distance Shipping, 1720–1815

UPPSALA
UNIVERSITET

ABSTRACT

Müller, L. 2004: Consuls, Corsairs, and Commerce. The Swedish Consular Service and Long-distance Shipping, 1720–1815. Acta Universitatis Upsaliensis. *Studia Historica Upsaliensia 213.* 268 pp. ISBN 91-554-6003-8.

Eighteenth-century Swedish consuls played an important role in the establishment of Sweden's trade links with the Mediterranean and, after 1780, with the 'West Indies' – the latter including the young American republic. However, historians have paid scant attention to their role. *Consuls, Corsairs, and Commerce* attempts to fill this gap. The consular service is analysed as part of an institutional framework, helping to reduce the transaction costs of Swedish actors in long-distance trade and shipping.

The book focuses on the establishment of the Swedish consular service in two specific areas: the Mediterranean after 1720, and the United States after 1783, and it links the establishment of the service to Sweden's ambitious contemporary commercial policy.

Special attention is paid to the growth in Swedish shipping activities. Traditionally, its growth in the eighteenth century has been associated with protectionism, as embodied in the Swedish Navigation Act (1724). *Consuls, Corsairs, and Commerce* instead focuses on the role of the consular service, in particular in reducing the threat from North-African corsairs, and on the role of Sweden's neutrality in the late eighteenth century. The book argues that neutrality was a crucial factor in the growth of Swedish shipping in the course of the wars between the great powers.

ISSN 0081-6531
ISBN 91-554-6003-8

Boken utges med stöd från Sjöhistoriska samfundet och Sune Örtendahls stiftelse och ingår i Forum navales skriftserie som nr 10 med ISBN 91-974015-8-7.

Typesetting: Uppsala University, Electronic Publishing Centre
Printed in Sweden by Elanders Gotab, Stockholm 2004
Distributor: Uppsala University Library, Box 510, SE-751 20 Uppsala
E-mail: acta@ub.uu.se
Web: www.uu.se
urn:nbn:se:uu:diva-4550 (http://urn.kb.se/resolve?urn:nbn:se:uu:diva-4550)

To Eva

Contents

Illustrations, tables, figures, and abbreviations

Illustrations

Tables

Figures

Abbreviations

BoT SNA Board of Trade, Swedish National Archives (Kommerskollegium, Huvudarkivet, Riksarkivet Stockholm)

SNA Swedish National Archives (Riksarkivet Stockholm)

SOIK Swedish East India Company (Svenska Ostindiska Kompaniet)

UUL Uppsala University Library (Uppsala universitetsbibliotek)

d.s.m. dollar silver money (daler silvermynt)

d.c.m. dollar copper money (daler kopparmynt)

rdr bko riksdaler banko

rdr rgs riksdaler riksgäld

SBL Svenskt biografiskt lexikon

St Bart St. Barthélemy

Acknowledgments

The idea of a book on the role of consuls in Swedish eighteenth-century shipping and trade dates back to the period of my dissertation. However, the actual researching and composition first became possible when, in 2000, I received a three-year grant from the Swedish Research Council. The Council has also covered a substantial part of the costs of printing, and of the extensive language editing required for this book. The Swedish Society for Maritime History (*Sjö-historiska samfundet*) also covered part of the printing costs. I would like to express my gratitude for this financial support.

Financial support is an important matter, but grants do not help greatly without intellectual inspiration, encouragement and—not least—debate with people sharing the same interests. Here I owe my greatest debts to Professor Jan Glete (Stockholm), Jari Ojala (Jyväskylä), and Dan H. Andersen (Copenhagen). Readers will notice that their works have had a significant influence on the perspective presented in this book. They also read and commented extensively on preliminary versions of the manuscript. In addition, Dan H. Andersen was helpful in providing me with many less accessible Danish works.

Together with Jari Ojala, we wrote a paper on the Nordic consular service, presented at a conference in Hull in 2001 and at the XIII Economic History Congress in Buenos Aires 2002. Even if this book presents a partially different perspective on the consular service, I owe a real debt of gratitude for Jari's cooperation. Another piece of the research, a preliminary study of Swedish transatlantic connections after 1780, was presented at the III International Congress of Maritime History (2000) in Esbjerg, and appeared in the International Journal of Maritime History. I am grateful to all who commented on my paper.

I must also thank many others who read and commented on the manuscript, or helped in other ways to improve or complete it. In particular I am indebted to: Professor Stellan Dahlgren, Hanna Hodacs, Professor Torkel Jansson, Professor Yrjö Kaukiainen, Stefan Lundblad, Professor John J. McCusker, Steve Murdoch, Anders Nordström, Pierrick Pourchasse, Göran Rydén, Xavier Labat Saint-Vincent, Louis Sicking, and Carmel Vassallo.

In the course of the years that I have spent with this project, I have worked, first, in Mitthögskolan, Östersund, as a Lecturer in history, and since 2001 in the Baltic and East European Graduate School, Södertörn University College in Stockholm, as a Research Associate. In Mitthögskolan I presented the first ideas for the project and I received many stimulating responses from both my colleagues and students. I am especially grateful to the students, who forced me to look at the subject from a different perspective. I also owe a substantial debt to Svenbjörn Kilander, with whom I have often discussed the topic of Swedish consuls. The Baltic and East European Graduate School provided me with an accommodating and supportive environment. I wish especially to thank Professor David Gaunt, Lena Arvidson, and Nina Cajhamre, whose support made the completion of this project easier in many ways.

Additionally, I am deeply indebted to Dr. Damon Hager for the language correction of the book. With English as my third language (after my native Czech and my second language, Swedish) it became his task to polish my text, and render my reasoning clear and comprehensible.

Finally, my greatest thanks go to my family: my wife Eva, and our daughters Klara, Sara, and Kristyna. Without them, and especially without their endless patience with my moods, this book would never have seen daylight. My family has always been a harbour of departure and return in my historical adventures, a place confirming that, in addition to the allure of Swedish consuls, Spanish and French privateers, Barbary corsairs—and of course pirates of the Caribbean—there are also other, even more important things worth returning to.

I have accumulated many other debts during the last four years. Historical works are never solely the result of solitary writing and sedentary archival research—even if some seem to believe that. Historical books are very much—and probably more than works of other genres—collective products. However, this statement is not the author's way of seeking to elude responsibility for the final product. I alone am responsible for any remaining errors and shortcomings that the reader may find.

L. M. May 2004

CHAPTER 1

Introduction

Hee that commaunds the sea, commaunds the trade, and hee that is Lord of the
trade of the world is Lord of the wealth of the worlde.

Sir Walter Raleigh[1]

1.1 Why study eighteenth-century Swedish consuls?

The Cinderella service—this is how the historian Desmond C.M. Platt has
described the British consular service in his outline of its history since 1825; an
ironic way of illustrating the discrepancy between humble consuls and high-
level diplomats.[2] It is clear that the same social gap separated the Swedish consuls from their more upper-class colleagues at the Department of Foreign Affairs. While high-level diplomats were recruited from Sweden's aristocratic circles, consuls generally had, by contrast, relatively modest mercantile back-
grounds. And while grand issues of foreign policy preoccupied career diplomats; consuls helped shipmasters to pay port duties in Lisbon or Livorno, or
mailed the latest issues of price currents from New York. Consuls did not make
important political decisions, and did not participate in the political game at
Stockholm—with some notable exceptions.

Indeed, historians have seldom considered consuls as significant and interesting actors; this perhaps is the reason why the history of the consular service has
received such limited attention in Sweden's diplomatic history.[3] The only historical context in which the Swedish consular service has been studied more
deeply centres on the break-up of the union between Sweden and Norway in
1905. In the 1890s, the conflict concerning appointments of Swedish-Norwegian consuls and the organization of the consular service became a serious

---

[1] Padfield 1999, p. 2.
[2] See Platt 1971.
[3] For general reviews see Jägerskiöld 1957; Tunberg 1935, for consular service specifically see
Almqvist 1912–13.

threat to relations between the two states, and is usually seen as the primary cause of the end of the Scandinavian union.[4]

One of the aims of this study is to redress this limited perspective. With the help of new theoretical tools, and via a combination of diplomatic and economic history, I will examine the role that the Swedish consular service played between 1720 and 1815.

The starting point of the study, the 1720s, marks the traditional turning point in Sweden's history. By 1718–21, Sweden had lost its great power status, and political interest shifted from military to commercial priorities; in a way, the active economic policy of the 1720s and 1730s was a substitute for military expansion. The Mediterranean and the Iberian Peninsula played an important role in this new policy. This region was interesting from the point of Swedish commercial expansion but, at the same time, was an area where the Swedes lacked established contacts. The establishment of the consular service was a putative solution to this problem.

Southern Europe, in particular, is an interesting area from other points of view: for example, Sweden's semi-diplomatic relations with the North-African states, and the active role of Swedish shipping in the endemic warfare in the Mediterranean. In the established accounts of Swedish trade with southern Europe, the commodity exchange has received major attention; shipping, on the other hand, has been seen as a necessary, but not especially profitable or unprofitable complement.[5] Because of its own Navigation Act, so the argument runs, Sweden had to build up sufficient shipping capacity to enable the country to carry its exports and import salt and other southern-European commodities. In contrast, I will argue that shipping and commodity exchange complemented each other in a rather complex way; in fact, in specific situations the commodity exchange might be a less profitable complement to highly profitable shipping. Therefore, in the first case study (chapters 3, 4, and 5), much more attention than in previous research will be paid to Swedish shipping and its relationship to commodity trade.

The concluding point of this case study is the end of the Napoleonic Wars. After 1815, the Mediterranean and the Iberian Peninsula lost much of their importance in Sweden's shipping and trade. On the one hand, this might be explained by the lost basis of neutrality for Sweden's shipping after 1815. On the other hand, different geographical areas, in particular the Baltic and Britain, reappeared as leading areas of trade growth.

The second case study (chapters 6 and 7) concerns the establishment of the Swedish consular service in the United States, and Swedish transatlantic trade and shipping after 1783. There are two important reasons for this choice. First, the establishment of transatlantic contacts in the 1780s followed the same policy as the establishment of the consular service in southern Europe after 1720;

---

[4] There is an extensive literature on the subject of the union's dissolution; see, for example, Weibull 1962; Boberg 1968; Nilsson 2000; Eliaeson and Björk 2000.
[5] Heckscher 1940; Högberg 1964; Högberg 1969.

in addition, Swedish transatlantic shipping developed as an extension of Swedish shipping in southern Europe. Hence, we may investigate whether these twin policies entailed the same results. Second, after 1800, the US became one of Sweden's major trading partners, due to the rapid expansion of Swedish iron exports to North America, and a key question is whether the early-established consular contacts played a role in that process. In particular, the focus will be on the relationship between consuls' economic functions and the development of Sweden's transatlantic trade and shipping.

The major focus of the whole book is on the period between 1721, the year of the Russo-Swedish Peace after the Great Northern War, and 1815, the year of the Congress of Vienna, which ended the extended period of Franco-British warfare. The period 1721–1815 also marks those years in which Sweden could fully employ the strategy of neutrality shipping.

This study has two major purposes. The first is descriptive. I aim to show why and how the Swedish consular service was established in these two specific areas and how it functioned. The second purpose is more analytical; to relate the establishment of the consular service to the issue of neutrality shipping and, at a theoretical level, to the question of protection costs and the productivity of Swedish shipping.

The book focuses on only two, rather specific cases of interaction between the consular service and the development of Swedish trade and shipping, and in additon, addresses these cases over a rather limited period. It is a legitimite question to ask why I have not examined the history of the Swedish consular service up to the year 1906, when it was reorganised in a very different way. In addition to the motives mentioned above, there is also a quite practical reason. The consular archives of the Swedish Board of Trade, the major source here, contain a vast volume of consular reports, especially reports concerning the nineteenth century and reports from the big commercial centres such as London, Amsterdam or Hamburg.[6] It has not been possible to explore this material comprehensively, in the available time and with the available means. Quite simply, I found it more valuable to concentrate on the two selected cases, and to study them in depth.

How to study Swedish consuls? The creation of the Swedish consular service was a part of the state-building process in Sweden, and one way to study consuls is to write an administrative history of the service. There is indeed such a study, written by Johan Axel Almqvist. It provides a detailed account of the consular service between the mid-seventeenth century and the administrative reform of 1906, including data about specific consulates and consuls.[7] How-

---

[6] The list of all Swedish consulates until 1906 (in Appendix A) provides some impression of the amount of the reporting. Parallel, some consuls sent reports to the Department of Foreign Affairs, see Diplomatica Collections in SNA (Portugallica, Turcica, Tripolitana, Tunisica, Algerica and Maroccana). With exception of the collection Americana, these reports have not been exploited in this study.
[7] Almqvist 1912–13.

ever, it is a typical administrative history. It does not set the consular service in the broad context of Sweden's economic policy, nor of the long-term historical developments connected to it.

The rising number of consulates dating from the beginning of the eighteenth century can also be perceived as an aspect of the process of bureaucratisation. This is the approach used by Stefan Håkansson in his study of the Swedish consular service, although focusing on a much later period (1906–21).[8]

Another way of placing the consular service in the context of the state-building process is to approach it from a neo-institutional perspective; to examine the consular service as a formal institution. For example, many consular duties might be comprised in the concept of transaction costs, the key concept of neo-institutional economic theory. First, consuls collected business information (on prices, market situations, business opportunities, etc.) and forwarded it either to the sending state authorities, the Board of Trade in Sweden (*Kommerskollegium*), or directly to economic actors, hence affecting information asymmetries between actors of the sending state and foreigners. Second, they also assisted subjects of the sending state in handling contacts with local authorities and business partners in their district, hence reducing costs for contract enforcement. Third, they affected the 'protection costs' of the sending state's subjects, by informing them of risks, and taking measures to diminish such risks. They frequently represented absent shipowners at court when a ship or cargo was declared a prize. Due to their semi-diplomatic status, they might directly affect the security of commerce and shipping (for example, by the negotiation of peace treaties with, and the forwarding of gifts to, the North-African rulers). Thus, the consular service might be seen as a formal institution that externalised and tentatively diminished the transaction costs of actors engaged in Sweden's foreign trade and shipping.

Another aspect of the institutional approach is to see the consular service as a typical 'mercantilist' institution. The express purpose of the consular service was to promote trade between Sweden and the receiving country, which was also a typical task of mercantilist policy. As the Swedish consular service was established as a component of the new protectionist trade policy after 1718, it must be perceived in the context of other measures of that same policy: for example, the Swedish Navigation Act, the protection of domestic industries, and the establishment of chartered trading companies. Overall, the neo-institutional perspective appears to be the more fruitful method of conceptualising the consular service, so it will be to the fore here.

---

[8] Håkansson 1989. Håkansson's study concerns with transformation of the Swedish consular service after 1905, after the dissolution of the union between Sweden and Norway.

1.2 Protection costs and Swedish neutrality shipping

The concept of transaction costs is useful in seeing the consular service as a general phenomenon. All national consular services aimed to reduce information, contract and other costs. In this sense, the Venetian consular service had no different function to the French, English or Swedish. From a specifically Swedish point of view, the concept of protection costs is especially valuable. The present writer's hypothesis is that Sweden benefited comparatively more from its lower protection costs than other, even more highly developed maritime states, and that these low protection costs were the single most significant factor in the growth of Swedish shipping in the late eighteenth century.

The eighteenth century was a century of warfare. The period 1689–1815 is sometimes referred to as the Second Hundred Years War.[9] Sweden, in spite of its traditional alliance with France, was successful in remaining outside many eighteenth-century conflicts, and this neutrality made the Swedish flag more secure, consequently diminishing the protection costs of Swedish shipping.[10]

Yet it is also important to underline the relative nature of Sweden's neutrality. Britain and the other naval powers of the period either did, or did not, recognize third party neutrality, depending on their own interests; therefore the interpretation of neutrality was under permanent dispute among the states concerned, and many Swedish ships and cargoes were seized in spite of declared neutral status. In the end, neutral status depended on British goodwill.

Looking at the consular service via a protection-costs perspective reveals it as primarily an institution created for the needs of shipping. There were, of course, other functions (notarial duties and state service), but from the economic point of view, the issue of shipping is crucial. The fact that until the mid-nineteenth century nearly all Swedish consulates were established at seaports confirms the significance of shipping.[11]

Between the sixteenth and the mid-nineteenth centuries sea transport and the dominance of the seas played a crucial economic and political role. With the introduction of the ocean-going sailing ship about 1500, the seaborne trade expanded. Shipping was generally the cheapest and fastest means of transportation goods and people over large distances. However, with the increasing importance of seaborne trade, states' concerns about the control of sealines of communication increased in parallel. Sir Walter Raleigh's statement, quoted at the beginning of this chapter, would be valid for the British—and not only British—view of the relationship between naval force and commerce for three

---

[9] McCusker and Menard 1985, p. 366; McCusker 1997, p. 316; Bonney 1995, p. 320 (see also the note).
[10] Generally on the use of neutrality in early modern Sweden see af Malmborg 2001, pp. 28–44.
[11] There are some few exceptions, Russian towns and Vienna in the seventeenth and eighteenth centuries. From about 1840 a number of inland German towns got consuls: Frankfurt, Berlin, Dresden, Leipzig and others. Yet this new policy of appointing inland consuls was also marking the end of period when seaborne trade had dominated international exchange. see Table 4.1 and Appendix A.

hundred years. Between 1700 and 1900, Great Britain exerted an efficient naval mastery over the seas, and its expanding trade and shipping went hand in hand with this dominance.

The Scandinavian countries did not stand aloof. Despite their peripheral location and remote distance from the European economic core, Sweden, as well as Denmark-Norway, became involved in early modern commercial expansion. The reason was not only the western-European demand for Baltic commodities, but also the Scandinavians' access to the seas. Without the possibility of sea transport, neither Swedish iron, nor Finnish tar and pitch nor Norwegian timber would have reached the Amsterdam and London markets.

Long-distance trade and shipping as factors of modern economic growth have been an issue of economic historical debate, and it is clear that the question is highly relevant in Swedish economic history, even if the research so far undertaken has been rather limited. Perhaps the cause of historians' lack of interest in eighteenth-century Swedish shipping is still the shadow of Eli F. Heckscher. Heckscher, the dominant figure of economic historical research in Sweden and one of the great names in the economic history discipline, had dealt in a number of works with Sweden's eighteenth-century shipping and, in particular, with its important precondition, the Swedish Navigation Act (*produktplakatet*).[12] Like the liberal economist he was, he criticised the Act as a typical protectionist measure. In this perspective, then, Sweden's protected shipping had been seen as inefficient, and indeed as consuming resources that could have been better employed elsewhere. Even if Heckscher's view of Swedish mercantilism has been re-examined in many other sectors, his view of shipping as inefficient and the Navigation Act as a typically protectionist measure has been reproduced by many historians.[13] The most recent account of Scandinavian shipping in the late eighteenth century, by the Danish historian Hans Christian Johansen, also reproduces this view. On the one hand, Johansen admits that Swedish shipping capacity was impressive in comparison with other seafaring nations; on the other hand, he explains this via a combination of bulky export commodities and strong protectionism (the Navigation Act and protectionist duties on trade). However, he does not point out the Swedish role in tramp shipping:

> The relatively large size of the Swedish merchant navy seems thus to be a result of a combination firstly of the natural resources of the kingdom which made possible the export of bulky commodities in great demand in western Europe, and secondly of a determined protectionist policy which ensured that this export took place in Swedish vessels. The two factors complemented each other, since natural resources themselves would not have been sufficient as the Russian case clearly demonstrates. In many respects the Swedish policy was similar to the British and had as much success.[14]

---

[12] Heckscher 1922; Heckscher 1940 and Heckscher 1949, vol. 2, pp. 670–678.
[13] On the debate see Carlén 1994 and Carlén 1997, pp. 247–270.
[14] Johansen 1992, pp. 484–485.

Shipping and foreign trade in the eighteenth century have received rather limited attention from economic historians in Sweden. Instead, the focus of research has been on domestic economic sectors: agriculture, proto-industries
and eighteenth-century iron production. The situation is different as regards
the second part of the nineteenth century and Sweden's industrialization.[15] The
discrepancy between the focus on either the domestic sector or exports is reflected in two explanatory models of Sweden's industrialization. The so-called
export model highlights, as one might expect, the role of exports.[16] The export
boom between 1850 and 1890 is perceived as the prime-mover of contemporary industrialisation. The 'export model' also connects the starting point of
Sweden's industrialisation to the expansion of world trade after 1850, and (in a
shipping perspective) to the transition from sail and wood to steam and iron.
Sweden's eighteenth-century trade and her early integration within the Atlantic
economy does not appear to have much importance.

The second model, the so-called 'domestic market model', points out that
the process of Sweden's industrialization was much more drawn-out, and that
the post-1850 export boom did not play as important a role as its advocates
have argued. Instead, the focus is on the role of the transition in agriculture, the
growth of proto-industrial activities, and of broad consumption and the domestic market. This model also lays emphasis on institutional change, especially the shift from the protectionist institutions of the early modern period to
the nineteenth-century's more liberal institutions. Instead of seeing Sweden's
industrialization as a revolutionary shift, mainly caused by external factors, this
model stresses the drawn-out, evolutionary, and basically internal/domestic
character of the change.[17] Neither of the two models investigates in depth the
role of Swedish trade and shipping between 1720 and 1815: the export model
because it ascribes the first significance of foreign trade to the period from the
mid-nineteenth century onwards, the domestic market model because it focuses on internal factors of industrialization and economic growth.

The Swedish export and domestic market models of economic growth reflect
the ongoing international discussion regarding the character of globalization,
which has its roots in the 1970s, when Immanuel Wallerstein published his
seminal work on the modern world system.[18] Even if the present debate does
not deal with the same issues of dependency and underdevelopment, as in the
1970s, there is a perceptible discursive connection. The present debate is also
concerned with the importance of long-distance trade before 1800, and in
general, the role of early modern European expansion. On the one hand, some
scholars see the role of long-distance trade before 1800 as vastly exaggerated.
According to this point of view, the modest volume of trade, of capital invested

---

[15] For recent overviews of Swedish economic history see Magnusson 1996 and Schön 2000.
[16] Jörberg 1961, on the two models see Schön 2000, pp. 34–37.
[17] See especially, Schön 1997; Schön 2000; Krantz 1987; Isacson and Magnusson 1987; Magnusson and Nyberg 1995; Magnusson 1996.
[18] Wallerstein 1974–89.

and of people engaged in the expansion were of limited importance for domestic economies and, consequently, of limited importance for modern economic growth. Alternatively, other scholars claim that a fixation with quantitative evidence obscures highly significant qualitative changes; for example institutional innovations, the establishment of trading networks between different parts of the world, etc. Even if volumes of traded commodities before 1800 were rather limited, this trade could entail very substantial consequences for domestic markets.[19] It is not appropriate to reconsider this debate extensively here: I will therefore focus on only one aspect of the debate—the aspect of the putative early modern transport revolution.

1.3 An early modern transport revolution?

Transport costs are a critical factor in the development of trade, especially in long-distance and bulk trade, and consequently they are also a critical factor in the development of the market economy. High transport costs function as efficient trade barriers; low transport costs promote trade. Hence, the decline in transport costs has been seen as one of the preconditions of modern economic growth; a factor of the same importance as the decline in commodity production costs. The lower the transport costs, the greater the integration of markets. Above all, it has been pointed out that the introduction of the ocean-going sailing vessel about 1500, and its dominance as a means of transportation for 350 years, effected significantly the development of foreign exchange in the early modern period, but there is no broad agreement on this issue. In fact, many economic historians do not see declining transport costs as a factor of economic growth at least until the mid-nineteenth century.

The American historian Russell Menard, in his analysis of transport costs in European and transatlantic trade between 1300 and 1800, arrives at the conclusion that there was only a modest decline in transport costs during the period. In fact, declining commodity prices and different methods of packaging appeared as more important factors in the growth of long-distance trade than the productivity of shipping. In other words, there was no transport revolution in the early modern era.[20]

Knick C. Harley's analysis of transport costs between 1740 and 1913, based mainly on British and American freight rates, confirms Menard's picture. There was a very modest decline in transport costs prior to the mid-nineteenth cen-

---

[19] There is vast literature on the subject. For a short survey of the myth of early globalization in the Atlantic economy see Emmer 2003, see also O'Brian 1982 and Kennedy 1989 (Paul Kennedy's and Patrick O'Brien's debate in *Past and Present* 1989; however, O'Brien has partly modified his view) For a differing view of the Atlantic economy, see McCusker and Menard 1985; McCusker 1997; McCusker and Morgan 2000; Hancock 1997. Also Kenneth Pomeranz points at the significance of foreign trade, especially transatlantic trade, for modern economic growth, see Pomeranz 2000.
[20] Menard 1991. On the effects of stowage factors, see French 1987, pp. 632–637; McCusker 1997, pp. 64–65.

tury. The first crucial drop in freight rates occurred between 1850 and 1913, and it is attributed to the transition from sail and wood to steam and iron vessels. Hence, the transport revolution first occurred in the mid-nineteenth century.[21]

Kevin H. O'Rourke and Jeffrey G. Williamson have used the lack of productivity growth in shipping before 1850 as evidence for the late market integration of the Atlantic economy.[22] However, in addition to the analysis of freight rates, these two authors have examined the price convergence among a number of globally traded commodities. If the gaps between prices in different markets indicate different levels of transport costs, then the convergence between global prices should also indicate declining transport costs. O'Rourke's and Williamson's data show that there was no such price convergence between 1500 and beginning of the nineteenth century. On the other hand, there is abundant evidence of such price convergence from the mid-nineteenth century.

In the early modern period, world trade grew not because of any decline in trade barriers but in spite of them.

> ... [E]ven for non-competing goods, there is no convincing evidence of a wide-spread transport revolution before 1800, or any inter-continental commodity price convergence.[23]

It was in the earlier decades of the nineteenth century that, for the first time and as a consequence of the technological revolution in both land and sea transport, the world's trade became truly integrated and global. Globalization began after 1800. It is worth mentioning that O'Rourke and Williamson's arguments are consistent with both the models of Sweden's industrialization. In fact, Sweden represents an important case in O'Rourke's and Williamson's evidence.[24]

O'Rourke's and Williamson's focus on the issue of market integration shows how important it is to make a distinction between commodity production costs and transport costs. Whereas supporters of the concept of an early modern transport revolution, and of early globalization, indicate long-distance shipping as a dynamic part economic agent, supporters of the post-1850 transport revolution do not perceive much dynamism in that sector in the early modern period. However, they do not suggest that there was no growth in commodity exchange. On the contrary, there could be, and there was, a significant growth in commodity exchange; but this growth has to be explained by large price differences between commodities and/or by a decline in commodity production costs in one area, and not by the integration of markets as a conse-

---

[21] Harley 1988.
[22] O'Rourke and Williamson 1999; O'Rourke and Williamson 2002a; O'Rourke and Williamson 2002b.
[23] O'Rourke and Williamson 2002a, p. 46.
[24] See especially their analysis of relationship between migration and capital flows on the one, and international trade on the other hand, O'Rourke and Williamson 1999.

quence of declining transport costs.[25] The focus on the development paths of commodity production and commodity costs, on the one hand, and of productivity in long-distance shipping and transport costs, on the other hand, of course also effects the perception of the transport and production sectors as either dynamic or stagnant.

Another group of economic historians has, contrary to the view adumbrated above, found evidence of a significant decline in transport costs even before the age of iron ships and steamers. The arguments for a decline in transport costs before 1800 combine two patterns of reasoning. First, there is the factor of overall shipping costs. Improved ship design, the better operation of ships, increasing tonnage per man ratios, and shortened turn-around times in harbours are all identified as crucial factors in the decline in transport costs. Second, there is the factor of protection costs. The reduced threat of piracy or privateering, international treaties on shipping, established insurance practices: all these factors reduced the protection costs of shipping.

However, in reality, decline in the two variables of transport costs is difficult to discern. For example, the introduction of the flute in Dutch shipping by 1600 might be seen as a mainly technological achievement, substantially reducing overall shipping costs. (The craft and its sails were designed to carry much larger cargoes with much smaller crews.) On the other hand, the introduction of the slow flute manned by a smaller crew was first made possible when the North and Baltic Seas became safe enough for shipowners to dare employ such a craft.[26]

The majority of the authors who have identified a decline in transport costs before 1800/1850 therefore combine the two variables of a decline in overall shipping costs with a decline in protection costs. Douglass C. North, the leading scholar of neo-institutional economic theory, has studied the relationship between the decline in transport costs and economic development in the United States. His analysis was based, like Menard's, Harley's and O'Rourke and Williamson's, primarily on the study of ocean freight rates. However, North's conclusion was different; instead of a long stagnation and then a dramatic decline in freight rates in the mid-nineteenth century, he uncovered a stable and quite rapid decline during the whole 1750–1900 period.[27] Later, North complemented his study of freight rates with other measures of productivity change, in particular, the average size of ships and ratios of ton per man. The results of this more complex analysis are consistent with his previous conclusions.

According to North the productivity growth in ocean shipping during the early modern period cannot be explained by new technology alone. Until the mid-nineteenth century, ocean shipping used basically the same technology, introduced by the Dutch 250 years before. Hence, North had to find some

[25] O'Rourke and Williamson 2000b.
[26] North 1968, p. 964; Glete 2000, p. 125.
[27] North 1958.

other, non-technological, explanation, and he consequently turned to institutional factors (a decline in piracy and privateering, the improved operational performance of ships, the decline of mercantilist restrictions, Navigation Acts) as forming a more proper explanation of productivity growth in shipping before 1850.

> The conclusion which emerges from this study is that a decline in piracy and an improvement in economic organization account for most of the productivity change observed.[28]

North's studies of ocean freight rates became a starting point for much of the subsequent research on sea transport. Harley's article of 1988 was primarily a re-examination of North's data—with differing conclusions. There are many other studies confirming North's conclusions, while using a different empirical basis. Gary M. Walton's research followed North's arguments closely. Simon Ville, in his analysis of coal shipping in Britain, 1700–1850, studied a number of productivity factors. His results convincingly show a significant increase in productivity before 1850.[29]

Many of the works discussed above have been based on freight rate analysis, which (as it appears to the present writer) entails a number of problems. The construction of freight rate indices includes too many variables to be fully convincing. The same empirical basis can provide widely divergent results, depending on the variables included or excluded (commodity price movements, packaging, etc.). Another problem connected with the use of freight rates is that the data sets used include freight rates for a limited number of routes, which is hardly representative. Much shipping (not least Danish and Swedish) took the form of tramp shipping from port to port, rather than the shipping in shuttle routes that provided the major data for freight rates. Furthermore, if shipowners took higher profits, productivity gains did not necessarily lead to lower freight rates. The decline in freight rates in the mid-nineteenth century occurred in a highly competitive environment; in such an environment, it was difficult to turn productivity gains into higher profits.

Measuring tons-per-man ratios appears a more robust method of estimating productivity change, and thus of addressing the question of stagnating or declining transport costs in early modern long-distance shipping. However, even this method entails many problems. Jan Lucassen and Richard W. Unger recently provided an account of labour productivity in ocean shipping between the fifteenth and late nineteenth centuries based on tons-per-man ratios. Their data are based on estimates of labour engaged in shipping and on estimates of the merchant tonnage of leading maritime states, and not merely on freight rates on a limited number of shuttle routes. Moreover, they do not only provide a general view of labour productivity in shipping; their data also afford a basis

---

[28] North 1968, p. 953; see also North 1958.
[29] Walton 1967; Shepherd and Walton 1972; Ville 1986.

for comparisons of labour productivity between different merchant marines. They found evidence of a significant growth in labour productivity in shipping between the fifteenth and nineteenth centuries.

This growth was not continual, and the growth rates differed between countries. The authors divided the whole period into four phases, each representing a specific kind of shipping pattern. The first phase, the late Middle Ages, is characterised by mixed fleets of oared and sailing ships, and low tons-per-man ratios, about five tons per man. The second phase, between the mid-sixteenth and mid-eighteenth centuries, was a period of Dutch dominance in shipping, with ratios of about ten tons per man. By the late seventeenth century, the Dutch reached an astonishing average of twenty tons per man, but this was a short-lived achievement and Dutch labour productivity declined in the following decades. The other merchant marines emulated the Dutch shipping and by the mid-eighteenth century the British and Scandinavians achieved ratios of about ten tons per man. During the third phase (1780–1850) the ratios grew by some 70 per cent, to seventeen tons per man. This growth occurred on a fairly broad basis, including all the leading European merchant fleets. The fourth phase started in the mid-nineteenth century, and is marked by the breakthrough of steam and iron ships, and consequently by a dramatic increase in labour productivity to thirty and more tons per man.[30]

The increase in labour productivity during the last phase is consistent with the technological shift examined in the studies of Harley, O'Rourke and Williamson and others. But Lucassen and Unger's data also indicate that there was a very substantial increase in labour productivity between 1450 and 1850, which, on the other hand, supports the conclusions of North, Walton, Ville and others. This growth in labour productivity is attributed to a number of factors. Size of vessel and destination are the most important. However, even the design of vessels and improvements in technology played an important role, particularly in the first and second stages. Other factors were the functioning of the labour market and the quality of sailors. By contrast, however:

> There was no specific technical advance in the late eighteenth century to explain the leap into the third phase; other factors, it would seem, created an environment that was conducive to advancement.[31]

This is exactly the period in which Scandinavian neutrality shipping expanded.

Lucassen and Unger's analysis of labour productivity in shipping focuses on a decline in overall shipping costs. The factor of protection costs played some role, they maintain; for example, the difference between Dutch labour productivity in the Baltic and in the Mediterranean is attributed to the safety of seas, but this is not the crucial factor in their long-term account.[32]

---

[30] Lucassen and Unger 2000, p. 134.
[31] Lucassen and Unger 2000, p. 139.
[32] Lucassen and Unger 2000, pp. 136–137.

There is no study of Swedish shipping focusing on the question of productivity development in the eighteenth century, yet the Finnish historian Jari Ojala's research on eighteenth and nineteenth-century Finnish shipping is highly relevant for Sweden too, due to the similarity of shipping conditions and, of course, due to the fact that, until 1809, Finland was a part of Sweden. Ojala, in parallel with North, sees the productivity development before 1850 as a combination of technological and organizational factors. As regards the technological factors (size, speed, manning levels per ship, etc.) there was a stable but not particularly rapid productivity growth. As regards the organizational factors, Ojala primarily focuses on the issue of information costs. State mercantilist policy is perceived mainly as a factor diminishing information costs and effecting information asymmetries between actors. In this development, the consular service played a significant role, diminishing actors' information costs. Ojala's analysis of the long-term economy of Finnish shipping is consistent with Douglass C. North's conclusions positing a significant increase in the productivity of shipping even before 1850. Ojala stresses, too, the combination of the transaction cost and the production cost approaches. However, he seems to pay rather limited attention to the issue of protection costs and to the importance of Sweden's neutrality for Finnish shipowners.[33]

1.4 Fiscal-military states and protection of shipping

It is clear that the factor of protection costs is a significant element in the explanations of the pre-1850 growth in the productivity of shipping. In North's and Walton's studies this factor is highlighted as the single most important, while other authors merely acknowledge its significance. The reason, perhaps, is the difficulty of defining it. Protection costs are included, but hardly discernible, in overall shipping costs. A decline or increase in protection costs affects those important production factors of shipping, a vessel's average size and available cargo space, its number of crew members, the crew's wages, insurance premiums, and even freight rates. All these factors are quantifiable, but not the protection cost element within them.

The difficulty for economic historians in dealing with protection costs also has to do with the difficulty integrating the role of the state in their analyses. The state and its capacity to protect its shipping interests were, of course, crucial factors affecting the level of protection costs. It is impossible to imagine the formidable growth of British trade and shipping in the eighteenth and nineteenth centuries without British naval mastery over the seas; and it is more than reasonable to expect that that mastery entailed lower protection costs for British shipowners and merchants.[34] But how may one compare, from this perspective, the protection costs of a British shipowner in comparison with a French or

---

[33] Ojala 1999, pp. 423–424. See also Ojala 1997a and Müller and Ojala 2002.

Spanish shipowner? How may we relate the comparatively high level of British duties on foreign trade to the comparatively low protection costs of a British shipowner and merchant?

Frederic C. Lane, the maritime and economic historian of Venice, made the first attempts to link the concept of protection costs to the efficient use of state violence. Within his perspective, the state was seen as a producer and seller of protection. The stronger the state and the state's control of sea-lines of communication, the lower the protection costs for the merchants and shipowners of that state.[35] The concept of the state as a protection vendor means that a militarily powerful state can provide its subjects with a better and safer economic environment than a weak state, even if the subjects concerned have to pay for this benefit through by higher taxes and duties.

Jan Glete, the Swedish maritime historian, employed this perspective in his study of the relationship between the rise of fiscal-military states and maritime conflicts in the early modern period.[36] He contrasts the different paths of development in the Mediterranean and in the Baltic, and explains the divergences with the help of a protection costs approach. The economic decline of the Mediterranean and the rise of north-western Europe is related to the growth of strong fiscal-military states in the latter, and to political fragmentation and the decline of states in the former, areas. The sixteenth-century rise of Denmark and Sweden to become the two dominant powers on the Baltic Sea made seaborne trade there much safer, particularly compared to other parts of Europe.

> By the 1570s and 1580s the Baltic had become a unique haven for seaborne trade in Europe where civil wars, piracy, loosely controlled privateering and unpredictable royal actions causing high protection costs for shipping were the norm. The Baltic, only a few decades earlier a rather backward area, suddenly enjoyed the benefits of unhindered peaceful trade.[37]

In the course of the seventeenth century Sweden and Denmark developed into efficient fiscal-military states with formidable navies. And the income drawn from duties on foreign trade played an important role in financing this development, at the same time as this income served as an important motive for the states' mercantilist policy. But merchants were willing to pay the concomitant costs provided the Baltic remained safe. The high productivity of Dutch shipping in the North and Baltic Seas indicates significantly lower protection costs there than in other parts of Europe. The Baltic Sea enjoyed a relative safety, which persisted over the course of the eighteenth and nineteenth centuries.

The Mediterranean developed in precisely the opposite way. The two dominant empires of the region, Spain and the Ottoman Empire, failed to transform

---

[34] This is the point stressed by Paul M. Kennedy in the debate on benefits and costs of British imperialism, see Kennedy 1989.
[35] Lane 1950 and Lane 1958.
[36] Glete 1993b; Glete 2000 and Glete 2002.
[37] Glete 2000, pp. 125–126.

themselves into efficient fiscal-military states. Their struggle for control of the Mediterranean did not result in a balanced and safe environment. Instead, the drawn-out conflict transmuted into coastal raids, semi-official privateering and piracy; a kind of warfare known as *guerre de course*. Constantinople's control over its North-African vassals declined, and the Barbary coast became a centre of corsairing. On the Christian side, Malta and Livorno played similar roles. In conclusion, the sixteenth- and seventeenth-century Mediterranean world was dominated by sea warfare and violence, with too many actors involved but no efficient control. The high protection costs of Mediterranean shipping appear at least partly to explain the low shipping productivity there.[38]

Jan Glete's analysis of fiscal-military states ends in 1650. However, his approach—which considers states essentially as protection-selling actors—is certainly also applicable for eighteenth-century shipping. With the rise of fiscal-military states, some of the protection costs of seaborne trade were transferred from the level of economic actors (merchants or shipowners) to the state level. These were primarily military costs. However, the question of protection costs concerned not only military but also political and diplomatic issues. Merchants argued that they needed state protection, and they often had political power and the means to press their claims. As regards protection costs, the military and economic aims were met. For example, the Navigation Acts in Sweden and Britain were not only measures protecting domestic shipping, trade and industries; they were also a component of the states' naval policy. Politicians were aware of the fact that considerable merchant fleets meant many well-trained sailors would be available for their navies.

Peace and trade treaties with the North-African states and neutrality pacts are examples of how diplomacy could reduce the protection costs of shipping. Due to their importance for the development of Swedish shipping in the course of the eighteenth century these two topics—neutrality and relations with the North-African states—will receive detailed attention here.

North and Walton, as well as Lucassen and Unger, found a significant productivity growth in ocean shipping in the late eighteenth century, entailing lower transport costs. When considering strong naval states as protection providers and sellers, it is possible to attribute a substantial share of these gains to a decline in the protection costs of shipping. At the global level, the decline might be attributed to British naval mastery. This eighteenth-century naval mastery, even if much more vulnerable than the nineteenth-century *Pax Britannica*, made seas safer for British vessels, but vessels of other flags could also draw benefits from it—providing they were not at war with Britain. Piracy in the West Indies disappeared, and even the Mediterranean became much safer in the course of the eighteenth century.

The view of the state as a protection vendor is also valid as regards eight-

---

[38] Glete 2000, pp. 107–111, see even Barbour 1996 (reprint), and North 1968, p. 964 employed the same arguments.

teenth-century Sweden. First, Sweden implemented, during most of the period in focus, a consistent and rather successful neutrality policy. In addition to this, the state signed a number of treaties with North-African and European states, which entailed relatively lower protection costs for Swedish vessels. However, if Sweden's neutrality was to impact on protection costs it had to be respected; neutrality shipping presupposed a navy that commanded the respect of other nations. Indeed, Sweden's eighteenth-century navy was relatively large.[39]

However, maintaining the navy and occasionally using it for convoying was costly. The peace treaties with North-African states were also expensive affairs in the long term, not least due to the consulates that needed to be established in connection with these treaties. Thus a *tentative* decline in protection costs for individual economic actors resulted in a very significant *real* increase in protection costs for the state. The drawn-out Swedish debate on the benefits and costs of long-distance shipping and trade shows that politicians understood this relationship well.

But protection costs are only one cost factor of shipping. We have to relate comparatively low Swedish protection costs to the overall costs of Swedish shipping. Here the labour productivity of Swedish shipping is the most interesting issue. If one takes Heckscher's conclusions about the Swedish Navigation Act as a starting point, the productivity of Swedish shipping should be comparatively low, due to the protection of the domestic shipping market. Consequently Swedish vessels should be crowded out of the international market for tramp shipping. This question will be addressed in chapter 5, which includes a detailed analysis of the labour productivity of Swedish shipping in southern Europe, and also comprises comparisons with other merchant marines. Chapter 5 further includes estimates of overall costs and benefits of Swedish shipping in southern Europe, in relation to state protection costs. Fortunately, the state's activities connected with providing protection for Swedish ships in southern Europe (convoying, peace treaties with and consular service in North-African states) were carried out under the umbrella of one institution—the Swedish Convoy Office (*Konvojkommissariatet*). Therefore the Office's outlays provide a fairly accurate reflection of the state's total protection costs in the area.

1.5 A note on the book's structure

This book consists of the introductory section and two case studies. The introduction (chapter 1) presents the subject of the study, the Swedish consular service, and sets it in the context of neo-institutional theory and the recent debate on the early modern transport revolution and productivity in shipping. The focus here is on the shipping sector, instead of the commodity trade sector.

---

[39] For the comparison with Denmark and Russia, her potential enemies in the Baltic and partners in the so-called Alliances of Armed Neutrality in the eighteenth century, see Glete 1993b, pp. 295–305.

One hypothesis is that shipping was, in fact, a more dynamic, a more important and, at least in the late eighteenth century, a more profitable sector of Sweden's foreign commercial activities than commodity exchange. In particular, the present writer highlights that part of the debate which lays emphasis on the factor of protection costs. This study argues that the factor of protection costs is particularly significant for the Swedish case, due to Swedish economic policy and due to Sweden's situation as a predominantly neutral state in the period. The two other parts of the book, the case studies of southern Europe and North America, should be examined in the light of that debate.

Chapter 2 provides a short outline of the Swedish consular service from the mid-seventeenth century to 1906. This outline shows that the build-up of the Swedish consular service occurred in a number of distinctive phases. The first phase of development, after some initial attempts in the second part of the seventeenth century, started about 1720 when Sweden established a number of consulates in southern Europe (the Mediterranean, the Iberian Peninsula and France). By the late eighteenth century, the Americas had become another region of interest, and Swedish consulates appeared in the new American republics soon after their liberation from British and Spanish control. The third phase in the establishment of the consular service is discernible in the mid-nineteenth century. New consulates appeared in Africa, southeastern Asia and the Pacific, following in the footsteps of the second wave of imperialism. Notably, almost all these consulates were located in seaports, serving Swedish and, after 1814, also Norwegian shipping interests. Parallel with these three specific areas, the consular service in Europe first developed in great commercial centres (Amsterdam, London, Hamburg), and then in many other more or less important seaports.

After this general introduction to the Swedish consular service, the focus is on two specific areas in which the consular service in particular could impact on the aspect of protection costs: consular services in southern Europe and in the United States. Thus, chapters 3 and 4 examine the establishment and functioning of the consular service in the Mediterranean and the Iberian Peninsula. Chapter 3 deals mainly with the motives and aims of Swedish policy in southern Europe. Special attention is paid to the role of the Swedish Navigation Act, which had considerable impact on the development of shipping between Sweden and southern Europe. The peace treaties with the Ottoman Empire and the North African states are another key issue dealt with in this chapter.

Chapter 4 examines in depth how the Swedish consular service in the Mediterranean and the Iberian Peninsula functioned. It starts with an account of the Mediterranean consular system, with which all national consular services originated. After that, it describes in detail how the Swedish service was established and what duties and rights the Swedish consuls had. Finally, the chapter describes in narrative form the activities of four leading consulates in the region (Lisbon, Cadiz, Livorno, and Marseilles) and of consulates in North Africa (Algiers, Tunis, Tripoli, and Morocco). The purpose of these narratives is to unveil, at an actor's level, the specific demands and problems encountered at different seaports (consular districts).

Chapters 3 and 4 are rather descriptive, since they show what consuls did or what they were supposed to do, and what they reported to Stockholm; but the account of the consular service at the actor's level cannot fully address the issue of the service's overall impact on Swedish economic development. Chapter 5 includes an overall analysis of both Swedish foreign trade and shipping activities in southern Europe; but the major focus is on shipping. With the help of the lists of Algerian Passports (passports issued for all Swedish-flagged ships sailing beyond Cape Finisterre), the pattern of Swedish shipping is unveiled and related to three factors: (1) economic policy and institutions (Navigation Act); (2) external environment and foreign policy (Swedish neutrality); and (3) the labour productivity of Swedish shipping. The productivity of Swedish shipping in the area is compared with the productivity of other merchant marines. This section also includes a rough estimate of overall costs and benefits of Swedish shipping in southern Europe.

The second case study (chapters 6 and 7) deals with the establishment of the Swedish consular service in North America and with Swedish transatlantic trade and shipping. The starting point of the American case study is the recognized fact that, after 1800, the United States replaced Britain as the largest buyer of Swedish iron.[40] Due to iron's importance for Sweden's economy, the shift to transatlantic markets was a crucial factor for Swedish economic development in the first decades of the nineteenth century and, beyond question, a factor that affected US-Swedish relations in the nineteenth century. Chapters 6 and 7 investigate whether there was any link between this shift in iron sales and the early establishment of Swedish diplomatic contacts with the United States: Sweden was one of the first states to sign a trade treaty with the United States, and the first Swedish consuls to the United States were appointed as early as 1783. More specifically, chapter 6 examines the motives and objectives of Swedish policy in the Americas in the 1780s and 1790s. It is apparent that the establishment of the consular service in the United States was part of a broad strategy that even included the acquisition of a colony in the West Indies (St. Barthélemy). Sweden intended to enter into the trade of the dynamic transatlantic triangle.

Chapter 7 then transfers attention to the pattern of American trade and shipping after 1800; and it shows that the Swedish 'West Indian' strategy had a rather limited impact on the establishment of the iron trade with the United States. Instead, Sweden's (and specifically Gothenburg's) role in the Continental blockade is indicated as the decisive factor in shaping the pattern of post-1800 Swedish-American trade. Once more, it was Sweden's neutrality that provided the Swedish actors with a comparative advantage, but in the case of iron exports to the US, this did not concern Swedish shipowners. Nevertheless, after

---

[40] Attman 1958, pp. 6–21; Adamson 1969.

1815 neutrality was no longer an advantage, and exchanges between Sweden and the United States developed according to a different pattern.

In conclusion, chapter 8 relates the results of the two case studies to the theoretical debate on productivity change in shipping, and on the timing and character of the transport revolution. It sets the build-up of the Swedish consular service, Sweden's neutrality and her protectionism in the context of a broader development of European long-distance shipping.

CHAPTER 2

The Swedish consular service: a summary, *c.* 1600–1900

2.1 1600–1718

The first data concerning the establishment of the Swedish consular service are from the first half of the seventeenth century, when the young 'great power' began to develop its diplomatic representation abroad. This process was a part of Sweden's military expansion and foreign policy in the 1620s and 1630s, and thus the first representatives were appointed at places of major importance for Sweden. This first rather simple and unorganised representation comprehended three major levels: ambassadors, residents (envoys) and correspondence agents; it was the latter category that most resembled the later consuls. One of the primary duties of these first representatives was to collect useful business information, a typical consular duty.

The establishment of diplomatic representation was also an outcome of the system of bilateral treaties which the Swedish kingdom began to build from the beginning of the seventeenth century. Thus the first Swedish representative in the Dutch Republic, at the rank of ambassador, was appointed soon after the conclusion of the defence and peace treaty between the Dutch Republic and Sweden in 1614. In consequence of this early measure, diplomatic relations between Sweden and the Dutch Republic were long lasting. The first Swedish residents were based at the Hague and not at Amsterdam, the world's economic centre, which indicated their primarily diplomatic function. However, from about 1640 there was even a Swedish agent in Amsterdam.[1]

After Amsterdam, Hamburg and Elsinore also became important centres of Swedish representation. In 1621 Anders Svensson Ödell was appointed Swedish agent at the Sound, to represent Sweden's commercial interests at Elsinore.[2] From the Swedish point of view, Elsinore was not only a key site for obtaining intelligence about Baltic trade and shipping. Elsinore, like Hamburg, was a crucial node in the early modern mail network between the continent and Sweden. The Swedish representatives at Elsinore functioned as royal mail

---

[1] Tunberg 1935, pp. 68–73.
[2] Ödell 1971.

agents.[3] Hamburg's role as a place of intelligence exchange and as a hub in the European mail network was the reason why that city was also an early recipient of a Swedish representative. After 1620 there was a Swedish resident there, whose duties were to supervise the mail destined for Sweden, and to gather valuable information from the Holy Roman Empire. Indeed, the Swedish correspondence agents at Elsinore and Hamburg had many different duties, from spying on Sweden's enemies to searching out new credit sources for the Swedish crown. Sweden's representative in Hamburg, Johan Adler Salvius, appears a typical example for this period.[4]

Russia was another state with which Sweden established early diplomatic contacts, as early as 1631. In fact, economic interests played an important role in Russia too: in this case they concerned supplies of grain for the Swedish army. The first Swedish representative in Russia (Petter Krusebjörn) was appointed a 'resident' at Moscow and Novgorod. During the 1620s and 1630s, Sweden also obtained its first representatives in England and in many German cities, as a consequence of her involvement in the Thirty Years War.[5]

Very unclear conditions of service were a typical feature of this early representation. Nevertheless, the collection of different kinds of information was the crucial duty that the first Swedish representatives discharged, even if this information was not gathered and forwarded in a systematic way. The aforementioned correspondence agents were appointed in states bordering Sweden, or in states of considerable economic and political importance for Sweden (the Dutch Republic, England). The agent networks grew naturally in parallel with Sweden's military expansion.

An interesting and different case, indicating the future importance of southern Europe, was the Swedish representation in Lisbon. This post was a direct result of the commerce and friendship treaty between Sweden and Portugal, signed in 1641, just a year after Portugal won its independence from Spain, and there was also a clear political interest in establishing diplomatic and commercial links between these two states. Portugal was a member of the same anti-Habsburg camp as Sweden, still engaged in the Thirty Years War. Portugal, indeed, is highly interesting from the point of view of the consular service.

The first Swedish representative in Portugal was Lars Skytte. He moved to Lisbon in 1641, together with the Portuguese mission that signed the aforementioned treaty in Stockholm, and he remained at his post until 1647. In addition to his representative function he was instructed to report on commercial opportunities in Portugal. Nevertheless, during Skytte's tenure, the overwhelming Swedish interest in Portugal related to the conflict with Spain.[6]

---

[3] Tunberg 1935, pp. 78–82; Rimborg 1997.
[4] Tunberg 1935, pp. 89–95; Droste 1999.
[5] Tunberg 1935, pp. 73–78, 82–98.
[6] Mellander 1926, p. 135; Mellander 1927, pp. 335–341; Tunberg 1935, p. 106. An unexpected episode, which concluded Skytte's period as Swedish representative there, was his conversion to Catholicism, marking the most important difference between Catholic Portugal and Protestant Sweden.

The next Swedish representative in Portugal, Johan Friedrich von Friesendorff (resident in Lisbon 1649–52) made attempts to win access to Portugal's colonies for Sweden, and after his return to Stockholm he also championed the promotion of Swedish trade in the Mediterranean and Levant.[7] In 1669, after almost two decades without an official representative, Nils Simons was appointed Swedish representative in Lisbon and received the title of 'consul'. In light of its continual operation since the 1660s, the Lisbon consulate may be considered the oldest branch of the Swedish consular service.[8] This consulate retained its role as one of the key points in the Swedish consular network in the eighteenth century; its history and role will be investigated in detail in chapter 4.

From the second half of the seventeenth century we can start to distinguish more clearly between properly diplomatic and consular functions. An important stage in this bifurcation was the creation of the Swedish Board of Trade in 1651. The Board became the central institution of the new economic policy, which worked much more consciously for the promotion of Sweden's foreign trade and shipping.[9] The consular service was formally connected to the Board—one of the reasons why consular correspondence was sent to the Board of Trade until 1906, and preserved at its archives.

As early as its first meeting, on 21 November 1651, the Board discussed the appointment of correspondence agents at the leading European commercial centres. The proposed cities were: London, Paris, Cadiz, Lisbon, Venice, Florence and Livorno. This selection shows us that, even as early as 1651, the Swedish authorities identified the potential for Swedish commerce in southern Europe. However, with the exception of Lisbon, no agent was appointed at that time. There were other attempts to establish a correspondence agent in Paris (1652), comprising a huge 'district' covering all the western Mediterranean, and a further attempt for Venice (1670).[10]

During the second half of the seventeenth century, Sweden already had an established and relatively stable network of diplomatic representation, but there were few agents with purely consular duties. In Denmark, representation was reorganised. From 1662 onwards, a new envoy was established at Copenhagen, near the Danish royal court, while the correspondence agent at Elsinore carried out consular duties. This separation of diplomatic and consular duties should be seen as a model for the future organization of Swedish representation.[11] In the Dutch Republic too, representation was dividend between a diplomat at the Hague and an agent in Amsterdam.[12]

---

[7] Mellander 1927, pp. 355, 373–374. After von Friesendorff the diplomatic functions were carried out by Henrik Bummellman. Yet there are also some other official documents appointing Michael Appelius (in 1658) and Adrien Abraham Vanderhoeven (undated) to Swedish consul in Lisbon.

[8] Almqvist 1912–13, pp. 30, 410.

[9] Gerentz 1951.

[10] Ekegård 1924, p. 156.

[11] Tunberg 1935, p. 133.

[12] Almqvist 1912–13, p. 30.

During this period, Swedish representation abroad was characterised by an eclectic mixture of titles, and by unexpected shifts in levels of representation. The title of 'consul' had primarily been used in states in which 'consuls' had been known for centuries—i.e. southern Europe. Therefore Lisbon and Cadiz were the first places where the title was used for Swedish representatives.[13] The traditional organization of the consular service in the Mediterranean was a model for consular services in all western European states, and the Swedish system developed in the same manner. This model will be described later (chapter 4).

In conclusion, we may say that in the second part of the seventeenth century, Sweden build up a system of regular diplomatic representation, which also carried out typical consular duties: the gathering and forwarding of business information, the promotion of Sweden's trade and shipping, and assistance to Swedish subjects abroad. Despite the early ambitions of the Board of Trade to establish a separate consular service, there was no clear distinction between the 'ordinary' representation and consuls. Both the titles and the functions were mixed, and the situation remained largely the same until the end of the Great Northern War.

2.2 1718–1815

The Great Northern War marked the end of Sweden as a great power and, of course, the decline in Sweden's international position had many internal political consequences. We will highlight only two here, in view of their impact on the future of the Swedish consular service. First, the shift of political power from the king to the *riksdag* and the royal council gave the commercial elite much more political influence. After 1718, this social group could participate more actively in shaping Sweden's economic policy than in the seventeenth century: consequently, the interests of different mercantile groups became an integral part of Sweden's policy. Second, in some ways, the eighteenth-century's commercial expansion replaced the seventeenth-century's military expansion. There was of course a substantial difference between the ambitions of the post-1718 Swedish state and the concomitant reality. However, it is clear that the Swedish authorities after 1718 implemented a policy of commercial expansion, and that southern Europe was accorded a very special place in this policy. The motives and aims of Sweden's economic policy after 1718 will be examined in detail in chapter 3. Here we will only furnish a general description of the expansion of the consular service, as a component of this policy.

The increasing number of consulates in the Mediterranean from the 1720s onwards clearly reflects the special role of this area in Swedish designs. As a consequence of the peace treaties ratified with the Barbary states and with the

---

[13] Tunberg 1935, pp. 148–152.

Ottoman Empire, Sweden established consulates in Algiers (1729), Smyrna (1736), Tunis (1737), Tripoli (1739) and Morocco (1764). Yet the treaties with the Barbary states were merely a precondition of safety for Swedes in the Mediterranean. They would not in themselves result in any inevitable increase in trade and shipping. To promote trade and shipping in the area, the Swedish authorities established a number of consulates on the northern coast of the Mediterranean and on the Iberian Peninsula. Thus Swedish consuls were appointed in Livorno in 1720, Marseilles in 1731, Venice in 1735, Malaga in 1737, Alicante in 1738, Cagliari (Sardinia) in 1743, Barcelona in 1744, Genoa in 1748, Naples in 1749, Cette and Montpellier in 1750, Madrid in 1754 and Cartagena in 1759. In addition, there were some further consuls appointed outside the Mediterranean. In 1735 the Board of Trade appointed a consul at Santa Cruz on Tenerife, but the Spanish authorities never accepted this appointment.[14] Even El Ferrol in northern Spain received a Swedish consul (1759). Consulates were also established on the north-western coast of France, at Rouen (1726), La Rochelle (1741), Nantes (1747), Dunkirk (1751), Bayonne (1760), and Le Croisic (1757). It should be pointed out here that an appointment did not necessarily result in consul's establishment in his district. Moreover, some consulates were left vacant after the first appointed consul returned home or died. In the same way as the appointment of a consul did not inevitably mean active consular service, the consular service itself did not necessarily entail an increase in trade and shipping. The policy of appointments should be seen mainly as an articulation of mercantilist ambitions.

Table 2.1 clarifies the overall picture of appointments between 1720 and 1815. It confirms the significance of southern Europe. The expansion of Sweden's consular service before 1815 can be divided into two clearly discernible phases. Until the 1780s, southern Europe was the major area of appointments, clearly in accordance with Sweden's offensive commercial policy. The independence wars in the Americas, first in North America, and later in Latin America, resulted in a number of consulates being established in this area.

Whereas the establishment of consulates in north-western Europe, Russia and the Baltic was more a result of practical concerns and of the traditional importance of these areas (these markets dominated Swedish foreign trade), the consulates in southern Europe and in the Americas were the result of conscious policy. The question is, first, whether the policy was successful or not, and, second, if there really was a significant increase in trade and shipping, was this a product of the consular service or were there other, more important factors?

---

[14] Almqvist 1912–13, p. 427.

Table 2.1: *Swedish consular service 1600–1850*

Periods	North-western Europe	Southern Europe	Americas, Asia	Baltic and Russia	Year of appointment
1600–1700	Amsterdam Hamburg	Lisbon		Danzig Elsinore Moscow Novgorod Pskov	
1701–1750					
		Cadiz			1703
	Bordeaux				1705
		Livorno			1720
	London				1722
	Rouen				1726
		Algiers			1729
		Marseilles			1731
		Santa Cruz (Tenerife)			1735
		Venice			1735
		Smyrna			1736
		Malaga			1737
		Tunis			1737
	Vienna*				1738
		Alicante			1738
		Tripoli			1739
	La Rochelle and St. Martin				1741
				Lübeck	1741
		Cagliari			1743
		Barcelona			1744
	Nantes				1747
		Genoa			1748
		Naples			1749
		Cette and Montpellier			1750
1751–1800					
	Dunkirk				1751
		Madrid			1754
	Le Croisic				1757
		Cartagena			1759
		El Ferrol			1759
	Bayonne				1760
				St. Petersburg	1761
		Morocco (Sale and Tangier)			1764
		Trapani			1764*
	Havre de Grace				1773
		Gibraltar			1774
	Honfleur				1775
	Lorient				1776
				Riga	1776
		Constantinople			1777
		Modena			1777

Table 2.1: *Swedish consular service 1600–1850 (cont.)*

Periods	North-western Europe	Southern Europe	Americas, Asia	Baltic and Russia	Year of appointment
	Rochefort				1778
		Lyon			1778
		Trieste			1779
	Ostend				1781
		Nice			1781
		Thessaloniki			1781
				Viborg	1781
		Calais			1782
		Rome			1783
			Boston		1783
			Philadelphia		1783
			Charleston		1784
				Libau	1784
				Narva	1786
	Kristiania				1787
				Flensborg	1787
				Copenhagen	1788
		Paris			1789
				Königsberg	1789
				Rostock	1789
			St. Barthélemy		1790
				Memel	1790
		Malta			1792
	Frankfurt*				1794
	Rotterdam				1796
		Madeira			1796
				Kronstadt	1796
	Antwerp				1798
			Batavia		1798
		Setubal			1799
			New York		1799
				Stettin	1799
	Middelburg				1800
1801–1850					
		Civita Vecchia			1804
	Leith				1808
			Rio de Janeiro		1808
			Canton		1812
				Åbo (Turku)	1813
		Ancona			1815
				Archangel	1816
				Reval	1816
				Kiel	1816
		Palermo			1818
	Berlin				1818
				Stralsund	1818
		Bilbao			1819
				Aalborg	1820
	Bremen				1822
		Messina			1824

43

Table 2.1: *Swedish consular service 1600–1850 (cont.)*

Periods	North-western Europe	Southern Europe	Americas, Asia	Baltic and Russia	Year of appointment
		Trapani			1824
				Odessa	1824
		Corfu			1826
		Alexandria			1827
			Port au Prince		1830
		Athens			1831
				Rönne	1833
			Buenos Aires		1834
		Florence			1836
			Montevideo		1836
			Pernambuco		1838
			Manila		1839
			Cape Town		1839
			Havana		1839
			Caracas		1840
		Aleppo			1842
	Dresden				1842
			Jamestown		1843
			Calcutta		1845
			Valparaiso		1847
			Panama		1847
			Quebec		1850

Sources: The dates of appointment are based on Almqvist 1912–13, pp. 137–138, and on Högberg 1981, pp. 295–296. Trapani*, first consular report received according to data in the Consular Report register, BoT SNA.

Notes: In some cases appointments did not result in any consular activity, either because a consul was not accepted by the second party (for example, at Santa Cruz on Tenerife) or because he never settled in his consular district (for example Charleston in the US). Perhaps the division of the Swedish consular services into four major areas is over-simple and rather confusing in some cases. Consulates in France have been divided between the Mediterranean and Atlantic coasts, whereas the whole of Spain is included in southern Europe. Vienna and the German inland towns have been included under the heading of north-western Europe. See also Appendix A for dates of the first report received at the Board of Trade.

Yet the rising number of Swedish consulates after 1718 was not only a result of the state's active economic policy. The leading Swedish merchants had an interest in doing business with people they could trust and, from the Swedish point of view, a Swedish consul at Lisbon or Cagliari was more trustworthy than a local. This was particularly important in southern Europe, the area where Swedes traditionally lacked contacts. The English merchant, James Shastoe, was well aware of this when, in 1735, he applied for the position of Swedish consul at Cagliari (Sardinia), an important centre for the purchase of salt. He wrote to the Board of Trade in thus:

> Undoubtedly the Lordships has been informed of the misusage of strangers in this plase, as several Sweds have experienced in being obliged to pay 14 & 16 Rixdollars courtage to person, no ways qualified, nor in capacity to give them satisfaction,

by reason in first place he understands no language but his mother tongue; in the next place, an entire stranger to trade or commerce pay [*sic*] even to honesty.[15]

The issue of consuls' appointments, their duties and their relations with the Board of Trade, merchant communities and other consuls will be studied in detail in chapter 4. In general, the description of the situation for Swedish consuls in southern Europe is applicable to the whole Swedish consular service. The consular services of the European states were organised according to the model of the Mediterranean consulates.

In southern Europe, the Swedish consular system appeared to have been completed by 1800. Of course, new consulates were established there even after this date, but the pace of establishment was now slower than in other areas.

2.3 1815–1906

The period between the 1780s and the 1850s marks another phase in the formation of the Swedish consular service. The most remarkable feature of this phase is the establishment of consulates in the Americas, which followed in the footsteps of the local independence movements. Thus, the first Swedish consuls appeared in the United States (in Philadelphia and Boston) in 1783, the same year as the United States' independence was recognised, and in Charleston in 1784. New York (1799) and Baltimore (1810) followed after. After 1800, Latin America began its struggle for independence. The first Swedish consul to Brazil was appointed in 1808. French Haiti (Saint Domingue), which won its independence in the same period, received a Swedish consul in 1830. By 1850, the Swedish authorities had appointed consuls in Buenos Aires (1836), Montevideo (1836), Pernambuco (1838), Havana (1839), Valparaiso, (1847) Caracas (1840), Panama (1847) and Quebec (1850).[16]

Of the total number of thirty-three appointments in the period 1815–50, ten were made in the young American republics. However, there were also a number of new appointments in Europe, the Mediterranean and Asia. It is apparent that this world-encompassing system was not designed merely for the interests of Sweden's foreign trade. The extension of the consular service after 1815 indicates that the system was re-shaped primarily to accommodate shipping interests. Part of the explanation lies with the union with Norway. The consular system after 1814 served both parts of the union, and in Norway the interests of the shipping industry played a significantly larger role. However, Sweden also had considerable shipping interests.

After 1814, policy concerning consular issues increasingly took Norwegian interests into account. Thus, the new ordinary consular instruction (*konsul-*

---

[15] James Shastoe to BoT, 15 December. 1735, Cagliari, Ansökningar om konsulattjänsten (Consulate applications) E XVII g:1, BoT SNA.
[16] On the Swedish policy in Latin America after 1800, see Swärd 1949 and Hildebrand 1950.

stadgan), issued in March 1830, was prepared in cooperation with Norwegians. This instruction replaced the first consular instruction dating from 1793. For example, it gave the Norwegian merchant and shipowner associations the same opportunity to propose new consuls as the Swedish merchants had had before.[17] However, after 1836, proposals for new consular appointments were prepared separately by the Swedish and Norwegian governments and sent to the king for their final decision.[18]

The balance between Norwegian and Swedish interests in the consular service was later to become a crucial issue, not only in terms of the future of the consular service but also, to an increasing degree, in terms of the future of the Scandinavian union. One of the consequences of balancing Swedish and Norwegian interests was the decline of the role of the Swedish Board of Trade. The new instruction for the Board of Trade, issued in 1831, made a clear distinction between consular economic issues (trade, shipping), which were still under the Board's authority, and political issues (for example, consular reports on local political situations), which were now under the authority of the union's Department of Foreign Affairs.[19] In 1840, the Board of Trade lost its right to issue letters of authorisation for consular appointments. Instead, the right was transferred to the Department of Foreign Affairs. According to another instruction, issued in 1858, all consular matters that concerned both areas of the union were taken over by the Department of Foreign Affairs. Only those questions that exclusively concerned Swedish economic affairs were still subject to the Board of Trade's authority.[20]

The transformation of the consular service after 1815 also entailed more stable and unified regulations. This concerned, for example, consular payments. In the eighteenth century, there were no general rules as to when, how and how much consuls would be paid. Consular fees were specified in a consul's letter of authorisation, and so they varied from place to place and from appointment to appointment. The nineteenth-century consular service was much more unified. In instructions of 1834 and 1850, equal fees per last of registered tonnage were introduced for all Swedish-Norwegian consuls.[21]

The consular service was reformed once again in 1858, according to the proposal of the consular committee of 1855.[22] One of the important issues discussed by the committee was the introduction of a system of salaried consuls. In general, in the course of the eighteenth century, the only salaried consuls were those working in the Barbary states. The reasons were quite logical. As there was insignificant Swedish trade and shipping in North Africa, consuls could not make a living from consular fees or from their own private business,

---

[17] Almqvist 1912–13, p. 197.
[18] Almqvist 1912–13, p. 248.
[19] *Betänkande* 1876, p. 6.
[20] Almqvist 1912–13, pp. 252–254.
[21] Almqvist 1912–13, pp. 249, 252, for detailed data on fees see *Betänkande* 1876.
[22] *Betänkande* 1857.

though at the same time their representation was necessary for the maintenance of peaceful relations with the states and for the safety of shipping in the Mediterranean. Swedish consuls in North Africa were paid by means of the Swedish Convoy Fund (*konvojkassan*), not by the Department of Foreign Affairs. This system will be described and analysed in detail in chapter 4.

The new instruction of 1858 comprised, conversely, a new system of financing, with a common consul fund, which replaced the one-hundred-and-fifty-year-old Convoy Fund and ended the special consular system in North Africa.[23] However, it was to take another decade for the system of salaried consuls to be introduced. The first such salaried consulate was in London, in 1869, followed by Cardiff, Liverpool and Newcastle in 1871.[24]

The Swedish consular service continued to expand after 1850. Over forty new consulates were established in the phase spanning the years 1850 to 1906. The majority of these consulates were located in Asia, Africa and the Pacific, reflecting the ongoing world trade boom and also the interests of Norwegian tramp shipping. But the consular service also expanded in Europe—especially in Germany and central Europe—and in Latin America. On the other hand, southern Europe, which had been so important for the establishment of the service in the eighteenth century, lost its significance.

In fact, the world trade boom after 1850 strengthened the divergence in the development paths of the Swedish and Norwegian economies. The Norwegian merchant fleet expanded at a remarkable pace. It increased, between 1854 and 1874, by 360 per cent, from 167,000 to 600,000 lasts. The Swedish merchant fleet increased by 280 per cent in the same period—an impressive growth rate, but the total tonnage in 1874 was still only 123,000 lasts. The Norwegian merchant fleet was almost six times larger, and it was growing significantly faster. On the other hand, Swedish exports were almost twice the value of Norwegian.[25] The divergent interests of shipping in one part of the union, and of foreign trade in the other, inevitably entailed differing views regarding the role of the consular service.

To solve the problem of this rising discrepancy between Swedish and Norwegian interests, another consular committee was appointed in 1875. The committee consisted of three Swedish and three Norwegian representatives. The committee's report, published in 1876, provides an excellent outline of the history and contemporary problems of the Swedish-Norwegian consular service, but it apparently failed to solve the problems which it addressed. The new instruction for consular service was first issued in November 1886, ten years after the committee's report. It strengthened even further the control of the consular service under the aegis of the common Department of Foreign Affairs. However, the Norwegians were disappointed, and the new instruction became an indirect cause of the break-up of the Swedish-Norwegian union in 1905.[26]

---

[23] *Betänkande* 1876, pp. 11–12.
[24] Håkansson 1989, pp. 21–22.
[25] *Betänkande* 1876, p. 4.

The reorganization of the consular service in 1906, as a consequence of the disunion, once again highlighted the question of the purpose of the service. On the one hand, the economic actors required the new service to work primarily for the promotion of Swedish economic interests, especially in distant markets (Asia, Latin America).[27] And, of course, they required the service to be as cheap and efficient as possible. On the other hand, by 1906, the consular service had already become an integral part of the bureaucracy of the Department of Foreign Affairs. The employees within this system (i.e., the salaried consuls) defended their interests. They argued that consular duties concerned many non-economic issues, and they attempted to preserve the system as it had existed before 1905. The result was a compromise between the interests of the diplomatic bureaucracy and those of commercial enterprises. Yet, after 1906, the consular service played a minimal role in promoting Swedish economic interests abroad. Swedish enterprises found other ways to reach distant markets. Thus, in the long-term perspective, the reform was a 'failure'.

The consular service's separation from the Board of Trade also confirmed the fact that, after 1906, it lost much of its economic purpose. When, in the mid-seventeenth century, the first steps in the establishment of a Swedish consular service were made, the service was part of a conscious mercantilist policy. The same reasoning lay behind the extension of the consular service in the eighteenth century. The service was integrated with the Board of Trade, and it grew in accordance with the priorities of Swedish commercial interests. It was shaped according to the traditional methods of doing business in the Mediterranean. An independent Swedish consular system was a necessary precondition for any Swedish commercial activities in the area. The same mercantilist reasoning explains the late eighteenth-century and early nineteenth-century extension of the consular service. But, under changing trade conditions, and in particular after 1850, the system became more and more obsolete for the purposes it had once been established for. Moreover, the differing paths of economic development in Sweden and Norway entailed rising tensions regarding the purpose of the consular service.

The modern Swedish consular service, established in post-1905 Sweden, still has many similarities with its eighteenth century predecessor. Consuls are still often recruited from among local businessmen, and the promotion of business contacts still plays an important role. However, the general economic importance of the service has naturally declined, due to the completely different methods of conducting modern business, and also because there are now so many other ways of obtaining economic information in comparison with the eighteenth century. Nevertheless, liaising with local authorities still has its place among the important functions of the consuls, even if troubled shipmasters have these days been replaced by tourists.

---

[26] *Betänkande* 1876; Almqvist 1912–13, pp. 255–263.
[27] On Swedish export interests in Asia and Latin America about 1900 see Larsson 1977, Runblom 1971.

CHAPTER 3

Sweden's eighteenth-century policy in southern Europe

I find not that Algier can be otherways beneficial to Sweden than that by having peace with them it gives free liberty to our Ships to go safely on the coasts of Spain and Portugall and to all ports of the Mediterranean with our own Cargoes and have the benefit of being employed and freighted by other Merchants with the same safety… I must beg leave to acquaint and inform your Lordships that I find no other method or possibility of keeping a firm and secure peace with the kingdom of Algier than now and then that is once in two or three years to give some handsome presents to the Dey and Leading men of the Government to keep them steadfast in our friendship which is what is practiced by the French by the Hollanders and all other nations in peace with them.

George Logie to the Board of Trade, 2/13 October 1738, Livorno.[1]

3.1 Preconditions, motives and aims of Sweden's economic policy in southern Europe

Early in the morning, on 30 July 1709, two Barbary corsairs attacked a group of seven merchant ships sailing off the coast of Portugal. With the exception of one Genovese ship, the merchantmen were sailing under the Swedish flag. Five ships managed to escape, but the two slowest, the Genovese vessel and a Swedish ship called *Stora Jernvågen*, were caught and forced to fight. The Genovese ship was soon overpowered by the enemy, but the Swedes fought with courage for almost an hour. At the end, a fire on board the Swede reached the powder room, and the ship and its unlucky crew were blown up.

The incident is reported in Joachim de Besche's letter to the Board of Trade, dated some days later. As de Besche, the Swedish consul in Lisbon, explains, the misfortune was partly a consequence of the Dutch peace treaty with Algiers. After the treaty was signed, thirty Barbary corsairs arrived in the Portuguese and Spanish waters looking for non-Dutch merchant ships, which usually followed the Dutch convoys. *Stora Jernvågen* became one of their victims.[2] How-

---

[1] George Logie to BoT, 2/13 October 1738, Livorno E VI aa 229, Consular Reports, BoT SNA.

ever, many more Swedish ships were in danger. The Barbary corsairs did not dare to sail as far as the Channel and to North Sea. This made commerce insecure for small seafaring states, such as Denmark, Sweden, Hamburg, Lübeck and Danzig. On the other hand, English and Dutch shipping could exploit the situation. In his report, de Besche asked for Swedish convoy vessels to make shipping more secure, but he was aware of the difficulties facing the Stockholm government in 1709, and he did not hope for much. Sweden was in middle of the long drawn-out Great Northern War (1700–21), with King Charles XII abroad, and with the country facing an increasing shortage of resources.

The misfortune of *Stora Jernvågen* shows how dangerous sailing to Portugal and to the Mediterranean could be for the Swedish crews. Even if Swedish shipping to Portugal was in danger, however, it was a very substantial element of Swedish shipping activities—in the course of the Great Northern War, as at other times. Portugal was Sweden's major supplier of salt. Due to its special character, as both a non-substitute commodity and a daily necessity, salt *had* to be acquired, regardless of cost. From this point of view, salt can probably be seen as the main determinant of Swedish policy toward southern Europe.

In the course of the eighteenth century, Swedish trade with the Iberian Peninsula and the Mediterranean changed character. The Iberian and Mediterranean markets began to import increasing quantities of Swedish staple commodities: iron, sawn timber, tar and pitch. There was also a substantial growth in shipping activities; and Swedish ships, to an increasing degree, began to carry the goods of other states. Sweden became a serious competitor to other middle-sized commercial shipping states, principally the Danes.

The interests of commerce and shipping in southern Europe became an important issue in Swedish politics. Decisions concerning Swedish economic or foreign policy could not be made without taking into account Mediterranean affairs. Sweden signed a number of peace and trade treaties with countries all around the Mediterranean. Furthermore, her commercial and shipping interests in southern Europe became a powerful argument behind Sweden's neutrality policy after 1721. Apparently, the Mediterranean was now included in the orbit of Sweden's interests. One clearly visible indicator of these interests was the rapid expansion of the network of Swedish consulates in the area. The consular network in southern Europe was the best organised and most developed part of the Swedish consular service. There are obvious reasons for this fact, which will be explained in detail later. First, we have to examine the preconditions for the Swedish presence in southern Europe and the motives for Sweden's political activity in the area after 1718. The subsequent chapter will then focus on the functions of the consular service in the area, and will provide a detailed account of some of the leading consulates.

---

[2] Joachim de Besche to BoT, 3 August 1709, Lisbon, E VI aa 223, Consular Reports, BoT SNA.

3.2 The Swedish presence in the Mediterranean in the seventeenth century

During the seventeenth century, Sweden established quite frequent commercial contacts with southern Europe. As we have mentioned above, the most important reason was the salt trade. In the course of the century, the traditional Lunenburg salt was increasingly replaced in Sweden by high quality salt from Setubal and, to balance the exchange, the Swedes began to export iron and naval stores to Portugal. Testimony for these relatively early contacts between Sweden and Portugal is provided by the trade treaty between the two countries, signed as early as 1641.[3] Even if the political importance of Portugal's independence was obvious to Swedish politicians, the political motives for the treaty should not be exaggerated. The major interest behind the Swedish-Portuguese alignment was commercial, specifically salt supplies.[4] As previously stated, the Swedish government also showed interest in obtaining access to Portugal's overseas colonies, though without much success.[5]

In the second half of the seventeenth century the direct trade between Sweden and Portugal developed quite satisfactorily. The fleets of merchantmen destined for Portugal and Spain usually left Stockholm in convoys during the autumn. They sailed out with cargoes of weapons, bar-iron, timber and tar, and returned with salt. These salt vessels were among the largest vessels in the Swedish merchant marine.[6] In later part of the century, about Swedish twenty vessels a year visited Portugal's ports.[7]

The Portuguese salt trade was monopolised by the king and a small merchant consortium. This form of organization, together with the changing conditions of salt production, resulted in violent price fluctuations, which made the market situation unpredictable for salt buyers. Consequently, many of them entered the Mediterranean to look for cheaper salt, as did the Swedes. There was a Swedish proposal, dated 1693, to buy salt in Ibiza (Ivica) and La Matta (near Alicante). Two years later, the Portuguese king decided to increase salt prices by 265 per cent at a stroke.[8] Following this price shock, Swedish vessels began to sail into the Mediterranean on a regular basis, albeit under the protection of convoys. Discussions in the Board of Trade also testified to the changed attitude towards shipping in the Mediterranean. Not only the salt trade was now encouraged, but also trade with Italian ports and even with Smyrna.[9]

---

[3] Mellander 1926, p. 109, Ekegård 1924, p. 71; Tunberg 1935, p. 105. Friendship and trade treaty between Sweden and Portugal, dated Stockholm, 1641, July 29. *Sveriges traktater med främmande magter, 1632–1645*, 1909, pp. 487–506.
[4] Mellander 1927, p. 338.
[5] Mellander 1927, p. 362.
[6] Bjurling 1951, pp. 6–7.
[7] Ekegård 1924, pp. 70–71.
[8] Börjeson 1932, p. 132.
[9] Ekegård 1924, pp. 75–76.

1. Map of the Mediterranean (undated, the eighteenth century) (UUL)

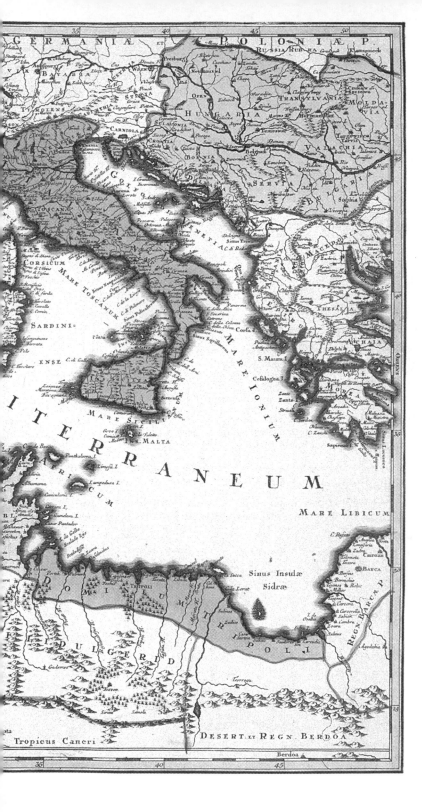

53

However, as the Swedes knew, the Mediterranean waters were among the most perilous in the world. There was still the matter of the ongoing *guerre de course*—the war between Christian and Muslim corsairs. This war actually continued in the tradition of crusades: thus on the Christian side, the Maltese knights were still among the most active participants. Many Christian sailors became slaves, or more exactly captives, in the North African states on the so-called Barbary coast.[10] This does not necessarily mean that the prisoners were taken in the Mediterranean. The Barbary corsairs sometimes sailed north along the European coast, and could reach as far afield as the fishing banks of Newfoundland. In the early seventeenth century they raided Iceland and the Faeroes (1627).[11]

There were also Swedes among these captives; however, the captured Swedes had not only been serving on ships of the Swedish flag. Indeed, many were captured while under service aboard foreign ships. According to a document dated 1662, about a hundred Swedish seamen were kept as captives in North Africa at this time. In 1690, double this number of Swedes were identified as prisoners.[12]

From the Christian point of view, *guerre de course* was more or less Muslim piracy with the economic aspect to the fore. But for the Muslim rulers of Algiers, Tunis, Tripoli and Morocco, it had another highly important function. Seen as a part of the holy war against the infidels, corsair activities legitimised the political power of the rulers and the semi-independence of the Barbary states within the Ottoman Empire[13]

Concerning this *guerre de course,* it should be noted that Sweden was not simply an innocent victim in this struggle between the Christian and Muslim worlds. It had the will, if not the resources, to participate in it, as the following episode clearly illustrates. In 1663, a secret Swedish privateer company was founded with the purpose of capturing Muslim ships in the Red Sea. Participants in the company were the Queen Dowager and a number of councillors (*riksråd*). Instructions for the privateer expedition were issued in September 1663, and two ships, under the command of Admiral Hans G. Sjöhjelm, were sent to the Red Sea. One of them, *Falken*, eventually reached the Red Sea after a lengthy voyage around Africa, and was successful in taking two richly-laden Muslim vessels. The expedition ended in Goa in Portuguese India, where Admiral Sjöhjelm sold the Swedish vessel and the captured Muslim cargoes. Papers detailing the proceedings and examined after Sjöhjelm's death show that, from the investors' point of view, the expedition was no success.[14]

Basically there were two ways to make shipping in these dangerous waters

---

[10] For a recent overview of the relationship between British Empire and the Barbary states, see Colley 2002, pp. 23–134.
[11] Helgason 1997; Andersen 2000, p. 41. Newfoundland is mentioned in Gøbel 1982–83, p. 74.
[12] Börjeson 1932, p. 132.
[13] Windler 2000, p. 172.
[14] Krëuger 1856, pp. 25–26.

safer: convoying, and peace treaties with the Barbary states. Both practices were used by other states and both had been discussed in Sweden. As regards convoying, this was a well-established and quite common practice, even for Swedish shipping to the Iberian Peninsula. According to Swedish Maritime Law, ships sailing to Spain and Portugal had to sail in convoys.[15] As the rising salt prices in Setubal and Lisbon pushed the Swedish merchants into the Mediterranean, the need for convoying in these waters became a pressing problem. In 1695, the convoying vessels received an order to convoy Swedish merchants through Gibraltar and along the eastern Spanish coast, to La Matta and other destinations.[16]

Treaties with the Barbary states were the other means of rendering shipping safer. The idea of concluding peace treaties with the Barbary states had been under discussion as early as 1667 and 1668.[17] However, these were so far merely paper proposals. The first serious attempts to sign treaties with the Barbary states were made much later, after 1721.

Although the salt trade between Sweden and Portugal was already well established in the mid-seventeenth century, Swedish merchants did not enter the Mediterranean more extensively until the late 1690s, and even then they did so with hesitation. Concerning treaties with the North-African states, as we have seen, the Swedish authorities discussed the question, but did not make any serious attempt to negotiate with the Barbary states in the course of the seventeenth century. However, the situation was to change during Charles XII's reign.

3.3 The diplomatic game with the Ottoman Empire

The previously-cited Swedish attempts to enter the Mediterranean were founded on primarily economic considerations. The Swedes were searching for cheap salt, and for potential markets for Swedish staple commodities. However, there was another, more political aspect to the Mediterranean initiatives. The southern and eastern parts of the Mediterranean were controlled—more or less formally—by the Ottoman Empire. And the Ottomans were seen in Sweden as a potential ally against Russia. Therefore Sweden made a number of attempts to strengthen this alliance of interest and establish closer cooperation with the Ottomans, not least in the economic sphere.

During the seventeenth century, there were some attempts to establish diplomatic relations with the Sublime Porte, and also to open direct commercial links with the Levant and Persia. During Charles X's reign, Claes Rålamb organised a diplomatic mission to Constantinople.[18] In 1671 a Tartar emissary,

---

[15] Bjurling 1951, p. 6.
[16] Ekegård 1924, p. 76.
[17] Ekegård 1924 , p. 78.
[18] Olán 1921, pp. 9–10; Rålamb 1963.

Haga, proposed the opening of direct trade between Sweden, the Levant and the Black Sea.[19] In 1687, a group of Armenian merchants visited Stockholm with the aim of establishing direct Swedish trade with Persia.[20] Yet none of these attempts resulted in real commercial exchange. One of the reasons was still the overwhelmingly negative image entertained of the Ottoman Empire, as the enemy of all Christians.

This attitude towards the Ottoman Empire changed during Charles XII's years of sojourn at Bender, within Ottoman territory. For Charles XII, relations with Constantinople had combined political, economic and cultural aspects. On the one hand, he saw the Ottoman Empire as a key ally in his struggle against Russia, and he aimed to transform the relationship with Constantinople into a form of military alliance against Russia. On the other hand, there was an economic interest in developing Swedish trade with the Levant, and with the eastern Mediterranean in general. The frequent contacts between Swedes and Turks during Charles's Bender period also stimulated cultural and religious interest in the Ottoman Empire.[21]

The outstanding supporter of commercial exchange with the Ottoman Empire was Johan Silfvercrantz, an official of the Swedish Board of Trade. Since 1705 Silfvercrantz had been travelling around Europe searching for commercial opportunities for Swedish manufactures and trade. Among other destinations, he visited Marseilles and Livorno, and he could see for himself the importance of Levant trade in these ports. In 1710, Silfvercrantz presented his report on the improvement of Swedish commerce to Charles XII at Bender. His ideas primarily concerned the development of manufactures within the kingdom, but the Levant also played an important role. He saw it as a future market for Swedish products. According to Silfvercrantz, Sweden possessed many products in demand in the Levant. And Sweden could purchase commodities there (especially silk), which were otherwise imported by foreigners. Silfvercrantz's proposal for organizing Swedish trade with the Levant centred on following the examples of states with a well-established Levant trade. His favourite example in this regard was the English Levant Company.[22]

In 1711, the king sent Silfvercrantz to the Levant, to continue to assemble information on the local commercial opportunities Unfortunately, Silfvercrantz died there the next year. His work had not been completed as planned, but his studies were nonetheless an important precondition for the foundation of the Swedish Levant Company in 1738.[23]

The second string of Charles XII's Bender policy concerned diplomatic relations with the Sublime Porte. The king strove to link a trade treaty with the Sublime Porte with a formal treaty of alliance directed against Russia. Soon

---

[19] Börjeson 1932, p. 130.
[20] Ekegård 1924 , p. 91.
[21] Karlsson 2000, pp. 197–225.
[22] Ekegård 1924, p. 102.
[23] Ekegård 1924, pp. 100–112; Florén and Karlsson 1998, p. 76.

after the king's entry into Ottoman territory he sent his envoy, Martin Neuge-bauer, to Constantinople to discuss this issue. Neugebauer was authorised to negotiate the terms of the treaty. In addition, he was supposed to negotiate with the Ottoman authorities regarding Sweden's relations with the Barbary states, which formally belonged to the Ottoman Empire. After a promising start, the negotiations failed in 1713. The major reason seemed to be Charles XII's wish to connect the trade treaty with a military alliance.[24] It took an additional two decades before the treaty could be signed.

The question of a trade treaty with the Sublime Porte was raised again in the 1720s, after the death of Charles XII. Then a significant hindrance for the establishment of commercial ties between Sweden and the Ottoman Empire was the royal debt. During his stay at Bender, Charles had borrowed substantial amounts of money from Constantinople. In 1729, when the first Ottoman envoy visited Stockholm, the debt was set at 2 million d.s.m., and the debt had to be paid before a treaty between the states could be signed.[25]

In 1734, the Board of Trade sent two young Swedes, Edvard Carlson and Carl Fredrik von Höpken, to Constantinople. Among other matters, they were authorized to negotiate the terms of the debt repayment and to discuss the trade treaty. With the help of an influential Frenchman working for the Otto-mans, the count de Bonneval, they reached a solution to the debt issue. Instead of a cash payment, Sweden promised to send to the Sublime Porte a fully equipped man-of-war with 72 guns; in addition, 30,000 firearms and items of war equipment should be supplied.[26]

Even if the proposed solution was very satisfying for the Swedish Treasury, it was not, at least at first sight, politically acceptable for two reasons. First, the Ottoman Empire was still seen as a major enemy of the Christian world, and the idea of supplying Constantinople with ships and weapons encountered many protests. Second, the proposed solution had an anti-Russian thrust, which was not acceptable to the Caps. The Swedish *riksdag* in the 1720s and 1730s was dominated by the Cap party, which worked for peaceful and friendly relations with Russia.

Despite these domestic protests a man-of-war, *Sverige,* was equipped in the navy's shipyard at Karlskrona, and sent to Constantinople, together with the supply ship *Patrioten.* However, *Sverige* was shipwrecked on the Spanish coast and only *Patrioten* reached Constantinople. After some additional negotiations the Sublime Porte accepted *Patrioten* instead of *Sverige* and, in 1737, the trade treaty could finally be concluded.[27]

Gustaf Kierman, the Stockholm merchant and leading Hat politician, was deeply involved in the negotiations, and he played an important role in estab-

---

[24] Ekegård 1924, pp. 103–104, 113.
[25] Olán 1921, p. 26.
[26] Olán 1921, p. 29.
[27] Trade and shipping treaty between Sweden and Turkey, dated 10 January 1737 *Sveriges trak-tater med främmande magter. 1723–1771*, 1922, pp. 238–247.

lishing of Swedish-Levant trade. He paid for Carlson's and Höpken's stay in Constantinople, and he equipped *Patrioten,* partially using it for his own cargo destined for Constantinople. He was one of the great supporters of the idea of the Swedish Levant Company, and one of the company's founders.[28]

It is clear that Sweden's foreign political interests played an important role in establishing commercial links with the Levant and Constantinople. It has been stated that Charles XII's project of a military alliance between the Ottoman Empire and Sweden finally became a hindrance, and, after 1721, the Caps' Russian-friendly foreign policy made it difficult to sign a treaty with Constantinople.

In these negotiations, very little real attention was paid to the Barbary states, even if they were mentioned, and even if the Swedish side attempted to persuade Constantinople to exercise its influence in North Africa. Therefore, it is not surprising to find that the first peace treaties with the Barbary states were signed outside this diplomatic game balancing Russian, Swedish and Ottoman interests, and before the conclusion of the treaty with the Sublime Porte.

The major reason for Sweden's fresh engagement in the issue of peace treaties with the Barbary states was the changed situation of Swedish shipping in the Mediterranean in the late 1720s. As mentioned above, Swedish ships sailing into the Mediterranean were wont to join the Dutch convoys. But, after 1726, this became impossible. In this year, after twelve years of war, the Dutch concluded a peace treaty with Algiers.[29] The Dutch-Algiers treaty forbade the Dutch convoys to protect non-Dutch merchantmen. This made Swedish shipping much more vulnerable. The issue of Swedish shipping's protection appeared the following year in front of the Swedish Secret Committee—the parliamentary committee dealing principally with foreign affairs. A peace treaty with Algiers appeared to be the best solution. Consequently, George Logie, the Scottish merchant resident in Sweden and possessing detailed knowledge of Mediterranean affairs, was empowered to negotiate the peace treaty on Sweden's behalf, a commission which he successfully discharged.

In October 1727, Jean von Utfall, appointed the official Swedish emissary for Algiers, left Sweden to conclude the treaty. Von Utfall was also instructed to conceal his mission as far as possible from foreign powers. In April 1729, the peace, trade and shipping treaty between Algiers and Sweden was officially signed by von Utfall and the *Dey* of Algiers (the Algiers ruler).[30]

The treaty was shaped along the lines of other treaties between European states and Algiers—the most recent Dutch treaty of 1726, but also the older English treaty from 1682.[31] The Swedish treaty regulated the obligations and rights of Swedish and Algiers subjects in detail, as regards shipping and commerce in their respective countries. Typically, the treaty avoided mentioning

[28] Haugard 1947, pp. 27–29; Börjeson 1932, p. 298.
[29] Andersen 2000, p. 43.
[30] *Sveriges traktater med främmande magter. 1723–1771,* 1922, pp. 99–106.
[31] Ekegård 1924, pp. 475–476.

the Swedish obligation to send gifts or tributes to the Algiers ruler, even if this was a self-evident part of the agreement. This highlights the ambiguous character of gift exchange in the contemporary settling of relations between Christian powers and Muslims. According to Muslim legal tradition, the gifts of the Christian powers were perceived as a tribute confirming Christian submission to the Muslim order. Naturally, the Christian powers made the effort to stress that these gifts were not regular tributes, and were not expressive of Christian obedience to the Muslim order. From the Christian point of view, gifts were exchanged between two equal partners. In particular, two leading European powers, France and Great Britain, even if they continued to hand over gifts to the Muslim rulers, interpreted them to an increasing degree as voluntary.[32] The ambiguous distinction between payment of a tribute or ransom, on the one hand, and the exchange of voluntary gifts, on the other, continued over the course of the entire eighteenth century. The different views of these relationships also reflected different legal traditions: Muslim customary law and European international law.[33] The exchange of gifts shows how complex the diplomatic interplay between Europeans and Muslim rulers was. The Swedish agreement with Algiers also followed exactly the same pattern as other Christian states' agreements. It encompassed substantial Swedish gifts to the Dey of Algiers, a practice perceived as a natural accompaniment of the treaty.

Two aspects of Sweden's treaty with Algiers are worthy of more attention: the consular service and the system of Algerian passports. The treaty gave Sweden the right to appoint a consul to Algiers. This was the beginning of the regular consular service in North Africa, an important precondition of Swedish shipping in the Mediterranean. The organization of these North-African consulates differed from other areas of the Swedish consular service, due to the fact that consuls in the Barbary states had a diplomatic function, whereas their economic function was rather limited.

The other aspect concerns the so-called Algerian passports. The treaty stipulated the corsairs' right to stop and search Swedish vessels, and the duty of the Swedes to prove the ship's nationality via a special passport—the Algerian passport. To prevent misuse of the passport by other shipping flags, the process of issuing passports was strictly regulated and controlled. Only the Swedish Board of Trade could issue the passports, and a passport's validity was limited to only one voyage. These strict control procedures make the passport register a very good source for the analysis of Swedish shipping in southern Europe, not only in the Mediterranean but also, more generally, south of Cape Finisterre in north-western Spain (see section 5.4).

What was the reaction of the other shipping states to Sweden's treaty with Algiers? Outwardly, the various foreign powers had no significant objections to a Swedish treaty with Algiers. The Dutch consul informed his government of

---

[32] Colley 2002, pp. 43–72.
[33] Windler 2000, pp. 175–177.

the Swedish diplomatic activities in Algiers, but did nothing to hinder them. The French consul even helped von Utfall conduct the negotiations.[34]

George Logie, who played the leading role in preparing the treaty, was appointed as first Swedish consul in Algiers.[35] Quite soon after the treaty with Algiers was signed, Logie also opened negotiations with another Barbary state, Tunis. He employed a similar strategy as in Algiers. First, the parties had to reach agreement on the conditions of the treaty, which included the form and value of the Swedish gifts. In parallel with Algiers, the gifts consisted mainly of arms, gunpowder and sawn timber, valued in Sweden at 10,000 d.s.m. The treaty with Tunis was signed in December 1736.[36] The next step was Tripoli. Here too the negotiations followed a similar path and the conditions were similar to those obtaining in the Algiers and Tunis treaties. It took Logie another four years before this treaty could be signed, on 15 April 1741.[37]

With the conclusion of the treaty with Tripoli, the first phase of the establishment of relations with the Barbary states was over. However, Sweden lacked a peace treaty with the most powerful Barbary state—Morocco. It took another twenty years before an agreement could be reached with the Moroccan Empreror, after treaties with Morocco had already been signed by the Dutch and the Danes.[38] The peace treaty with Morocco was much more expensive than those with the other Barbary states. The final cost of peace with Morocco was about 350,000 rixdollars, compared to about 125,500 rixdollars for the three other states.[39]

The peace treaties with the North African states gave Sweden the necessary degree of safety for her shipping in the Mediterranean. In fact, these treaties provided Swedish ships with a comparative advantage to offset their other relative disadvantages. Sweden lacked expertise of long-distance shipping in southern waters. In addition, Sweden was situated in the northern periphery of Europe, with a short sailing season, at a distance from the key European markets and from the Mediterranean Sea. Sweden's important competitor for the shipping market in southern Europe was Denmark. It is worthy of mention that the Swedish system of peace treaties with the Barbary states was established before the Danish; Denmark signed its first treaty with Algiers in 1746.[40]

---

[34] Ekegård 1924, p. 474.

[35] He was appointed 19 May 1729. Almqvist 1912–13, p. 387.

[36] Peace and trade treaty between Sweden and Tunis, dated Tunis, 23 December 1736, *Sveriges traktater med främmande magter. 1723–1771*, 1922, pp. 224–235.

[37] Peace and trade treaty between Sweden and Tripoli, *Sveriges traktater med främmande magter. 1723–1771*, 1922, p. 300. On Tripoli, see also Borg 1987.

[38] Olán 1921, p. 56, on the Danish-Moroccan treaty, see Andersen 2000, pp. 57–59, and Wandel 1919.

[39] Olán 1921, p. 57, peace and trade treaty between Sweden and Morocco, dated 16 May 1763, *Sveriges traktater med främmande magter. 1723–1771*, 1922, pp. 859–870.

[40] Andersen 2000, pp. 41–54.

3.4 Swedish Navigation Act 1724

As mentioned above, the system of peace treaties with the Barbary states was established without much regard for Sweden's grand diplomatic strategy towards Russia and the Ottoman Empire. It is more correct to see this system primarily as a part of the shipping promotion policy pursued in the 1720s by the Board of Trade. In this section we will focus on this policy. Without doubt, the most important instrument of eighteenth-century Swedish economic policy with regard to shipping was the Swedish Navigation Act (*produktplakatet*), approved on November 10, 1724.[41] The Act was a result of intense debate about the contemporary problems and future direction of Sweden's foreign trade and shipping, a debate conducted between 1719 and 1723. In typical Swedish manner, the Act was shaped with prevalent western European shipping policy as its model, and in particular, the role of the English Navigation Acts should be noted.[42]

The Swedish debate followed a classical pattern. The major problem of Swedish foreign trade was recognized as a trade deficit, and this deficit was caused, among other things, by the Dutch and English dominance of shipping from and to Sweden. On the one hand, the debate was carried out in the Board of Trade, where Jacob Olofsson Hökerstedt in particular sharpened his statistical arguments for a more protective policy.[43] In 1721, according to the calculations of the Board of Trade, Sweden had a large current account deficit of about 2.5 million d.s.m.

The second forum, much more important for the outcome of the debate, was provided by the sessions of the Swedish parliament, the *riksdag*. In particular, the 1723 *riksdag* played an important role in introducing a new policy. This *riksdag* paid much attention to trade and shipping questions, and it also decided the question of the Swedish Navigation Act. There were two groups with widely differing interests engaged in the issue. On the one hand, there was the group of the major Stockholm merchants and shipowners. The Navigation Act was, of course, in their interest. This group cooperated closely with Hökerstedt and the Board of Trade. On the other hand, there were representatives of small port towns, without sufficient shipping capacity or capital rapidly to buy or build new tonnage. These men feared that shortage of domestic tonnage would entail a shortage of salt and other import commodities. Both sides argued for their respective points of view, and the *riksdag's* solution was a compromise. The parliament did not yet approve any new policy; it merely ordered the Board of Trade to prepare a Navigation Act for consideration.[44]

Taking the baton from the 1723 *riksdag,* the Board of Trade took over the

---

[41] Gerentz 1951, p. 178.
[42] Heckscher 1940, p. 21.
[43] On Hökerstedt, see Vallerö 1971–73, pp. 710–712, see also Vallerö 1969; Ekegård 1924, p. 274. Hökerstedt was one of the leading Swedish economic thinkers of the time and he contributed to development of economic statistics.
[44] Ericsson 1985.

issue of the Navigation Act and worked for its rapid passing. In 1724, the board prepared the Act's draft and rejected the objections of the small towns' representatives. On 10 November 1724, the Navigation Act—to be effective from January 1725—was signed by the king. Nevertheless, small towns continued to apply for exemptions to allow them to hire foreign ships. To reinforce the Act, the original version was supplemented on 28 February 1726 with a coda dealing with foreign shipping in Sweden.[45]

The Swedish Navigation Act prohibited imports and exports to and from Sweden on any vessels other than Swedish ships or ships of those countries where the cargoes originated or were destined for. It was directly modelled on the English Navigation Act, which was also frequently mentioned in the debate. Its primary target was Dutch shipping. During the Great Northern War, the Dutch took a large share of Swedish foreign shipping, and the Act's aim was to reduce this encroachment. On the other hand, the Act could not change much in terms of the trade and shipping balance between Sweden and Britain, which had different features from trade between Sweden and the Dutch Republic.

The debate on the Navigation Act focused on two key, and space-requisite, commodities—iron and salt. These should be carried in Swedish hulls, to save money and to develop a strong merchant marine. As the Act only concerned transit shipping, it did not, in fact, touch on the iron carried on British ships to Britain. But it hit the Dutch transit shipping of salt heavily. As mentioned above, Swedish salt supplies came primarily from Portugal and the Mediterranean, not from the Dutch Republic. With the introduction of the Navigation Act, all this trade could only be carried in Swedish hulls.

The statistical data indicate that Dutch shipping to and from Sweden collapsed. The Sound Toll Register shows over a hundred Dutch ships passing the Sound on their way from Sweden in 1719 and 1720 (Finland not included). In 1725 and 1726 the number of Dutch ships passing the Sound from Sweden declined to six and three respectively. At the same time there were almost two thousand Dutch ships passing the Sound to and from non-Swedish ports.[46] Without doubt, immediately after 1724, a large part of the Dutch decline and the Swedish increase can be attributed to a mere change of flag, but in the long run there was a real increase in Swedish-built and -manned tonnage. The path of shipping development was established.

Even if the Board of Trade played an important role in framing the arguments, in the end it was large merchants, ironworks owners and shipowners who carried these measures through the parliament. This means that the Navigation Act was not a result of abstract economic thinking on the part of administrators in the Board of Trade. It expressed and served the interests of the Stockholm mercantile elite. The same group of Hat-oriented politicians then

---

[45] Ericsson 1985, p. 310.
[46] Bang and Korst 1930, pp. 60–67.

played a key role in carrying out other parts of Sweden's mercantilist policy in the Age of Liberty, concerning manufactures, protectionism, price and exchange regulations, and so on.

As the first and perhaps most distinctive measure of Swedish protectionist policy after 1721, the Navigation Act attracted a good deal of public attention during the eighteenth century. There were many early critics (Christopher Polhem, Emmanuel Swedenborg, Lars Salvius, Pehr Niclas Christiernin and others). An investigation conducted by Johan Jacob Westberg for the Board of Trade was also very critical of the Act. In addition, the Act received much attention during the political struggles of the 1760s. At that time, Anders Chydenius, the Swedish 'Adam Smith', was its most renowned opponent.[47] The major argument against the Navigation Act was that Swedish shipping could not compete with that of the more developed maritime states, such as the Dutch or the British. The carriage of goods on Swedish ships had to be more expensive, which in the end caused higher commodity prices, both at home and on foreign markets. The commodities particularly in question were salt and iron. The critical question was whether the Navigation Act was an economically rational institution, benefiting the whole Swedish economy, or merely another costly instrument disturbing the market balance, while promoting the interests of small selfish elite.

The contemporary debates, even when they relied heavily on the use of statistical evidence, could not provide a definitive answer. The evidence was insufficient and was, as was the debate, too highly coloured by the political interests of the combatants. However, the question has also attracted the attention of modern economic historians. For Eli F. Heckscher the Swedish Navigation Act was a favourite subject, to which he returned many times.[48] Heckscher stated that as regards the number of registered Swedish ships, the volume of shipping, and particularly the geographical expansion of Swedish shipping, the Act was, in fact, a great success. But, at the same time, this success led to high salt prices in Sweden. Moreover, the Navigation Act supposedly had a similar effect on grain prices, in particular during periods of grain shortage. It occasionally happened that the Navigation Act was suspended in periods of dearth, to help secure adequate grain supplies.

On the export side, the Act supposedly made Swedish iron more expensive and so less competitive on the British market. These market problems for Swedish iron could also have been related to another major issue of Swedish economic history in the same period—the loss of dominance in the iron trade to Russia. In summation, Heckscher argued that, despite the spectacular increase in the number of ships and in shipping volume, the primary consequence of the Navigation Act was increased freight costs.[49] Using institutional

---

[47] Chydenius 1765. On Chydenius, see Virrankoski 1995, on criticism in general, see Gerentz 1951, p. 182–183; Carlén 1997, p. 249 and Högberg 1964, p. 16.
[48] See, for example, Heckscher 1922; Heckscher 1940 and Heckscher 1949, vol. 2, pp. 670–678.
[49] Heckscher 1940, p. 25.

terminology, we can say that, according to Heckscher, the new institution (Navigation Act) did not diminish, but rather increased the transaction costs of the Swedish economy.

Heckscher also compared the Swedish Navigation Act with the English version, relating his criticism to Adam Smith's relatively positive view of the English Navigation Act. Smith appreciated the value of the English Navigation Act, because of its importance for the British navy. Even when the use of merchantmen in naval warfare declined, the large, heavily-manned merchant fleet provided a supply of experienced sailors who in time of need could be enrolled in the navy. However, according to Heckscher, no such argument could be used in the case of the Swedish Navigation Act. It was a purely mercantilist measure made in the interests of a small merchant elite.[50]

Heckscher's view of mercantilist policy, and not least his picture of Sweden's eighteenth-century economy, has been questioned for at least fifty years,[51] but his view of the Navigation Act has been widely accepted, with few exceptions. The Swedish economic historian, Stefan Carlén, who has provided the most detailed analysis so far of Heckscher's arguments against the Navigation Act and economic statistics, did not find any evidence of a price effect on the iron and grain trades.[52] And Carlén's detailed study of Swedish salt prices has shown that they in fact declined in the long term, both relative to other Swedish prices and to foreign salt prices (the Dutch Republic).[53] In other words, there is no evidence that the Navigation Act entailed increased transaction costs for the Swedish economy.

However, in addition to the price factor, there is another important factor to which Heckscher did not pay attention. In the case of the English Navigation Act, Adam Smith stressed its military significance, which he, in the end, saw as being more important than the purely economic profitability of the institution. We may not see the Navigation Acts, English, Swedish and otherwise, exclusively as economically rational or irrational measures. There are other factors involved, which must compromise any purely economic perspective. A large merchant fleet provided manpower for the navy, and a strong navy was a precondition of that naval mastery that made it possible for the British to shape the shipping market according to their interests. Thus, in spite of the fact that seventeenth-century Dutch shipping was much more efficient than that of the British, in the course of the eighteenth century British shipping increased, whereas the Dutch declined.[54] The reasons here were not economic, but political and military.

There was also a clearly military aspect to the introduction of the Swedish Navigation Act. A large merchant marine was seen as a guarantee that the

---

[50] Heckscher 1940, p. 26.
[51] See, for example, Nyström 1955; Magnusson 1994 and Carlén 1997.
[52] Carlén 1997, p. 255.
[53] Carlén 1997, pp. 255–263.
[54] Barbour 1996; Lucassen and Unger 2000, p. 130.

Swedish navy could quickly recruit experienced seamen and officers at home in case of war.[55]

The introduction of the Navigation Act touched on many different issues. Here, in particular, the author will stress the link between the Navigation Act and Swedish salt imports, and between the Act and shipping to the Mediterranean and the Iberian Peninsula.

3.5 Convoying and the Convoy Office

Another institutional arrangement necessary for Swedish shipping in the Mediterranean Sea was convoying. In this case, Sweden followed the Dutch example, even though the concept of convoying as an instrument of shipping protection had long been familiar. The convoy system in the Netherlands had been in use as early as the 1550s, before the Dutch Revolt. At that time, it had been employed in the rich westerly trade with the Iberian Peninsula and France, and had followed a pattern established by Spanish shipping to the New World.[56] After the Revolt, the Dutch improved the convoy system and placed it on a stable financial basis. The common Dutch duty on the financing of convoys was introduced in 1582.[57]

In the Mediterranean, the Dutch convoy system reached perfection in the mid-seventeenth century. In contrast to the English, who sailed in large, heavily manned and well-armed vessels, the Dutch sailed to the Mediterranean in convoys consisting of considerable numbers of small merchantmen, usually accompanied by two men-of-war.[58] The use of convoying, to some extent, was a consequence of the introduction of a new and highly cost-efficient ship design, the flute.[59]

The system was apparently efficient as the Dutch, steadily replaced the English in the Mediterranean. In the second half of the seventeenth century, the convoy system was introduced in the English shipping organization, especially in the Mediterranean, and by 1700 convoying had become widely established practice. Sailing in convoy significantly reduced insurance premiums for shipping.[60] However, the system also had its disadvantages. Convoys were slow, as the slowest ship determined the speed of the entire convoy, and turnaround times at ports were extended.

The practice of convoying ships passing the Sound was established in Sweden in the mid-seventeenth century. Axel Oxenstierna issued the first ordinance regulating convoying in 1653.[61] According to this ordinance, Swedish ships

---

[55] Gerentz 1951, pp. 175–178; Müller 2000, pp. 348–349.
[56] Sicking 1998, pp. 106–146.
[57] Vries de and Woude van der 1997, p. 98.
[58] Israel 1989, p. 229.
[59] Barbour 1996, pp. 122–123.
[60] Davis 1962, p. 318.
[61] Olán 1921, p. 77.

sailing to England, the Dutch Republic, and France should meet at Gothenburg on Sweden's western coast. When a sufficient number of vessels was assembled, the convoy sailed away, accompanied by one or two men-of-war. As mentioned above, Swedish ships also frequently joined the Dutch convoys travelling to Portugal and Spain. During the period of armed neutrality in the 1690s, there was co-operation between Denmark and Sweden in organizing convoys.[62]

Conditions for Swedish shipping deteriorated during the Great Northern War, especially after 1709 when Denmark again entered the war. The Swedish ships became potential booty for the Danish privateers west of the Sound. However, as the story of *Stora Jernvågen* shows, Swedish ships could also be taken by Barbary corsairs. By 1720, in particular, the Barbary corsairs had begun to take many Swedish ships.[63] The need for convoying Swedish merchantmen was widely recognised.

A reorganization of the Swedish convoy system was discussed by the same *riksdag* (in 1723) as had promulgated the Navigation Act. The session agreed to establish a new system for financing convoys, based on a special duty, the so-called *extra licenten*. The Board of Trade proposed that the following duty should be paid on all imports and exports: 1 per cent on all imports, and ½ per cent on all exports. Of course, merchants trading in the Baltic Sea, who had no use for convoying, opposed this proposal, and the *riksdag* finally decided to reduce the duty on Baltic imports and exports by a half.[64]

The duty was collected in the Convoy Fund (*Konvojkassan*) which was used to pay for convoys, for peace treaties with the Barbary states, and partly also for the release of Swedish seamen in Africa. The question of whether the Convoy Fund was an institution useful to the whole kingdom, or whether it was created merely in the interests of the mercantile elite engaged in the Mediterranean trade, recurred many times. For example, in 1745, during the ongoing negotiations with Tripoli, many were critical of Anders Plomgren, one of the merchants with interests in the Mediterranean, when he proposed that all merchants should contribute to the Convoy Fund according to their financial situation.[65]

Before 1724, the convoys had usually been organized through cooperation between the Admiralty and the Board of Trade. With the new ordinance for convoy organization, a new office was created with its seat at Gothenburg—the Convoy Office (*Konvojkommissariatet*). It included representatives of burghers (merchants and shipowners) and of the Admiralty. The Presidents of the Office were always drawn from the ranks of the navy's admirals.[66]

According to the instructions issued by the Board of Trade and the Admi-

---

[62] Ekegård 1924, p. 252.
[63] Ekegård 1924, p. 310.
[64] Ekegård 1924, pp. 311–312.
[65] Hahr 1966, p. 66–69.
[66] Olán 1921, pp. 88–89.

ralty, convoys should consist of two men-of-war, with at least 50 guns each. Earlier, it had been usual for only one ship to accompany convoys. Convoys were supposed to sail twice a year—in spring and autumn. The first place where ships met was Gothenburg. Swedish convoys were then supposed to wait at Plymouth for all merchant vessels that asked for protection, and then they sailed directly to Portugal, keeping close to the Portuguese coast. Men-of-war were expected to continue their voyage to Cadiz, but not to sail past Gibraltar into the Mediterranean. On their return voyage, the men-of-war were supposed to assemble Swedish ships waiting in salt ports, such as Lisbon and Setubal.[67]

Typically, convoy organization encountered continual problems. On the one hand, there was a constant lack of resources. The costs of the expeditions were much larger than the collected duty of the *extra licenten*. On the other hand, Stockholm merchants in particular were reluctant to use convoys. Convoying was always connected to long waiting periods and turnaround times, which made ships less efficient. Therefore many shipmasters refused to wait for convoys and sailed without protection, or in the convoys of other countries.

Despite frequent public criticism and lack of resources, the Convoy Office survived for over a hundred years. However, the organization went through many changes. First, it was moved from Gothenburg to Stockholm in 1741–42.[68] There the Office continued in it activities until the 1780s, when, as a result of an investigation, its closure was proposed. Between 1790 and 1797, the Convoy Office's duties were taken over by the State Office. But, quite soon, it became clear that the new organization was even more expensive, and no better at protecting shipping than the Convoy Office. Thus, in February 1797, the Convoy Office was re-established in a similar form as before, and it continued into the first decades of the nineteenth century.[69]

As mentioned above, the activities of the Office were theoretically financed by the duty of *extra licenten*. But the resources thereby collected were insufficient. Therefore, the *extra licenten* level was doubled in 1747, and again in 1760.[70] In addition, the Office was allowed to finance its activities via loans. However, all these attempts to secure its finances proved inadequate. Clearly, it was impossible to balance rising expenditure with available income. For example, in 1759 the Convoy Office's income was roughly 100,000 d.s.m., but its outlays amounted to almost 162,000 d.s.m.[71] The total debts of the Office were steadily rising. Repeatedly, when the situation became acute, the state took over the Office's debts and wrote them off. Hence, in 1766 the state wrote off a debt of 923,448 d.s.m.

The situation did not much improve during the Gustavian period (1772–

[67] Ekegård 1924, p. 355.
[68] Krëuger 1856, p. 27.
[69] Carlson 1971, pp. 8–9.
[70] Carlson 1971, p. 7.
[71] Krëuger 1856, p. 29.

1809). In 1776, the Office received a subsidy of 666,666 rixdollars specie. In spite of this, the debts continued to rise, and in 1778 it was once again necessary to write them off, this time to the tune of 364,723 rixdollars specie. These continuous problems with finances were among the reasons why the Office was closed in 1790.

The financial problems of the Convoy Office were the result of the fact that it was employed in too many areas. First, there was convoying—the most important task. The Office was responsible for manpower aboard the navy's convoying ships and for supplying the equipment for voyages. The navy's ships also had to be returned to the Admiralty in good shape, which entailed repair costs. Thus the total costs of a single convoy could be dauntingly high. For example, the first convoy of autumn 1724, including the two 54-gun ships *Verden* and *Öland*, cost the Convoy Office 35,286 d.s.m.[72]

Second, there were the costs of peace treaties with the Barbary states, which, indeed, made the biggest hole in the Office's accounts. As mentioned above, from the first contacts with the Barbary states onwards, the Convoy Office was seen as the institution which should provide for these outlays. This meant that the treaties and the institutional arrangements surrounding them, including the work of Swedish diplomatic representatives, the gifts and the consular services, were seen by the Stockholm authorities as a part of the same institutional arrangement for the Mediterranean shipping as was convoying. In modern institutional terminology, both could be labelled protection costs.

The third task of the Convoy Office was the payment of ransoms for, and hence the freeing of, Swedish captives in North Africa. However, the resources for this purpose were not only provided by *extra licenten*. Every year, money was collected in all Swedish churches for the freeing of Swedish subjects from Muslim slavery.[73] As late as 1726, the king issued an ordinance to the effect that four times per year money should be collected in Swedish churches to free these helpless Swedish subjects.[74]

To make the convoy system less costly, Sweden occasionally co-operated with Denmark, the latter being in exactly the same situation. Such joint convoys were already being organised in the 1690s, during the first period of armed neutrality.[75] Similar attempts were made after the Dutch treaty with Algiers in 1726: at that time the Danish envoy in Stockholm proposed organising joint Danish-Swedish convoys to the Mediterranean. However, in 1728, when it became clear that Sweden would soon sign a treaty with Algiers, Stockholm lost interest in joint Danish-Swedish convoying.[76]

It should be mentioned here that the Danish protection system was organised in a partially different way. There was no Danish Convoy Office, and the

---

[72] Krëuger 1856, p. 43.
[73] Ekegård 1924, pp. 253–254 (note).
[74] Olán 1921, p. 108.
[75] Ekegård 1924, p. 252.
[76] Ekegård 1924, p. 482.

Danish consular service and the release of Danish captives were implemented via other institutions. In 1725, there was a proposal to pay for convoys to Portugal and Spain via a special duty on shipping—quite similar to the Swedish *extra licenten*—but the proposal failed.[77] Perhaps the notion that all Danish vessels should pay for convoys used by only a limited number of ships was not acceptable to the absolute state. The same idea, however, could find support in the Swedish *riksdag* of the Age of Liberty.

Payments of ransoms for Danish captives in North Africa were carried out by a special Slave Society (*Slavenkassen*), established in 1715.[78] The funds were collected from a duty paid on each ship, according to its tonnage. Indeed, the Danish Slave Society was the institution which first proposed signing a treaty with the Barbary states: the proposal of a treaty with Algiers in 1736. This proposal clearly had the Swedish treaty of 1728 as its model, and perhaps the Society's representatives also had contacts with the Swedes engaged in the Swedish negotiations.[79] Yet it took another ten years before the Danish treaty became a reality.[80]

Balancing the convoying of ships with the maintenance of peaceful relations with the Barbary corsairs was a complicated task. The main reason for signing the treaties with the Barbary states was the protection of shipping in southern Europe. It was argued that treaties would reduce the costs of convoying and increase security for the ships. However, convoying did not disappear; instead the Convoy Office was obliged to pay for both peace treaties and convoying.

The Swedish convoying system concentrated the many tasks of shipping protection (convoying, peace treaties and consular service in Algiers, Tunis, Tripoli, and Morocco) in one institution—the Convoy Office. According to the original concept, the Convoy Office was supposed to finance its activities by a special duty on all Swedish foreign trade. However, this income was never enough, and hence the outlays of the Office, and so the whole Swedish protection system in southern Europe, were more or less obviously paid for by the state. Looking at the system from a protection costs perspective, we may conclude that it modestly reduced the overall protection costs of Swedish shipping and trade in southern Europe (See section 5.6 and Appendix E). To be sure, it transferred the protection costs of private enterprises (Swedish shipowners and merchants with interests in the area) to the state: a private issue was thereby turned into a public concern. This became possible due to the political power of the Stockholm mercantile elite, which had the strongest interest in the development of commercial contacts with southern Europe. But a number of examples show that the public acceptance of the system was not wholly unproblematic. The history of the Swedish Convoy Office includes many attempts to change its organization and reduce its costs.

---

[77] Andersen 2000, p. 43.
[78] Andersen 2000, p. 42.
[79] Andersen 2000, p. 43.
[80] On the Danish relations to the Barbary states, see Wandel 1919.

3.6 The Swedish Levant Company

Salt supplies have been identified as probably the single most important factor behind Sweden's engagement in southern Europe. However, there was another, commercial motive for such activities—the Levant trade. As in the case of the salt trade, Swedish interests in the Levant had a long history. Some of the initial contacts have been mentioned in the section above, dealing with diplomatic relationships with the Sublime Porte. We have mentioned Johan Silfvercrantz's plans to establish a Swedish Levant trade during Charles XII's stay on Ottoman territory, and the reasons for their failure.

In parallel with the diplomatic negotiations with the Sublime Porte in the 1730s, some leading Stockholm merchants were planning the prompt opening of Swedish trade with the Levant, and when the question of Charles XII's debt was resolved and the trade treaty with the Sublime Porte concluded, there were no more obstacles to this ambition. Thus, a year later, in February 1738, the Swedish Levant Company was founded in Stockholm.[81]

In many ways, establishing the Levant company was a controversial issue, a fact reflected in the *riksdag* of 1738. There was a deep political split over the issue between the old Cap regime of Arvid Horn, and the rising party of the Hats. Not coincidentally, the supporters of the company idea were without exception leading Hats. Firstly, the controversy had diplomatic implications. The establishment of the Levant Company was impossible without improved relationships with the Ottoman Empire (the trade treaty), which met with the disapproval of the Caps' ally, Russia, and even with that of some other states. And in this sense the establishment of the Company may be interpreted as an important platform in the Hats' aggressive anti-Russian policy.

Second, and in this context perhaps more important, was the organizational aspect. Should the Levant trade be organized according to a chartered company model, following the example of the English Levant Company, or should it be left free, following the model of the Dutch? The Stockholm merchant community was divided on the question. Some minor merchants argued for a free trade form of organization. However, the merchant elite argued for a chartered company on the English model, and their proposal, although in partially reduced stature, finally won through in the *riksdag*.[82]

Third, there also was a more general mercantilist aspect to the Levant trade debate. Adversaries argued that Sweden had no true commercial interests in the Levant. Levant commodities (e.g. silk) were seen as unnecessary luxuries, and so one of the roots of Sweden's unfavourable balance of trade. Instead, the Swedes should consume products made in Sweden, in Swedish manufactures; and, even if consumption of Levant commodities were allowed, foreigners could import them at lower cost.

---

[81] Olán 1921, p. 42.
[82] Hahr 1966, p. 47, see also Olán 1921. For the Danish Levant trade see Andersen 1992 and Andersen 2000, pp. 59–77.

Analysing the privileges included in the Company charter of 1738, we can see that the final version of the charter was a kind of compromise between monopoly and free trade. The Company's monopoly was not complete. It concerned only the Levant coast—meaning that commerce in western area of the Mediterranean basin was left free. In addition, individuals could purchase a special Levant trade licence from the Company (for a fee of 15 per cent of the cargo value).

The charter gave the newly-appointed Swedish consul in Smyrna, Henrik Hackson, an important role. On the one hand, the consul was made an official Swedish representative there. His duty was to register all Swedish cargoes entering and leaving the harbour, and to inform the Board of Trade about trade and shipping there. The Convoy Fund paid him 2,000 rixdollars annually, which showed that the Smyrna consulate was a part of the same consular system as the consulates at Algiers, Tripoli and Tunis. At the same time, the consul was appointed by the Company's directors, and he worked for the Company.[83] Hackson also took an active part in the discussions about the future shape of the Swedish Levant trade and, not surprisingly, he preferred a chartered company form of organization.

The Levant Company was the second chartered company founded in Sweden during the Age of Liberty, the first being the Swedish East India Company (1731). However, despite a superficial, external similarity in organization, there were substantial differences between the Levant and East India Companies. First, the monopoly rights given to the East India Company were much more exclusive. In contrast to the Mediterranean trade, there were no real opportunities for private East India trade from Sweden. Second, the scale of operations and the capital stock invested were of different magnitudes. The starting capital of the Levant Company was a modest 200,000 d.s.m., compared to 5.5 million d.s.m. for the Swedish East India Company.[84] The difference in capital stock can be explained not only by the scale of operations of the East India Company, but also by foreign interests. In particular, during its first decades, foreign investments in the East India Company played a crucial role, and the Company staff included many foreigners. On the other hand, the Levant Company does not appear to have attracted any foreign investors or employees.

The business of the Levant Company did not develop according to the high-flown expectations of its founders. When, after the first ten years, the charter was renewed, the monopoly for the Levant coastal trade was made even more exclusive, to improve the Company's financial condition. But that did not help. After 1752, the Company's operations more or less ceased, and after another three years the *riksdag* (1755–56) decided to withdraw the company charter, and thus 'liberated' Swedish trade with the Levant. The charter was bought back by the state. During its 18 years existence (1738–56), the Levant Company sent the tiny number of fourteen vessels to Smyrna.[85]

---

[83] Olán 1921, pp. 42–43.
[84] Olán 1921, p. 59; Åberg 1988, p. 31.
[85] Olán 1921, p. 63.

The failure of the Levant Company strongly contrasts with the overall increase in Swedish shipping to the Mediterranean. The fourteen vessels cited above can be compared with over 3,000 Algerian passports issued in the 1739–59 period by the Board of Trade.[86] Why did the Levant Company fail? In 1752, the *riksdag* asked the directors for an explanation of the miserable conditions of the Company business. The reasons given by the directors exactly reflect the general problems experienced by Swedish long-distance trade compared with other states. There were too many disadvantages. The value of an average Swedish cargo was much lower than an average foreign cargo. Swedish cargoes destined for the Levant was never valued over 15,000 d.s.m., while the Dutch and English cargoes were usually valued at about 100,000 d.s.m. The explanation lies in the composition of Swedish cargoes. The Swedes mainly exported bulky commodities (iron, iron manufactures, tar, pitch, sawn timber), demanding of space but relatively cheap. The Dutch and English, on the other hand, exported textiles and other high-value goods. Whereas bar-iron was the major commodity for the Swedes, the Dutch used it as ballast, so that it was free of freight cost. In addition, sailing from Stockholm to Smyrna took much longer than a voyage from Amsterdam or London, which made the Swedish voyage relatively uneconomic. Moreover, the Swedish company was financially too weak, and hence it was obliged to buy Levant commodities on worse terms than its financially stronger competitors.[87]

The Company directors also highlighted the well-known structural disadvantages of Swedish long-distance trade and shipping. It was scarcely novel to argue that Swedish ships had to sail much further than Dutch or English ones. Neither was the capital weakness of Swedish merchants or the unfavourable composition of their cargoes news. This did not explain much. Perhaps a better explanation of the failure of this enterprise lays in the fact that the Company was not successful in exploiting all the opportunities and advantages that the Swedes had in the area of Mediterranean shipping. It was also dissolved before the Swedish ships could fully exploit the advantages of neutrality shipping.

Neither did the consulate at Smyrna promote trade as had been intended. The first consul at Smyrna, the above-mentioned Henrik Hackson, apparently spent much time in Sweden. He was appointed consul in March 1736, even before the peace and trade treaty with the Sublime Porte was concluded.[88] However, as early as 1737 he was in Stockholm, taking part in the debate about the future shape of the Levant trade. As mentioned, the Company charter gave him a position as the Company's commission agent. In 1742, Hackson sent his resignation to the Board of Trade. In his place, Johan Henrik Kierman took over the consular duties, but he does not seem to have received the official appointment document from Stockholm. Kierman was a stepson of Gustaf Kierman, who played so important a role in the payment of the Swedish debt

---

[86] Algerian passport registers. (*Sjöpassdiarier för åren 1739–1768*), C II b, BoT SNA.
[87] Olán 1921, pp. 61–62
[88] Almqvist 1912–13, p. 430.

to the Sublime Porte, and was already deeply engaged in the Levant trade in the early 1730s. Gustaf Kierman was also one of the founders and directors of the Company.

Despite the fact that he lacked an official appointment, Kierman junior worked to promote Swedish trade with the Ottoman Empire. And he highlighted out neutral shipping as the major Swedish advantage. In his report to the Directors of the Company of September 1744, he wrote of the profitable prospects for Swedish shipowners in shipping between Smyrna, Thessaloniki, even Alexandria, and other parts of the eastern Mediterranean. Because of the lack of shipping capacity, local merchants rented ships from Naples and Venice—only too well aware of the danger, as the Neapolitan and Venetian ships were favourite targets of the Barbary corsairs. Swedish ships were much safer and, due to their lower insurance premiums, they were better paid for freight. Kierman mentioned the fact that for the Smyrna-Livorno voyage, the insurance premiums for the Swedish ships were 3–4 per cent, whereas the Venetian ships paid premiums of 6, 8, or even as much as 10 per cent.[89] Unfortunately, the young Kierman did not manage to realise many of his ideas. In October 1744, just two years after taking over the consulate, he was murdered in a robbery near Smyrna.[90]

Other reports for the area also testify that the most profitable opportunity for the Swedes was not the commodity trade between the Levant and Sweden, but shipping for foreigners in the Mediterranean Sea. Edvard Carlson, who after the successful negotiations with the Sublime Porte became the Swedish envoy in Constantinople, reported in August 1744 on the plans of Marseilles merchants to hire Swedish ships for trade with Thessaloniki and Smyrna.[91] The failure of the Levant Company should therefore be seen mainly as a failure of the direct trade between the Levant and Sweden. It did not demonstrate any general failure of Swedish policy for the Mediterranean.

3.7 Conclusions

It is clear that the Mediterranean became, in the early eighteenth century, a high-priority area for the Swedish authorities and Sweden's merchants. Swedish ambitions encompassed both the western and eastern basins of the Mediterranean Sea, and they had a primarily commercial, but also partly a political character. In the western basin of the Mediterranean, the Swedes were first of all interested in salt supplies. Second, they were searching for new markets for Swedish staple commodities, such as iron, sawn timber, tar and pitch. The major motive for establishing contacts with the eastern basin of the Mediterra-

---

[89] Report 9/20 September 1744. Levant Company 1741–1754, E XVII aa 1, BoT SNA.
[90] Butini to BoT, 18 December 1744, Marseilles, Consular Reports, Marseilles 1732–1814, E VI aa 331, BoT SNA.
[91] Carlson to BoT, 22 August 1744, Levant Company 1741–1754, E XVII aa 1, BoT SNA.

nean was the Levant trade; but, in this area, the balance of foreign political interests between the Ottoman Empire and Russia decided the timing and extent of Swedish engagement.

To promote these ambitions, Sweden implemented a number of measures, which can be described as institutional modernization. Nevertheless, even if this institutional modernisation was new for Sweden, it was not original in an international context. In fact, all the 'new' Swedish institutions mimicked the well-tested Dutch and English prototypes.

First, the Swedish Navigation Act was launched in 1724. Second, the Swedish convoy system was reorganized, and a new Convoy Fund and Convoy Office were established. Third, Sweden signed important peace and trade treaties with the Barbary states and the Sublime Porte. The consular service in North Africa appeared as an immediate outcome of the peace treaties, and a complement to the rising number of consulates on the northern coast of the Mediterranean Sea and on the Iberian Peninsula. Fourth, the Swedish Levant Company began operation business in 1738.

The institutional framework described above fits comfortably under the umbrella of that eighteenth-century economic policy labelled mercantilism. A question that naturally flows from this, and one naturally related to the old debate about the character of mercantilism, is: did this institutional framework provide an efficient foundation for the growth of Swedish trade and shipping in southern Europe, and of the Swedish economy in general, or should it be seen as a distortion of the 'market balance', and perhaps a result of political egotism by some self-interested actors? In other words, did the institutional framework entail a reduction or increase in transaction costs for Sweden? Answering these questions, however, requires a quantitative analysis of both the Swedish commodity trade and shipping activities in southern Europe. In addition, such an analysis must be related to the general development of European long-distance shipping. An attempt to address the issue is made in chapter 5, but before that we will look more closely at the Swedish consular service in southern Europe: its models, origins and functions. Not least, we will closely examine the history of some major Swedish consulates in the area.

CHAPTER 4

The Swedish consular service in southern Europe

In the few days that I have been here in Livorno I find that this is the Generall Magazine of Commerce that supplies not only all Italy but most parts of Africa with all sorts of European American and Asian Merchandize & manufactures, corn is also laid up here from Sicily the Levant and often from England for supplying Spain and Portugall in their necessities [...] the reason why this place is so much frequented by all nations Is that the customs and charges upon goods inwards and outwards is very insignificant it being also the principal and most convenient Scala Franca in all the Mediterranean.

George Logie to the Board of Trade, Livorno, 2/13 October 1738[1]

4.1 Early consular services in the Mediterranean

Violet Barbour described the seventeenth-century shipping world as divided into two quite distinct fields.[2] Shipping in northern Europe was characterised by bulky commodities, by large merchant fleets and by high average tonnage per vessel. It was also a relatively safe world, with few seamen on board an average ship and low insurance premiums. It was a world dominated by the Dutch flute.

The second field encompassed the remaining shipping world: southern Europe, the Canaries, Madeira, Africa, and the East Indies. Barbour might also add the Caribbean and the Americas. Commerce in these regions had been characterised by 'rich trades'. The shipping of high-value commodities did not require such large shipping capacity as the northern trades in bulkier commodities, but on the other hand, long-distance sailing and especially sailing in dangerous waters required many hands on board; insurance premiums were high. In spite of the fact that the shipping world changed and expanded substantially, Barbour's characterisation also largely works for the eighteenth century. The Mediterranean Sea belonged, of course, to the latter field of shipping, notwith-

---

[1] George Logie to the BoT, 2/13 October 1738, Livorno, Consular Reports, Livorno 1725–1822, E VI aa 229, BoT SNA.
[2] Barbour 1996, pp. 107–108.

standing that much of the shipping in the Mediterranean also had the character of 'bulky' trade.[3]

Swedish trade and shipping had for centuries been conducted in northern Europe. Swedish merchants and sailors knew the conditions of shipping, as well as the institutional environment in the area. The Mediterranean, which they had entered more extensively by the late seventeenth century, was a different proposition. Business activities in southern Europe were carried out in a different institutional environment from northern Europe. This environment was the result of much longer historical development dating back to the ancient period, but it was also an environment characterised by a large degree of uncertainty, both on the seas and in relations with local authorities.

One of the particular features of this strange institutional environment was the consular system. The system united commercial, legal and—partly—also diplomatic functions. Consulates were originally tribunals, with representation from both merchants—either local or from abroad—and from local authorities. In this form, consulates were already known in the late thirteenth century.[4] Consulates solved disputes concerning all aspects of maritime trade. They were supposed to solve conflicts between merchants and authorities, but also between different merchants, or merchants and their employees (captains, seamen, etc.).[5] Consuls, in fact, were representatives of the merchant community at a specific seaport, and were usually elected by the merchant community of that seaport.

Because of the international character of the merchant communities all around the Mediterranean, many elected consuls were foreigners. In conflicts with local authorities, they then represented not only the interests of commerce but often also the interests of their own national groups. In this way the distinction between two categories of consuls arose. The overseas consuls (*Consul de Ultramar*) obtained a representative function. They defended and assisted citizens of their respective countries, and they represented their state in its contacts with the local power. On the other hand, the consuls of the sea (*Consul de Mar*) fulfilled a legal role in the resolution of conflicts concerning the Mediterranean maritime world.[6] Here the focus will be on the group of overseas consuls. In particular, north-western European countries developed overseas consular services in the course of sixteenth and seventeenth centuries, which then served as a model for the Swedish consular service.

An interesting area, as regards the rise of overseas consuls, was the Levant coast: on the one hand, part of the Ottoman Empire, on the other an area of

---

[3] On the difference between armed shipping in southern waters and relatively safe shipping, without need of armed ship in the North and Baltic Seas see also Glete 1993b, pp. 113–119, 196–197.

[4] Carmel Salvo mentions that the regulations of the Consulate of the Sea of Messina could be dated as early as to 1282 or 1283, Salvo 2000, pp. 17, 218

[5] Sebastian Vella provides a detailed description of consulate's duties at Malta. Vella 2000, pp. 69–80.

[6] Vassallo 1996, p. 51

great commercial importance for Europeans since the Middle Ages. Ottoman administration often came into conflict with European merchant communities. Therefore the consular system in the Levant may serve as a classic example of how the consular services of the European powers operated.

In the sixteenth and seventeenth centuries there were four states with consular representation in the Levant: Venice, with its traditionally well-established exchange with the area; France, with its consular service established in 1535/36; England, with a consular service since 1583; and the Dutch Republic, with a consular service since 1613.[7] The consular representations were based on treaties with the Sublime Porte, but these treaties had a different character compared with the European treaty system. Relations with the Sublime Porte should not be seen in the same perspective as inter-European diplomatic relations based on international law. Relations between European consuls and local authorities followed Muslim customary law, regulating the legal situation of infidels under Muslim sovereignty. This feature is also important as regards the later Swedish treaties with the North-African states.

The non-diplomatic character of the consular service in the Ottoman territories is confirmed by the fact that, in the course of the sixteenth century, European consuls were not exempt from local jurisdiction. As late as 1596, the local authorities in Alexandria could execute a French consul.[8] Provision for the diplomatic immunity of consuls was first included in the renewed English and French treaties in 1601 and 1604 respectively.

The consuls were perceived by the Ottoman authorities primarily as the leaders of foreign merchant communities, not as representatives of European states. Therefore they could be handled quite arbitrarily. For example, it was usual to see unilateral increases in the duties paid by consuls, without proper explanation. In addition, a typical feature of the authorities' attitude to consuls was collective responsibility. Communities of foreign merchants and their leaders—consuls—were responsible to local authorities for the behaviour of individual community members.

In a similar manner as the consuls of the sea (*Consul de Mar*), European consuls in the Levant functioned as judges. They ruled on conflicts within European merchant communities. In the course of time, they became more and more independent from the local jurisdiction. In special cases consuls could even send defendants to their home countries for trial.

It has been stressed that the European consuls had a role mainly as representatives of their national merchant communities. Nevertheless, they were authorised to act as consuls by the governments of their home countries. They had to receive official appointments, otherwise they were not taken seriously by the local authorities. So an official appointment letter was drawn up to confirm a consul's diplomatic role, although this role was not the same as that of diplomats in western Europe.

---

[7] Steensgaard 1967.
[8] Steensgaard 1967, p. 18.

This ambiguous position—as a representative of a merchant community, and as a quasi-diplomatic representative of a state—was frequently a cause of conflict of interest.[9] For example, typical Venetian consuls seldom had commercial ties with Venetian merchants at the place of appointment. They had usually seen prior service as officials in Venice. The Venetian consular service seems to have been more professionalised than the services of other states. According to Niels Steensgaard, who analysed the European consulates in the Levant, the reports of Venetian consuls to their government were of better quality than those of their French, Dutch and English counterparts.[10] The Venetian consuls also obtained a fixed state salary, and were not allowed to take part in local commerce. All these features stress their position as official diplomatic representatives of the Venetian Republic more than as leaders of any merchant community.

This professional system contrasted with the French consular service. French consuls had much closer relationships with their merchant communities. The state tried to strengthen its control over the consular institution, but it was not very successful. The French consulates frequently passed from one family member to another in a way typical of other offices in seventeenth-century France. This was the reason why the French consular service was seen as less efficient than the other states'. French consuls in the Levant did not receive any salary, and were supposed to obtain their living from the 2 per cent duty on imported French goods. To improve their financial situation, French consuls had to take part in commerce, although this meant less independence and lower social status.[11]

The Dutch consular system more closely resembled the French than the Venetian model. Dutch consuls also originated from well-established merchant families. They did not receive any salary, and so they were dependent on consular duties and on their own business affairs.[12]

The English consular system in the Levant was completely different from any other. It was built up on the basis of the different organization of the English Levant trade, and the special role of the English Levant Company within it. English consuls represented neither England, nor the English merchant community (English 'nation'). They represented nothing other than the Levant Company and its interest, even against other English subjects in the Levant. The company was also entitled to appoint the English consuls and vice-consuls in the Levant, despite the criticism of the independent English merchants in the area. This inflamed the relationship between Englishmen living in the Levant and the London directors of the Levant Company.[13]

The cases of the Venetian, French, Dutch and English consular services obviously demonstrate that the consular institution could be organised in quite

[9] Steensgaard 1967, p. 25.
[10] Steensgaard 1967, p. 26.
[11] Steensgaard 1967, pp. 26–28, 31.
[12] Steensgaard 1967, p. 33.

different ways. The Swedish consular service in the Mediterranean was to include different pieces of these models, depending on the consulate's location.

By the seventeenth century, international commerce in the Mediterranean had acquired a partially different character in comparison with previous centuries. The traditional corsair *guerre de course* between the Christians and Muslims was receding. France, due to its early diplomatic relations with the Ottoman Empire, played a key role in this development. At the same time, northern-European shipping and commerce acquired a large share of Mediterranean trade.

In comparison with the Mediterranean states, the northern-European merchants (first the Dutch and English, but later, also the Danes and Swedes) had more spacious ships, more tonnage per man on board, and a more efficient shipping organization. However, one of the key preconditions of northern-European shipping in the Mediterranean Sea was the increasing security and predictability of trading activities. Treaties with the Ottoman Empire and its vassals in North Africa created this security, and it appeared easier for such treaties to be signed by Protestant northern-European powers than by Catholic Mediterranean states.[14] Consular services played a key role in creating this more secure commercial environment, at least for the Dutch, English and French.

The Swedish consular service, established after 1720, clearly combined the Dutch and English consular models—in the same way that the Dutch and English treaties with the Barbary states served as a model for defining Swedish relations with the Muslim states in the Mediterranean. In the following sections we will describe in detail how the Swedish consular service was shaped, which individuals were appointed as Swedish consuls in the area, and which duties and general functions Swedish consuls discharged.

4.2 Appointment procedures in the Swedish consular service

The expansion of the Swedish consular service in southern Europe was more a result of political and economic ambition than a response to the specific needs of Sweden's foreign trade and shipping in the area. To some extent, consuls were appointed for areas where the authorities wished to develop Swedish trade. But the consular service had also expanded, even if less rapidly, in areas where Swedish trade was already established: Britain, France and the Dutch Republic.

---

[13] For example, in 1630, when the English consul in Smyrna died, the 'nation' consisting of local English merchants elected a new consul, without the Company's approval. In this specific case a compromise was reached and, at the end, the Company's representatives approved the locally elected consul. Steensgaard 1967, pp. 34–36.

[14] Colley 2002, p. 81.

An interesting aspect of the Swedish consular service in the eighteenth century is the issue of nationality. On the one hand, the employment of local merchants of non-Swedish origin as Swedish consuls was very common. They usually had better knowledge of the local trade and political situation than the Swedes. They were quite often also interested in becoming Swedish consuls. Foreigners did not only aspire to the post of Swedish consul because of their commercial interests. Consular appointment also entailed diplomatic immunity, and thus exemption from the local jurisdiction. Consuls enjoyed a high degree of personal security and esteem within the local merchant communities. However, within France it was forbidden to appoint as consul an individual who was not a French subject. Therefore all Swedish consuls in France were Frenchmen.

The Swedish Board of Trade preferred Swedish subjects. These were perceived as better guarantors of the promotion of Swedish interests. As early as November 1719, the Swedish Board of Trade was arguing that young Swedish merchants should be preferred as consuls abroad. In 1723, the royal instruction concerning the consular service once again expressed the aspiration that Swedes rather than foreigners should be employed. Consuls were also asked to report in the Swedish language and this, of course, was easier for a Swedish-born consul. Nevertheless, a considerable volume of consular correspondence to the Board of Trade was in English or French. In the course of the eighteenth century, the proportion of foreigners slowly declined. In 1789, foreigners made up only seventeen of forty-eight active consuls.[15]

The rising number of Swedish-born consuls was not only a result of the Board's appointment policy, but also a sign of interest on the part of Stockholm's leading merchant families. Swedish consuls in the key commercial centres often belonged to these families. The Lisbon consulate is a good example of this phenomenon. After Joachim de Besche (1704–21), Anders Bachmanson Nordencrantz, a prominent politician and merchant (1727–38) served as consul. After Nordencrantz came Arvid Arfwedson (1738–56) of the well-known Stockholm family, and later Jean Bedoire (1757–78), member of another prominent city family. Between 1782 and 1808, and again from 1816 to 1860, the Lisbon consulate was served by the Kantzow family, yet another leading Stockholm family.[16] The same situation will be found in other parts of the Swedish consular services. The key consulates in London were served by members of the Grill and Tottie families for almost a hundred years (1777–1869). The consulate in Amsterdam was managed by the Hasselgrens. All three families belonged to the very highest stratum of the Stockholm merchant elite.[17]

---

[15] Almqvist 1912–13, pp. 132, 139.
[16] Almqvist 1912–13, p. 410, see also Högberg 1964; Jansson 1964 and *SBL*, vol. 20, 1973–75, pp. 609–613.
[17] Almqvist 1912–13, pp. 356 and 405. For information about the families see Samuelsson 1951; Müller 1998; Müller and Ojala 2002, pp. 37–39, and *SBL*.

However, the leading merchant circles of Stockholm had quite an ambiguous view of the consular service. In some parts of Europe, they perceived consuls as a necessity; in particular, this was true for the Mediterranean. Here, the consular service was necessary because it was a part of the traditional fabric of doing business—as described above. So, if Sweden wished to take part in Mediterranean commerce, it had to conform to this same system. On the other hand, in northern and eastern Europe, areas without any tradition of consular service, exchange could be carried out without consuls. Hence consular service in these areas entailed little more than new costs. Perhaps the long period of vacancy of the London consulate may be explained by the unwillingness of merchants to fill it. Despite the first official appointment in 1722 (Jonas Alström), the consulate was in fact vacant for 50 years. Jonas Alström promptly returned to Sweden in 1723, and the next consul, Peter Christian Algehr, received his official appointment in 1772.[18] London business could be carried out with or without a consul.

To reach a concord between the enthusiastic appointment policy of the Board of Trade and the more practical attitude of the merchant community, all appointments were made in consultation with merchant representatives. Usually, the Board asked the merchants for a recommendation on the question of an appointment, and usually followed their recommendation. In the first part of the eighteenth century, the Stockholm merchants chose between six and twelve representatives, who drafted these recommendations. From 1770 on, the recommendations were signed by the Stockholm Merchant Association (*Grosshandelssocieteten*). Beginning in 1813, other Swedish port towns were even asked to comment on the appointments of new consuls.[19] This proves that the Stockholm merchant elite played a key role in the appointment policy.

Merchants' statements concerning the appointments of new consuls are preserved in the archives of the Board of Trade. They provide us with a detailed picture of how the Stockholm merchant elite approached the question. It seems that quite often they were opposed to new consulates, new costs being the main reason. The following cases show in detail how the process of consideration could play out.

In 1775, Gustaf Baumgart applied to the Board of Trade for appointment as a Swedish consul in Valencia in Spain, and as usual, the Board sent his application to the Stockholm Merchant Association for comment. The Association response stated that Swedish trade in the district of Valencia had not developed as merchants wished, and that the reason was 'the lack of National consuls'. So, in general, the Association was positive regarding the creation of a new consulate. Nevertheless, it also stated that the new consulate should not impose any new fees on Swedish trade and shipping.[20] The application was subsequently

---

[18] Almqvist 1912–13, p. 136.
[19] Almqvist 1912–13, pp. 136, 195.
[20] Stockholm Merchant Association to BoT, 9 November 1775, *Ansökningar om konsulattjänsten* E XVII g:1, BoT SNA.

declined. Yet it is worth mentioning that this same Baumgart became Swedish consul at Cartagena some twenty years later, in 1792.[21]

Statements of the Association also show that its members recommended only individuals whom the Stockholm merchants knew and trusted. Of course, one natural consequence of this priority was that the recommended applicants were frequently of Swedish origin, and were very often members of one of Stockholm's leading mercantile families, as previously observed. So, when the Association was asked to make a statement regarding applicants for a vacant consulate at Genoa, in 1778, it recommended the Swedish-born Carl Holmberg, well known to them from his business activities in Genoa. They also expressed the hope in their statement that 'through Holmberg a good national [Swedish] merchant house could be established at Genoa'. But once again, the representatives stressed that the appointment must not entail new consular fees.[22]

Another example of the importance of personal knowledge for recommendation is the case of an English officer named J. Labot. In 1813, Labot applied for the position of Swedish consul at Malta (La Valetta). The Association's answer was dated June 1814. The merchants stated that the applicant was completely unknown to them, and they could not recommend him for the post.[23]

A strong reason for preferring a well-known and trustworthy individual was the employment of consuls as commission agents. A recent analysis of the role of Swedish consuls as commission agents for Finnish merchants reveals that about half of the consuls dealing with Finnish cargoes in the late eighteenth and early nineteenth centuries had Scandinavian names.[24] They were simply more trusted. This implies that Swedish-Finnish merchants preferred Swedish consuls before foreigners, mainly because of their personal knowledge of the consul or his family.

But the importance of Swedish origin should not be exaggerated. There were at least two strong arguments for appointing foreigners. Firstly, they usually had much better expertise *vis-à-vis* the local trade conditions than did Swedes. This advantage was especially apparent in the early part of the eighteenth century, and in those areas where Sweden had no established contacts. The establishment of the consular service in North Africa would not have been possible without the experience of the Scottish merchant George Logie. Secondly, foreigners were simply more interested in getting the job. The Board of Trade had problems recruiting Swedish nationals, and it blamed the rich merchants as being unwilling to settle in foreign countries, or to send their sons there.[25]

---

[21] Almqvist 1912–13, p. 428.
[22] Stockholm Merchant Association to BoT, 5 June 1778, Application concerning Genoa's consulate, *Ansökningar om konsulattjänsten* E XVII g:1, BoT SNA.
[23] Stockholm Merchant Association to BoT, 7 June 1814, Application concerning Malta consulate, *Ansökningar om konsulattjänsten* E XVII g:1, BoT SNA.
[24] Ojala 1999, pp. 264–265.
[25] Almqvist 1912–13, p. 139.

4.3 Payments and 'consulade' fees

The Swedish consular service was not a lucrative option for ambitious merchant sons. It was too badly paid. The majority of Swedish consuls, in contradiction to their Venetian counterparts, were not paid officials (career consuls), but so-called honorary consuls.[26] This meant that they had primarily to earn their living on their own accounts, as merchants and commission agents. But they also had the right to claim 'consulade'—a fee paid by every national ship visiting a consul's district. In addition, they could collect some other special fees for assisting Swedish subjects abroad.

The system of payments was not unified. Consequently, the conditions varied from district to district, and sometimes from appointment to appointment. The prevalent level of consulade in a specific district was decided on the occasion of the appointment of a consul, but it usually conformed to the previous conditions. Consulade fees comprised a never-ending saga in the correspondence between consuls, the Board of Trade and the merchant representatives. In fact, the question of consulade fees is one of the most frequently raised in consular reports to the Board of Trade.

The only salaried consulates in the course of the eighteenth century were those in Algiers, Tunis, Tripoli and Morocco. Nevertheless, these salaries were a consequence of the very special character of these consulates. In the Barbary states, consuls had a primarily diplomatic function: they negotiated with the local rulers; they organised the delivery of the gifts/tributes; they represented their government. On the other hand, they had a very limited commercial function, simply because the trade between Sweden and these states was insignificant. They could not make a living as commission agents, which was the usual practice in other consulates. The salaries of the Swedish consuls on the Barbary coast were paid from the resources of the Convoy Office Fund, which indicates how closely this system was connected with the issue of the security of Swedish shipping.[27]

Because Swedish honorary consuls could not survive without conducting their own business, the Board of Trade did not limit consuls' mercantile activities—in spite of the fact that they could become entangled in a conflict of interest between their roles as consuls and as merchants. However, there were some prohibited areas. Consuls were forbidden to participate in freight shipping. Yet again, there were exceptions even here, so that consuls in the Barbary states were allowed to participate in freight shipping.[28]

The question of the durable financing of the Swedish consular service was not resolved in the eighteenth century. The fees (consulade) were a permanent conflict issue between consuls and merchants; the latter often argued, in fact,

---

[26] On distinction between honorary and career consuls, see for example, Ojala 1997b, p. 336; Müller and Ojala 2002, p. 27.
[27] Almqvist 1912–13, p. 134.
[28] Almqvist 1912–13, p. 134.

that fees created a real hindrance for Swedish trade. The conflict between Stockholm merchants and the Lisbon consul Anders Bachmanson Norden-crantz in the 1730s seems to have been particularly tough. This conflict will be described in detail in the section concerning the Lisbon consulate.[29] Looking at the consular fees from the merchant perspective, one may argue that the consular service did, in fact, increase the transaction costs of Swedish shipping and trade. Yet the competing arguments are difficult to evaluate. Here, the question will primarily be treated as a conflict of different interests. However, the dispute clearly reflects the ambiguous (and in a sense untenable) situation of consuls as both professional state bureaucrats and independent businessmen.

As late as 1789, the Board of Trade proposed that those applicants would be preferred who could take over the business of a former consul, so that the appointee could make a living from the same merchant firm as his predecessor. The Board also argued for salaried consulates in districts in which commerce was insufficient to satisfy an independent Swedish merchant house. Another recommendation was to make a clear distinction between consulates with primarily diplomatic functions, which should be linked more directly to the Department of Foreign Affairs, and consulates with predominantly commercial functions.[30]

The lack of common rules for the consular service increased the confusion. There was no general instruction regarding consular duties or rights until 1793. Consequently, each appointment included a more or less specific description of conditions and payment in the specific consular district, even if these frequently did no more than repeat the old instruction. The first general Swedish consular instruction (*konsulstadgan*), issued in January 1793, summarised and confirmed the existing practices. It pointed out the required qualities of a consul, his duties and rights, and it defined the rules of selection of applicants.[31]

The distinction between salaried (career) and honorary consuls is indicative of the important difference between consuls' diplomatic and commercial functions. Yet there are also some other distinctions worthy of discussion. There existed three different ranks in the Swedish consular service: general consuls, consuls and vice-consuls. Consuls were appointed by the Board of Trade in Stockholm, and the appointment was confirmed by a royal letter, which provided the consul with his diplomatic rank. Vice-consuls were often appointed by the consul to help him in his duties, for instance in far-flung areas of the consular district, or during the consul's absence. Hence, vice-consuls lacked the 'official royal letter'. The payment of vice-consuls was also decided locally.

The highest rank of consular representation was general consul. Like that of a with consul, the general consul's status was confirmed and defined in an official appointment and confirmed by a royal letter, these documents delineat-

[29] Nilzén 1987, pp. 38–49.
[30] Proposal of BoT dated 21 July 1789, Almqvist 1912–13, p. 140.
[31] Dated 31 January 1793, Almqvist 1912–13, p. 140.

ing the general consul's rights and duties. The major difference between consul and general consul lay in the extent of territory. The district of a general consul comprised a whole state, and a general consul often lived in the capital, whereas the district of a consul was much smaller, usually comprising a specific port town and its hinterland.

It has been pointed out above, in the description of the origins of the Swedish consular service in the seventeenth century, how different functions and titles were mixed. In the seventeenth century, there was no clear distinction between consuls, merchant agents and envoys. In Sweden, the term 'consul' was in use from the second part of the seventeenth century onwards—for example, in Lisbon (1669), and Amsterdam (1688).[32] However, it is clear that the term was broadly used by other nations, even in the Baltic area.[33] In Sweden, more general use of the term, and a clear distinction between consular and other forms of representation, is first apparent after 1720. From 1801 the title of 'merchant agent' (*handelsagent*) replaced that of 'consul'. The Swedish authorities did not wish to arouse the ire of the great French consul. Yet in 1815, when Napoleon's power was no more, all Swedish 'merchant agents' were once again designated 'consuls'.[34]

4.4 Reporting and other duties

Looking at consular duties from the state perspective, the process of reporting to the Board of Trade was one of the most important functions. These reports could concern many different subjects, depending very much on the consul's personality and interests. However, the most important subject was the description of the conditions of trade and shipping in a consul's district.[35]

Consuls provided information about price developments *vis-à-vis* the key local commodities, and those commodities important for Sweden. They could also inform the Board of important events, and of new regulations (e.g. new duties) that impacted on the market situation. It was quite usual to enclose price currents, cuttings from local newspapers, or cargo lists with a consular report. From the Swedish point of view, each specific market had some interesting commodities to purchase, or some interesting opportunities for sales. Such topics were the focus of the reports. Hence, the Lisbon reports dealt overwhelmingly with salt: salt prices, conditions of salt production, duties, weather conditions—all the factors affecting salt supplies and prices. However, in the

---

[32] Almqvist 1912–13, p. 30.
[33] See appointment of Patrick Leyel 'in the Consuls office' for all British subjects in Denmark, 4 March 1686, DRA (Danish Rigsarkivet) TKUA, England, AII *Akter og dokumenter fra forhandlinger med den engelske konsul I Helsingo[e]r Patrick Leyel*. I thank Steve Murdoch for the reference of the use of 'consul' in this way.
[34] Almqvist 1912–13, p. 141.
[35] On the employment of consular reports in general see Barker 1981. On the quality and employment of Swedish consular reports, see Högberg 1964 pp. 25–26 and Högberg 1981.

2. Livorno Price Current (in Swedish), August 11, 1777 (Peter Vilhelm Törngren's reports, Livorno, BoT SNA)

same Lisbon reports we will even find information on incoming Brazilian fleets and their cargoes.

On the other hand, reports from Cadiz or Marseilles paid the bulk of their attention to the market for Swedish staple commodities: iron, sawn timber, tar and pitch. At the same time, however, they were also concerned with market conditions for grain, and the consequences of market changes for Swedish tramp shipping in the area. Reports from the Barbary states were mainly concerned with the political situation.[36]

Due to the importance of the political situation for commerce and shipping, consuls paid a good deal of attention to the diplomatic relations between the great powers, particularly when the outcome could affect freight rates, insurance premiums and (eventually) the demand for Swedish shipping. For neutral Sweden, warfare always meant a potential increase in business. Therefore much space in the reports was allotted to rumours about possible conflicts.

Another aspect of reporting specifically concerned the data on Swedish shipping and trade. Consuls were obliged to report on every Swedish ship entering and leaving their district. They reported on cargoes, conditions of cargo sales and suitable return cargoes. They informed the Board of conditions of shipping (freight rates and insurance premiums) and advised Swedish shipowners as to when and where shipping was profitable. The reports show that the consuls had a very good overview of the movements of Swedish ships, not only in their own districts but in the whole Mediterranean area. Occasionally, reports included annual accounts or shipping lists.

Cases of the capture of Swedish ships were a very frequent topic within consular reports. It was the consul's duty to defend the interests of Swedish subjects in court when a ship was declared a prize. Consuls sent warnings to Stockholm as to when and where privateers and corsairs could be expected.

Another important aspect of reporting concerned the health situation in the consul's district. Particularly by the late eighteenth century, consuls had begun to give information about epidemics, quarantine periods and regulations, so the Swedish merchants could decide if the voyage to the district was secure or not. All this was highly important business news for shipowners and merchants in distant Sweden.

Evidently, the scope of reporting was very varied, and so was the quality. Some consuls wrote frequent and lengthy letters, some others just a few short letters annually. Some consuls paid attention only to commercial information, others focused on political events. Some consuls preferred to write in an abstract general manner, some others restricted their reporting to practicalities. One could find consuls sending lengthy, high-flown proposals for increasing Swedish trade and shipping in a district; others only detailed necessities. Consuls were obliged to keep records of the Swedish shipping and trade in the district, and to report them. Therefore some reports include quantitative data on Sweden's shipping, trade, and even seamen. Other reports do not pay any attention to such issues. Such a widely differing quality in the reports makes it difficult to carry out any systematic analysis based on these data (see chapter 5). At the same time, the reports do provide a good picture of the consuls' daily activities. The concluding part of this chapter will give a narrative account of these daily activities in key Swedish consulates in the Mediterra-

---

[36] Respective reports from Lisbon, Livorno, Marseilles, Tunis, Tripoli and Algiers. BoT SNA.

nean, but first we should say something more about the other duties comprised in the consular service.

The consuls' notary duties are an obvious element here. Consuls had the right to issue passports and documents testifying to the Swedish nationality of ships and people. However, they had also to take care of the documents of lost and sold ships. As regards the aforementioned Algerian passports, there are many examples of situations in which a ship was either lost or sold in the Mediterranean. The local Swedish consul had to collect the ship's documents and send them back to the Board of Trade. This was very important in order to avoid abuse of the Swedish flag. For example, in his letter of 23 May 1753, the Cadiz consul Jacob Martin Bellman informed the Board of Trade of a number of passports from ships which had been lost or sold in his district in recent months. Of the five ships mentioned, two were lost at sea (*Enigheten* and *Änge-len*), two were sold (*Printz Gustav* and *Freden*) and one was captured by priva-teers and brought to Ceuta (*Westerviks Vapen*).[37]

A duty we have mentioned was that of helping Swedish subjects in local courts. The most frequent cases concerned the capture of Swedish ships. Here, consuls represented shipowner's interests, and tried to prevent a ship or cargo being declared a prize. And if this did occur, the consul could even try to purchase the prize back. The capture of Swedish ships seems to have been among the most common incidents regarding which consuls had to deal with local authorities. We will return to some of these cases in the detailed account of the consulates in Lisbon and Cadiz.

Helping his nation's subjects was always among a consul's primary duties. For present-day consuls, this might mean helping lost tourists; in the eight-eenth century it almost exclusively meant providing assistance to captured or otherwise stranded seamen. Consuls helped those seamen who got into diffi-culties as the crew of putative prize ships, or as captives in North Africa. A typical consequence of privateer activity was the local appearance of released and unemployed Swedish crews. Consuls had to cover the costs of local author-ities in keeping the released seamen in quarantine, jail or hospital. For instance, in 1805, the Swedish consul in Livorno, Joachim Grabien, was involved in freeing Swedish seamen taken by French privateers. Because of the local health regulations, the Swedes were kept in quarantine, and the consul was charged for their sojourn there. Grabien mentioned in his reports that the released seamen frequently took work on foreign ships, when their own ship was de-clared a prize. Consuls usually strove to find some employment for seamen on returning Swedish ships, but it was not always possible. By 1800, American ships had become a favoured option because of their much higher wages.[38]

---

[37] Jacob M Bellman to BoT, 23 May 1753 Cadiz, see also Bellman to BoT, 17 June 1745 Cadiz, concerning the documents of Swedish ship *Carolus*, Consular Reports, Cadiz 1719–1802, E VI aa 67, BoT SNA.
[38] Grabien to BoT, Letters 16 December 1805, 31 January 1806, 4 April 1806, 31 January 1806. Livorno, Consular Reports, Livorno 1725–1822 EVI aa 229, BoT SNA.

The cases of Swedish seamen captured by the Barbary corsairs were of course much more moving. Even here, consuls did their best to help the Swedish subjects in captivity. The following example illustrates how such help might be provided. It concerns a group of Swedish captives in Tangier in 1740. In October 1739, the Lisbon consul Arvid Arfwedson received a letter from Tangier, written by five Swedish seamen who had been captured by Morocco corsairs while on their way from Cadiz to Sweden. The consul reported the case to the Board of Trade and the shipowner, and he also sent money to the captives from his consulate's charity fund, as well as taking the first steps to get them released. However, it was to be another three years before the men were allowed to leave. In April 1742, two of them—the others probably died in Morocco—arrived in Gibraltar on board an English ship. They received food, clothes and travel money from the Lisbon consul for the journey to Setubal, whence they could catch a Swedish ship bound for home.[39]

Nevertheless, consuls could also represent absent shipowners at court against their escaped crew members, or again, they might intercede in conflicts between Swedish seamen and the local authorities. In April 1774, the Cadiz consul Hans Jacob Gahn reported on the subject of two Swedish seamen who had found their way into the jail in Cadiz. One of them, the crew member on a Swedish East India ship, seemed to be suspected of smuggling, some goods into Cadiz. Fortunately, the matter appeared to be a mistake, and the man was freed with the consul's help. Another Swedish seaman apparently tried to smuggle tobacco into Cadiz. In this case, the man sat in jail for a longer period, not daring to ask the consul Gahn for help. It is not clear how the affair ended.[40]

Consuls were supposed to provide a solution in critical situations concerning Swedish interests—for example, when a Swedish shipmaster died or became incapable of commanding his ship. Thus, in January 1729, the Lisbon consul Bachmanson Nordencrantz had to decide what to do with the ship *Concordia* and its crew, when the vessel's master suddenly died. Apparently in this situation his consular instruction was of no help to him. On his own initiative, Bachmanson Nordencrantz organised a meeting of all the Swedish shipmasters who were then in Lisbon, and asked them if they could recommend that *Concordia's* mate take over the ship's command.[41]

Consuls were also supposed to keep records of all Swedes living in their districts, and they regularly informed the Board of Trade of the number of Swedish subjects there. Hence the Cadiz consul Gahn's reports from the 1770s and 1780s included detailed information on all Swedish subjects living in his

---

[39] Arfwedson to BoT, 6 October 1739, 9 February 1740, 10 April 1742, Lisbon, Consular Reports, Lisbon 1731–1778, E VI aa 224, BoT SNA.
[40] Hans Jacob Gahn to BoT, 15 April 1774, Cadiz, Consular Reports, Cadiz 1719–1802, E VI aa 67, BoT SNA.
[41] Bachmanson Nordencrantz to BoT, 26 January 1729, Lisbon, Consular Reports, Lisbon 1694–1697, 1709–1730, E VI aa 223, BoT SNA.

district.[42] Consuls even had to take care of the estates of deceased Swedes—those who had died in their district, or (much more commonly) on board. Typically, a majority of the tasks concerned shipping and seamen in one form or another.

One of the specific conditions of consular service in southern Europe was the right to observe the Swedish Church's services in the consul's home. We must remember that the Barbary states were Muslim, and the Christian coast of the Mediterranean and Iberian Peninsula was Catholic. The right to observe the Swedish service was usually included in the peace and trade treaties regulating the relationships between the local power and the Swedish consulate. For example, the treaty with Algiers of 1729 clearly stipulated the right of the Swedish consul to have a Swedish priest and to observe services at the consul's house. It was permissible for all Swedish subjects in Algiers to participate in these services—including captive Swedish seamen.[43]

On the other hand, the religious freedom guaranteed by treaty could be violated, as Joachim de Besche, the Swedish consul in Lisbon, discovered. In 1717, the Portuguese Inquisition accused him of providing a public Protestant service in which all nations could participate. The Inquisition approached the Portuguese king and asked him to intervene. De Besche was called to court to explain himself, and in the end he was forced to send his priest, Andre Silvius, home to Sweden.[44]

Apparently, then, consuls had many duties. Reporting and the duties connected with the aforementioned everyday concerns reflected their role as the nation's representatives. But, of course, consuls were also businessmen, even if these two functions often came into conflict. Business activities provided the means of earning one's living, and so were a precondition of consular service. In the next section we will look more closely at consuls' function as commission agents and merchants.

4.5 Consuls as commission agents

The basis of a Swedish consul's personal economy was usually provided by commissions from Swedish merchant houses. Evidently this was such a well-established practice that the Board of Trade presupposed it. Many letters of appointment include an article forbidding the consul to take a consulade fee from a ship consigned to him.[45] Of course, this practice increased the costs for merchants who did not consign their cargo to a consul; they had to pay both a

[42] Hans Jacob Gahn to BoT, 8 January 1779 Cadiz, Consular Reports, Cadiz 1719–1802, E VI aa 67, BoT SNA.
[43] Article 17 of the treaty, *Sveriges traktater med främmande magter. 1723–1771*, 1922, pp. 99–106.
[44] Joachim de Besche to BoT, 16 January 1717 Lisbon, Consular Reports, Lisbon 1694–1697, 1709–1730, E VI aa 223, BoT SNA.

commission to their local commission agent and a consulade fee to the consul. To avoid such double costs, merchants and shipowners were obliged to consign their cargoes to a consul, without regard to his qualities as a businessman.

The policy may also be seen as a typical mercantilist means of controlling trade. It had been argued—by the Board of Trade and by consuls—that it was better to monopolise sales of Swedish staple commodities in one strong national house at a port (district, country) rather than to divide them among many weak commission agents, who might in addition often be foreigners. One strong national house could guarantee that commodities could be sold for the best prices and at the right moment. As early as 1712, the Lisbon consul de Besche criticised the fact that Swedish iron reached Portugal from many different places (the Dutch Republic, England, Hamburg) and was imported by many merchants. If the iron was retailed through one house, he argued, the price would be much better.[46] In 1740, George Logie argued in a letter from Livorno that Swedish iron could receive a much better price if sold through one Swedish firm.[47] Another Lisbon consul, Anders Bachmanson Nordencrantz, also expounded—in the context of his schemes for the development of the Swedish-Portuguese exchange—on the virtues of having one strong Swedish merchant house. Bachmanson Nordencrantz mentioned the English organization of trade as a model.[48]

Of course, the regulations concerning consulade fees strengthened the position of the consul as commission agent. This is not to say that merchants were happy about it. They saw these regulations as a violation of their right to choose whichever agent they wanted. The problem was not an issue if the appointed consul already worked as a commission agent in the locale—not an unusual situation—and if the merchant representatives in Stockholm supported the appointment. However, this became a serious problem when the consul appointed lacked experience and the support of the Swedish merchants. He then received few commissions and was more dependent on fees, which annoyed both merchants and shipowners. Their annoyance swelled when the consul argued for higher consulade fees.

Commissions became such a troubled issue for the consul Arendt Dreyer.

---

[45] For example, Anders Bachmanson Nordencrantz mentions in his letter of 28 December 1728 that he has right to get consulade fee only from ships which are not consigned to him, according to instruction issued for Jean Bedoire, appointed consul at Lisbon, no consulade fee should be paid for cargoes consigned to consul's office. Jean Bedoire to BoT, 18 April 1758 Lisbon. Consular Reports, Lisbon 1731–1778, E VI aa 224, BoT SNA. Instruction for 'merchant agent' (consul) in Cadiz, of November 1803, mentions that only ships which are not consigned to consul will pay consulade fee, as it has been usual under former consul Gahn. Circular of consul Scherman, dated Hamburg, 8 November 1803, Consular Reports Cadiz 1803–1810, E VI aa 68, BoT SNA.

[46] De Besche to BoT, 16 January 1717, Lisbon, Consular Reports , Lisbon 1694–1697, 1709–1730, E VI aa 223, BoT SNA.

[47] Logie to BoT, 10 October 1740/ 27 October 1740 Livorno, Consular Reports, Livorno 1725–1822, EVI aa 229, BoT SNA.

[48] Bachmanson Nordencrantz to BoT, 25 February 1730, Stockholm, *Berättelse om Sveriges rikes handel med Portugal*, Consular Reports, Lisbon 1731–1778, E VI aa 224, BoT SNA.

Dreyer, consul in Cadiz in 1767–73, was apparently appointed in spite of his weak connection with the Swedish trade in Cadiz. From 1772, he engaged in a bitter struggle over commissions with his own vice-consul, Anders Hagström. Dreyer accused Hagström of taking the most profitable commissions whereas he, the consul, got only the scraps. Of course, in his accusations Dreyer did not mention the fact that Hagström was an experienced and successful merchant who had lived in Cadiz for many years. In fact, Hagström's experience of local business and knowledge of Spanish were the main reasons why Dreyer had employed him as vice-consul. In his reports to the Board of Trade, Dreyer revealed that Hagström also worked as vice-consul for the French. These French commissions seemed to be the key problem in the quarrel. But the cause of Dreyer's problems was not lack of French commissions. He appeared simply to be a bad businessman, as his losses even of Swedish commissions testified.[49]

The Lisbon consul Bachmanson Nordencrantz got into difficulties with the Stockholm merchants because of similar problems. His case will be analysed in depth in the section on the Lisbon consulate (section 4.6.1). Nevertheless, the cases of Dreyer and Bachmanson Nordencrantz appear to be exceptional. The majority of consuls seem to have been quite successful as commission agents of Swedish firms. Part of the explanation is of course that many of them belonged to established merchant families, as noted above.

An indirect testament to the commission trade's importance for consuls is provided by merchant accounts in Sweden. The Finnish historian Jari Ojala has analysed the ledgers of Abraham Falander, a large Swedish-Finnish merchant and shipowner. Falander's accounts show that in the period 1785–1815, about one-third of his transactions abroad were made via the commission of consuls. Consuls also accounted for about one-quarter of all the correspondents with whom Falander was in contact. In 1790, about a half of Falander's foreign trade's value was made through consuls' commissions. Yet data for the year 1790 is partly misleading, due to the dominant role of one single partner, the Amsterdam consul Conrad Adrian Hasselgren. Analyses of the correspondence of other Swedish-Finnish merchants (Matts Johanson Sovelius in Finland, and the Stockholm-based Carlos and Claes Grill) also prove the important role of consuls as correspondents and commission agents.[50]

The examples above are drawn from merchant correspondence and account books. It is difficult to get this kind of evidence from consular reports, simply because the aim of these reports was the provision of information for the Board of Trade—not reportage on the consul's private business. However, a few con-

[49] Dreyer to BoT, 1 December 1772, Cadiz, concerning Anders Hagströms' dispute with Dreyer, Cadiz 1719–1802, E VI aa 67, BoT SNA.
Anders Hagström to BoT, 14 July 1772 Cadiz, dispute with Dreyer, Hans Jacob Gahn to BT, 20 April 1773 Cadiz, Consular Reports, Cadiz 1719–1802, E VI aa 67, BoT SNA, Almqvist 1912–13, p. 425.
[50] Müller and Ojala 2002, pp. 37–39; see also, Ojala 1997b, p 336–337.

Table 4.1: *Ship cargoes consigned to Hagström and Gahn, Cadiz, 1777–95*

Year	Total number of ships	Hagström	Gahn
1777	31	21	
1778	41	35	
1785	83	18	56
1795	45	7	36

Source: Shipping lists for Cadiz 1777, dated 6 January 1778; and for 1778, dated 8 January 1779; and for 1785 (probably dated 27 January 1786); and for 1795, dated 15 January 1796. Consular Reports, Cadiz 1719–1802, E VI aa 67, BoT SNA

sular reports mention to whom the Swedish cargoes were consigned and these confirm the major role of the consul as a commission agent. The reports of the aforementioned vice-consul Anders Hagström are such an exception. His reports clearly show that he dominated Swedish trade in Cadiz in 1777 and 1778. (In 1778 and 1779 the appointed consul Gahn was visiting Sweden.) But the situation changed when Gahn returned. Gahn's reports of 1785 and 1795 show that the consul and his vice-consul controlled a major share of Swedish cargo consignments in Cadiz. It seems that the longer Gahn worked as Swedish consul in Cadiz, the stronger was his grip on Swedish trade in this important city.[51]

The Lisbon consul Arvid Arfwedson also seemed to keep control of consignments of Swedish cargoes. In 1741, 66 Swedish ships were consigned to him, and only 19 to other firms. In 1742, 52 Swedish ships were consigned to the consul, while only 12 were consigned to other firms.[52] The Swedish consuls in Marseilles enjoyed a similar position. In the course of the eighteenth century, the firm Butini and Fölsch controlled a major part of Swedish trade in iron in this key Mediterranean port. Members of the Butini and Fölsch families worked as Swedish consuls for nearly 150 years, from 1735 to 1881.[53] Due to the ambiguity of the consuls' situation, as both state officials and businessmen, it is difficult to state whether they became consuls because of their business experience, or whether they became successful businessmen because of the consular post itself. Cases of failure, such as Dreyer's and Bachmanson Nordencrantz's, prove that the first option was rather possible.

---

[51] See the source in table 4.1, On Gahn's firm see also Gonzalez 2000.
[52] Notes on the charity money received in 1741 and 1742 from Lisbon, Setubal and Oporto, Arvid Arfwedson to BoT, Lisbon, Consular Reports, Lisbon 1731–1778, E VI aa 224, BoT SNA.
[53] Almqvist 1912–13, p. 384; Hildebrand 1957, pp. 141–142.

4.6 Swedish consulates in Lisbon, Cadiz, Marseilles, Livorno, and North Africa

The concluding part of this chapter focuses on the Swedish consulates in leading southern-European ports: Lisbon, Cadiz, Marseilles and Livorno, and on the consulates in North Africa. The four former consulates represented Sweden's major markets in the area. However, the purpose of this section is not to provide a comprehensive analysis of Swedish trade and shipping in the key markets; this will be a topic of chapter 5. Instead, the consulates and their consuls will be presented in a narrative fashion, extensively employing the consular reports preserved in the archives of the Swedish Board of Trade. Consequently, the following accounts of the specific consulates should primarily be seen as examples of how consuls carried out their daily duties, and of what issues they considered as significant for Sweden, and so worthy of reporting to Stockholm. Much attention will be paid to issues of shipping, and especially neutrality shipping.

As stated, the following narratives are primarily based on the consular reports. One advantage of this source is that it provides a rich, detailed description of daily consular pursuits. A disadvantage is that the picture is sometimes too detailed, and conversely, sometimes very superficial. It depends, of course, on the widely varying quality of the reports. The eighteenth-century reports very much mirror the consul's own interests and ideas. This affects the final picture, and explains why, in the narrative, some consuls and some activities are covered in much more detail than others. The consular reports are complemented by some other primary sources (e.g. Angerstein's reports), and by literature.

4.6.1 Lisbon

As noted above, Lisbon had the privilege of obtaining the first Swedish consul in southern Europe.[54] This depended partly on Portugal's importance as a salt supplier. Nevertheless, even the early establishment of diplomatic relations between Portugal and Sweden was of moment. The consul in Lisbon was also the only Swedish diplomatic representative in Portugal, which meant that he played a role in high-level diplomacy.[55]

The first consul whose reports have been preserved in the Board of Trade's collection was Nils Simons (Nicolas Simon), officially the consul between 1669 and 1704. His preserved reports from the 1690s bear witness to the vital Swedish traffic in Lisbon and Setubal.[56]

Joachim de Besche was Sweden's Lisbon consul over the course of the Great

---

[54] Almqvist 1912–13, p. 28.
[55] Jägerskiöld 1957, p. 28.
[56] Nicolas Simon to BoT, Lisbon, Consular Reports, Lisbon 1694–1697, 1709–1730, E VI aa 223, BoT SNA.

Northern War. His reports provide us with a very detailed picture of the salt market and salt production in Portugal, as well as of the political game behind the decisions regarding annual prices. These issues were regularly addressed in de Besche's reports. In particular, great attention is paid to salt prices. Usually, de Besche notes salt prices in Setubal and in Lisbon, the latter being much higher. He also makes a distinction between prices paid within the city and the so-called free-on-board prices, including all duties.[57]

Another frequently mentioned topic is the weather and its impact on salt production. In September 1712, rain damaged salt production so much that the supplies were not sufficient for more than 130 ship cargoes. The reports testify to the fact that salt was without doubt the most important Portuguese commodity for the Swedes.

But there were also other recurring issues. From the beginning of his period in Lisbon, de Besche paid much attention to the activities of Barbary corsairs. After the tragic incident with the ship *Stora Jernvågen*, described above, there was a strong sense of danger. In a letter of 1710, de Besche describes a problem with a crew which refused to sail out of Lisbon because of the corsair threat, so that the shipmaster was forced to acquire the salt cargo in the city, which was extremely expensive. The feeling of insecurity was strengthened by the shortage of news from Scandinavia. A Swedish captain might well be afraid not only of Barbary corsairs, but also of Danish privateers. The solution in this specific situation was to sail to England and wait there for more information.[58] The danger of being captured increased in 1712, when the Dutch signed another treaty with Algiers. Usually, the Swedish ships followed the Dutch convoys. After the conclusion of the Dutch-Algiers treaty, the consul reported, the French, English and Dutch sailed in safety, whereas Swedish, Danish and Hamburg ships were open to capture.[59]

De Besche stressed in his letters that Swedish ships employed in the salt trade were only flutes, with limited defensibility. Yet he was aware of the difficulty of organizing the convoy service—as long as the country was at war and Charles XII abroad. De Besche instead proposed arming some bigger ships to serve as defensive vessels for other Swedes.[60] In the late 1710s, it appears that the safety of Swedish shipping improved; at least de Besche did not report on the issue so often.

One of the frequently mentioned topics in De Besche's reports was Portugal's trade with Brazil. Thus, the consul wrote about the probable arrival dates of the

---

[57] The prices fluctuated from 4,150 *rees* per moy in 1711 to 2,100 in 1720. De Besche to BoT, 17 October 1711 and 19 March 1720, 1 *rees* is accounting money in Portugal. According to Angerstein 1 *rees*=90 d.c.m. (Angerstein 1996b, p. 88). 1 *moy*=2.2 Swedish barrel (*tunna*).

[58] De Besche to BoT, 16 April 1710, Lisbon, Consular Reports, Lisbon 1694–1697, 1709–1730, E VI aa 223, BoT SNA.

[59] De Besche to BoT, 12 September 1712, Lisbon, Consular Reports, Lisbon 1694–1697, 1709–1730, E VI aa 223, BoT SNA

[60] De Besche to BoT, 3 August 1709, Lisbon Consular Reports, Lisbon 1694–1697, 1709–1730, E VI aa 223, BoT SNA.

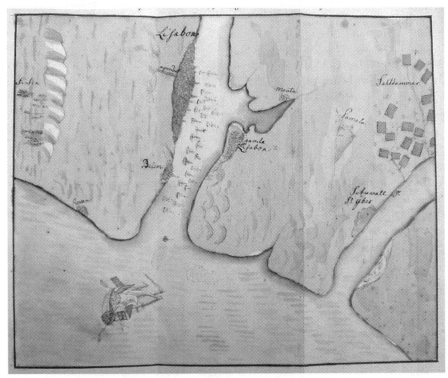

3. Lisbon and Setubal (Reinhold Angerstein's report, BoT SNA)

so-called Brazilian fleets, and he wrote in detail about the number of ships in each fleet, quantities and values of cargoes and the like. For example, in October 1712, he reported on the return of the Brazilian fleet consisting of 84 ships, carrying large quantitites of sugar, tobacco, leather and gold.[61] It is difficult to see how the arriving Brazilian cargoes were of major significance for Sweden's trade with Portugal.

At the same time, de Besche appeared to pay relatively scant attention to the trade in Swedish staple commodities. Before 1715, there were rather few references to the iron trade. Concerning this trade, he reported on prices and demand. The consul also analysed the trade, and made proposals for improvement. According to him, the major problem was the fact that iron and other Swedish staple commodities were carried to Portugal on ships of so many different nations (the British, Dutch, Hamburg). The situation would improve if the Swedes managed to concentrate trade in Swedish staple commodities in their own hands.[62]

Whereas the next Lisbon consul, Carl Henrik Harmens (1721–27), left very

---

[61] De Besche to BoT, 12 September 1712, 18 October 1712, Lisbon, Consular Reports, Lisbon 1694–1697, 1709–1730, E VI aa 223, BoT SNA.
[62] De Besche to BoT, 16 January 1717, 4 January 1718, 19 March 1720, Lisbon, Consular Reports, Lisbon 1694–1697, 1709–1730, E VI aa 223, BoT SNA.

4. Anders Bachmanson Nordencrantz, consul in Lisbon (1727–1738) (UUL)

few reports, and these mainly relating to his consulade fees, the third consul, Anders Bachmanson Nordencrantz, forwarded a huge flow of papers to the Board of Trade. This is not surprising. Anders Bachmanson Nordencrantz was one of the most productive—as regards volume—Swedish writers of the eighteenth century. After his years as the Lisbon consul he became one of Sweden's most influential, if also most controversial, economic thinkers and politicians. Bachmanson Nordencrantz is a very interesting even if rather untypical consul. Therefore we will pay his Lisbon years more detailed attention.

Bachmanson Nordencrantz began his career as a merchant and ship agent in

London, in the years 1722–24. After his return home, he published an influential work on Sweden's economy, *Arcana oeconomiae et commercii*. He began also his political career as a burger representative of a small port-town, Sundsvall, in the 1726–27 *riksdag* session; and on the recommendation of this *riksdag*, he was appointed consul in Lisbon.[63] It is obvious that his appointment was based on his political credentials, and its political character is even more evident, when one knows that another applicant was Arvid Arfwedson, an experienced Swedish merchant in Lisbon.

The new consul was certainly an interesting economist and an active politician, but he was not a good businessman. He lacked the practical expertise of trade in southern Europe and, in addition, he lacked contacts with the Swedish firms engaged in this trade. He was also short of necessary capital. Apparently, he was appointed consul against the competition of a representative of one of the leading Stockholm mercantile families. This was not good grounds for a successful business career at Lisbon. Therefore, much of his reporting to the Board of Trade concerned three issues: proposals on how to re-organise Sweden's trade with Portugal; applications to increase the consulade fees, because he could not manage to live on the existing ones; and complaints about shipmasters and merchants who refused to pay or otherwise avoided his consulade fees.

His proposals were directed against the traditional manner of doing business in Lisbon, dominated by other Swedish firms and foreigners. Bachmanson Nordencrantz argued in his schemes for the reorganization of Swedish-Portuguese trade in terms of the necessity of monopolising the trade in one national house. The only way to improve the profitability of trade—he claimed—was to concentrate it in one pair of hands. It is an irony of history that, in the 1760s, the same man became the bitterest enemy of trade monopolies.

Bachmanson Nordencrantz made extensive calculations as to how much Sweden was losing through the current trade system, and how much the country would benefit from his reorganization. It is very difficult to evaluate the consul's figures (see table 4.2)—due to his own interest in the issue—yet they provide us with some kind of general picture. According to the consul's figures for trade between October 1728 and 1729, Sweden exported about 12,100 ship pounds of bar-iron to Lisbon. Considering the total Swedish exports of bar iron, over 250,000 ship pounds in these years,[64] the Lisbon market made up about 5 per cent of the total; a quite impressive share. Not surprisingly, iron was the dominant Swedish commodity. In value, iron, including bar-iron, steel, cannon balls and nails, made up 87 per cent of Swedish imports to Portugal. Another typical Swedish staple commodity was sawn timber, which made up almost 13 per cent of the export value. Surprisingly, 246 barrels of tar were listed at only 0.34 per cent of the total import value.

Swedish imports consisted of over 150,000 *moy* of salt, equal to 68,000 Swedish barrels. According to the accounts provided in Portuguese currency,

---

[63] Nilzén 1987; Magnusson 1989, pp. 11 ff.
[64] Hildebrand 1957, p. 92.

Table 4.2: *The Swedish-Portuguese trade (October 1728–October 1729)*

Exports	in d.c.m.	Per cent
12,100 ship pounds of iron	641,300	79.90
540 ship pounds of steel	45,900	5.72
30 ship pounds of nails	2,400	0.23
5,250 pieces of cannon balls	3,500	0.44
246 barrels of tar	2,706	0.34
4,602 dozen double-deals	50,622	6.30
8,275 dozen deals from Gothenburg	49,653	6.19
Masts, spires, deals	6,500	0.81
Total exports	802,581	99.93

Imports	in d.c.m.	Per cent
151,158 *moy* of salt	20,608	69.43
286 ox-heads of wine	4,290	14.45
1,055 boxes of fruit	1,582	5.33
sugar, olive oil, sweets	3,200	10.78
total imports	29,680	100.00

Source: *Räkning över Sveriges handel på Portugall* (from 8 Oct 1728 to 8 Oct 1729), Bachmanson to BoT, Consular Reports, Lisbon 1731–1778, E VI aa 224, BoT SNA.
Notes: 1 barrel salt =2.2 *moy*

the salt made up about 70 per cent of the import value. Moreover, wine comprised an important import item, at about 15 per cent. The remaining share consisted of fruits, sugar, olive oil and other commodities. In terms of cargo space, of course the dominance of salt was almost total. A striking feature of the Bachmanson Nordencrantz account of the Swedish-Portuguese trade is the huge discrepancy between export and import values. The discrepancy reflects Portugal's capacity to pay in cash.[65]

This trade between Sweden and Portugal was carried on 25 ships that made 27 voyages in total. Ten of these ships even sailed for freight, four from Sweden to Holland, three from Sweden to London, one from Riga to London, and two from Porto to Hamburg. According to Bachmanson Nordencrantz, the ships sailing for freight earned an additional 60,000 d.c.m.[66]

There is also the next year's account (October 1729–October 1730) sent by the consul to the Board of Trade, which provides quite a similar account of the exchange.[67] One significant difference was the much lower level of iron exports (7,890 ship pounds). Even in 1730, one-third of Swedish ships entering Lisbon were engaged in tramp shipping. The consul also made some calculations to

---

[65] Högberg 1964, pp. 21–22.
[66] Sweden's trade with Portugal (from 8 October 1728 to 8 October 1729), Bachmanson Nordencrantz to BoT, Lisbon, Consular Reports, Lisbon 1731–1778, E VI aa 224, BoT SNA.
[67] Sweden's trade with Portugal (8 Oct. 1729 to 8 Okt 1730). Bachmanson Nordencrantz to BoT, Lisbon, Consular Reports, Lisbon 1731–1778, E VI aa 224, BoT SNA.

provide the Board with a picture of the profitability of the Swedish business in Portugal. It is, however, difficult to grasp his reasoning, with the exception of the conclusion—that trade should be concentrated in Swedish hands, and more exactly, in those of the consul.

As mentioned above, one of Bachmanson Nordencrantz's problems, and also the major issue in his reports, was consulade fees. He complained that the fees were not sufficient to provide the means for a proper standard of living for Sweden's national consul. He complained that he could not afford a proper house in the centre of town. Another typical topic of his complaints was seamen's attempts to avoid payments of fees. A usual practice seemed to be that a Swedish ship used the Swedish flag when sailing in open waters; but before it reached Lisbon the captain changed flag to avoid consular fees.[68] For example, in October 1730, Bachmanson Nordencrantz complained about the ship *Diligence*, anchored in Lisbon under the English flag. According to the consul, the captain Samuel Volsey admitted that the ship sailed for Lisbon under the Swedish flag but changed it in Lisbon.[69]

Yet, it seems that the major difficulty with Stockholm merchants began with rising salt prices in 1732. In this year the salt price was set at 4,000 *rees* per *moy*, whereas normal salt prices fluctuated between 2,000 and 3,000 *rees*. According to Bachmanson Nordencrantz, high Swedish demand was blamed for the high price, and so he negotiated with the Portuguese authorities to push salt prices down. And indeed, the next year salt prices declined to 3,300 *rees*.[70] The consul claimed that the lower price was a result of his successful negotiations with the Portuguese, and he sent a bill for his negotiations to Stockholm, to the tune of 8,085 d.c.m. Yet the bill and the consul's arguments met with an angry answer from the Stockholm Merchant Association. The merchants sent a letter to the Board of Trade in which they made it very clear that Bachmanson Nordencrantz's negotiations had had no impact on the salt price. Instead, the declining salt price in Portugal was a consequence of the new strategy of the Swedish merchants; instead of buying expensive salt in Portugal they went to more distant salt markets within the Mediterranean. In addition, they harshly criticised Bachmanson Nordencrantz's proposal for *repartition*, the salt contract with Portugal. The idea of this contract was to concentrate all Swedish salt purchases within one large contract.[71]

In their next step, the Stockholm merchants accused Bachmanson Nordencrantz of taking fees which exceeded the fixed ½ per cent of cargo value. The

---

[68] Bachmanson Nordencrantz to BoT, 28 December 1728, Lisbon, Consular Reports, Lisbon 1694–1697, 1709–1730, E VI aa 223, BoT SNA.

[69] Bachmanson Nordencrantz to BoT, 17 October 1730, Lisbon, Consular Reports, Lisbon 1731–1778, E VI aa 224, BoT SNA.

[70] Bachmanson Nordencrantz to BoT, 9 March 1733. According to Stockholm merchants the prices declined even more to 2,960 *rees* per moy, see the Merchant Assocation's Report, 1 August 1734.

[71] Stockholm Merchant Association to BoT, 1 August 1734 Stockholm, Lisbon, Consular Reports, Lisbon 1731–1778, E VI aa 224, BoT SNA.

fight over excessive fees had, in fact, already begun in 1729, yet it continued until 1734. In 1734, the consul was allowed to leave Lisbon to resolve the conflict, and he never returned. The lawsuit between the Stockholm merchants and the Lisbon consul continued until 1736, when Bachmanson Nordencrantz lost. Yet he appealed against the decision, and pressed on with the case.[72]

In 1738, Bachmanson Nordencrantz formally left his consular post in Lisbon. Arvid Arfwedson, his old rival and a member of the leading Stockholm merchant family, was appointed as new consul. This appointment must inevitably have disillusioned Bachmanson Nordencrantz greatly. Perhaps the roots of his later political ideas, his political struggle against the Stockholm merchant elite and the party of Hats that represented it, might be found in this period of his life.

With Arfwedson, the consular business in Lisbon returned to more standard conduct. There are no new proposals and schemes as to how to increase and reorganise Sweden's trade. Arfwedson's reports showed clearly that in the late 1730s the shipping between Sweden and Portugal increased significantly, in comparison with the years 1729 and 1730. For example, only in the period between May and December 1738 did the number of Swedish ships entering the Portuguese ports reach 74: 36 ships destined for Setubal, 26 for Lisbon, and 12 for Porto.[73]

In parallel with de Besche and Bachmanson Nordencrantz, even Arfwedson showed an interest in the Brazil trade.[74] But in his case, this interest might reflect a family consideration. Arvid was a younger brother of Abraham and Jacob Arfwedson, who managed a very active merchant house in Stockholm. Among the brothers' business projects—one as yet unrealised—was the foundation of a Swedish West India Company. In 1745, the Arfwedson brothers were granted the Swedish monopoly trade rights on 'all African and American ports [...] on which the other nations have free trade or which have no trade with European nations'.[75] The project failed due to Spanish protests. The family's contact with the brother in Lisbon must at least have helped to keep the Arfwedson's firm in Stockholm well informed about colonial trade.

In contrast to his predecessors in Lisbon, Arfwedson paid much attention to the international political situation. The reason was the War of the Austrian Succession (1739–48), which involved both Britain and Spain and thus provided Swedish shipping with a profitable opportunity. In August 1739, Ar-

[72] Nilzén 1987, pp. 44–45.
[73] Arfwedson to BoT, 13 January 1738, Lisbon, Consular Reports, Lisbon 1731–1778, E VI aa 224, BoT SNA.
[74] For example, in May 1739, he reported on the Brazilian fleet, consisting of two men-of-war and ten merchantmen. The cargo of the fleet consisted of 5 ½ million crusados in gold and about 13 million crusados in colonial goods (sugar, boards, skins, jacaranda timber, etc.) Arfwedson to BoT, 19 May 1739 Lisbon, Consular Reports, Lisbon 1731–1778, E VI aa 224, BoT SNA.
[75] Simonsson 1920, pp. 158–161.

fwedson was already mentioning the rumours about the upcoming conflict, and in October he reported on the declaration of war with considerable satisfaction: 'As the war between Spain and England is now declared one hopes that Swedish Navigation shall profit in it.'[76]

Even if neutrality shipping gave rise to profitable opportunities, it certainly also entailed serious risks. In 1740, Arfwedson reported on many captured vessels. One of the more curious cases concerned the ship *Hoppet*, home at Västervik on Sweden's east coast. The vessel was travelling between Cadiz and Spanish Tenerife, which proves that Swedish vessels were employed in the inter-Spanish trade. The vessel was taken to Madeira (Portugal) by a British privateer, where it was declared a prize. The captain, Nils Bauman, did not accept the decision at Madeira's prize court and he went to Gibraltar to appeal it. He was successful, even managing to get his freight costs paid by the British authorities.[77]

Neither did the Spanish hesitate to capture Swedish ships. Just a week after the case of *Hoppet*, Arfwedson wrote of another Swedish ship, *Svenska vapnet*, which was captured on its way from Livorno to Lisbon, with a cargo consigned to Arfwedson. The ship was taken to Genoa by two Spanish privateers and sold there. Arfwedson accused the French in Livorno and Genoa of conspiracy. According to him, the French had tried to bring the Swedish flag into dishonour to discourage other merchants from employing Swedish shipping. In this specific case the Swedish crew members were forced to admit, under torture, that they were sailing under an English passport, which was not true.[78] Even if the correspondence provides evidence of Swedish neutrality shipping, this appears to have been less active than in the second half of the century. The rather limited employment of neutrality shipping in 1739–48 is also confirmed by the issuing of Algerian passports (see figure 5.2 and table 5.7).

In 1752, the Swedish traveller Reinhold Angerstein visited Lisbon. His journey was financed by the Swedish Association of Ironmasters (*Jernkontoret*), and he was supposed to collect information about iron industries and the iron trade abroad.[79] During his rather lengthy visit to Lisbon (from April to July), he was a frequent guest at Arfwedson's house and he met Arfwedson's partners Reuter and Hornsten. He obtained much detailed information about Lisbon's and Portugal's economic life from the consul, yet he travelled around Lisbon's environs on his own. For example, he made a trip to Setubal and its renowned saltpans.[80]

Angerstein left a detailed description of trade conditions in Lisbon, and spe-

---

[76] Rumors about the war in Arfwedson to BoT, 18 August 1739 and 6 October 1739 Lisbon, Consular Reports, Lisbon 1731–1778, E VI aa 224, BoT SNA.
[77] Arfwedson to BoT 7 June 1740, Lisbon, Consular Reports, Lisbon 1731–1778, E VI aa 224, BoT SNA.
[78] Arfwedson to BoT, 14 June 1740, Lisbon, Consular Reports, Lisbon 1731–1778, E VI aa 224, BoT SNA.
[79] On Reinhold Angerstein's travels see Florén and Rydén 1996 and Florén and Rydén 2002.
[80] Angerstein 1996a, pp. 89–131.

Table 4.3 *Angerstein's estimate (value) of the Swedish-Portuguese exchange, by 1752*

Swedish exports	in d.c.m.	Per cent
Bar-iron	1,447,026	52.30
Steel	73,250	2.65
Nails, band-iron	166,500	6.02
Copper-sheets, brass, blind mint, metal wares	177,500	6.42
Tar	33,325	1.20
Boards	668,175	24.16
Estimated income of freights	200,000	7.23
Total Swedish exports	2,765,776	100.00
Total Swedish imports	500,000	
Turnover	3,265,776	

Source: Angerstein 1996 (1752), p. 142.

cifically the Swedish-Portuguese exchange. He also made proposals on how to develop Swedish commerce, which did not differ much from the schemes of Anders Bachmanson Nordencrantz, put forward twenty years earlier. Yet Angerstein's report also included an estimate of the Swedish-Portuguese turnover, which it is interesting to compare with Bachmanson Nordencrantz's figures for 1728 and 1729.

In comparison with Bachmanson's figures, Angerstein's estimate shows significant changes. Firstly, there was a significant increase in the export value, from 0.8 million d.c.m. to 2.8 million d.c.m.. Even if part of the increase can be explained by rising prices, there was evidently a significant boom in business activities. The increase in trade was not primarily connected to the iron trade. Angerstein estimated the volume of bar-iron exports at 15,000 ship pounds, which was somewhat more than the 12,000 registered by Bachmanson Nordencrantz: in value bar-iron exports doubled. Portugal's demand for Swedish bar-iron was already saturated. Angerstein estimated Portugal's total bar-iron imports at 15,000 to 18,000 ship pounds, of which some three-quarters were already coming from Sweden. But, at least according to Angerstein, there was still an opportunity to increase the export of Swedish steel. The steel market in Portugal was dominated by steel from Corinthia. The Swedish steel makers and merchants could increase their share on the Corinthian steel account.[81]

The most important shift in trade occurred in the area of sawn timber exports, the value of which increased seven-fold, from roughly 100,000 d.c.m. in 1728–29 to almost 680,000 d.c.m. in 1752. Another important change concerned the role of freights, which in 1752 were estimated at 200,000 d.c.m., or about 7 per cent of Swedish exports.

---

[81] Angerstein 1996a, p. 98.

It must be stressed that Angerstein's calculations are based on estimates, which if anything seem to be set too low. He mentioned in his report that, according to word of mouth reports, the consular fees for the Swedish charity fund at Portugal reached 10,000 d.c.m. in some years (0.2 per cent of all trade), which more probably indicates a total turnover of 5 million d.c.m., instead of the estimated 3 million d.c.m.(table 4.3.).

As regards the organization of Swedish trade in Portugal, Angerstein's view did not differ from the other observers. He observed that trade was dispersed in too many hands and he proposed to limit this by establishing a national *Contoir* directed from Stockholm—a proposal not substantially different from Bachmanson Nordencrantz's ideas. As mentioned above, Angerstein's travels were financed by the Swedish Association of Iron Masters, which explains why an overwhelming portion of his attention is devoted to the iron trade and production. Angerstein did not pay much attention to the conditions of shipping.

Arfwedson carried out his consular duties until his death in 1756, four years after Angerstein's visit. Unfortunately, there are no Arfwedson reports from the 1750s, and consequently nothing about Lisbon's earthquake of 1755, which had such major consequences for European commerce.[82] According to his successor in the consulate, Jean Bedoire, Arfwedson lost many commissions at the end of his life and his economic situation deteriorated.

Jean Bedoire, like Arfwedson, belonged to an outstanding Stockholm merchant family. Bedoire was officially appointed in February 1757 but his first report was dated April 1758. It concerned, as usual, the pitiable economic conditions of the Swedish Lisbon consulate.[83] He complained about the general high expenses of living in Portugal, especially the housing. The consul's income was absolutely insufficient for paying all the necessary costs for employees, for his house, for bribes to the Portuguese authorities and all other necessary outlays. He complained, not surprisingly, about low consulade fees.

In comparison with his forerunner, Bedoire left relatively few reports, and there are large gaps in his reportage: 1759–69 and again 1769–75. Bedoire appeared to spend much of his consular period in Sweden. From 1776, there was a rising number of reports concerning the American War of Independence, which provided the Swedes with profitable opportunities. For example, Bedoire reported on an American privateer sailing along Portugal's coast and taking English ships. Another conflict, which also provided the Swedish shipowners with a profitable opportunity, was the Dutch-Moroccan war the same year.[84]

Neither did the next Lisbon consul Adolf Ludwig Ström leave many reports. He took over the consulate officially in November 1778, still in a period when

---

[82] On Lisbon's import of Swedish timber after 1755 see Högberg 1964, p. 23.
[83] Jean Bedoire to BoT, 18 April 1758/31 May 1758, Lisbon, Consular Reports, Lisbon 1731–1778, E VI aa 224, BoT SNA.
[84] For example, Jean Bedoire to BoT, 10 September 1776, Lisbon, Consular Reports, Lisbon 1731–1778, E VI aa 224, BoT SNA.

5. The snows *Resolution* and *L'Apparance* attacked by the British between Lisbon and Madeira, December 1793 (*Svenska flottans historia*, vol. 2, 1943, p. 527)

Swedish shipping was expanding, as, for example, reports from Cadiz show. Yet we will not find much evidence of this in Ström's reporting. In 1781, Johan Albert Kantzow, from another well-known Stockholm family, was appointed Lisbon consul. Members of the Kantzow family then maintained the consular position in Lisbon until 1860, with the exception of only three years (1813–16) when the consulate was held by Lorentz Westin.[85]

Johan Albert Kantzow was a very young man, a mere twenty-two years old, when he settled in Lisbon. Apparently, there was no Swedish house in the city at that time.[86] Kantzow was also supposed to make his living mainly from trade commissions, and he seemed to do so quite succesfully in the 1780s. His situation deteriorated in the 1790s during the French Revolutionary Wars. In 1798, he got into such profound difficulty that the firm Kantzow and Co. was declared bankrupt. The major reason for the bankruptcy appears to have been French debts. Kantzow had extensive exchange with the French merchants who belonged to one of the most important national groups in Lisbon, and as a consequence of the French Revolution many of the French failed to repay their

[85] Almqvist 1912–13, p. 410.
[86] Jansson 1964, p. 50; Högberg 1964, pp. 26–29.

debts. Strangely, despite the bankruptcy, Johan Abraham Kantzow continued to work as the Swedish Lisbon consul.

Kantzow stayed in Lisbon until Portugal's occupation by Napoleon in 1808. Then, he followed the Portuguese king Joao to Brazil, where the royal court found a safe haven in the years of the French occupation of Portugal. The consul Kantzow continued to carry out his diplomatic duties in Rio de Janeiro and he became the first Swedish envoy in Brazil. Yet he left, at his post in Lisbon, his younger son Carl Adolf Kantzow. In 1811 Johan Albert Kantzow returned from Brazil to Sweden, but just a year later, in 1812, he was appointed as the Swedish representative to the USA. Meanwhile, the son Carl Adolf Kantzow continued to manage the Lisbon consulate. He was officially appointed the new consul in 1816. Not surprisingly his older brother's (Johan Albert Kantzow Jr.) Stockholm firm became one of the largest Swedish houses in engaged in trade with Portugal, Latin America and even East Indies in the first decades of the nineteenth century.[87]

With Johan Albert and Carl Adolf Kantzow the consulate in Lisbon stayed in the hands of one merchant family for almost eighty years. For the first time, the consulate was also connected with a truly successful firm, despite the elder Kantzow's bankruptcy. As we shall see later (chapter 7), the Kantzow firm in Stockholm, Kantzow and Biel, was also one of the leading iron exporters to the United States, a very different kind of trade than the traditional salt imports from Lisbon.[88] The Kantzow firm appeared to be among those Swedish firms that adapted rather quickly to the changing conditions of trade before 1800, and it took part in the transatlantic trade, especially the sectors in which the Swedes had competitive advantages. This happened at the same time that Sweden's trade with the Mediterranean declined; tramp shipping became more dangerous than profitable, and salt lost its importance as a strategic commodity.

4.6.2 Cadiz

The second consulate to which we pay more detailed attention is that of Cadiz. This large city's role as Spain's major trading hub was a result of its role as the port with exclusive rights for trade with Spanish America. Cadiz was the entrepôt of American and Caribbean colonial goods, and so, significantly, also a place where the Spanish American fleets were equipped and repaired. Hence, Cadiz was also an important market for Swedish naval stores. After 1731, when the Swedish East India Company was established, Cadiz also became important as a place where the Swedish East India vessels acquired their silver, before undertaking the voyage to Canton. As with other European enterprises, the

---

[87] Kantzow and Biel, the firm of Johan Abraham Jr. was the first Swedish firm with direct contacts to India and China in the 1820s and 1830s, after the abolition of monopoly of the Swedish East India Company. Johan Abraham Kantzow, *SBL*, vol. 20, 1973–75, pp. 612–613.
[88] Adamson 1969, p. 81

Swedish East India trade was also mainly paid for in bullion, primarily Spanish American silver.[89]

From the Swedish point of view, Cadiz was also a very different market compared to Lisbon. Even if there was significant salt production in the environs, Cadiz was not at all as important a salt-supplier as Setubal, Lisbon, Cagliari or Ibiza. In addition, bar-iron, the key Swedish staple commodity, had limited demand in Cadiz. Spain had its own, well-protected iron production in the Basque countries and in Catalonia.

As mentioned in chapter 2, there were already loose plans to appoint a Swedish correspondent at Cadiz in 1651. However, the first consular reports from Cadiz, preserved in the Board of Trade collection, are from 1719. These were written by the consul Isaac Rouyer, appointed the consul in Cadiz in the same year.[90] Rouyer's reports mainly concerned conditions in the Cadiz trade, particularly the trade in naval stores (boards, tar, pitch and cannons), yet he also informed the Board of Trade of the prices of salt, wine, olive oil, cochineal, etc.[91] Isaac Rouyer officially left his position in 1736.

The next consul, Jacob Martin Bellman, received his appointment eight years later, in 1744. Bellman was a Swede; however, he had been living abroad since 1732, and had obtained his business experience long before the appointment. He held the Cadiz consulate until his retirement in 1766. He then married a Spanish merchant's daughter and became a Catholic. He died an eighty-year-old man, in 1786, near Cadiz. It is worth mentioning that consul Bellman was an uncle to the outstanding Swedish poet-musician Carl Michael Bellman.[92]

How did Swedish trade develop in the course of Bellman's consulate? In one of his first reports (May 1745) Bellman reviewed the general situation in commerce, and he paid special attention to iron. Firstly, he complained about the recent increases of duties that made Swedish iron more expensive, compared to that of the Basque region. This duty issue was seen as so important that Bellman asked the Swedish ambassador in Madrid to take action in response. As regards the other commodities the situation appeared better. In particular, the market was favourable for boards.[93]

The aforementioned Reinhold Angerstein also visited Cadiz in 1752, just before his journey to Lisbon. In accordance with his instructions, he paid major attention to the trade in steel and bar-iron in Cadiz. He noted that the bulk of steel arrived via Venice, Genoa and Livorno, and was of Austrian origin, like that of Lisbon. Angerstein made a rough calculation which seemed to prove

---

[89] Ahlberger and Mörner 1993.
[90] Ysak Rouyer to BoT, 30 October 1719 Cadiz, Consular Reports, Cadiz 1719–1802, E VI aa 67, BoT SNA According to Almqvist there were three appointed consuls already the late 1690s: Christian Bratt, Alexander Bredal and Carlos Panhuysen. Almqvist 1912–13, p. 425.
[91] Rouyer to BoT, 28 February 1724 Cadiz, Consular Reports, Cadiz 1719–1802, E VI aa 67, BoT SNA.
[92] On Jacob Martin Bellman, see Simonsson 1922.
[93] Bellman to BoT, 11 May 1745/pres 4 June 1745, Cadiz, Consular Reports, Cadiz 1719–1802, E VI aa 67, BoT SNA.

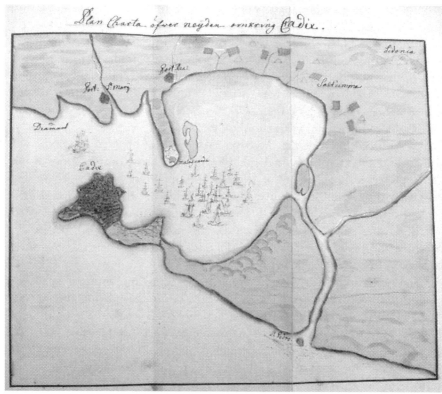

6. Cadiz (Reinhold Angerstein's report, BoT SNA)

that Swedish steel could find a much better market in Cadiz.[94] Nevertheless, he was less hopeful regarding the market for Swedish bar-iron. Spain produced large quantities of iron, and it protected this production. Angerstein estimated total Spanish production at 73,000 ship pounds, of which about a half was exported, mainly to the American colonies and France. Between 6,000 and 7,000 ship pounds of foreign iron, mainly of Swedish origin, reached Cadiz.[95]

If the trade in iron received less attention than expected, tramp shipping then played a rather important role. Already, in his account of the Cadiz commerce in May 1745, the consul Bellman had discussed international shipping conditions in the Mediterranean. The ongoing War of the Austrian Succession, a great European conflict with potentially useful consequences for Sweden, was at the forefront of his considerations. For example, he mentioned rumours about the approaching outbreak of war between the Dutch Republic and France, which—he suggested—should much benefit Swedish trade. In the same context he complained about the relative lack of Swedish shipping capacity.

---

[94] Angerstein 1996b, p. 11.
[95] Angerstein 1996b, pp. 28–29.

Nevertheless, shipping in wartime conditions was not only profitable, but very risky. The correspondence in the following years (1745–47) concerned to a high degree the capture of Swedish vessels, taken by both Spanish privateers and the British Royal Navy. In September 1745, Genoa entered the War of the Austrian Succession on the Spanish and French side. The British began to declare Swedish vessels destined for Genoa as just prizes, and soon two Swedish vessels were taken. The first one was *Resolution* (owned by Carlos and Claes Grill) under master Lars Böcker, with a cargo of sugar and coffee beans from Genoa. The second vessel, commanded by Anders Kjellberg, was sailing from Lisbon to Genoa with an unknown cargo. Both were boarded near Genoa and taken to Livorno.[96]

The Spanish did not behave differently. In September 1746, Bellman reported the case of the ship *Westerviks Vapen* taken by a Spanish privateer and sold as a prize in Ceuta. In this case the reason for capture was the fact that the neutral Swedish ship had on board an English-owned cargo destined for Livorno.[97] However, the case of *Westerviks Vapen* was not yet over. The owners appealed to the court in Madrid, and proceedings were ongoing for many years. Bellman, for this case, even hired a Flemish merchant, Jean François van der Lepe, who was supposed to help the Swedish envoy with proceedings in Madrid.[98] In 1752, the case of *Westerviks Vapen* still was not closed.

The Seven Years War was the next large European conflict. In this war, Sweden was involved on the French side and the Swedish army was engaged in limited operations against Prussia. Apparently, the involvement also affected Swedish shipping in southern waters. In 1759, a Prussian privateer from Emden (14 guns, 100 men) cruised in the Mediterranean, chasing the Swedish vessels. The Prussian captured at least three Swedes and took them to La Coruna, Gibraltar and Cartagena. For the protection of Swedish shipping, the man-of-war *Sparre* and the frigate *Falken* were sent to the Mediterranean.[99]

The war years also provided Swedish shipowners with profitable opportunities, but Bellman's reports show that the Swedes were expanding their tramp shipping even in peacetime. Cadiz appears to have been a typical place for Swedish ships to be hired for shipping within the Mediterranen. Typical voyages of these hired ships were to Livorno and Genoa, with Spanish colonial goods as usual cargoes. Yet Swedish ships were even hired by the Spaniards for voyages to northern Spanish ports. For example, in 1753, Swedish ships carried salt from Cadiz to the northern Spanish provinces of Galicia and Asturias.[100]

[96] Bellman to BoT, 14 September 1745, Cadiz, Consular Reports, Cadiz 1719–1802, E VI aa 67, BoT SNA.

[97] Bellman to BoT, 12 September 1746 Cadiz, Consular Reports, Cadiz 1719–1802, E VI aa 67, BoT SNA.

[98] Bellman to BoT, 4 September 1753 Cadiz, Consular Reports, Cadiz 1719–1802, E VI aa 67, BoT SNA.

[99] A. Williamson (instead of Bellman) to BoT, 1 August 1759/5 September 1759, Cadiz, Consular Reports, Cadiz 1719–1802, E VI aa 67, BoT SNA.

[100] Bellman to BoT, 4 September 1753 Cadiz, Consular Reports, Cadiz 1719–1802, E VI aa 67, BoT SNA.

By the late 1760s, Swedish ships were hired for even more spectacular voyages. They were transporting Spanish troops to America. In 1769, the consul Arendt Dreyer reported on six ships that had been contracted for these transports, and four other ships that were expected to return soon. From this report, it is not clear if all the ships were contracted for troop transports to Cuba, but from letters dated the next year, we know that the ship *Pehr Öhrenshield* returned from Havana in February 1770, and that this ship was contracted for troop transports.[101] The Spanish authorities also employed foreign ships, not only for shipping in Spanish coastal waters, but also for shipping to Spanish America. Perhaps it was in this trade that Swedish seamen obtained their first experience in transatlantic shipping. This pattern also shows that Swedish ships entered transatlantic shipping as an extension to tramp shipping in southern Europe.

In 1767, the retired Bellman was replaced by Arendt Dreyer, who was not very well prepared for his consular position, as has already been observed. He lacked a social network in Cadiz, and, apparently, also expertise in terms of Swedish trade in the Mediterranean. Dreyer's first preserved reports are dated April 1769, and they very much concern Morocco. The peace and trade treaty between Sweden and Morocco was only signed in 1761, and it was a very expensive treaty. Nevertheless, in 1769, the Moroccan Emperor raised new claims against Sweden, and in Cadiz there were rumours about a forthcoming war between Morocco and Sweden (23 May 1769). In August 1769, Dreyer heard from the Dutch consul that if the Swedes did not send their gifts to the Emperor by the end of October, war would be declared. Such rumours were affecting Swedish shipping, as correspondents were advising their customers to avoid Swedish vessels.[102] But other national consuls in Cadiz also had the same problems. Morocco was already at war with Great Britain and Portugal, and the conflict did not develop well for Europeans. The Moroccan Emperor conquered a Portuguese fortress, which boosted his ego, and after this success he increased his claims against all European states.[103]

The bulk of Dreyer's reports to the Board of Trade were about his problems with captains who resisted paying consulade fees, and about his increasing problems with his vice-consul, the highly successful merchant Anders Hagström. Due to Dreyer's lack of business contacts, Swedish ships were usually consigned to merchants other than him, for example to Hagström. Hence, although captains were obliged to pay consulade fees to Dreyer, they frequently avoided it. For example, in April 1769, captain Daniel Ell anchored at Cadiz with a cargo of grain consigned to the Cadiz house of Rey and Brandenbourg.

---

[101] Dreyer to BoT, 18 April 1769, 27 February and 12 July 1770, Cadiz, Consular Reports, Cadiz 1719–1802, E VI aa 67, BoT SNA.
[102] Dreyer to BoT, 23 May 1768? (letter-writer's error), 8 August 1769, Cadiz, Consular Reports, Cadiz 1719–1802, E VI aa 67, BoT SNA.
[103] Dreyer to BoT, 29 August 1769, Cadiz, Consular Reports, Cadiz 1719–1802, E VI aa 67, BoT SNA.

7. Hans Jacob Gahn, consul in Cadiz (1775–1800) (UUL)

He refused to pay a consulade fee to Dreyer, and left Cadiz without documents signed by the consul. The same month, three other captains refused to pay the fee.[104]

In 1772, the conflict between the consul and his vice-consul intensified. It primarily concerned the fact that Hagström was a well-established merchant with many contacts and many commissions, especially from France, whereas the consul's commissions were few. The rivals turned to the Board of Trade for a decision. The Board appeared to accept Hagström's interpretation of the conflict, and Dreyer left Cadiz in 1773, after just four years in office.[105]

The next consul, Hans Jacob Gahn, was officially appointed in 1775.[106] However, Gahn seems already to have been in Cadiz in April 1773, when he sent his first report to the Board of Trade. In this letter he mentioned that he had received from Dreyer all the documents relating to his new position.[107]

Like other Swedish consuls, Gahn also started his reporting activities from Cadiz with a general account of Swedish trade in the area. In the beginning of

[104] Dreyer to BoT, 18 April 1769, 25 April 1769 Cadiz, Consular Reports, Cadiz 1719–1802, E VI aa 67, BoT SNA.
[105] Dreyer to BoT, 23 July 1772, 11 December 1772, Anders Hagström to BoT Cadiz 14 July 1772/2, Cadiz, Consular Reports, Cadiz 1719–1802, E VI aa 67, BoT SNA.
[106] Almqvist 1912–13, p. 425.
[107] Gahn to BoT, 20 April 1773, Cadiz, Consular Reports, Cadiz 1719–1802, E VI aa 67, BoT SNA.

the 1770s, commercial conditions appeared to be quite disappointing from the Swedish point of view. Demand for Swedish staple commodities was declining, and the competition from Russian iron was tough.[108] Moreover, neither were the conditions of shipping very profitable. Gahn noted that the profitable shipping to the West Indies had stopped, as the Spanish crown now employed its own ships. Even shipping in the Mediterranean had declined and some large Cadiz houses were going bankrupt.

Another issue often mentioned in Gahn's reports, which threatened Cadiz's commerce, were the royal plans deregulate trade between Spain and the Spanish Americas. Gahn was interested as to what possible consequences free trade could have for the Swedes. For example, he described in detail how the situation developed in the Caribbean when the Cuban trade was 'set free'. For the whole of Spanish America, trade was deregulated in 1778.

In the second half of 1774 and in the beginning of 1775, the situation for Swedish business radically improved. Gahn was now reporting on improved sales conditions for Swedish commodities, especially for sawn timber, and on the improved shipping market. Iron was not by any means as profitable.

Gahn's unusually detailed shipping lists not only provide information about cargoes, but also reveal ship-movements in Cadiz and the Mediterranean. They illustrate the means by which Swedish tramp shipping in the Mediterranean was carried out. Usually, the Swedish ship arrived in Cadiz with a cargo of Swedish staple commodities. Then it was hired for a voyage to the Mediterranean. Some ships, as also indicated in Bellman's correspondence, might be carrying salt cargoes from Cadiz in northern Spain. Gahn's shipping lists show that many ships stayed in the Mediterranean for more than one season. A good example of the shipping pattern is the snow *Pelikan*, of 75 lasts and a crew of ten, which anchored in Cadiz in December 1776. *Pelikan* left its homeport of Norrköping in August 1775. The vessel was in Bordeaux in December 1775, and in Ancona in Italy in May 1776. From Ancona it sailed back to Alicante in Spain (18 July 1776), to Genoa in northern Italy (14 September 1776), to Palermo in Sicily (2 October 1776), and finally to Cadiz. *Pelikan* left Cadiz on 15 December for Setubal, whence it most probably continued home with a cargo of salt.[109]

The outbreak of the American War of Independence led to a dramatic change in Swedish commerce. The first rumours about the oncoming war in America appeared in July 1776, with consequent increases in the prices of colonial products. And, even if war between Spain and Britain did not break out until 1779, Swedish shipping was already flourishing in 1776 and 1777.[110]

---

[108] Gahn to BoT, 23 April 1773, Cadiz, see also the letter of 19 October 1773, Cadiz, Consular Reports, Cadiz 1719–1802, E VI aa 67, BoT SNA

[109] Gahn to BoT, Shipping list dated 3 January 1777, Cadiz, Consular Reports, Cadiz 1719–1802, E VI aa 67, BoT SNA.

[110] Gahn to BoT, 23 July 1776 Cadiz, Consular Reports, Cadiz 1719–1802, E VI aa 67, BoT SNA.

In 1778, Gahn was in Sweden, and vice-consul Anders Hagström replaced him for a short period. Yet, as soon as January 1779, Gahn was back in Cadiz. In February 1779, Gahn wrote:

> Hence the ongoing war is a favourable occasion for the neutral states' flags, it has not failed to influence our shipping and commerce here and it is important to exploit this opportunity as much as possible. [111]

Swedish ships were chartered at high freight prices. But the situation could turn very quickly. In summer 1779, Gahn still was reporting on the profitable situation, with the prices of Swedish products increasing by 12 to 15 per cent, and the prices of American colonial products increasing by as much as 50 per cent. However, he also mentioned that, as far as neutral ships were concerned, the French correspondents preferred Dutch ships due to the Netherlands' better relations with Britain. They were afraid to hire the Swedes. This changed when the Dutch Republic entered the war on the French and Spanish side, in 1780. To discredit Swedish shipping, competitors also spread rumours about a Swedish conflict with Morocco—the same strategy as had been employed in the late 1760s.

Great Britain was the most dangerous state for the Swedish neutral flag, because the British applied their own restricted interpretation of neutrality shipping rules. Whereas other states followed the rule 'free [neutral] ship equals free goods', the British defined naval stores (including boards, tar and pitch) as contraband even if carried on a neutral ship.[112] But there were also other states hostile to neutrals.

In June 1779, Spain entered the war on the French side, and this damaged the neutrals' position. Spanish privateers were cruising in the Gibraltar straits, and taking neutral ships. In his letter of October 1779, Gahn reported the case of three Swedish ships taken by Spanish and French privateers to Algeciras, the Spanish naval base. Two of them had British cargoes; *Gubben Noah* had a cargo from Exeter destined for Genoa and Livorno, and *Regressen* was destined for Gibraltar with coal from Newcastle. But the third ship, *Maria Elisabeth*, was carrying cargo from St. Petersburg consigned to Naples, and so was unquestionably neutral.[113] The latter ship was set free, after fifty-two days of waiting in Algeciras.

In the winter months of 1779/80, the Spanish blockade of Gibraltar seemed to be almost complete. Between September 1779 and April 1780, thirteen Swedish vessels were taken to Algeciras, three to Ceuta, and sixteen to Cadiz.[114]

---

[111] Gahn to BoT, Cadiz 17 February 1779, Consular Reports, Cadiz 1719–1802, E VI aa 67, BoT SNA.

[112] Jägerskiöld 1957, p. 281. See also the British reaction on Armed Neutrality 1780, Scott 1918, p. 317

[113] Gahn to BoT 23 October 1779, Cadiz, Consular Reports, Cadiz 1719–1802, E VI aa 67, BoT SNA.

[114] List of captured Swedish ships at Algeciras between 26 September and mid-April 1779–1780, Gahn to BoT Cadiz 18 May 1780, Consular Reports, Cadiz 1719–1802, E VI aa 67, BoT SNA.

Table 4.4: *Swedish ships calling at Cadiz, 1778–1800*

1778	41
1785	83
1791	25
1792	18
1793	40
1795	45
1796	80
1800	22

Source: Carl O. Christiernin's and Gahn's shipping lists, Consular Reports, Cadiz 1719–1802, E VI aa 67, BoT SNA.

Even if most of the vessels were set free, the arrests caused costly delays and they damaged the reputation of Swedish neutrality shipping. This damaged reputation was the major reason for Gahn's strong reaction. He argued that the Swedish authorities had to take greater responsibility for convoying merchant ships and they also had to act more forcefully in Madrid.

Even Russian and Danish shipping was damaged by Spanish privateering, and the deteriorating situation of these three states' shipping was a motive for the armed neutrality coalition of Denmark, Sweden and Russia, signed in summer 1780.[115] The neutrality coalition appeared to strengthen Sweden's position. In 1780–83, the privateer activities against the neutrals declined and Swedish shipping in the Mediterranean thrived. The positive trend also continued after 1783. In 1785, as many as eighty-three Swedish ships visited Cadiz.[116]

The shipping lists from period of the French Revolutionary Wars indicate how volatile business conditions were (table 4.4). The commodity trade manifests the same unpredictability. Hence, in 1795, the Swedes exported the tiny amount of 909 ship pounds of iron to Cadiz, in comparison with over 3,000 ship pounds ten years before. However, as early as the next year, 1796, Swedish ships arrived with over 5,700 ship pounds of iron. Trade in sawn timber showed even more volatility. The number of 'dozen' (*tolfter*) deals increased from 2,813 in 1795 to 14,892 in 1796.

The instability of trade and shipping has of course to be linked to wartime conditions. In the 1790s, commerce was profitable but dangerous. Once again, the consular reports were full of cases of captured ships and complaints about the weakness of Swedish policy against the combatant countries. Lists of captured ships show that French and Spanish privateers were very active.

There is a list of seventeen ships taken by the Spanish privateers to Algeciras in the first half of 1793 alone.[117] In addition to these, there were captured ships

---

[115] Svensson 1943, p. 525; Jägerskiöld 1957, pp. 283–284.
[116] Shipping list for 1785, dated probably 27 January 1786, Consular Reports, Cadiz 1719–1802, E VI aa 67, BoT SNA.
[117] The list of captured Swedish ships at Algeciras 1793, Consular Reports, Cadiz 1719–1802, E VI aa 67, BoT SNA.

in Ceuta. In September 1797, the Cadiz consul reported on all the 68 Swedish vessels taken by the Spanish in the course of the Spanish-British war (1796–97). As in the American War of Independence, the ships were eventually set free, but delays were expensive and privateers damaged the credibility of Swedish neutral shipping.[118]

In October 1798, Gahn wrote to the Board of Trade about the British blockade of Cadiz. The Royal Navy was then in full control of the Mediterranean, and, according to the consul, the only neutral state whose neutrality the British respected was the United States.[119]

Gahn died in October 1800 after his long consular service. It took three years for the Board of Trade to appoint a new consul. This consul, Zacharias Scherman, was also supposed to make his living primarily as a merchant and commission agent. His reports from the Napoleonic years do not provide the same rich picture of Swedish activities as Gahn's correspondence, but it is worth mentioning the fact that they regularly included printed price lists from Cadiz.[120]

Due to its role in the Spanish commercial system, Cadiz was a very important entrepôt for the Swedish trade and shipping activities in southern Europe. The Cadiz consulate appeared to function as a kind of information centre concerning both the profitable shipping opportunities in the Mediterranean and Spanish shipping contracts. Many hiring contracts were mediated via Cadiz houses. And, of course, Cadiz was also an important market for Swedish staple commodities, even if this role was not as crucial as that of Lisbon.

4.6.3 Marseilles

Most probably, Marseilles was the leading Mediterranean entrepôt, and certainly the key French city-port in the area. But the Swedish presence in Marseilles dates from a significantly later period than in Portugal, Spain, and even Italy. This most probably resulted from the fact that, at least in the beginning of the eighteenth century, Swedish commerce in Marseilles was of limited importance. Indeed, the foundation of the Swedish consulate in Marseilles appeared to be connected with the establishment of peaceful relationships with the Barbary states. From the beginning, Marseilles functioned as a base for the Swedish negotiations with Algiers. Another important motive for the establishment of the Swedish consulate at Marseilles had to do with the Levant trade.

---

[118] 20 Swedish ships were taken to Ceuta, 6 to Cadiz, and as much as 42 to Algeciras. List of captured ships 26 September 1797, Cadiz, Consular Reports, Cadiz 1719–1802, E VI aa 67, BoT SNA. Spain declared war to Great Britain in October 1796, already in February 1797 the Spanish navy was defeated.

[119] Gahn to BoT, 12 October 1798 Cadiz, Consular Reports, Cadiz 1719–1802, E VI aa 67, BoT SNA.

[120] On Gahn's death, see Christiernin to BoT, 10 October 1800 Cadiz, Consular Reports, Cadiz 1719–1802, E VI aa 67, BoT SNA; For Scherman's reports see Consular Reports, Cadiz 1803–1810, E VI aa 68, BoT SNA.

Marseilles was the centre of the European Levant trade, which was also an important motive behind Swedish engagement in the Mediterranenan.

The first Swedish consul in Marseilles was appointed in 1731, two years after the peace treaty with Algiers. The consul was not of Swedish origin. Consuls of foreign nations in France had to be French citizens. The consul's name was Nicolas Sollicoffre, and he belonged to a well-known Marseilles merchant family.[121] In 1735, the Swedish consulate was taken over by Jean Antoine Butini and from his period Sweden's Marseilles consulate stayed in the hands of the families Butini and Fölsch for almost 150 years (until 1881). Butini and Fölsch were also well-known members of the Marseilles merchant elite and the leading commission agents of the Swedish firms.[122]

There is also another striking difference, compared to Lisbon and even Cadiz. The consulates in Cadiz and especially in Lisbon were of large political significance. In France, consuls did not have the same role. France was Sweden's traditional ally, with well-developed contacts at a high diplomatic level. The Swedish diplomatic representation in Paris was doubtless Sweden's most important, and Swedish ambassadors to France were important Swedish politicians. The status and functional discrepancy between the consular service on the one hand, and the high-level diplomatic representation on the other, was greater in France than in other states.

In the first years, the Swedish Marseilles consul seemed mainly to transmit the correspondence of George Logie from Algiers to the Board of Trade.[123] Trade with the Barbary states and the Levant was the most important aspect of the consul's own business. For example, in 1735, when the consul Butini gave a general account of the conditions of Swedish commerce in Marseilles, he focused on the Levant and Barbary coast trade.[124] In particular, he paid attention to the Levant trade, in which the Butini firm was a large actor. According to Butini, Swedish ships could be employed by French merchants in shipping between Levant and Marseilles; then the Swedes migh import Levant commodities from Marseilles. The idea seemed to attract the attention of some Stockholm merchants. Butini was in frequent contact with Thomas Plomgren and Gustaf Kierman, major supporters of the project of the Swedish Levant Company.

In addition to the Levant and Barbary coast commerce, the consul commented on the market conditions of Swedish staple commodities. On the one hand, Marseilles was not a good market for Swedish iron. Direct iron exports from Sweden were seldom profitable, because Swedish iron in large quantities reached Marseilles on Dutch ships. On the other hand, there was a rather

---

[121] Carrière 1973.

[122] Almqvist 1912–13, p. 384; Carrière 1973; Hildebrand 1957, p. 140; Müller 1998, p. 204.

[123] Gaspar et Nicolas Solicoffre Som. to BoT, 21 July 1732 Marseilles, Consular Reports, Marseilles 1732–1814, E VI aa 331, BoT SNA.

[124] Jacques [Jacob] Butini to BoT, 23 March 1736 Marseilles, Consular Reports, Marseilles 1732–1814, E VI aa 331, BoT SNA.

satisfactory market for tar and pitch. As in other southern European markets, the situation for Swedish commodities worsened over the course of time, due to quantities of Russian iron and naval stores reaching the western Mediterranean on Dutch ships.

In 1739, Butini sent a proposal to the Board of Trade to concentrate all trade in Swedish commodities at Marseilles in the hands of one house. The Swedish and French courts would make a deal according to which the French naval bases (Toulon, Port Louis, Rochefort and Brest) should exclusively purchase all naval stores from Sweden.[125] However, there are no indications that the scheme was seriously discussed.

The reports indicate that Swedish ships called rather frequently at Marseilles. Between 1736 and 1740, 27 Swedish ships called at Marseilles, an annual average of eight ships. According to other sources, Sweden was in fact the third northern-European shipping nation at Marseilles, after Britain and the Dutch Republic.[126]

As in the case of the correspondence from the Lisbon and Cadiz consulates, the Marseilles consuls' reports frequently included news about the capture of Swedish ships. Wartime years were once again filled with reports on French privateers and on shipping conditions generally. The Seven Years War provided, at least initially, a profitable opportunity for Swedish shipowners. Swedish and Danish ships were hired for shipping between the southern and western coasts of France. And, in 1756, Butini reported on the granting of permission for Swedish ships to sail to French colonies, especially in the French Caribbean—a similar pattern to that in which Swedish tonnage was employed by the Spanish authorities for shipping to Spanish America.[127]

However, the lucrative circumstances of neutral shipping also tempted some less honest businessmen. Particular examples illustrate how delicate the balance between legal and illegal neutrality was during wartime. In March 1757, Butini received a letter from master Olof Aschenborg, of the ship *Resolution*, which was currently at Genoa. The master informed the consul of a strange Swedish-flagged ship, which had recently anchored at Genoa. The captain of the ship, named Wengren, was a burgher in Garezze, where the vessel's owners also lived. The vessel was built in England, contrary to regulations for Swedish-flagged ships, and it had a fake Swedish Algerian passports. There were no Swedes on board and no other Swedish documents. Aschenborg was terrified by such an obvious abuse of the Swedish flag and he was afriad that if such a Swedish-flagged ship was taken in the open sea, all Swedish ships would be in danger. Butini immediately sent the details of the case to the Swedish consuls in

---

[125] Butini to BoT, 29 June 1739 Marseilles, Consular Reports, Marseilles 1732–1814, E VI aa 331, BoT SNA.

[126] Butini to BoT, 14 September 1740 Marseilles, Consular Reports, Marseilles 1732–1814, E VI aa 331, BoT SNA. The average is confirmed at Carrière 1973, p. 1061, see also Desfeuilles 1956, pp. 327–349.

[127] Butini to BoT, 29 March and 8 September 1756 Marseilles, Consular Reports, Marseilles 1732–1814, E VI aa 331, BoT SNA.

Livorno, Cadiz, Alicante, Cagliari, and Lisbon, and of course to the Board of Trade.[128] There was no Swedish consul in Genoa at the critical moment.

The 1757 reports showed a rising number of captures of Swedish ships by French and British privateers. Even the Barbary corsairs seemed to make use of the wartime opportunity. In 1759, Butini also mentioned a Prussian privateer from Emden; it must have been the same one as is mentioned in the Cadiz reports.[129] Thus the post-1756 shipping boom was short-lived. The French historian Charles Carrière's statistical record of entries of Swedish ships in Marseilles harbour suggests the same thing. After a peak in 1756, with 61 registered ship entries, the number of Swedish ships declined rather quickly to 37 (1757), 12 (1758), and 13 (1759).[130]

Butini was a very frequent correspondent and his reports provide a vivid account of Swedish affairs in Marseilles and in the Barbary states. He continued as Swedish consul until 1763 when his son-in-law, Henrik Jacob Fölsch took over the consular post—on Butini's recommendation. Henrik Jacob Fölsch continued to report extensively to Stockholm, commenting on roughly the same subjects as his father-in-law. In comparison with those of the Lisbon and Cadiz consulates, however, the reports from Marseilles did not include much trade and shipping data. Between 1781 an 1814, another member of the Fölch family, François Philip Fölsch, managed the Marseilles consulate. Hovewer, there are no reports preserved for the period between 1783 and 1803, the two decades of his office.

The establishment of the Marseilles consulate was connected to Sweden's grand commercial strategy towards the Levant and the Barbary coast. Yet it soon became apparent that these plans were over ambitious. The Swedish Levant Company disappeared and Swedish trade with the Barbary states was not successful. Nevertheless, Swedish commerce at Marseilles developed differently. As the strategic entrepôt in the western Mediterranean basin, Marseilles became a frequent point of call for Swedish ships sailing between Sicily, Livorno, Genoa, Sardinia and of course Spain and Portugal. Moreover, it also became an important market for Swedish products.

4.6.4 Livorno

Livorno began its rise as the central shipping port of north-western Italy in the late sixteenth century, assisted by the economic policy of the Tuscan dukes. It became a centre of foreign—mainly Dutch and English—commerce in the Mediterranean, and it held this position throughout the seventeenth and eighteenth centuries. Due to its free port status, the harbour functioned primarily as

---

[128] Butini to BoT, 21 March 1757 Marseilles, Consular Reports, Marseilles 1732–1814, E VI aa 331, BoT SNA.
[129] Butini to BoT, 19 January 1759 Marseilles, Consular Reports, Marseilles 1732–1814, E VI aa 331, BoT SNA.
[130] Carrière 1973, p. 1061.

a staple market for foreign merchants, while its links with the economy of Tuscany appeared rather weak.[131]

In Sweden, Livorno was apparently perceived as a leading Mediterranean port as early as the mid-seventeenth century. Livorno was mentioned as the possible site of a Swedish correspondent in the discussions of the Board of Trade in 1651,[132] and we have mentioned the visit to Livorno by Silfvercrantz during Charles XII's reign. In 1719, another Swedish traveller, Peter Sahlgren, visited Livorno. He made contact with the German merchant, Paul Lochner, who applied for the position of Swedish consul at Livorno. In August 1720, Lochner was duly appointed the first Swedish consul there, and consequently also the first Swedish consul in the Mediterranean.[133]

Lochner appears to have been an ambitious man. He made proposals for developing Swedish trade in the Mediterranean, especially with the Levant. He asked for the right to appoint Swedish vice-consuls in Italy. He also made an offer to the Board of Trade to represent Sweden in negotiations with the Barbary corsairs, in cases relating to captured Swedish ships and crews.[134] In 1722, the consul was authorised to start peace talks with the Barbary states. However, the slow progress in Lochner's negotiations did not fulfil Stockholm's expectations. After four years, in 1726, Lochner reported that the Barbary states were indeed showing interest in an agreement with Sweden, but only for a limited number of years and for a limited number of ships annually. In addition, the cost of the negotiated peace was high. At the same time, Lochner got into economic difficulties. He went bankrupt, and he embezzled money from the Swedish Convoy Fund, which was intended to ransom Swedish captives in North Africa. Lochner entirely lost his credibility. In the negotiations with the Barbary states, he was replaced by the aforementioned George Logie, and he lost his consular appointment in January 1727.[135]

The Swedish consulate in Livorno was then officially vacant for almost twenty years. Finally, in 1745, Pierre Jean de Bertellet was appointed consul.[136] Nevertheless, the collection of Livorno consular reports includes a number of letters from 1738–40, written by George Logie, who apparently used Livorno as a base in his further negotiations with Tunis and Tripoli—after signing the peace with Algiers.[137] Logie's reports are very valuable. They provide a detailed account of trade conditions in the Barbary states and Livorno. For example, Logie's report dated October 1738 provides an extensive account of conditions of commerce in Algiers. Logie was rather unenthusiastic regarding the prospects of trade in Africa, but rather hopeful regarding trade in Livorno and Italy.

---

[131] Engels 1997, pp. 39–46.
[132] Almqvist 1912–13, p. 28.
[133] Ekegård 1924, pp. 125–126.
[134] Ekegård 1924, pp. 258–259.
[135] Ekegård 1924, pp. 458–460.
[136] Almqvist 1912–13, p. 395.
[137] Logie to BoT from Livorno, Consular Reports, Liverpool Livorno 1725–1822, E VI aa 229, BoT SNA.

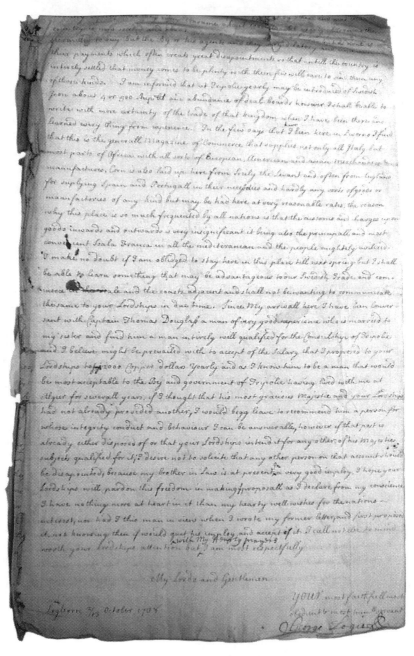

8. George Logie's letter to the Board of Trade (George Logie's reports, Livorno, BoT SNA)

The report is not only full of detailed information on trade conditions: it reveals Logie's view of the Algerians. He characterised the people and conditions of trade in Algiers in the following manner:

The Algerians being a people whose minds are entirely given to plunder and piracy are very little inclinable to trade themselves or give any encouragement to others to carry on any advantageous trade and what trade here is carried on with great uncertainty in so much that often when goods are in demand and imported by private persons at the same time arrives the Cruisers who being in prize abundance of the same sorts of goods and those are often sold so cheap that vendors the lawful purchased goods invendible [...][138]

This report also provides a detailed picture of the demand for different commodities in Algiers. As regards Sweden, there was a market for naval stores: tar, pitch, boards, cordage, and iron. However, the required quantities were limited and the conditions of sale unpredictable, as obvious from the quotation above. It is clear that the reason for maintaining relations with Algiers was not commodity exchange but the safety of Swedish shipping in the Mediterranean waters.

In a similar way Logie described the conditions of trade and shipping in Tripoli and Tunis, where negotiations were ongoing. Even if the focus of his letters was on the Barbary states, he also paid some attention to the conditions in Livorno, and not least to the Swedish trade there. In 1740, he summarised the situation of Swedish commerce in Livorno in the preceding two years. He mentioned that between 3,000 and 4,000 ship pounds of iron were brought into the port annually on Swedish ships, which was less than 1 per cent of Sweden's total iron exports. On the other hand, large quantities of Swedish and Russian iron reached Livorno on Dutch ships.

Steel sold at Livorno was from Austria, as was that in other Mediterranean ports, and it was difficult to find buyers for Swedish steel, as customers were familiar with the Austrian products. The situation was better for the tar and pitch trade. In the two years of Logie's stay at Livorno, between 3,000 and 4,000 barrels of tar were unloaded and sold at a good price. There was always substantial demand for Swedish sawn timber.

Another important commodity in the Swedish trade in the area was Cagliari salt from Sardinia. The salt trade in the Kingdom of Sardinia was organised in the same manner as in Portugal, which meant that the king controlled the conditions of sale. According to Logie, the Swedish merchants were the largest buyers of Sardinian salt and so were in a good negotiating position. He made a proposal to co-ordinate the Swedish purchases of Sardinian salt with Sardinian purchases of guns, muskets, cannon balls and copper. Logie also argued for a Swedish consulate in Cagliari.[139] As mentioned above, James Shastoe, who applied for the position as early as 1735, failed to be approved, and it took some years, until 1743, before the first Swedish consul to Cagliari was appointed.[140]

---

[138] Logie to BoT, 2/13 October 1738 Livorno, Consular Reports, Liverpool Livorno 1725–1822, E VI aa 229, BoT SNA.
[139] Logie to BoT, 3 August 1739 Livorno, Consular Reports, Liverpool Livorno 1725–1822, E VI aa 229, BoT SNA.
[140] Almqvist 1912–13, p. 393.

In his two years in Livorno, Logie also proposed two new consuls to the Board of Trade: first the husband of his sister, captain Thomas Douglass, as a new consul in Tripoli; and second Conrad Biehusen, a merchant in Livorno, as a consul in that city.[141] Nevertheless, none of his proposals resulted in an actual appointment. In 1740, Logie returned to North Africa and the Livorno consulate continued to be vacant.

The correspondence of Pierre Jean de Bertellet, the Swedish Livorno consul from 1745, dealt very much with issues of shipping. In addition to the usual flow of reports on captures, privateers and corsairs, he left interesting information regarding Swedish crews. Apparently, it was rather common for Swedish seamen to be hired on foreign ships. For example, in February 1747, he reported on two Swedish sailors who had run away from their ship to take hire on a British vessel. He also reported on problems with crews who refused to sail because they were afraid of corsairs.[142]

In the 1764–75 period, the Livorno consulate was occupied by Johan Reinhold Wije. Only two letters are preserved in the archives of the Board of Trade from this time. In his second letter (December 1772), he excused his infrequent correspondence by stating that there was nothing to report.[143]

The next consul, Peter Vilhelm Törngren, who was appointed in 1776, conversely left a very rich stream of reports, at least from the earliest years of his stay. Even in Livorno, Swedish trade and shipping thrived in the years of the American War of Independence. As early as October 1776, the consul was reporting on British problems. American privateers were cruising in the Mediterranean and taking British ships, which affected the insurance premiums of British vessels. Moreover, ships travelling between London and Livorno had to carry weapons. The British problems with shipping capacity strengthened the demand for neutrals. Hence, Swedish ships were frequently chartered immediately after their arrival; both for voyages within the Mediterranean and for shipping routes to Bremen, Hamburg and other northern-European ports. Törngren expressed his wish of seeing more Swedish ships in Livorno, to exploit the demand for shipping capacity.[144] Nevertheless, despite the consul's appeals, there were few Swedish ships calling in Livorno. Shipowners were well aware of the fact that neutrality shipping was profitable only when neutrality was respected.

Yet between 1778 and 1780, the French, Spanish and British openly attacked neutral ships. Even if the cargo was neutral and set free by the decision

---

[141] Logie to BoT, 2 October 1738 Livorno, related to Thomas Douglass, and 15 August 1740 Livorno, related to Conrad Biehusen, Consular Reports, Liverpool Livorno 1725–1822, E VI aa 229, BoT SNA.
[142] Bertellet to BoT, February 1747, 22 December 1755 Livorno, Consular Reports, Liverpool Livorno 1725–1822, E VI aa 229, BoT SNA.
[143] Almqvist 1912–13, p. 395, Wije to BoT, 21 December 1772 Livorno, Consular Reports, Liverpool Livorno 1725–1822, E VI aa 229, BoT SNA.
[144] Törngren to BoT, 21 October 1776 Livorno, Consular Reports, Liverpool Livorno 1725–1822, E VI aa 229, BoT SNA.

of a prize court, the voyage's economic viability could be damaged. In 1779, Törngren reported on the case of the ship *Victoria*, based in Stockholm, which sailed with a cargo of herring from England to Livorno. On the way, the vessel was taken by an American privateer and carried to a French port. After months of waiting, the vessel was set free to continue its voyage to Livorno. Yet, on the remaining part of the voyage, it was inspected many times by Spanish and other privateers, and when it finally arrived in Livorno the cargo was decayed.[145]

It is clear that the Swedish consul took an active part in finding profitable charters for Swedish ships. He recommended ships for freighters; he had the latest news on freight rates and he reported on them to Stockholm. He knew what kind of ships were in demand. For example, large vessels were normally chartered only for salt and grain cargoes in western parts of the Mediterranean—on routes to Sicily, southern Spain, etc. Smaller vessels (brigs) were, on the other hand, frequently chartered for very lucrative routes to Bremen, Hamburg, and the Baltic. These vessels often carried diverse and valuable cargoes.

Törngren continued to manage the consulate in Livorno until his death in 1800. Unfortunately, after 1780, there are no reports preserved in the Board of Trade archives. Thus we have no detailed information about Törngren's business during the French Revolutionary Wars, but most probably it did not differ from that of other wartime years in other consulates.

The narratives of the four leading consulates in the four major markets in southern Europe provide a detailed picture of consular activities, primarily from the point of view of the consular reports. This means that the narratives were based very much on the information that consuls wished to send and/or were supposed to send to the Board of Trade, and—via the channel of the Stockholm Merchant Association—to Swedish merchants. On the other hand, the reports provide very limited information on issues not properly within their remit—for example, the consuls' own businesses. Due to the detailed but scattered character of the reporting from a mere four consulates, it is also difficult to grasp the nature of these activities in their entirety. There were, of course, differences between consulates as well as between individual consuls. Nevertheless, the reports from other consulates do not provide a widely differing picture of consular life from that portrayed in the reports from Lisbon, Cadiz, Marseilles, and Livorno.

---

[145] Törngren to BoT, 4 October 1779/1 November 1779 Livorno, Consular Reports, Liverpool Livorno 1725–1822, E VI aa 229, BoT SNA.

4.6.5 Algiers, Tunis, Tripoli, and Morocco[146]

As mentioned above, the consular service in North-African states differed from the consulates on the northern coast of the Mediterranean basin. Their major aim was to keep up 'diplomatic' relations with these states. These diplomatic relations consisted primarily of forwarding tributes—ransom should perhaps be the term—to the local rulers to keep them in a good mood. Swedish consuls did not differ from the established pattern. Even if the Swedish authorities had ambitious plans to develop commerce with the North-African states, there was a weak demand for Swedish commodities. Logie, in his reports from Livorno cited above, described the situation quite exactly. So it was apparent that a Swedish consul in North Africa could not make a living as a commission agent. He was a state representative, paid by means of the Convoy Office.

The treaty with Algiers was signed in April 1729, and Logie's first task, as the Swedish consul to Algiers, was to prepare the exchange of gifts confirming the treaty. Even in terms of this operation, Sweden followed the pattern developed by other states. The exchange itself was a manifestation of Sweden's naval power. Therefore Sweden sent the ship-of-the-line *Verden* to Algiers, under the command of captain Cronhaven, and two merchant ships loaded with gifts: *Götha Lejon* and *Taxestis*. The cargoes-gifts consisted of 40 guns, 800 sabres, 1,600 cannon balls, masts and anchors, valued at a total of 20,980 rixdollars specie. The Algiers ruler expressed his satisfaction with the gifts and reciprocated with a liberated slave, two lions, three hyenas and a wild cat.[147]

The character of this gift exchange says much about the unequal relationship between Algiers and Sweden, and about the situation of Sweden as a tribute-paying party. There was a clear disproportion in the value and usefulness of the gifts. The Swedish gifts were highly useful for the Algerian naval force—the corsairs. On the other hand, the Algerian gifts had symbolic value only. Wild animals, especially lions, symbolised the dignity of the Dey, according to recognised, contemporary symbolic code. Weapons and ammunitions were gifts associated with the weakness of European power, stressing their position as tributaries of a Muslim ruler. Great powers, such as France and Britain, avoided these kinds of gifts. Thus, for example, the French gifts to North-African rulers consisted of jewellery, wine, sweets, textiles and presents, and gifts illustrating France's superior technology, such as mechanical watches, cartographic works, etc. Nevertheless, the demonstration of French technological superiority was not displayed only in the exchange of gifts. As early as 1784, a year after the successful balloon flight of the Montgolfier brothers, the French vice-consul in Tunis engaged two captains to launch a hot-air balloon in Tunis. The flight was

---

[146] There are rich report collections at BoT archives from all consulates in Barbary states (Tanger, Tripoli, Tunis, Algiers). Nevertheless, as these reports already were extensively employed I will use, in this section, primarily the secondary sources. Krëuger 1856, Olán 1921, and more critically Borg 1987).

[147] Krëuger 1856, p. 234.

a great success, and an excellent illustration of how technological expertise was used in diplomacy.[148] Sweden's ambitions to display national greatness were much more modest, not involving the manifestation of technological superiority. As we have seen in the case of Logie's gift exchange, Sweden largely accepted its position of a 'tributary'.

In 1732, the Dey who had signed the first peace treaty with Sweden died, and his successor soon came to Logie with new claims. This was a part of the game: to demand new tributes as soon as any change in the government occurred. It meant that not only the death of rulers—either in Europe or on the Barbary coast—but also changes in consular posts and similar events entailed new claims from the North-African rulers. Thus in 1735, Sweden sent another two ships to Algiers, loaded with jewels, silk and cloth, and once again ammunition and weapons. These cargoes were valued at 26,000 rixdollars.[149] In 1745 and 1746, another three ships anchored in Algiers with gifts. In total, in the 1735–46 period, Sweden sent tributes to Algiers valued at 68,000 rixdollars.

In 1736, consul Logie left Algiers for Tunis, to initiate peace negotiations with the next Barbary state. In his absence, vice-consul Gedda carried out his consular duties. After some trouble with Logie's Scottish partner, George Gordon, Gedda returned to Stockholm, and he left a detailed report on Algiers affairs, which provided the Swedish authorities with the first detailed description of Algiers' fortifications and naval force. The local navy did not impress him very much. Algiers had only eight or nine ships carrying guns, and between twelve and fifteen galleys. In Gedda's opinion, three European frigates would be enough to blockade Algiers harbour.[150] The character of the information provided shows that the Swedish authorities, if necessary, were prepared for a quick change in their Algiers diplomacy. Yet Swedish-Algiers relations continued to be peaceful in the next decade.

Logie first returned to Algiers in 1743, after six and half years' absence. As we have seen, he spent this time partly in Livorno, partly in Tunis. For the last three years of his absence (1740–43), he was negotiating a peace treaty with the third Barbary state, Tripoli. Logie apparently had a very good relationship with the Dey and a strong position among the European consuls in Algiers. For example, in 1740, he was employed in the delicate negotiations between France and Algiers. A couple of years later, the Dey personally used Logie's own vessel for a voyage from Algiers to Constantinople and back. The Swedish Convoy Office was charged for this.[151] Yet a consul's life in Algiers was not easy, even if he were among the Dey's friends. In the course of Logie's years in Algiers, there was a failed rebellion against one Dey, while another was murdered by his own soldiers.

---

[148] Windler 2000, pp. 189–194.
[149] Krëuger 1856, p. 236.
[150] Krëuger 1856, p. 238 (note).
[151] Krëuger 1856, p. 240.

In 1758, after a long and successful career, Logie left Algiers and returned to Sweden. Erik Brandel became the new consul. Brandel was an anticipated choice. He had worked as consular secretary in Algiers since 1754, and moreover, he was married to Logie's daughter. As usual on the occasion of the appointment of a new consul, the Dey handed a new list of expected gifts to the Swedes, which included, among other things, guns, balls, gunpowder and boards. In 1763, the ship carrying the required goods entered Algiers. This time the gifts/tributes were valued at 27,000 rixdollars.

In 1764 the Swedish consular representation changed again. Henrik Gottfried Brandel was appointed as the new consul, and Erik Brandel left Algiers for Sweden. Two years later, in 1766, the new Dey raised new claims, and this time he threatened the consul with war. To meet these claims, Sweden sent ships to Algiers more or less regularly every two years. In the same way the relationship between Sweden and Algiers continued to develop during the 1760s and the 1770s. The Swedes were forced to pay again and again, but in comparison with other nations, for example the Danes and the Spanish, they at least avoided an open war. Generally, relations involving the Algiers Dey could be characterised as an ongoing ransom game between him and the European consuls—but also among the consuls themselves. Due to the competition in shipping, an Algerian war against one nation meant shipping profits for the others. Consequently, the consuls kept the Algerian ruler informed of other nations' aims and strategies. For example, when one nation intended to impress the Dey by sending a fleet of naval ships, other consuls were quick to inform him of the coming demonstration of power and to explain the background.

Particularly, during the great European wars (1756–63 and 1778–83), the Algerians profited from their intermediary position. It became common practice for English, French and even Spanish privateers to bring captured ships to Algiers and sell them as prizes. Then the same ships that were as prizes set sail again under neutral flag. Naturally, the Algerians made money on such operations.[152]

The steady flow of consular reports to the Board of Trade of course also included information on the strength of the Algerian navy. In 1776, Brandel reported on the Algerian navy, in a similar way as had Gedda. This time the Algiers naval force consisted of eighteen vessels in total, mainly so-called schebecks and galleys. The fleet was not only employed in piracy against Christian ships. Occasionally the Algerians also plundered the Spanish and Italian coasts.[153]

The peaceful relationship between Algiers and Sweden ended in 1791, when Algiers declared war on Sweden. The cause, according to the Algiers Dey, was that Sweden had not sent proper gifts. Due to the declaration of war, the consul Brandel had to leave the country. He went to Livorno, whence he informed all

---

[152] Krëuger 1856, p. 254.
[153] Krëuger 1856, p. 252.

Swedish consuls in the area of the Algerian declaration of war. Moreover, Robert Anderson, the Swedish consul in Gibraltar, sent out a vessel which, cruising in the Gibraltar Straits, warned Swedish-flagged ships of the danger from the Algerian corsairs. The dissemination of information was successful; the Algerians failed to capture a single Swedish ship.[154]

The same year, Brandel was temporarily dismissed and the Board of Trade appointed Matthias Sjöldebrand in his place. The new appointment was necessary because the Algerians no longer recognized Brandel as Sweden's consul to Algiers. Sjöldebrand's first task was to conclude peace as soon as possible. The Algiers ruler substantially increased his claims in comparison with previous years. He claimed that Sweden should pay as much as the other smaller shipping nations: Venice, Denmark and the Dutch Republic. The Swedish consul essentially accepted the Algerian claims, and so the peace was concluded rather quickly, on 25 May 1792. Yet the cost of the peace substantially exceeded the former agreements. The total cost, in cash and cargoes sent to Algiers, was estimated at 175,000 rixdollars specie (see also section 5.6).[155]

Despite the new peace treaty the relationship between Sweden and Algiers continued to be tense in the 1790s, primarily due to the Dey's ambition to exploit European warfare as much as possible for his own advancement. Both Sweden and Denmark were forced to pay many extra tributes to keep the peace with Algiers. After 1795, even the United States signed a peace treaty with Algiers. Henceforward another neutral flag took part in the profitable shipping in the Mediterranean.

Sweden also maintained its consular representation in Algiers in the course of the Napoleonic Wars. Despite the volatility in shipping, the consulate was seen as useful. The pattern of conduct and reportage did not differ from the consul's business before 1800. In fact, the pattern of gift exchange between Sweden and Algiers was in operation until 1830, when France occupied Algiers.

Tunis was the second Barbary state with which Sweden signed a peace treaty. Here too, George Logie played the key role in negotiations. As mentioned above, he made the first contacts in the summer of 1736. The ruler of Tunis, entitled *Bey*, initially claimed the same tribute as Algiers, but he reduced his claims after some time. Tunis was a minor power in comparison to Algiers.

In December 1736, the treaty—the text of which closely followed the treaty with Algiers—was concluded. This peace seems to have been much cheaper than the peace with Algiers. According to the Board of Trade, the total costs of negotiations, including the tributes, was 14,070 rixdollars. The first consul, Olof Rönling, arrived in Tunis in April 1738. He had already had some experience of consular duties. He had served as a bookkeeper in the London consulate under consul Jonas Alström, and he had been recommended for his new

---

[154] Krëuger 1856, p. 257.
[155] Krëuger 1856, pp. 258–260. For details concerning the total Swedish outlays see Åmark 1961, pp. 762–775.

position by Logie, who knew him from his London days. Rönling stayed in Tunis for the following two decades, until 1758.

The Tunis consulate appears to have been a rather quite place over the course of the century. There were no large changes in Tunis-Swedish relations. An exception was the delaration of war in 1763 by the Bey. Because of the ongoing Seven Years War, that year the Swedish ships with their gifts were delayed on their voyage to Tunis, and because of this Tunis declared war on Sweden. However, the war appears to have ended as soon as the ships loaded with gifts arrived in Tunis.[156] In the 1790s, as with Algiers, the Tunis rulers increased their claims against all the European powers. War was declared on Spain, France, and Denmark. However Sweden, despite many threats, was successful in avoiding an open conflict.

In the same way as in Algiers, the major duty of the Swedish consul in Tunis was to send gifts/tributes, and to keep the rulers in good humour. The consuls reported to Sweden, but mainly on the political events in the area. There was not much opportunity for Swedish trade and shipping in Tunis.

The peace treaty with the third Barbary state, Tripoli, was also concluded by the dynamic George Logie. He had already investigated conditions in Tripoli during his 1736–37 stay in Tunis. Preparing the ground for the coming negotiations, he sent a Swedish ship loaded with guns to the Tripoli ruler, *Pasha* Ahmed Karamanli. In the next step, the pasha sent a list of expected gifts to Logie. The list included 30 guns, gun balls, gunpowder, boards, sabres and tar. However, it took an additional four years before the ship *Maj,* loaded with the requested gifts, reached the Mediterranean. The ship sailed first to Livorno, where Logie and the recently appointed Tripoli consul, Isaac Bergh, were waiting.[157] After the ship's arrival in Tripoli, the final stage of negotiations was opened. In April 1741, the peace and commerce treaty between Sweden and Tripoli was signed. There were no significant differences between this treaty and the treaties with Algiers and Tunis.

Bergh did not serve in his new post for long. The next winter, Tripoli was hit by an unknown plague that also killed the Swedish consul. A year later, in 1743, Jöns Wijnberg, Bergh's business associate and friend, was appointed in his place. For the remaining six decades of the century another four consuls managed the Swedish consulate in Tripoli—Christian Bagge, J.G. Burgman, Joh. Widell and—for a short period of negotiations after 1798—a navy captain named Cöster.[158]

The duties of the Swedish consul in Tripoli did not differ in any significant way from the business of the consulates in Tunis and Algiers. They forwarded gifts/tributes, reported on the political shifts at the Tripoli court and tried to

---

[156] Krëuger 1856, pp. 357–359 and 361; Almqvist 1912–13, p. 388.

[157] For the negotiations related to Tripoli peace treaty, see Krëuger 1856, pp. 399 ff, and Borg 1987. Borg provides the detailed history review of Tripoli's Swedish consulate based on reports to BoT.

[158] Krëuger 1856, p. 463; Borg 1987, p. 25

9. The frigate *Camilla* in Marseilles, 1806 (*Svenska flottans historia*, vol. 2, 1943, p. 345)

find business opportunities for Swedish merchants and shipowners. However, in one way, Swedish-Tripoli relations were distinctive. In contrast to other North-African states, the Tripoli rulers expressed the desire to have representation in Sweden. Hence, in the early 1740s, the Pasha proposed to send a diplomatic representative to Sweden, to strengthen the friendly and peaceful relationship between the states. In 1744, his envoy Ali Hogia Effendi began Tripoli's diplomatic mission to the Nordic kingdom. He reached Sweden in September the same year, and he stayed for twelve months, at Sweden's expense. He returned to Tripoli on board the Swedish frigate *Fama,* that also carried new gifts. This exotic mission to Sweden ended to the satisfaction of Tripoli's ruler.[159] This was not the last visit of Tripoli representatives. There was another visit in 1757, and a third representative visited Stockholm in 1772. The Tripoli missions received a good deal of attention in Stockholm. Even Carl Michael Bellman, the well-known poet-musician of the Gustavian period and relative of the Cadiz consul, wrote a poem about the exotic Tripoli envoy Abderrahman.[160]

As with Algiers and Tunis, even the Tripoli rulers increased their claims in the 1790s. However, in the case of Tripoli, the claims resulted in a number of declarations of war against Sweden and in an extended conflict in 1802, during which Sweden blockaded Tripoli. The Swedish co-operation with another neu-

---

[159] Borg 1987, pp. 29–30.
[160] Borg 1987, pp. 59, 69–75; Carl Michael Bellman, *Fredmans sånger* nr. 30.

tral flag in the area—that of the United States—was an interesting aspect of this 'war'.

The period 1798–1802 saw substantial activity from the Swedish navy in the Mediterranean, as it carried out the tasks of demonstrating Sweden's naval power, defending Swedish merchantmen, and delivering gifts/tributes. From December 1801, four Swedish frigates, *Thetis, Fröja, Camilla* and *Sprengporten*, were cruising in the area. In January 1802, a period of co-operation with the American navy was initiated by the Swedish commander, Rudolf Cedeström. It concerned the joint blockade of Tripoli and the convoying of merchant ships. American and Swedish consuls carried on the necessary information exchange between the commanders and the merchant ships.

The Swedish Tripoli consul, Per Niklas Burström, left a detailed description of the 1801–02 conflict. His letters reveal that the joint US-Swedish blockade of Tripoli was not successful. Tripoly corsair galleys appeared to go out of and return to the harbour as they wished; and they continued to take American and Swedish prizes. The consul, who in the course of the war was in Tripoli and in official contact with the Pasha, noted that the blockade even improved the ruler's mood.[161]

At the same time, both the Swedes and the Americans continued to negotiate with the Pasha. The Swedish negotiations were concluded in October 1802. The final peace was one of the most expensive that Sweden signed with the Barbary states. According to the accounts of the Convoy Office, the price of the peace treaty was 650,000 rixdollars, which substantially increased Sweden's protection costs for shipping in southern waters.[162]

Not surprisingly, American comments on the Swedish peace treaty were unenthusiastic, and the Secretary of State and future President, James Madison, described the Swedish agreement as dishonourable.[163] The war between the United States and Tripoli continued for additional three years, at large cost to the Americans, but it ended successfully. According to the new peace treaty of June 1805, the United States was forever released from the duty of sending gifts to Tripoli.[164]

At least in brief, we should mention the Swedish consulate in Morocco. Morocco was the strongest North-African state. In the Swedish documents the Moroccan ruler is styled Emperor (*kejsare*), which also marks his independence from the Ottoman Empire. Three decades after Logie's treaty with Algiers, in 1761, peace negotiations with Morocco were started. As mentioned in chapter 3, the Swedish negotiations followed the pattern of the Danish and Dutch peace treaties with Morocco. The Swedish side was represented by Peter Kristian Wulf, previously an official of the Swedish Bank, who also became the first

---

[161] Burström to BoT, 1801–1803 letters, Tripoli EVI aa 467, Consular Reports, BoT SNA. See especially letters dated 1 August, 15 September and 6 October 1802.
[162] Åmark 1961, p. 775.
[163] Borg 1987, p. 262.
[164] Krëuger 1856, pp. 71–78; Borg 1987, pp. 230–279.

Swedish consul in Morocco. The treaty was signed after two years, in May 1763, and it was at that point the most expensive treaty concluded with a Barbary state. The consul Wulf settled in Sale, but after some time the consulate was moved to Tangier.

The Swedish consul to Morocco was salaried in exactly the same way as the Algiers consul, by means of the Convoy Office Fund. The consul was not entitled to take fees from Swedish ships visiting Morocco, but this does not indicate any substantial exchange between the countries. There are very few preserved consular reports from Tangier and Sale. The rare letters indicate that there was no exchange of significance between Sweden and Morocco. Nevertheless, some reports from Tangier include price currents, which inform us, among other things, of the price of Swedish iron.[165] After Wulf, who was permitted to return to Stockholm in 1774, another two consuls carried out consular duties in Tangier, Johan Magnus Wenström (1775–86), and Per Wijk (1787–1813).[166]

Sweden continued to pay tributes to the Barbary states until 1830, when France occupied Algiers and the Ottoman Empire strengthened its control of Tripoli. Yet even in the 1840s, the Swedish navy was still sending expeditions to the Mediterranean to carry on diplomacy and to make impression on the Barbary states. For example, in 1841 and 1844–45 the ship *Carlskrona* visited the Barbary coast. In the mid-nineteenth century, however, the relationship between the North-African coast and the European powers was perceived from a perspective of European colonialism, or in terms of a civilising mission. Sweden's consular service in North Africa was reorganised and integrated within the contemporary Swedish-Norwegian consular service. The Convoy Office, whose foundation had been connected with the Barbary corsair threat, in fact disappeared as late as 1867.[167]

4.7 Conclusions

This detailed account of the Swedish consulates in Lisbon, Cadiz, Marseilles, Livorno and North Africa does not mean that there were no other Swedish consuls in the area. We have already mentioned the specific role of the consulate at Smyrna, which was founded parallel to the establishment of diplomatic relations with the Ottoman Empire and the foundation of the Swedish Levant Company. Another result of Edvard Carlson's and Carl Fredrik von Höpken's journey to Constantinople was the consulate in Venice (1735).[168] The consulate in Naples was a consequence of the trade treaty with the Kingdom of the

---

[165] Wulf to BoT, 29 September 1768; Wenström to BoT, 20 January and 4 June 1776, Consular Reports, Tangier, Sale 1768–1822, E VI aa 460, BoT SNA.
[166] Krëuger 1856, p. 222; Almqvist 1912–13, p. 403.
[167] Åmark 1961, p. 757.
[168] Jägerskiöld 1957, p. 29; Almqvist 1912–13, p. 399.

Two Sicilies, of 1742; yet the first consul there, Carl Fredman, was first appointed in 1749.[169] Due to the major importance of the salt trade, Cagliari on Sardinia had had a Swedish consul since 1743. Swedish consulates were also established in Genoa and Barcelona.[170] In addition, the network of consulates was complemented by the vice-consuls: in Trapani, Algeciras, Setubal, Porto, and others ports. As we saw in the cases of Cadiz and Lisbon, consuls frequently made use of their privilege to appoint vice-consuls.

The picture presented in this chapter does not cover all these consulates and consuls. But the present writer does not believe that the overall picture would be significantly different if all the consulates were included. The widely varying quality and frequency of consular reports make any large-scale generalizations impossible. In addition, reports, the major source of these narratives, reveal only one side of the consular activities—that directed towards the Board of Trade. Still, in spite of the scattered narrative picture, there are some conclusions which may be drawn.

Firstly, consuls collected and forwarded to Stockholm a substantial amount of economically and politically useful information, and there is evidence (the connection between the Board of Trade and the Stockholm Merchant Association) that the information was available to merchants—at least to Stockholm merchants. Secondly, consuls apparently played an important role as commission agents, and as ship agents, in their districts. At the consulates we have examined, Swedish consuls appeared in the role of the leading merchants of Swedish commerce, with only a few exceptions (Dreyer, Bachmanson Nordencrantz). Thirdly, the attention paid to shipping and shipping conditions in the consular reports strengthens the impression that shipping was, in fact, a much more important sector of Swedish economic activities in southern Europe than the established view acknowledges. The fact that, in most consular districts, the consuls were prohibited from being shipowners indicates the sector's importance. And fourthly, the conditions of Swedish shipping depended very much on Sweden's neutrality in the wars between Britain and its foes. Neutrality increased the demand for Swedish shipping, yet it also entailed the threat of privateers. Balancing the benefits and hazards of neutrality shipping was an important, recurring issue in the consular reports.

The consular reports, however, do not provide proper quantitative evidence of commercial development. We cannot say if the Swedish consular service really promoted trade and shipping, and we cannot evaluate the role of shipping for freight. The search for answers to these questions will be one of the purposes of the following chapter.

---

[169] Trade- and shipping treaty between Sweden and Kingdom of the Two Sicilies. Paris, 19/30 June 1742, *Sveriges traktater med främmande magter. 1723–1771*, 1922, pp. 329–351. Almqvist 1912–13, p. 397.

[170]Almqvist 1912–13, pp. 394, 424.

CHAPTER 5

Neutrality and Swedish shipping and trade in southern Europe

In reality, this measure was suggested and in manner conducted by France; and is as extraordinary in its nature, as dangerous in its tendency. The Danes have, for many years, pretended to the enjoyment of those privileges that are granted to the Dutch, by the maritime treaty of 1674, and consequently to cover, by their neutral flag, the property of his Majesty's enemies [...] As to Sweden, they cannot have the least pretender to justify this demand, as the last treaty of commerce made with that power declares, in express terms, that, between the contracting powers, the flag of the friend shall not protect the property of the enemy.

The Earl of Holdernesse to Andrew Mitchell, 5 July 1757.[1]

5.1 Introduction

The preceding two chapters have provided a narrative picture of eighteenth-century Swedish policy in southern Europe and of the consular service there. We saw consuls in their daily business dealing with Swedish crews, and at courts working for the freeing of ships and cargoes. We looked more closely at the semi-diplomatic game between the consuls and the Muslim rulers in Algiers, Tunis, Morocco, and Tripoli. We examined consuls' schemes and proposals as to how to promote Swedish trade and shipping—and also examined the consuls' own interests. Nevertheless, a narrow description of daily consular practice does not greatly help in grasping the importance of southern Europe in eighteenth-century Swedish economic development. Nor does it say much about the fulfilment of grand Swedish ambitions from the 1720s and 1730s.

To set the daily consular practice in the context of Swedish economic history, it is necessary to provide data on the general development of Sweden's trade and shipping in southern Europe, and to analyse that data. This is the purpose of this chapter. Swedish economic activities in southern Europe will be examined from two perspectives: first, Sweden's commodity trade, mainly exports; second, Swedish shipping, and in particular, neutrality shipping.

---

[1] Hattendorf 1993, p. 329.

The overall picture of Sweden's commodity trade with southern Europe has been rather well explored. There are very good and easily accessible trade data, partly published; and there are several studies that have employed this source.[2] Due to this, the present account of Sweden's commodity exchange in southern Europe is mainly based on secondary sources. As regards shipping, the situation is less satisfactory. The literature is scarce and it very much follows Heckscher's standpoint on the Swedish Navigation Act. One purpose of the following analysis of shipping is a re-examination of this view; therefore, we will look at some hitherto unexplored sources. The Swedish registers of Algerian passports is such a source; rich, but seldom employed. Consular shipping lists and reports will be used as a complement to the registers.

Even if the following account makes a distinction between the sectors of commodity trade and of shipping it must be made clear that these two branches were deeply intertwined. Demand for bulky salt cargoes promoted the building of large ships, and shipowners looking for employment of free outward capacity found that sawn timber was in large demand in southern Europe. And, because neither the carrying of sawn timber nor the carrying of salt paid especially well, shipowners were looking for other profitable opportunities, and eventually they entered the market for tramp shipping in southern-European waters. They began to charter their vessels for voyages between ports in southern Europe. The commodity trade and tramp shipping were also intertwined. Profits or losses in one branch had to be weighed against the economy of the other branch. This connection between commodity trade and shipping, at least as regards sawn timber, is clearly proven by the fact that shipowners were often coidentical with dealers in sawn timber, as we shall see.

5.2 Swedish trade in southern Europe

Iron was the most important Swedish export commodity. It made up between 50 and 70 per cent of total Swedish exports by value, and was also a very important item in southern markets. Bachmanson Nordencrantz's figures for Lisbon, for 1729 and 1730, show that iron made up 80 and 75 per cent respectively of the overall Swedish export value (table 4.2).[3] However, iron exports were not a very dynamic part of Swedish foreign trade. From the mid-century, iron exports stagnated at a level of between 40,000 and 45,000 metric tons (300,000–337,000 ship pounds), partly as a result of conscious production regulations. In spite of the regulations, there was a vigorous growth in iron

[2] Data on Swedish foreign trade (*Berättelser om utrikes handel och sjöfart*) are part of the Board of Trade archives. Högberg 1969 is a classical study based on this source, but see also for published statistics: Boëthius and Heckscher 1938 and *Historisk statistik för Sverige*, 1972. For other aspects, see Samuelsson 1951; and for iron, in particular, Hildebrand 1957. Specifically for trade with southern Europe and the Mediterranean, also Högberg 1964 and Carlson 1971.
[3] Accounts on Portuguese-Swedish trade for 1729 and 1730, Consular Reports, Lisbon 1731–1778, E VI aa 224, BoT SNA.

Table 5.1: *Swedish iron trade to southern Europe 1725–99 (in ship pounds)*

Year	A	B	C	D	E	F	G	H
1725–28	255,000							
1730–34	276,000							
1738–39	302,000	29,000	10					
1740–44	310,000	44,000	14	26,500	800	6,500	8,700	1,200
1745–49	317,000	32,000	10	15,700	200	4,000	10,800	1,300
1750–54	302,000	37,000	12	18,100	1,000	7,200	8,700	700
1755–59	302,000	30,000	10	15,700	1,400	3,700	7,100	
1760–64	330,000	33,000	10	18,100	1,800	3,400	8,700	
1765–69	309,000	39,000	12.5	19,500	2,600	8,400	8,000	
1770–74	317,000	61,000	19.5	21,100	2,500	23,800	13,800	
1775–79	332,000	71,000	21.5	24,900	1,800	22,000	22,600	
1780–84	327,000	96,000	29	39,300	3,500	38,800	13,300	
1785–89	379,000	121,000	32	25,900	2,900	72,100	18,900	
1790–94	380,000	88,000	23	31,700	2,500	26,900	23,200	
1795–99	324,000	66,000	20	28,900	3,800	12,300	14,000	

Source: Hildebrand 1957, pp. 92, 96, and 134 (five-year averages). The sum total of Portugal, Spain, France, Levant and other Mediterranean areas differs from southern Europe; however, the difference is marginal (1 ton=7.4 ship pounds)
A=Total Swedish iron exports; B=Southern Europe incl. France; C=Percentage of total exports; D=Portugal; E=Spain; F=France; G=Other Mediterranean; H=Levant.

trade in the 1770s and 1790s, linked, as we will see, mainly to the southern markets. After this short revival the iron exports fell again. This time the reason was the industrial revolution in Britain.[4]

As regards the geography of iron markets, Great Britain dominated completely, with a share declining from 60 per cent in 1700 to about 40 per cent by 1800. Another formerly significant buyer of Swedish iron was the Dutch Republic; nevertheless, the Dutch share fell from 10 per cent in 1700 to a tiny 2–3 per cent in the late eighteenth century. The southern Baltic continued to buy between 20 and 25 per cent of Swedish iron.

The decline of the Dutch and British markets had to be compensated for, and Swedish iron exporters had to find such compensation in southern Europe. Until the 1760s, southern Europe had accounted for about 10 per cent of Swedish iron exports, but in the 1770s combined exports to France, Portugal, Spain, and Italy increased to one-third. In the period 1785–90, 32 per cent of Swedish iron went to these markets. Thus the revival of the Swedish iron trade must be linked to the increase of iron demand in southern Europe. In the last decade of the century iron exports to southern Europe declined again, to about one-fifth of the total.[5]

Not surprisingly, the trade data indicate that the growth in iron exports to southern Europe runs parallel to the growth in Swedish shipping to this area in

[4] Eklund 2001, p. 53; Hildebrand 1957, p. 96.
[5] Eklund 2001, p. 55; Hildebrand 1957, p. 96.

the 1770s and the 1780s, and this is connected with the American War of Independence. As we saw above, for example in Cadiz in 1779, iron prices increased considerably during wartime. But the wartime boom years were not responsible for the whole increase. The best export years were, in fact, the peaceful late 1780s.

Although iron was Sweden's major export commodity, in many ways it was a troublesome one. Demand for iron was not very dynamic and the Swedes often had problems in selling it. Moreover, iron was a substitute commodity; there were many competing iron suppliers and producers. On the one hand, there were protected local markets (France, Spain). On the other hand, there was Russian iron imported into the area in large quantities. In addition, other ships sailing to southern Europe with more valuable commodities used iron as ballast. The Swedish consuls reported on Dutch vessels carrying Swedish iron as ballast, and consequently free of freight charges.[6] In fact, the directors of the Levant Company mentioned this Dutch practice as one of the reasons for the Company's failure.[7]

Sawn timber exports were of a different character. By volume, Swedish sawn timber exports to southern Europe increased from 30,000 dozen deals in 1750 to over 80,000 by the mid-1770s. Yet this trade declined again in the 1790s, to between 40,000 and 60,000 dozen deals per year.[8] Lisbon was again the major destination, though Marseilles, Cadiz and Livorno also bought substantial quantities. The structure of the Lisbon trade shows that, by 1750, sawn timber made up roughly a quarter of Swedish exports by value (see table 4.3). In Cadiz and Marseilles, sawn timber must have been even more important.

Regarding the sawn timber trade, southern Europe was clearly Sweden's single most important market. Yet this trade had different significance for different parts of Sweden. Southern Europe was particularly important for Stockholm merchants. In 1731–35, 51 per cent of Stockholm sawn timber exports was destined for southern Europe, compared with 76 per cent in 1751–55, and as much as 78 per cent in 1781–85. On the other hand, the majority of sawn timber exports from Gothenburg went to Britain; and the south-Swedish regions (Småland, Gotland and Blekinge) mainly exported to the southern Baltic.[9]

The divergence between the major destinations for iron (Britain) and sawn timber (southern Europe) shows that sawn timber was not a packing material necessary in the stowing of iron cargoes. In trade with southern Europe, most sawn timber exports were not combined with iron. Another differing feature of sawn timber exports in comparison with iron was the fact that this trade was usually organised on the account of the shipowner. In 1760–80, about 80 per

---

[6] A vessel's cargo had to be loaded in proper combination of heavy and light commodities; which explains sometimes very strange combinations of commodities in a cargo: iron and tobacco, fish and stone, etc.; for examples see McCusker 1997, p. 63.
[7] Olán 1921, p. 61.
[8] Högberg 1969, p. 124.
[9] Högberg 1969, p. 138.

cent of the owners of timber cargoes destined for Portugal were actually owners of the ships being employed.[10] In the iron trade, the merchant and carrier functions were clearly separated.

This strengthens the link between the sawn timber trade and tramp shipping in southern Europe. A shipowner aiming to charter out his ship in the Mediterranean simply loaded it with sawn timber. It was not a very profitable cargo, but it was inexpensive to acquire, and in demand in the area. This is not to say that tramp shipping was the reason for Swedish sawn timber exports to southern Europe, but it is clear that the two businesses were closely intertwined. This link allows us to understand why sawn timber exports specifically for southern Europe were so important in Stockholm, the centre of the Swedish shipping industry. In addition, there was a close relationship between Swedish consuls all over southern Europe and the Stockholm merchant elite. As stated above, many consuls belonged to leading Stockholm families.

Tar and pitch were other key commodities in Swedish exports. As important naval stores, these were seen as strategic commodities and so the focus of political interest. The Baltic was the major supplier of masts, sawn timber, tar, pitch, hemp and flax, and Sweden, or more precisely Finland, became the major supplier of tar and pitch. Strategic naval stores were also one of the reasons why Portugal, Spain and France were so interested in trade with Sweden.

For the Swedish trade in tar and pitch, the eighteenth-century's endemic warfare was tremendously important. Demand for these commodities usually oscillated in parallel with wartime booms, and due to its conscious neutrality policy Sweden was usually one of the few possible suppliers.[11]

Between 1740 and 1800, Swedish tar exports trebled, from under 50,000 to about 140,000 barrels. The Seven Years War, the American War of Independence and the French Revolutionary Wars were periods of remarkable increase. The development in pitch sales was similar. Swedish pitch exports doubled, from 10,000 barrels in 1740 to over 20,000 barrels by 1800. It may be noticed that Sweden sold roughly five times more tar than pitch.[12] But there were differences between the markets. Southern Europe was a far more important market for pitch than for tar.

Like iron and sawn timber, tar and pitch sales boomed in the 1770s and 1780s, in connection with the American War of Independence, and fell after 1800. However, the boom in tar exports was not only the result of wartime conditions. The increase in tar exports must be linked to the strong development of tar shipping from Ostrobothnia (the north-eastern coast of Finland), which was the leading tar-producing area in the world. Until 1765, Stockholm kept a monopoly privilege, the so-called *bottniska handelstvånget*, over all export trade north of Stockholm; and Ostrobothnian merchants were forbidden to export tar directly. In 1765, the Ostrobothnian trade was deregulated, and

---

[10] Högberg 1969, pp. 126–129 (table 4.6).
[11] Högberg 1969, pp. 145–146.
[12] Högberg 1969, p. 146.

Table 5.2: *Swedish tar and pitch exports to southern Europe 1738/40–1801/08 (in barrels)*

Year	Total Swedish tar exports	Tar to southern Europe and France	Share of southern Europe in per cent	Total Swedish pitch export	Pitch to southern Europe and France	Share of southern Europe in per cent
1738/40	43,400	8,100	19	11,400	4,800	42
1741/50	65,100	11,000	17	12,100	4,200	35
1751/60	83,000	12,600	15	16,900	6,700	40
1761/70	88,700	16,800	19	15,700	5,400	34
1771/80	100,500	28,000	28	20,200	7,900	39
1781/90	124,500	34,700	28	23,900	10,800	45
1791/00	134,000	30,200	22	23,000	8,800	38
1801/08	142,300	22,100	16	20,300	5,600	27

Source: Högberg 1969, pp. 150 and 160 (southern Europe includes France, Spain, Portugal, Italy and other Mediterranean regions).

Table 5.3: *The Swedish annual demand for shipping capacity 1741–1805 (in heavy lasts)*

Year	Iron	Tar and pitch	Sawn timber	Herring	Total capacity
1741/50	18,000	5,000	10,000		33,000
1751/60	18,000	7,000	10,000		35,000
1761/70	18,000	7,000	12,000	8,000	45,000
1771/80	19,000	8,000	14,000	8,000	49,000
1781/90	22,000	10,000	18,000	11,000	61,000
1791/00	21,000	10,000	18,000	14,000	63,000
1801/05	23,000	11,000	25,000	8,000	67,000

Source: Högberg 1969, p. 21.

booming tar exports were one of the first consequences of this decision. Table 5.2 shows that tar exports doubled between the 1760s and 1780s, whereas total exports rose by 50 per cent. Pitch exports to southern Europe followed the same path as tar.[13]

Herring was the last key export commodity. From about 1750 onwards, it appeared as a typical product of Sweden's west coast. A proportion of Swedish herring was exported to southern Europe, yet for herring this market was not so important as it was for iron, sawn timber, tar and pitch.[14]

Table 5.3 shows the distribution of carrying capacity demand for Sweden's key export commodities. The distribution clearly reflects the relative stagnation of iron and the increase in demand for tar, pitch and sawn timber.

---

[13] On increase of Finnish shipping and tar trade, see e.g. Alanen 1957 and Kaukiainen 1993, p. 37.
[14] Högberg 1969, p. 175.

The composition of the Swedish export trade was also quite plain. The five aforementioned commodities, in addition to copper, made up almost all Swedish exports. On the import side, the situation was very different. On the one hand, imports consisted of a hotchpotch of very different kinds of goods. On the other hand, as regards southern Europe, salt totally dominated. Salt was a very different kind of commodity. Salt was a necessity and the maintenance of a sufficient supply of salt at home was an important political issue. The aim of Sweden's salt trade policy was to import as much as possible and to keep the salt price low; profitability was secondary. If import exceeded demand, salt could be re-exported.

It has already been argued that the salt trade was one of the major reasons for Swedish interest in southern Europe. As early as in the mid-seventeenth century Setubal and Lisbon sea salt had been preferred in Sweden, and this salt completely dominated during the eighteenth century. Salt was one of the major reasons for the enactment of the Swedish Navigation Act in 1724 and sufficient salt supplies were the reason for the foundation of the Salt Stores (*Saltkontoret*) in 1750.[15]

The data on Swedish salt imports seem to confirm that the salt policy was successful. There was a significant increase of salt imports, from an annual average of 150,000 barrels in 1740, to about 300,000 barrels by 1800. Essentially, nearly all salt (90–95 per cent) originated in southern Europe, half in Portugal and half in the Mediterranean. But, in contrast to the export side, the fluctuations in salt imports seem to have been large.[16] For example, the herring boom in western Sweden, in the period 1770–1800, caused a large increase in salt imports, because herring processing required enormous amounts of salt. During these decades, about one-third of Swedish salt, or between 70,000 and 90,000 barrels, was used in the herring industries. And Gothenburg's share in salt imports increased from 10 per cent in the 1740s, to almost 30 per cent in the 1790s.[17] The increasing discrepancy between incoming Swedish shipping and salt imports in the 1790s and the post-1800 period, indicates that salt was also carried on foreign ships.[18]

Salt required vast carrying capacity. In Sweden's total incoming shipping capacity, salt cargoes claimed about one-third, and salt only just took second place to the most demanding item—Baltic grain. The picture is very different when we look at import values. In value, bulky salt made up about 5 per cent of Sweden's imports in 1734–37 and 1769–71—after grain, textiles, groceries, tobacco, and even beverages.[19]

---

[15] Carlén 1997, p. 118.

[16] Högberg 1969, pp. 222–224; Carlén 1997, p. 53.

[17] Högberg 1969, p. 227.

[18] In 1799 the Navigation Act was abolished after complains about salt shortage. Yet already in 1802 it was introduced again. Carlson 1971, p. 6. More important for decline of salt import after 1800 were the Napoleonic Wars. In 1801–08, significant quantities of salt came from Britain, as re-exports. Högberg 1969, p. 224.

Table 5.4: *Incoming Swedish shipping from southern Europe and total salt imports*

Year	A	Year	B
1739/43	9,456	1741/50	10,000
1744/48	10,620		
1749/53	14,250	1751/60	12,000
1769/71	17,793	1761/70	15,000
1774/75	22,995	1771/80	17,000
1776/80	19,884		
1781/82	21,112	1781/90	19,000
1787/88,90	20,192		
1791/95	16,840	1791/00	19,000
1796/00	16,173		
1801/05	15,280	1801/05	20,000
1806/10	4,967		
1812/13	4,873		

Source and Notes: A=Incoming Swedish shipping from southern Europe (annual averages in lasts), (Heckscher 1940, p. 24); B=Swedish salt imports (ten-year averages in lasts), (Högberg 1969, p. 21).

This combination of large demand for carrying capacity and low commodity value was a typical structural feature of Swedish trade, and it says much about the economy of this trade. Staple commodities were bulky and heavy, consequently relatively expensive to carry. In contrast, the Dutch and English trades in southern Europe were dominated by luxury high value commodities, such as cloth, silk, cotton, wine and sugar.

The composition of Swedish cargoes was both an advantage and a disadvantage in competition with other states. In comparison with the Dutch, English, French and even the Danes, average Swedish value per cargo was low, and relative transport costs high. However, this low-value cargo forced the Swedish shipowners to employ large ships to push down their transport costs. Therefore, the Swedish shipping capacity for chartering was somewhat cheaper than in comparable nations. Nevertheless, this advantage should not be seen as the primary reason for chartering a Swedish ship. There was no 'average' Swedish ship; the large variation in capacity shows that there was room for very different crafts. Each charter contract combined many factors; and a ship's total capacity and freight cost were only one of them.

To summarise, in the course of the eighteenth century, the importance of southern Europe as a destination of Swedish exports unquestionably increased. In the iron trade, which was the major export sector in Swedish foreign trade, the data (table 5.1) indicate that, from the late 1730s to the late 1780s, iron exports to southern Europe at least doubled, and in the period 1770–1800, between 20 and 30 per cent of Swedish iron was destined for this market. Sawn

---

[19] Boëthius and Heckscher 1938, pp. 620–621; *Historisk statistik för Sverige*, vol. 3, 1972, (table 1.24).

timber exports also show a very dynamic pattern and southern Europe became the major destination for Swedish sawn timber. For Stockholm, sawn timber trade to the area was even more important; between 70 and 80 per cent of Stockholm sawn timber was destined for southern Europe. The trade in tar and pitch, crucial naval stores, also manifested both significant total growth and the rising share of southern Europe. The 1770s and 1780s were the most dynamic decades for all staple commodities.

This shift in Swedish foreign trade toward southern Europe was not the result of any dramatic shift in global demand. Instead, two other non-economic factors—one internal and one external—have to be mentioned. The internal factor was Sweden's ambitious trade policy. The encouragement of Swedish trade and shipping in southern Europe was a key element of Sweden's eighteenth-century economic policy. The new institutional framework, part of which was also the consular service, was its result.

The external factor was the international demand for, firstly, carrying capacity, and secondly, for Swedish staple commodities, especially during wartime. The endemic warfare between the great maritime powers created a market for neutrality shipping. From this point of view, the analysis of Swedish shipping in southern Europe is a very appealing task. One hypothesis is that the late eighteenth-century boom in demand for neutral shipping was a far more important factor in the growth of Swedish activities in southern Europe than demand for Swedish commodities or foreign trade policy. In this perspective, the growth of the Swedish commodity trade could primarily be explained as an effect of Swedish shipping activities. However, without comparisons of profitability between commodity trade and neutrality shipping, the answer is not unambiguous, and we have no established basis to allow us to make such a comparison.

5.3 Swedish shipping in southern Europe

In the course of the eighteenth century, Sweden's total volume of incoming and outgoing shipping capacity increased significantly. The total shipping volume between 1734/36 and 1801/05 nearly doubled, from 136,000 lasts to 240,000 lasts annually, and the data also reveal that Swedish shipping successfully displaced foreigners. The Swedish share in total in- and out-going shipping increased from a half at the beginning of the period to over 80 per cent in the 1770s.[20]

Another indicator of the successful development in shipping is the number of Swedish-registered ships, which quickly increased in the 1720s and 1730s. But, after this initial increase connected with the introduction of the Swedish Navigation Act, and after a plausible policy of change of flag in Dutch shipping, the number of Swedish vessels stagnated at a level between 400 and 500

[20] Heckscher 1940, p. 23; Högberg 1969, p. 12 (figure for 1718–19, 1720).

141

Table 5.5: *Swedish-registered ships 1693–1806 (in lasts and metric tons)*

Year	Number of ships	Total tonnage in lasts	Average tonnage per ship in lasts	Estimated tonnage per ship in metric tons
1693(a)	750			
1723(a)	228			
(1723)(b)	(100)	4,984	49.84	122
1724(ab)	348			
1726(ab)	480	21,000	43.75	107
1734(b)	329			
1744–49(b)		18,000–22,000		
1760(b)	456	26,003	57.02	140
1760(c)	572	32,667	57.11	140
1774(a)	664			
1783(e)	976	70,714	72.45	177
1785(b)	900	57,466	63.85	156
1785(e)	1,014	70,526	69.55	170
1786(d)	1,224	(169,000 tons)		(138 tons)
1790(b)	598	23,277	38.92	95
1795(b)	832	20,610	24.77	61
1795(e)	835	57,328	68.66	168
1799(b)	685	43,811	63.96	157
1800(c)	1,123	68,074	60.62	148
1800(e)	956	63,534	66.46	163
1804(e)	1,212	65,540	54.08	132
1806(e)	955	63,116	66.09	162

Sources: (a) Heckscher 1940, p. 22; It is not clear if the figure for 1693 also includes the Baltic Provinces. (b) Börjeson 1932, p. 265; (c) Carlson 1971, p. 18. (d) Johansen 1992, p. 484. A frequently cited estimate is that of the French government report dated 1786; the estimate ranks the Swedish merchant marine as Europe's fifth. (e) Johnson 1957, p. 247.

Notes: The data are only roughly comparable. The major part of the data relates to the number of issued registration letters (*fribrevsdiarier*).Carlson's data relate to the investigation of 1801. The registered tonnage of Swedish ships was measured in heavy lasts, equal to 2.448 metric tons. The Swedish-registered tonnage provides data on the carrying capacity (roughly deadweight tonnage) of Swedish ships.[21]

until the 1770s (table 5.5). It is also noteworthy that the figures for the 1720s and 1730s are not very impressive if compared to the shipping boom of the early 1690s, when there were 750 Swedish-registered ships. An average tonnage of a Swedish registered ship increased in the second half of the century, with the exception of the years after the Russo-Swedish War of 1788–90. Then the most likely explanation for the decline of average tonnage was the sale of Swedish ships. During this war, many Swedish-registered ships changed flag, and disappeared from the Swedish register. Most probably these sales concerned the large long-distance ships, which were abroad during this period of war.

---

[21] Measurement of early modern shipping capacity is a complex task. For measurement of shipping capacity, see Note on volume and weight units, measurement of shipping capacity, and money.

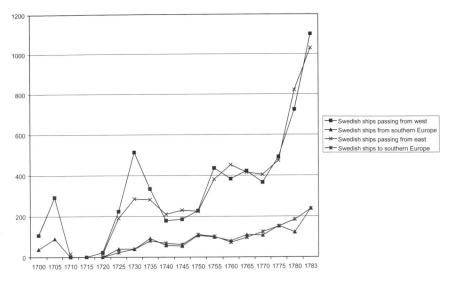

Figure 5.1 *Swedish ships passing the Sound, according to place of departure, 1700–83*
Source: Bang and Korst 1930 (see also Appendix B)

The Sound Toll Register indicates very well the consequences of the Swedish Navigation Act for Swedish shipping. It also clearly reveals the Act's effect on the Dutch shipping: between 1720 and 1730, the number of Dutch ships destined for Sweden declined from about a hundred to almost none. In the long run, the number of Swedish ships in the Sound increased from between 500 and 600 in 1700 to about 2,000 by 1783. According to Hans Christian Johansen's analysis of the Sound Toll Register in the 1784–95 period, the number of Swedish ships reached its peak in 1794, when 2,565 Swedish-registered ships (including Finland and Swedish Pomerania) entered the Sound. At that moment Sweden was the second largest shipping nation in the Sound, just behind Britain and before Denmark and the Dutch Republic.[22]

Due to shipmasters' obligation to give information about ports of departure and destinations, the Sound Toll Register provides data on the southern-European destinations and departures of Swedish ships. However, there is no guarantee that captains provided correct information and, in addition, the information provided was often very unspecific. Another problem with the Sound Toll Register, particularly as concerns southern Europe, is that it did not register the ships sailing from Sweden's west coast.

Figure 5.1 shows that about one-quarter of the Swedish ships passing the Sound was destined for southern Europe (on average 23.9 per cent according to place of departure, and 25 per cent according to destination). However, due to a higher average tonnage per ship, the share of southern Europe was in fact

---

[22] Johansen 1983, p. 18.

Table 5.6: *Swedish shipping to France, the Iberian Peninsula and the Mediterranean, 1739–1813*

Year	A	B	C	D
1739/43	9,456	35.5	9,829	34.4
1744/48	10,620	32.9	9,066	25.5
1749/53	14,250	41.5	13,535	34.5
1769/71	17,793	27.1	16,194	22.0
1774/75	22,995	40.1	22,443	35.4
1776/80	19,884	28.7	18,932	26.6
1781/82	21,112	26.2	23,111	25.2
1787/88,90	20,192	37.7	17,107	34.4
1791/95	16,840	30.4	24,914	28.4
1796/00	16,173	25.8	20,102	21.5
1801/05	15,280	22.2	19,782	19.5
1806/10	4,967	10.3	7,640	11.1
1812/13	4,873	10.0	14,379	16.4

Source: Heckscher 1940, p. 24.
Note: A=Incoming tonnage from southern Europe (in lasts); B= Percentage of total incoming Swedish shipping; C= Outgoing tonnage to southern Europe (in lasts); D= Percentage of total outgoing Swedish shipping

higher than the number of ships indicates. Eli F. Heckscher calculated the Swedish carrying capacity destined for southern Europe (France, the Iberian Peninsula, and the Mediterranean), and his data indicate that the share of tonnage destined for southern Europe was between 30 and 40 per cent.

The available data also point to two important conclusions: first, Swedish shipping increased substantially; second, southern Europe played a crucial role in that increase. The following section will analyse shipping to southern Europe from another perspective.

5.4 Algerian passports and shipping beyond Cape Finisterre

In its 'Article 4', the peace treaty between Sweden and Algiers mentions the duty of Swedish ships to prove their identity with a special passport issued by the Swedish Board of Trade. The regulation concerning this passport, the so-called Algerian passport, was published the following year (on 13 January 1730). As so many times before, the Swedish regulation followed the Dutch model, and served itself as a model for the Danish regulation of 1747.[23]

According to this regulation, all ships sailing beyond Cape Finisterre, the north-westernmost point of the Iberian Peninsula, had to carry an Algerian passport. Every passport was cut into two pieces, one of which was sent to

---

[23] Olán 1921, pp. 66–68. On the Danish Algerian passports see Gøbel 1982–83, p. 80.

10. Algerian passport issued for the brig *Sara* (Gothenburg), dated 12 June, 1799, Stockholm (*Svenska flottans historia*, vol. 2, 1943, pp. 528–529)

Algiers; the other one was kept on board ship. When corsairs inspected the ship, the captain demonstrated the ship's Swedish nationality with the requisite piece of the passport.[24]

The control of the issuing of Algerian passports was very strict, because any misuse placed in danger the entire Swedish policy towards the Barbary states. A passport was issued for only one voyage to southern Europe and it had to be returned to the Board of Trade as soon as possible after the ship's homecoming: both the dates of issue and return were noted at passport registers. When a ship

[24] Krëuger 1856, p. 27, Svensson 1943, p. 295; Börjeson 1932, pp. 271–273.

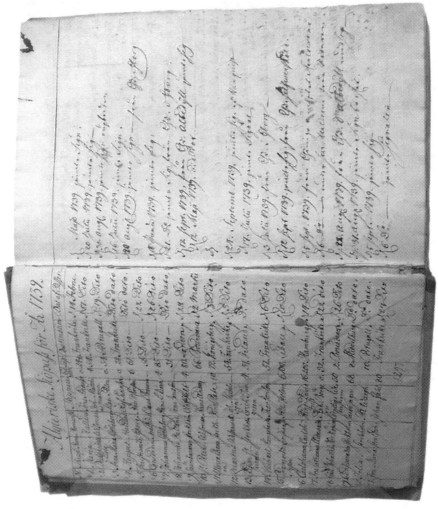

11. Algerian passport register 1739 (BoT SNA)

was sold or wrecked, the passport had to be saved and sent to the nearest consul, who forwarded it to Stockholm. In the course of the eighteenth century, Algerian passports became more or less the identity documents of ships sailing in southern waters. Therefore, in registers from 1765 onward, passports are no longer called 'Algerian'. The passports were issued until 1831.

Due to these strict procedures the preserved passport registers provide very detailed data on Swedish long-distance shipping between 1739 and 1831. Sailing beyond Cape Finisterre meant that registers included not only ships sailing to the Iberian Peninsula and the Mediterranean, but also ships engaged in transatlantic shipping and all Swedish East India Company vessels.

The first preserved passport register is dated 1739; from this year on, however, the series is complete for ninety-three years (1739–1831). In this period the Board of Trade issued 30,546 passports, encompassing data on over 30,000 Swedish voyages beyond Cape Finisterre, or more than 300 vessels annually.

Each entry in the series includes information on the name of the ship, captain, home port, number of guns (though not always), capacity, destination, and dates of issue and return of the passport. The quality of information can be examined from two perspectives. First, there is the question of reliability. Do the passport registers cover all ships destined for the area, or were there many ships sailing without passports? The comparison between the Danish Algerian passport registers and the Sound Toll Register proved that an absolute majority of ships provided with the passport were registered at the Sound as going to the reported destinations. Other comparisons made for the Danish data proved the Algerian passport register as being highly reliable.[25] We have no reason to regard the Swedish registers as less reliable. As mentioned above, the authorities had strong reasons for keeping the control of the passport issuing procedure as rigorous as possible.

The second question concerns the quality of data in register entries. It is clear that the most problematic information is the destination of the ship. First, many destinations were given very summarily as the 'Mediterranean' or the 'Western Sea'. Especially after 1800, destinations were seldom specified. Second, even if the specific destination was given, there is no guarantee that the captain really went there. Third, the given destination was normally the first port of call, which explains the strange fact that many ships applying for Algerian passports were destined for St. Petersburg and other Baltic ports.[26]

The following analysis of the Algerian Passport data focuses on the general trends in the development of Swedish shipping and especially the effects of neutrality. Detailed studies were made for only two specific years—1739 and 1786. Figure 5.2 shows the general pattern of increase, from 136 passports in 1739 to over 1,000 passports issued in 1815. Yet the increase was not steady; on the contrary, the development was marked by a high degree of volatility. Much of the volatility can be attributed to transition between peace and wartime.

During the War of the Austrian Succession (1739–48), the number of passports issued increased from 136 in 1739 to a maximum 173 in 1747, but it declined again as early as 1748. The figures indicate no significant exploitation of Swedish neutrality, and merely a minor decline during the Russo-Swedish War 1741–43. In the next conflict, the Seven Years War, Sweden was drawn in on the French side against Prussia, but it stayed neutral in relation to other states. Swedish engagement in the war was unenthusiastic and did not affect the shipping greatly—with the exception of the aforementioned Prussian privateers. Actually, during the war years the number of issued passports increased by 70 per cent, from 132 in 1755 to 225 in 1764, which shows that Swedish

[25] Gøbel 1982–83, pp. 91–92.
[26] Gøbel 1982–83, p. 99.

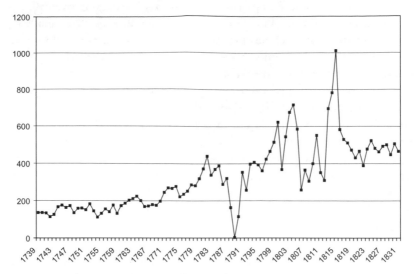

Figure 5.2: *Algerian passports issued in Sweden, 1739–1831*
Source: Appendix D

shipowners effectively exploited wartime conditions. After the war, the number of issued passports declined to about 200, but clearly shipping remained at a higher level than in the 1739–55 period.

During the American War of Independence (1776–83), the number of issued passports doubled, from 222 in 1775 to 441 in 1782. For Sweden and the remaining neutral flags, the situation became particularly profitable after the Dutch Republic's entry into the war, in 1780, and after Russia, Denmark and Sweden formed the Alliance of Armed Neutrality. The dramatic decline in the number of passports, in 1788–90, was, of course, a consequence of the second Russo-Swedish War. Nevertheless, as early as 1791, the number of issued passports reached the pre-war level (354 passports). Notably, the Danish merchantmen quickly exploited the gap created by the Swedish absence in these years.[27]

The period 1793–1815 was one of endemic warfare, with a short break after the Peace of Amiens 1802. On the one hand, the period provided neutrals with unusually profitable opportunities. On the other hand, during the French Revolutionary Wars, international law, and even neutrality itself, were not respected. But at least in the first period of the wars (1793–1800), Swedish shipping flourished. The number of issued passports increased from 257 in 1792 to 624 in 1800, in spite of the fact that the important area of French trade disappeared. From 1805, Sweden became involved in the pan-European conflict on the British side, but due to the country's relatively peripheral position, the Swedes avoided direct warfare and instead exploited the Continental System. For a couple of years, Swedish ports became loopholes of illicit traffic between Britain and the continent.

---

[27] Feldbæk 1997, p. 86.

148

Table 5.7: *Variations in the number of issued Algerian passports in wartime and peace, 1739–1815*

1739–1748 War of the Austrian Succession	0 %
1749–1754 peace period	- 30 %
1755–1764 Seven Years War	+ 70 %
1765–1775 peace period	+ 10 %
1776–1782 American War of Independence	+ 87 %
1783–1787 peace period	- 5 %
1788–1789 Russo-Swedish War	- 98 %
1792–1800 French Revolutionary Wars	+ 143 %
1802–1815 Napoleonic Wars	+ 86 %

Source: Appendix D

To illustrate neutrality's importance for Swedish shipping, the period 1739–1815 has been divided into nine peace and wartime phases (Table 5.7). To underline the scale of variation, upper and lower points of the curve have been chosen, which do not necessarily correspond to the beginning or the end of wartime. Shipping under neutrality conditions depended very much on accessible information—both rumours and reliable reports. Such information could affect a shipowner's decision even before the actual declaration of war.

Dan H. Andersen, the Danish maritime historian, has made a more detailed analysis of the Danish Algerian passport registers in the period 1747–1807, and his results do not diverge in any significant way from the view presented here. His analysis of the Danish passport registers contains data from 15,190 voyages. The lower number in comparison with the Swedish registers is due primarily to the fact that the Danes signed their treaties with the Barbary states later than Sweden (see above).[28]

Denmark carried out a more consistent neutrality policy than Sweden. It also seems to have exploited the wartime booms of the second half of the century more efficiently than Sweden. In the course of the Seven Years War, the number of Danish ships in the Mediterranean doubled, and it increased even more in the French Revolutionary Wars 1793–1800.[29] Despite its late start, by 1800 Denmark was a significantly larger carrier in southern waters than Sweden. The numbers of northern-European ships calling in Marseilles show how Danish shipping passed the Swedish level by the late decades of the century (figure 5.3).

Yet Figure 5.3 also shows that Swedish shipping really was an important player. According to Carrière's data there were a total of 1,466 Swedish ships calling at Marseilles in the period 1709–92, compared to 1,453 Danish, 2,749 British and 3,363 Dutch ships. The Scandinavian share is almost exactly one-third; yet these figures do not include southern-European merchant marines.

---

[28] In addition, there is a gap in the Danish sources in the years 1772–77. Andersen 2000, p. 13, and Appendix C, pp. 331–332.

[29] Andersen 2000, p. 2. For the Danish Mediterranean shipping, see also Johansen 1990.

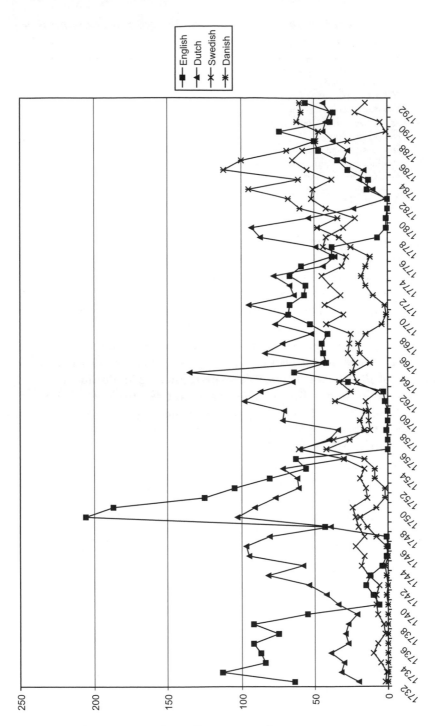

Figure 5.3: *Northern-European ships calling at Marseilles, 1709–92*
Source: Carrière 1973, p. 1061.

150

The figure confirms again the view of the Swedes as taking market shares from belligerents—in Marseilles especially from the British. Data for ships calling at Barcelona and Livorno show a similar pattern.[30] In fact, the importance of Scandinavian shipping in the Mediterranean was even greater because the Scandinavian vessels were on average larger than the British.[31]

Even if the similarities between Danish and Swedish neutrality shipping are many, there are also significant differences. Denmark lacked large export commodities, with the exception of Norwegian fish and timber, and salt did not play as crucial a role in Denmark as in Sweden. Danish vessels were primarily carriers of foreign goods.

Another noteworthy difference was the capitals' roles. In Sweden, Stockholm was disproportionately over-represented in shipping to southern Europe. The passport register of 1739 reveals Stockholm's total dominance in shipping beyond Cape Finisterre. Seventy-two vessels (53 per cent) came from Stockholm, and only eleven vessels (8 per cent) from Gothenburg, the second most important seaport. Two Finnish seaports, Åbo (Turku) and Fredrikshamn, which each sent out three large ships, are also worthy of mention.

A half century later, in 1786, Stockholm had lost much of its dominance. Partly, this was a consequence of the liberation of trade policy after 1765, for example the opening of the Ostrobothnian trade. There were 118 entries for ships registered in Stockholm (41 per cent) of a total 287 entries for this year. The number of entries for Gothenburg ships increased four-fold to 42 ships (15 per cent). However, the increase of provincial shipping was the most remarkable fact. For example, the Pomeranian seaports, Wolgast, Barth and Stralsund, sent out as many as 22 ships, of which nine were based at the tiny seaport of Barth. Many Pomeranian ships first went to the eastern Baltic (Riga, St. Petersburg, Pernau) to acquire cargo for their southern voyages. The pattern evinces some similarity with the shipping of the Danish Duchies.[32]

The opening of the Ostrobothnian export trade after 1765 is visible in over 20 passports issued in 1786 for ships from Jakobstad (Pietersaari), Uleåborg (Oulu), Gamla Karleby (Kokkola), Brahestad (Raahe) and Åbo (Turku). In contradistinction to the Pomeranian vessels, the Ostrobothnian ships were sailing with cargoes directly to the Mediterranean. They specialised in the carrying of bulky goods; their average tonnage was significantly larger than an average Swedish tonnage.

What were the major destinations of the ships according to the registers? An absolute majority of ships, about 70 per cent both in 1739 and 1786, declared France, the Iberian Peninsula and the Mediterranean as their first destinations. As regards the remaining 30 per cent, it is very likely that many of these ships

---

[30] Andersen 2000, pp. 4, 81.
[31] Johansen 1992, p. 482.
[32] Pomeranian merchant fleet made a very substantial part of the Swedish shipping capacity. According to the investigation of 1801, about one-quarter of the Swedish merchant tonnage was registered in Swedish Pomerania (Carlson 1971, p. 18).

Table 5.8: *Destinations of ships in Algerian passport registers*

Destination	Number of ships	Tonnage (in lasts)	Percentage of tonnage
1739			
Portugal	35	3,950.50	32.92
France	45	2,739.75	22.83
Mediterranean, Spain, Levant	25	2,291.00	19.09
Dutch Republic	10	910.00	7.58
'England and Ireland'	12	851.50	7.09
Remainder (including SOIK ships)	9	1,285.00	10.70
Total	136	12,027.75	100.00
1786			
Mediterranean	88	10,330.75	34.12
France	67	5,725.00	18.91
Portugal	43	4,738.00	15.65
Spain	12	1,903.00	6.29
'England and Ireland'	17	1,417.00	4.68
West Sea [*sic*]	27	2,182.00	7.20
North Sea [*sic*]	6	546.00	1.80
the West Indies, St. Barthélemy	4	454.00	1.50
Remainder (including the Baltic, SOIK ships)	23	2,979.00	9.84
Total	287	30,274.75	100.00

Source: See figure 5.2. There are many unspecified destinations (the so-called 'West Sea', the 'North Sea', the 'Spanish Sea', the Mediterranean, etc.).

continued from their first destination to the Mediterranean, especially the ships with their first call at St. Petersburg, Königsberg, Pernau or Riga.

In Denmark, Copenhagen did not play the same role in shipping, and trade in southern Europe was very much the business of the Duchies. In 1747–71, 57 per cent of Algerian passports were issued for ships from the Duchies, and only 17 per cent for Denmark proper (in fact, Copenhagen). The leading ports in Danish shipping in southern Europe were Flensborg, Altona and Åbenrå.[33] As we look at the total Danish merchant tonnage, we may see that Norway's share was a half, but from the beginning only about a quarter of the Algerian passports were issued for Norwegian-registered ships. The Norwegian share, however, increased and, in the period 1793–1807, the shares of the Duchies and Norway were equal, at 39 per cent each.[34] It is clear that the Copenhagen

---

[33] Andersen 2000, pp. 99–101, 221.
[34] Feldbæk 1983, p. 4.

shipowners did not play the same role in their country's Mediterranean shipping as did their Stockholm counterparts.

By 1806, there were about 2,400 ships over ten lasts registered in Denmark, Norway and the Duchies. The Danish tonnage was between 120,000 and 136,000 commercial lasts (250,000–350,000 long tons).[35] This may be compared to the 1,000 Swedish-registered ships in 1805 with a tonnage of 65,000 lasts (160,000 metric tons) (see table 5.5). It is clear that the Danish merchant marine was significantly larger in total; however, looking at the number of issued Algerian passports, and calls at Marseilles, Barcelona, Cadiz and Livorno, the difference in southern Europe was not as large. In southern Europe, the Danish and Swedish merchant marines were pretty equal. This also indicates that Sweden employed a comparatively larger share of its tonnage than Denmark in southern Europe.

Both the Danish and Swedish registers of Algerian passports bear witness to a spectacular increase in shipping activities. Denmark and Sweden took market shares from the combatant maritime powers—Britain, France, Spain, and partly also the Dutch Republic—and in both cases, neutrality was a crucial factor. However, both the Danes and the Swedes should have lost their market share as soon as the wars finished if neutrality had been the *only* explanation for Scandinavian shipping expansion.

The question has drawn much attention in Denmark. Since the late nineteenth century, there was an established view that the late eighteenth-century shipping boom was 'built on sand'. Contemporary Danish historians have questioned this view. For example, Hans Christian Johansen argued, in a number of works based on the analysis of the Sound Toll Register, that the increase in shipping was more stable and less dependent on wartime booms than has been stated. The underlying structural factors, such as Denmark's advantageous geographical situation, her low wages, and the demand for Norwegian timber and Norwegian fish, played the decisive role in the development of Danish shipping.[36] Ole Feldbæk, and recently Dan H. Andersen, have emphasized once again the importance of international political conditions, and they have highlighted the neutrality strategy as a key factors. Feldbæk's approach is mainly a combination of economic and diplomatic history, yet he, too, explicitly states that: 'Shipping and trade under the Danish flag during the eighteenth century were not in themselves based on the exploitation of neutrality.'[37]

In the case of Danish Mediterranean shipping, Dan H. Andersen and Hans-Joachim Voth have analysed the effect of Danish neutrality in comparison with the effect of the relative competitiveness of Danish wages. Their conclusion is that, 'No more than two-thirds of the rise in Danish shipping output can be attributed to the benefits of neutrality.'[38]

---

[35] Lindvall 1917, p. 422.
[36] Johansen 1983 and Johansen 1990, on the debate see Andersen and Voth 2000, p. 8.
[37] Feldbæk 1983, p. 7.
[38] Andersen and Voth 2000, p. 23.

The question of whether Danish shipping in the late eighteenth century was indeed 'built on sand' or not is also highly relevant for Sweden. As regards the importance of neutrality, the answer is clear. The effects of neutrality on the volume of shipping have been clearly demonstrated above (see especially table 5.7). However, to prove the sound economic basis of Sweden's shipping business in southern Europe we have to look more closely at its economic structure. We have to compare the productivity and, if possible, profitability of Swedish shipping with other competing merchant marines. We also have to weigh the total costs and profits of the shipping and trade sector (including public costs) against the other economic sectors.

5.5 Labour productivity in Swedish shipping in southern Europe

It has been noted (chapters 1 and 3, above) that the main reason for the rather pessimistic view of Swedish eighteenth-century shipping lay with Eli F. Heckscher's assessment of the Swedish Navigation Act. Heckscher presupposed that foreign shipping, notably Dutch shipping, was more productive than Swedish. However, his empirical arguments mainly concerned price indicators. He provides no direct evidence of low productivity in Swedish shipping, and there are no other studies which confirm his assumption. In addition, his evidence based on price indicators has been questioned.[39]

An attempt to analyse productivity, essentially labour productivity, in Swedish shipping will be made in this section. The analysis is related to two main questions. The first one concerns the comparative situation of Swedish shipping. How productive/competitive was the Swedish merchant fleet in comparison with other European merchant fleets? The second question is related to the first. This study has stressed that Swedish shipping grew substantially in the late eighteenth century, yet we do not know to what degree that growth should be attributed to factors of protectionism (stressed by Heckscher as the most important), of Sweden's neutrality (highlighted above), or of the productivity of Swedish shipping. The present writer's aim is not to evaluate the impact of those factors in quantitative terms; they complemented each other. Nevertheless it is clear that protectionism was a stronger factor in the first decades of the system, whereas neutrality became a large advantage mainly in the period 1776–1815.

There are many methods for measuring productivity in shipping. Perhaps the most reliable way is an analysis of records at enterprise level. Unfortunately, the research undertaken in this area in Sweden is rather limited, and relates mainly to later periods. Moreover, a high productivity level for one shipping firm does not necessarily allow us to posit a high overall productivity for Swedish shipping in general.

---

[39] Carlén 1997, pp. 247 ff.

Frequently, the measurement of productivity in early modern shipping combines a number of different methods (see part 1.3). The examination of freight rates is a classical method. Other measurement techniques focus on wage developments, tons-per-man ratios, tons-per-gun ratios, turnaround times in harbour, and other indicators.[40] The measurement of the average size of vessels and tons-per-man ratio will be employed here. The results, however, must be interpreted cautiously. First, the eighteenth-century shipping market consisted of many segments, dependent on the varying demand of agents. Hence, the impressive size of, or a high labour productivity level on, one particular vessel does not necessarily imply a high overall productivity level of a merchant marine.

Second, the measuring of average size of ship and tons-per-man ratios, and comparisons between different merchant fleets based on these ratios, entail many practical problems. The methods of measurement of a vessel's tonnage differ from time to time, and from state to state, which makes all calculations and comparisons tentative. The problems with measurement of tonnage are the major reason why all calculations here are made in lasts; conversions to metric tons (roughly long tons) are made only for the purpose of comparisons.

According to data presented in table 5.5, in the course of the century the average registered tonnage of an eighteenth-century Swedish merchant craft varied between 50 and 60 lasts. However, ships sailing beyond Cape Finisterre were much larger. In 1739, 136 ships were listed in the passport register, with a total tonnage of 12,100 lasts, which makes an average of 89 lasts per ship (220 metric tons). This average includes three very large Swedish East India Company ships; however, there were also other spacious vessels. For example, *Charitas* and *Fortuna* from Åbo had respective tonnages of 300 and 250 lasts (730 and 610 metric tons).

In 1786, five decades later, the number of ships with Algerian passports was 287, with a total tonnage of 30,270 lasts. The average tonnage per ship increased to 105 lasts (260 metric tons). There was also a notable increase in the average tonnage per craft; yet we have to be cautious in positing too rapid a rate of growth. First, the tonnage per craft varied between 30 and 300 lasts, and the calculated average increase of 16 lasts disappears easily within this range of variation. Second, the figures for Swedish ships entering the Mediterranean in the period 1774–92 (table 5.9) indicate no increase in average tonnage. The average tonnage of these ships oscillated around 120 lasts (290 metric tons).

An average Swedish vessel provided with an Algerian passport also had a tonnage of about 89 lasts (220 metric tons) in 1739 and about 105 lasts (260 metric tons) in 1786. Vessels entering the Mediterranean seem to have been larger, on average 120 lasts (290 metric tons), in the 1774–92 period. In spite of all the obstacles to comparison, these are rather impressive figures. Danish

---

[40] The majority of the articles focusing on productivity in shipping has been based on study of freight rates (North 1968; North 1994; Ville 1986; Harley 1988; Menard 1991).

Table 5.9: *Swedish ships in the Mediterranean, 1774–92*

Year	Number of ships	Total tonnage (in lasts)	Average tonnage per ship (in lasts)
1774	139	14,577	104.87
1775	142	21,901	154.23
1776	142	16,906	119.06
1777	131	15,773	120.40
1778	155	18,278	117.92
1779	116	14,594	125.81
1780	68	7,886	115.97
1781	96	11,966	124.64
1782	99	10,579	106.86
1783	151	17,692	117.17
1784	133	17,175	129.14
1785	205	23,699	115.60
1786	132	18,195	137.84
1787	227	27,621	121.68
1788	167	18,766	112.37
1789	113	11,737	103.86
1790	100	10,673	106.73
1791	182	20,548	112.90
1792	146	17,582	120.42
1774–92	2,644	316,148	119.57

Source: Desfeuilles 1956, p. 344.

vessels in the Mediterranean had an average tonnage of under 150 tons.[41] According to Ralph Davis's classic study of English shipping in the seventeenth and eighteenth centuries, a typical English-flagged vessel entering the Baltic in the 1760s had a tonnage of over 300 tons, and carriers in the English-Norwegian timber trade could have tonnages of between 300 and 350 tons. But English vessels employed in the southern-European trade had much lower tonnages. In 1766, the average figure was just above 100 tons for a vessel going to Spain and Portugal, and 148 tons for a vessel going to Italy and Greece.[42] London vessels employed in the transatlantic trade (1750–70) had tonnages varying between 168 and 182 tons.[43]

These figures highlight shipping in the northern waters as being something very different from Mediterranean or transatlantic shipping. The same discrepancy between Baltic or North Sea shipping and shipping in the Mediterranean or the Atlantic was also typical for the Dutch.[44] In general, the average size of

[41] Andersen 2000, pp. 294–298. The Danish tonnage data, in commercial lasts, express ship's carrying capacity; so they are comparable with the Swedish data.
[42] Davis 1962, on the Baltic shipping, p. 221; on the timber trade, p. 214; on Portugal and Spain, p. 243; and on Italy and Greece, p. 256. The most productive was shipping in England's coal trade (Ville 1986).
[43] Menard 1991, p. 261. For London/New York, London/Virginia and London/Jamaica routes, in the 1710–1769 period, see also French 1987, p. 630.
[44] Bruijn 1990, p. 180.

Table 5.10: *Tons-per-man ratios on board, based on shipping lists from Cadiz, 1777–95*

Year	Number of ships	Tonnage (in lasts)	Manpower	Lasts-per-man on board	Estimated metric tons per man on board
1777	28	4,652	497	9.36	23
1785	77	10,074	1,136	8.87	22
1795	45	4,143	497	8.34	20
Total	150	18,869	2,130	8.86	22

Source: Consul Gahn to the Board of Trade, Shipping lists 1777, 1785, 1795, Cadiz 1719–1802, E VI aa 67, BoT SNA.
Note: The Swedish East India ships have been excluded from the table, because of their much larger crews. An average tonnage calculation of this sample of 150 vessels gives 126 lasts per vessel.

ships on specific routes did not change greatly during the eighteenth century. Examples of both Baltic and transatlantic shipping indicate rather large variations and stagnant averages.[45]

Of course, an average tonnage figure does not say much about the labour productivity of shipping. When we look at tons-per-man ratios on board, we can compare labour productivity for the first time. The tons-per-man ratios for Swedish vessels in southern Europe can be calculated with the help of the shipping lists of the Mediterranean consuls, which, occasionally, included data on crews. These scattered data do not provide a basis for any long-term and systematic analysis. However, they are sufficient to indicate average crew sizes on Swedish vessels, and subsequently help us to estimate Swedish tons-per-man ratios.

The average ratio was also an impressive 22 metric tons per man on board; this is also about five men per 100 tons.[46] As usually, averages hide variations. Small vessels had notably higher manning levels than large vessels. For instance, the galleass *Anna Elisabeth*, 38 lasts (93 metric tons), home-port Udevalla, had a crew of seven. Its ratio of 13 metric ton/man was lower than the Swedish average. The ship *Resolution*, based at the same port, had a tonnage of 350 lasts (*c.* 857 metric tons) but a crew of only twenty-four men. Its ratio was almost 36 metric tons per man. This limited sample of 150 Cadiz ships and their crews also indicates that the Swedish merchant marine enjoyed rather a high level of labour productivity.

The Danish tons-per-man ratios, according to the calculations made for the 1748–69 period, were 10.5–15.51 tons per man. For the 1778–1807 period, more comparable with the Swedish data from Cadiz, the ratios were 13.18–

[45] Walton 1967.
[46] Another way to calculate labour productivity is in men/100 ton ratio, see for example, Kaukiainen 1991, pp. 106–107; Ojala 1999, pp. 164–165.

20.54 tons per man.[47] The tons-per-man ratios in transatlantic shipping were markedly lower. Christopher J. French's data for the 1710–1769 period indicate ratios of 8–10 tons per man, though increasing over the course of the time.[48] According to the estimates by Jan Lucassen and Richard W. Unger, the English, Dutch and French overall ratios varied between 10 and 18 tons per man in the course of the eighteenth century, also slightly lower than the Swedish average from Cadiz.[49] The Swedish ratios are also at least as high or even higher than those obtaining in the other merchant marines.

The sample of the vessels entering Cadiz also indicates that an average Swedish crew consisted of 14 men.[50] This is very close to the English average of 14 men on board for ships going to the Baltic. But English ships going to the Mediterranean had on average 32 men.[51] Reasons for these differences were, of course, connected to the different kinds of ships employed in the English Mediterranean trade. Again, the Swedish figures indicate rather high labour productivity.

The labour productivity of the sample is connected to the high average tonnage of vessels entering Cadiz; 126 lasts per ship, also slightly more than the average 120 lasts for the Mediterranean (table 5.9), and significantly more than the average 105 lasts based on the Algerian passports of 1786. The combination of small crews and large shipping capacity appears to be a consequence of the 'bulky' Swedish trade. Indeed, the introduction of the technique of bulk carrying, in combination with risk-reducing measures taken by the state, might be perceived as the typical Swedish pattern in southern-European shipping. The Dutch, English and French competitors of the Swedes carried out the same risk-reducing measures, but they shipped cargoes of high-valued commodities (silk, cotton, wine). In this trade, high tons-per-man ratios were not a decisive comparative advantage, and so hardly a priority.

In general, there was an increase in the productivity of early modern shipping but it was rather slow. The highly productive technique of carrying cheap bulky cargoes had been known and employed in northern Europe as early as the early seventeenth century, yet it was apparently difficult to introduce the technique on other routes.[52]

Low wages are also often mentioned as a comparative advantage of neutral shipping. In wartime, the British navy competed for able sailors with the merchant marine, with surging wage costs as a consequence. For example, the

---

[47] Andersen 2000, pp. 295–296. (The Danish commercial lasts were converted into tons by ratios 2–2.6 tons per last, due to the uncertainty of Danish lasts-per-ton ratio, and the hidden moderation of official tonnage by 1/6. Despite this cautious calculation the present Swedish averages per ship are significantly larger.)
[48] French 1987, pp. 630–631.
[49] Lucassen and Unger 2000, p. 131.
[50] Compare with manning of ships from Ostrobothnian seaport Gamla Karleby (Kokkola), Ojala 1997a.
[51] Lucassen and Unger 2000, p. 138.
[52] Davis 1962, p. 223; Menard 1991, p. 270; Bruijn 1990, pp. 74–75.

Danish wages were two-thirds of the British in peacetime. But during the French Revolutionary Wars the Danish sailors became as much five times cheaper than their British counterparts.[53] Yet it is also important to point out that even neutral wages followed wartime booms: the Danish sailors were much better paid in 1756–63, 1776–83, and after 1793, than in years of peace.[54]

Even the Swedish seamen's wages were significantly lower than wages in other merchant marines. The Swedish seamen leaving Swedish vessels abroad and taking hire on foreign ships provide indirect evidence of this fact. The reports of Swedish consuls are full of such cases.[55] Contemporaneous comparisons of wages provide more exact evidence. For example, information on wages dating from the peace year of 1768 tells us that Swedish wages were between one-half and one-third lower than the wages of competitors (Britain, France, the Dutch Republic, Venice and Denmark).[56]

In summary, the available data indicate that Swedish shipping beyond Cape Finisterre, and especially within the Mediterranean, had rather higher productivity and lower running costs than its competitors. Yet we should not overrate these comparative advantages. In the Swedish case, the pattern of shipping was linked to the rather unfavourable composition of inward and outward cargoes. And the factor of protection-costs reduction was more significant in southern-European shipping than in northern Europe. Basically, the economy of Swedish shipping in southern Europe rested on a combination of relatively high labour productivity, low costs and neutrality. Yet it is important to stress that these factors are inseparable. The introduction of the 'Baltic and North Sea–shipping pattern' by the Swedes in southern Europe was a consequence of the combination of low protection costs and the commodity structure of Swedish trade.

5.6 Costs and benefits of Swedish shipping

The Danish debate on the character of eighteenth-century shipping had its parallel in the Swedish discourse on the use and abuse of the Navigation Act. As noted above, there was criticism of the Act even before its enactment, and this critique continued throughout the remainder of the century. Two works may be cited as typical examples, one defending and one attacking the principles of Sweden's economic policy in shipping. The first is a speech given by Claes Grill at the Swedish Academy of Sciences in 1749, which defended the necessity of maintaining a Swedish merchant fleet, built in Sweden. Grill's arguments were

[53] Andersen 2000, pp. 287–288.
[54] Andersen 2002, pp. 27–30.
[55] Another indirect evidence is the recurrent issuing of *pardonplakat* for runaway seamen in the late eighteenth century; see Müller 2000, p. 350.
[56] Börjeson 1932, p. 345–347. Examples of crew costs of a Dutch and a Swedish vessel in Marseilles, in 1760, confirm the account. Dutch wage costs were about 380 guilders, whereas the wage costs of the Swedish ship was 234 guilders.

based on his expertise regarding Sweden's trading conditions. He simply calculated how much Sweden—supposedly—earned or saved by building and employing its own ships. Yet Claes Grill was a leading member of the Stockholm merchant elite—the so-called quayside-nobility—and a leading shipowner and shipbuilder. No doubt he was speaking in his own interest at least as much as in that of the country.[57]

In 1765, on the other hand, Anders Chydenius attacked the Navigation Act in a pamphlet revealingly entitled 'The source of the country's misery' (*Källan till rikets Wan-magt*). Neither can Chydenius be seen as an unbiased observer. His polemic was written in the heat of the political struggle between the Hats and the Caps in the 1760s, and Hat economic policy was one of his targets.[58] Above, we have already met another outspoken participant in this struggle, Anders Bachmanson Nordencrantz.

Despite the criticism of the 1760s, the protection policy and Navigation Act continued to survive in the Gustavian period (1772–1809). However, the debate over the costs and benefits did not disappear. During the Gustavian years, the debate concerned the most costly element of the protection policy, the Convoy Office. As mentioned earlier, the fees (*extra licenten*) paid to the Convoy Office Fund were completely insufficient to finance its duties, despite many increases over time. On a couple of occasions, the government attempted to reorganize the Convoy Office in order to make it less expensive, and in 1791, the Convoy Office was even closed down. Yet the new organizational structures which replaced it did not function any better, and in 1797 the Convoy Office was re-established with the same duties and organization as before.[59]

In 1801, an investigation was initiated with aim of analysing Sweden's protection system and comparing its costs and benefits. The investigation's conclusions, less partial than the previous debates on the issue, provided a strong argument for keeping the system alive. The investigation paid major attention to Sweden's protection system in southern Europe, including the consular service, the peace treaties with the Barbary states, and convoying: all functions carried out by the Convoy Office.

According to the conclusions of the investigation, the Swedish commodity trade was insufficient profitably to employ all of the Swedish shipping capacity, and so shipping in foreign service was necessary for the survival of the Swedish shipping industry. Yet Swedish ships would be chartered only if the Swedish flag were respected and secure. Therefore it was essential to keep the whole system, including the consular service and peace treaties, in being. According to the investigators, Swedish shipping within the Mediterranean employed a carrying capacity of between 12,000 and 15,000 lasts, and it gave jobs to 15,000 people. The overall shipping volume beyond Cape Finisterre was estimated at between 30,000 and 32,000 lasts. If Sweden abandoned southern European tramp ship-

---

[57]Grill 1749. On Claes Grill see Müller 1998.
[58] Chydenius 1765.
[59] Carlson 1971, pp. 8–11.

ping, the extra costs in salt carriage alone were estimated at one million rixdollars. In addition, the Swedish merchant fleet would be reduced by one-third, and numerous jobs would disappear. The investigators also noted that tramp shipping in wartime was highly profitable, and that income from tramp shipping during the American War of Independence significantly contributed to the success of the 1776 monetary reform, and it made possible to import large quantities of grain in the beginning of the 1780s. The conclusion was that, in spite of high costs, the system was profitable in the long term.[60] The protection system, as well as the Convoy Office, survived, and Sweden continued to employ its special maritime position even during the Napoleonic Wars.

The 1801 investigation's picture of Swedish shipping in southern Europe and of its overall importance does not differ from the account presented here. The analysis of the Algerian passports shows that, from the mid-1770s, there were between 300 and 400 ships sailing beyond Cape Finisterre annually. Due to the fact that many ships continued to sail with the same passport even in the following year, most probably the number of ships engaged in southern-European shipping at a specific moment was even greater. With an estimated tonnage per vessels of at least 100 lasts, this represents a total tonnage of between 30,000 and 40,000 lasts annually—with the exception of the years of the Russo-Swedish War. The Algerian passport registers indicate that, in the late eighteenth century, half of the Swedish merchant tonnage was regularly sailing beyond Cape Finisterre.

In the following section we will make a more specific attempt to compare the costs of Sweden's protection system with the 'guesstimate' of the capital employed in Swedish shipping beyond Cape Finisterre, and look at the likely business profitability of Swedish shipping. Due to the complete accounts covering the outlays of the Convoy Office, we are able to make an estimate of the state protection costs of Swedish shipping in southern Europe.[61] These costs did not include the protection costs of single shipping enterprises, such as insurance premiums, higher wages caused by wartime risks, cost of guns and powder, and other expenses. Nevertheless, the Convoy Office outlays indicate the level of the 'public' protection costs. They include three major items: expenditure on the consular service, gifts to the North-African rulers, and outlays for convoys. Both the total costs and the proportional shares of the major items varied. The consular service was the most stable item, whereas the cost of the gifts could fluctuate very widely.

Table 5.11 summarises the data for the Convoy Office outlays in the peace and wartime periods. It confirms the view that the outlays did not expand greatly until about 1760. The high average costs in the 1760s, above 500,000 d.s.m. annually, were a consequence of the expensive peace with Morocco

---

[60] Krëuger 1856, p. 31; Åmark 1961, p. 761; Carlson 1971, pp. 13, 17–19; Högberg 1964, pp. 19–20.
[61] The following analysis is based on the table of accounts of the Convoy Office 1726–1809 (Åmark 1961, pp. 762–775), see Appendix E.

Table 5.11: *The average number of Swedish ships and tonnage employed beyond Cape Finisterre 1739–1800. Estimates of the annual capital stock in tonnage and annual outlays of the Convoy Office.*

Years	A	B	C	D
1739–1748	146	14,600	2.19–4.38	0.07
1749–1755	149	14,900	2.24–4.48	0.14
1756–1763	173	17,300	2.6–5.19	0.30
1764–1775	217	21,700	3.26–6.51	0.55
1776–1783	316	31,600	4.74–9.48	0.47
1784–1787	342	34,200	5.13–10.26	0.33
1788–1790	93	9,300	1.4–2.79	0.26
1791–1792	305	30,500	4.58–9.15	0.09
1793–1800	449	44,900	6.74–13.47	1.17

Source: Figure 5.2 and Appendices D, E, and F.
Notes:
A: Average annual number of Algerian passports issued (See Appendix D)
B: Estimate of the annual Swedish tonnage employed beyond Cape Finisterre (in lasts). The calculation is based on the rough estimate of an average 100-lasts vessel and average number of Algerian passports issued.
C: Capital stock (in million d.s.m.) in the shipping beyond Cape Finisterre, based on (B) and a 'guesstimate' of ship value per last 150–300 d.s.m. (for guesstimate, see Appendix F)
D: Average annual outlays of the Convoy Office (in million d.s.m., see Appendix E). The figure for the 1739–48 period is based on an average of the 1726–48 outlays. Calculations for the 1778–1800 period are based on new rixdollars (1 rixdollar=6 d.s.m.)

(1764). Then, in the course of the 1770s and 1780s, the Office outlays declined. After the beginning of the French Revolutionary Wars, the protection costs of Swedish shipping increased very substantially, which factor explains both the attempts to reorganise the system and the investigation of 1801. The growth in cost was partly a consequence of new gifts sent to North-African rulers, partly a consequence of convoying. The average annual cost in the period 1793–1800 was over 1 million d.s.m. However, as the war and the following peace treaty with Tripoli revealed, costs could increase even more. Thus in 1804, the Convoy Office outlays reached 784,660 rixdollars (4.7 million d.s.m.), with the cost of the Tripoli peace alone accounting for 650,000 rixdollars.

Apparently the Convoy Office outlays, especially after 1792, were rather high compared to the estimated capital stock invested in shipping beyond Cape Finisterre. It appears that, even in the profitable 1770s and 1780s, the public protection costs per ship employed in southern waters were at least a 1,000 d.s.m.

If the state protection policy was so expensive how profitable was the shipping business at a micro-level? There is no specialised study of the profitability of a Swedish shipping enterprise from the eighteenth century. Yet there are some data on the profitability of specific enterprises from the thriving Ostrobothnian ports, which took part in the Swedish shipping to southern Europe.

Calculations of profitability by the Finnish historian Jari Ojala are based on the ship's value as capital stock.[62] For the first decades after 1800, the figures from Ostrobothnian shipping enterprises show that normal long-term levels of profitability were about 10 per cent. Yet during wartime, profitability was much higher. The shipping business of the merchant house of Donner from Gamla Karleby (Kokkola) in 1793–1815 had an astonishing return of 35 per cent on invested capital. In some cases the returns could be as much as 100 per cent, which means that the vessel paid for its building costs in one voyage.[63] Such profits, of course, were exceptional; yet they let us understand why the number of ships sailing to southern Europe increased so much in wartime.

There are other examples of the shipping profitability of neutral ships. In particular, the Danish case is enlightening, due to the similarity of business conditions. Detailed analysis of three Danish ships from Flensborg sailing in the 1783–1812 period again clearly reveals a very sharp difference between peacetime and wartime shipping. The first ship's (*Der Junge Hinrich*) seven voyages in the peacetime years 1783–91 ended in an overall loss. The two other ships (*Die Einigkeit* and *Die Harmonie)* sailed in the war years 1793–1807, and earned excellent profits. *Die Einigkeit*, a smaller vessel (valued at 22,000 marks in 1793) earned 2,000 marks annually, while *Die Harmonie* (building costs of 22,000 marks) earned 3,000 marks annually. The period 1801–07 in particular was a golden age, in which *Die Harmonie* earned 4,000 marks annually.[64]

Studies of long-term profitability in Dutch shipping in the eighteenth and the beginning of the nineteenth centuries show returns of 10 per cent and more. Yet, as in the case of the Ostrobothnian and Danish ships, the variations were huge. Of a sample of thirty-six ships analysed for the 1740–1830 period, one-third did not return invested capital, the remaining two-thirds made such profits that the total return of the sample's capital stock was over 10 per cent.[65]

Ralph Davis' examples of eighteenth-century English shipping provide evidence of modest profitability. By 1770 a typical English ship of 120 tons, in the Malaga trade, afforded a slim 4.8 per cent profit. Yet the profitability was very much dependent on whether peace or wartime conditions prevailed. For example, freight per ton of cargo destined for the Iberian Peninsula almost tripled from 30 shillings in 1754–55 to 80 shillings during the Seven Years War, giving substantial profits.[66]

---

[62] Ship values are based on building costs, probate inventories and sales of ships. The operating costs include wages, insurance, brokerage, port dues, outfit for voyage, and annual depreciation. Ojala points out the problem with cargoes owned by shipowners. In such a situation, it is extremely difficult to separate shipping from commodity trade. For details, see Ojala 1999, p. 427.

[63] Ojala 1997a, p. 18; Ojala 1999, p. 427.

[64] Ventegodt estimated the ship value of *Der Junge Hinrich* at 10,000 marks, which makes a loss rate 2 per cent, *Die Enigkeit* was valued at 22,000 marks in 1793, which makes a profit rate 10 per cent, and the building value of *Die Harmonie* was 22,000, with profitability 13.6 per cent until 1801 and 18 per cent 1801–07. The figures demonstrate clearly the differences between profitability of shipping in peace and wartime (Ventegodt 1989, pp. 36, 37, 190–238)

[65] Bruijn 1990, pp. 180–183.

[66] Davis 1962, pp. 362, 379.

The Swedish data do not provide any basis for such an estimate of profitability. However, the 1801 investigation mentions that in the 1790s only freights on the Portugal routes earned 250,000 rixdollars (1.5 million d.s.m).[67] In wartime, by 1800, the freight returns of Swedish shipping made up a half of Sweden's total export income.[68]

These examples of Swedish, Danish, Dutch and English ships say something about the character of the eighteenth-century shipping business in general. It was a business with a substantial initial capital stake (building and outfitting a ship) and quite high and predictable running costs (wages, victuals, port charges, repairs, and insurance premiums). For neutrals, such as Sweden and Denmark, running costs did not vary as much as for belligerents. Shipping under a belligerent flag had to contend with both increased wages, due to the competition for seamen between the navy and the merchant marine, and increased insurance premiums. The level of freight rates depended very much on whether peace or wartime conditions prevailed, and they were higher for both neutrals and belligerents in wartime. Consequently, ships made considerable profits during the wars and tried to keep afloat in peacetime. The central features of eighteenth-century shipping point to the general vulnerability of the whole business.

5.7 Conclusions

The concern of this chapter was to offer a description of the development of Swedish trade and shipping to, and within, southern Europe. The picture of the commodity trade presented here was based on the available studies, whereas the chapter's portrait of shipping combined established data with a fresh analysis of the Algerian passport registers and consular reports. Much more attention has been paid to the issue of shipping, especially neutrality shipping, not only because shipping has hitherto received limited attention in the economic history of eighteenth-century Sweden, but also because the shipping interests have been presented here as a more important driving force in Sweden's engagement in southern Europe.

In the course of the century, Swedish shipping became a means of balancing freight income against the unfavourable structure of the country's commodity trade, even if this was not the primary aim of trade policy from the 1720s. Not surprisingly, there are no useful official data on Swedish tramp shipping in southern Europe.[69] Nevertheless, there are data available that indicate the shipping industry's importance. First, there is qualitative evidence in the consular reports. Swedish consuls often reported both on Swedish tramp shipping in their regions and on the profitable shipping opportunities that Swedish ship-

---

[67] Carlson 1971, p. 19; Högberg 1964, p. 20.
[68] Schön 2000, p. 60.
[69] On the offical estimates of Swedish shipping income, see Högberg 1964, p. 21.

owners should exploit. Second, the rising number of Algerian passports and destinations within the Mediterranean, as well as the clear development pattern of neutrality shipping, provides some, albeit limited, quantitative evidence. Third, the rather high labour productivity in Swedish shipping beyond Cape Finisterre confirms that shipping productivity could not have constituted a Swedish disadvantage, as Heckscher thought. Swedish shipowners employed the same shipping pattern in southern-European tramp shipping—spacious ships and small crews—as had been used for centuries in the Baltic and North Seas. But such a strategy could work only if Swedish vessels could sail in safety.

Making Swedish shipping safer was the major motive for establishment of the Swedish consular service in North Africa. The connection is apparent—not least in view of the fact that the same institution that organised the convoying of Swedish ships, the Convoy Office, also salaried consuls and negotiated peace treaties with the Barbary states. In this way, the protection costs of private shipping enterprises were transferred to the state. This was ultimately a political decision. The private protection costs, including large crews, guns, arms, powder, higher wages and insurance premiums, were converted into 'public' protection costs, such as convoying, outlays for gifts to Barbary rulers and consular salaries. The price of the protection policy was substantial, and so it was often an issue of political debate, but in the end the policy survived.

Even if Sweden's protection policy reduced protection costs for private shipping enterprises, the institutional framework could not affect the foreign demand for Swedish carrying capacity. The transfer of protection costs from the private to the state sector was an internal factor of Swedish economic development. Yet there had to be a much stronger external factor that increased the demand for Swedish carrying capacity—the endemic warfare between the great maritime powers. Sweden was successful in standing aloof from major eighteenth-century conflicts, and in the exploitation of neutrality.

Even Sweden's neutrality can be seen from a protection cost perspective. No doubt a neutral flag was a cheaper means of protecting cargoes and ships than a navy. However, such cost-efficient protection presupposed that the belligerents, and especially Great Britain, recognized that neutrality. The profitability of neutrality shipping provides evidence that this was the case. In general, in spite of the fairly large numbers of captured neutral vessels, neutrality shipping was respected. The question of why Great Britain did respect Danish, Dutch, Swedish, and later American neutrality shipping is a complicated one, and belongs to the sphere of diplomatic and military history, and so will not be discussed here.[70]

Of the three factors discussed above—high labour productivity in shipping, an institutional structure that diminished transaction costs, and neutrality—the last was the most important. There is clear evidence that Swedish shipping increased in tandem with major maritime conflicts, whereas it is much more difficult to trace any such connection with the establishment of a specific consulate. However, it is also obvious that Swedish shipping could not operate without a proper institutional environment. The consular service in southern Europe did not only reduce protection costs. The consuls also functioned as commission and ship agents. They informed shipowners and captains of profitable freights and they arranged charter contracts. In their reports to the Board of Trade, consuls highlighted potential markets as well as shipping risks. Thus, from an institutional perspective, we may say that the consular service, in addition to cutting protection costs, also reduced information and transaction costs. However, such benefits are even more difficult to quantify than protection costs.

High labour productivity, low wages and cheap shipbuilding materials were factors that affected Swedish shipping growth in the long-term. However, even these factors were dependent on Sweden's low protection costs. The Baltic and North Sea-shipping pattern was more productive due to the safer environment of the northern seas.

In conclusion, the picture of the development of Swedish shipping in southern Europe presented above is consistent with the view established in the works of North, Menard, Bruijn, Feldbæk, Andersen and Voth, and others. The entrance of Swedish shipping into southern Europe was connected to the spread of a more productive shipping pattern, already developed in the Baltic and North Seas, which entailed an overall productivity growth in shipping by the late eighteenth century. Yet Sweden's entrance onto the southern scene was rendered possible by the combination of declining violence and Sweden's protection policy.

---

[70] In fact, in spite of all British successes in the eighteenth-century wars, the British naval mastery had never been granted. In the course of the period there was a balance of naval powers of France (or Bourbon France-Spain and their allies), and Britain. Thus the navies of the neutrals counted. For a general account of the British naval policy in the eighteenth century, see Kennedy 1976. From Danish point of view, the issue of neutrality has been treated in numerous works of Ole Feldbæk (e.g. Feldbæk 1977; Feldbæk 1980; Feldbæk 1983); for Swedish neutrality policy in the period 1776–1815, see Wahlström 1917; Svenson 1952; Gasslander 1954; Johnson 1953; Johnson 1957; Trulsson 1976; af Malmborg 2001, pp. 14–87.

CHAPTER 6

Transatlantic connection: colonial ambitions and neutrality shipping

[I]n such economic conditions Swedish ships travelling from this country [the United States] to the West Indies will make a good deal of money if they obtain their documents for St. Barthélemy, and they can always sail for the Spanish islands[...] The Spanish envoy here constantly asks me if there are any Swedish ships to be chartered. The English envoy Liston, who served as envoy in Sweden, has likewise shown me much politeness and confidence, and he assured me that he wishes to serve the Swedish Nation on any occasion as much as he can. He has received much respect since he arrived and many are attached to him—but I believe that he is more dangerous to them than the former envoy. Due to Liston's cautious behaviour this Government believes itself to be quite safe and strong as regards the protection of its ships, but if they will be ruined in their trade their whole Financial System will collapse and so too will the Government.

Richard Söderström to the Swedish Board of Trade, Philadelphia, 8 April 1797[1]

6.1 Introduction

In the late eighteenth century, the contacts between Sweden and America were rather limited, even if there was some historical connection. In the mid-seventeenth century, Sweden had established the colony of New Sweden in North America—present-day Delaware. However, New Sweden was lost to the Dutch as early as 1655, and the Dutch soon lost it to the English. After this interlude, Swedish-American contacts were merely sporadic. There was a population of Swedish-descent, living in Pennsylvania and Delaware, together with its Swedish Church Congregations. In fact, the Swedish authorities kept in touch with these Swedish descendants and provided the congregations of the Swedish Church with priests educated in Sweden.[2]

Nevertheless, contacts between the weakened Sweden of post-1721 and the

---

[1] Söderström to BoT, 8 April 1797, Philadelphia, Americana vol. 1, SNA.
[2] On the history of New Sweden, see e.g. Dahlgren and Norman 1988; on eighteenth-century Swedish congregations in America, see e.g. Lindmark 1999. Some preliminary results of the author's research on the Swedish consular service in the United States appeared in Müller 2002.

Americas were sporadic. Therefore it is surprising to see how quickly the situation changed during the Napoleonic Wars. In 1810, Swedish-American contacts were thriving. Gothenburg, which became one of the biggest loopholes of the Continental System after 1806—not dissimilar to Malta or Helgoland—was full of American merchants, shipmasters and ships. At this time, the United States was one of the few neutral states and American transit shipping played the major role in the illicit transit trade between the continent and the outside world. A significant part of this business was carried out via Swedish territories.[3]

Richard S. Smith, the future American consul in Gothenburg, later recalled the thriving atmosphere of the Continental blockade years in that seaport. He had first arrived in Gothenburg in 1810, and it had surprised him to see so many fellow countrymen from Philadelphia and New England. The town was full of Americans and the harbour was swarming with American-flagged ships. In 1810, the best year of the Continental System boom, as many as 169 American ships anchored in Gothenburg harbour.[4]

However, the declaration of the Anglo-American war of 1812 changed the situation once again. It dealt a heavy blow to the American neutrality trade in northern Europe. On the other hand, it provided entrepreneurial Swedes with great opportunities. The news of the outbreak of war reached Gothenburg in late July 1812. There were about forty American ships waiting for convoy. All of them stayed in the safety of Gothenburg harbour. The blockade of belligerents' ships in a neutral harbour was not unusual, and neither were the solutions employed. Many Americans changed their flag. Hence, the ship *Franklin*, which arrived in Sweden in June 1812, left Gothenburg the following summer as *Freden* ('Peace' in Swedish), under the Swedish flag and a Swedish master. Another ship, *Arabella*, became *Friheten* ('Liberty' in Swedish), and left the harbour under Swedish flag in September 1813. The official owner of the two ships was Olof Wijk, one of Gothenburg's leading merchants. However, his ledgers show that the true owners were indeed Americans: Thomas Fosdick from Boston, C.C. Haven from Portsmouth in New Hampshire, and Samuel Gair from Boston.[5]

At the same time, similar metamorphoses were taking place on the other side of the Atlantic. In the reports of the Swedish consul in New York, Henrik Gahn, we will find a number of American ships applying for Swedish documents. Between July and October 1812 alone, Gahn provided at least ten vessels with such documents (*Edmund, Diana Talbot* [*Susanna*], *Lydia, Mary* [*Maria*], *Prudentia, Ollongren, Passagerare, Stackelberg, Baron Stackelberg,* and *Regina Christina*).[6] An important role in these transactions was played by the

---

[3] For the organization of traffic under the Continental System, see also Marzagalli 1998.
[4] Tiselius 1935, pp. 1–3, 26.
[5] Adamson 1969, pp. 72–73.
[6] Gahn to BoT, 26 August and 21 October 1812, Consular Reports New York, E VI aa 352, BoT SNA.

12. The list of Swedish vessels in New York 1812 (Henrik Gahn's reports, New York, BoT SNA)

Swedish colony in the Caribbean, the island of St. Barthélemy. The new vessels were formally registered at the colony whose inhabitants became willing ship-owners. Their names often betray British or American origin. Many of them became Swedish citizens simply to make use of the colony's neutrality. St. Bar-thélemy became a place where illicit Anglo-American exchange was possible.

In the course of the Napoleonic Wars, St. Barthélemy acquired a very similar position in the Caribbean as Gothenburg possessed in northern Europe—a neutral place in which belligerents might find a safe haven. The wartime years were a brief golden age in the colony's history. Gustavia, the harbour and the only town of the colony, increased in the first decade after 1800 to about 5,000 inhabitants, which made it one of the biggest 'Swedish' towns—yet with very few native Swedes. By comparison, Gothenburg, Sweden's second city, had about 15,000–20,000 inhabitants in the same period.[7] On average over 1,000 vessels were calling at Gustavia annually.[8] However it has to be remembered that the majority of these vessels were only sailing between the Caribbean is-lands and America, and were significantly smaller than the craft employed in transatlantic trade.

---

[7] Andersson 1977b, p. 39.
[8] Tingbrand 2002, pp. 70–71.

The use of Gothenburg and St. Barthélemy as neutral loopholes for international trade during the wars shows that the neutrality strategy employed by the Swedes in southern Europe could also be used within Swedish territories. Not only Swedish vessels, but also those territories themselves could profit from the state's neutrality. The prior chapters have shown that Sweden became a significant shipping nation in southern Europe in the course of the eighteenth century. The transatlantic connections before 1800, together with the use of St. Barthélemy and Gothenburg as neutral entrepôts, reflect Sweden's endeavours to initiate trade with the Caribbean and the United States, which in Sweden were seen as a whole, and therefore called 'the West Indies'. The aim of the two following chapters will be to shed light on Swedish activities in 'the West Indies' and evaluate their importance, especially as regards the United States. The focus will again be very much upon the Swedish consular service, specifically the Swedish consular service in the United States.

The issue is no less interesting due to the fact that, as mentioned above, Sweden's transatlantic contacts before the American War of Independence were very limited. During the war, Swedish activities on the other side of Atlantic increased significantly. These activities were largely a result of the conscious policy of Gustav III's government, which had a number of purposes behind it. The promotion of the iron trade was one of them.

By 1800, the technological transformation in the British iron industry caused a dramatic decline in Swedish exports to Britain: it has been stressed how important this market was for Sweden. But instead of the disaster one might have predicted, Swedish iron exports shifted from Britain to America. After 1806, the USA took over Britain's role as the single most important purchaser of Swedish iron. In particular, iron producers and dealers from western Sweden were rescued by American demand. An interesting question is whether this shift was initiated by an informed Swedish policy during Gustav III's reign, or whether it was a consequence of more general changes on the global scene. Is it possible to trace any similar development between the expansion of trade and the increase in Swedish-flagged shipping as we can observe in southern Europe? These questions again relate, as in the case of neutrality shipping in southern Europe, to the interaction between the Swedish institutional framework and the international environment. Sweden's merchants, shipowners, shipmasters and seamen had to adapt to this environment and exploit its opportunities, but their capacity to affect it were insignificant.

6.2 Sweden's colonial ambitions

Sweden has never had a colonial empire worthy of note. With the exceptions of the tiny colony of St. Barthélemy (1784–1878) in the Caribbean, and the two failed attempts in North America and Africa in the mid-seventeenth century, there were no notable results for Sweden's colonial endeavours. However, a

13. A view of Gustavia, St. Barthelémy, 1793 (UUL)

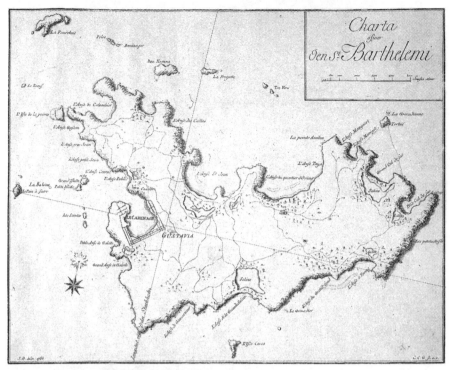

14. A map of St. Barthélemy, 1786 (UUL)

shortage of colonies did not mean that Sweden was short of colonial ambitions. In the course of the eighteenth century, there were many more or less serious attempts to gain a foothold in the colonial arena, especially in the West Indies, and to make Sweden a colonial power.

The reasons for these ambitious plans were both economic and political. In true mercantilist manner, some Swedish economists argued that Swedish colonies would supply the mother country with sugar, coffee and other colonial products, which otherwise had to be acquired from foreigners at great expense.[9] In a political sense, the possession of colonial domains would also confirm Sweden's status among the great European nations. This argument in particular became important during Gustav III's reign, due to his considerable political ambition. The examples of Great Britain, France and the Dutch Republic had frequently been used to show that successful powers also had to have colonial

[9] Johan Henrik Kjellgren, Swedish writer, published in 1784 an article (*Förslag till Nybyggens anläggande i Indien och på Africanska kusten*), in which he especially argued for importance of a Swedish colony in the West Indies. Hildebrand 1951, p. 41; see also Gerste 1994, p. 18 on Daniel Anders Backmann' dissertation (1754) on a colony in North America. Ulric Nordenskiöld wrote about colonial proposals in 1776, and perhaps also 1778, Nelson 1998, p. 40. Even Carl Linnaeus was highly interested in colonies and proliferated ideas about introduction of tropical and colonial plants (e.g. tea) in Sweden see Linné 1963 (1745), p. 32, see also Koerner 1999, pp. 113–139.

empires, and Sweden wished to count itself among such states. Hence, her colonial ambitions, regardless of their very limited real effect, revealed Sweden as a willing would-be participant in the European colonial enterprise. It is therefore useful to look more closely at these ambitions. They provided a backdrop for the establishment of Swedish contacts across the Atlantic—the subject of this chapter.

In the eighteenth century, the first serious attempt to add a new colony to Sweden's possessions took the form of Charles XII's contacts with Madagascar pirates in 1714. The pirate representatives were prepared to accept Sweden's sovereignty over Madagascar in exchange for protection. It is not clear what kind of interest Charles XII had in the affair, yet it was most probably not Madagascar. The king seemed primarily to be interested in the pirates' fleet, which explains why they received permission to capture Danish ships. Preparations of an expedition to Madagascar also continued after the king's death, yet these plans never came to fruition.[10]

After 1721, the majority of Swedish colonial plans focused on the West Indies. This area, with its booming production of sugar, rum, coffee, cocoa, and cotton, became in the course of the eighteenth century the most dynamic part of the European colonial system. One quite serious Swedish objective concerned the proposed colonization of a territory by the river Barima, near to the Orinoco's estuary, situated between Dutch and Spanish settlements in South America. In 1731 an expedition was sent to the area and a contract was signed with local tribes, but nothing further happened. The Barima idea was taken up once again in the 1770s. Johan Silander proposed to promote colonisation with a focus on sugar, coffee, cotton and cocoa production.[11]

The island of Tobago near the modern-day Venezuelan coast was another favoured object of Swedish colonial dreams. This was discussed as early as the 1690s, and more seriously in 1724. Daniel N. von Höpken, the secretary of state, saw Tobago, with its good harbour, as a future staple location for Sweden's West Indian trade. Tobago attracted the attention of Swedish politicians several times—in 1731, 1749, 1758, and most seriously during the American War of Independence.[12]

Colonial dreams became serious plans in the Gustavian period. And the royal interest attracted many foreign adventurers to Stockholm, aiming to sell their colonial schemes. Hence, in 1774, the Englishmen Andrew Orr and James Monsell visited Gustav III with a proposal to colonise Puerto Rico. They did not overly care that Puerto Rico had been a Spanish island for over two hundred years. In their opinion, Spain had no use for it and so might be willing to hand it over to Sweden. The Swedish ambassador in Madrid was instructed

---

[10] Sprinchorn 1921 and 1923 and others.
[11] Sprinchorn 1923, p. 122; Essén 1928, p. 227; Koninckx 1980, p. 37; Börjeson 1932, p. 277; Hildebrand 1951, pp. 1–2.
[12] Sprinchorn 1923; Koninckx 1980, p. 37. On Sweden's legacy, or more exactly the king Frederick I's legacy, to Tobago see Sprinchorn 1923, p. 112 (note).

to approach the Spanish court with the proposal. Madrid rejected the idea, unsurprisingly.[13]

As late as 1786, the Flemish adventurer Willem Bolts tried to sell Gustav III a project for the colonisation of an island in the Indian Ocean. His idea actually seemed to be among the more realistic. He was himself a former employee of the English East India Company, and familiar with the conditions of the East India trade. His idea was to turn the would-be Swedish island in the Indian Ocean into a neutral entrepôt of the same kind as the Dutch St. Eustatius in the West Indies. Yet his ambitious plans also included the putative colonisation of the Indus estuary.[14]

Other plans concerned Africa. In 1759 a Swedish naval officer, on his own initiative, made contacts with the native people on an ambiguously defined southern coast of Guinea.[15] Another attempt—much more serious, however—was made on the initiative of Gustav III in 1787. Three Swedes, Anders Sparrman, (a well-known Linnaeus disciple), Carl Bernhard Wadström and Carl Axel Arrhenius, were sent to Senegal on Gustav III's orders. The official purpose of the expedition was scientific, but, in fact, the Swedes were investigating the possibility of establishing a Swedish colony and direct Swedish slave trade to the West Indies. Just three years earlier Sweden had acquired the colony of St. Barthélemy. The journey did not result in any colony, and Wadström, influenced by first-hand contact with the conduct of slave trade, became a fervent abolitionist.[16]

Nevertheless, it is clear that the most serious Swedish colonial plans concerned the West Indies. The Swedish interest in the West Indies mirrored the huge economic importance of the area. The interrelated trade in sugar, slaves, North American provisions and European manufactures became enormously important for British, French, Spanish, Dutch, and Danish trading activities. Even if there are rather divergent views of the importance of this trade, as well as of the question of an integrated Atlantic economy, the West Indian trade was doubtless of huge importance for all the involved states. For example, in Denmark, despite the fact that the country possessed only three small Caribbean islands, the trade in sugar and slaves became very significant.[17]

It is important to point out that at this time the West Indies was one of the most dynamic areas in the world. From the French or British point of view, the West Indian colonies were much more important than North America. An

---

[13] Essén 1928, pp. 228–230.
[14] William/Willem Bolts is one of the more renowned adventurers of the late eighteenth century. He was mainly interested in East India trade, yet under non-British flag, therefore the proposal to Gustav III. See Everaert 1995; Furber 1997.
[15] Sprinchorn 1923, pp. 139–142.
[16] Wadström 1968 (1794); Nelson 1998.
[17] There is a huge volume of literature on the rise of the eighteenth-century Atlantic economy, and its different parts: on the British transatlantic trade see e.g. McCusker 1985; McCusker 1997; McCusker 2000; Hancock 1997; on the Dutch transatlantic trade see e.g. Klooster 1995; Enthoven 2003; on the Danish transatlantic trade see e.g. Gøbel 1983; Andersen 2004 (forthcoming); Feldbæk 1997, pp. 43 ff; Johansen 1992, pp. 488–489.

enlightening illustration of the weight of the Caribbean in comparison with North America is the French proposal at the peace negotiations in 1763. The French offered to the British either the small island of Guadeloupe (with a population of 80,000) or the whole of French Canada (with a population of 65,000).[18]

6.3 St. Barthélemy and the Swedish West India Company

A turning point in Swedish colonial aspirations was the American War of Independence. In spite of its official neutrality, Sweden supported France and the insurgent colonies. However, there were widely differing reactions to the outbreak of the war in Sweden. On the one hand, there was some sympathy for the political content of the colonists' struggle, as well as strong feelings against British hegemony. On the other hand, fifty years of Swedish proto-democratic experimentation during the Age of Liberty (1720–72) had not strengthened republican intellectual currents in Sweden.

Instead, there were other, more practical causes for Swedish support of the colonists. The traditional alliance with France was one such cause, the economic interests of the mercantile elite another. The conflict gave Sweden the opportunity of exerting pressure on France in colonial issues. Moreover, American independence was supposed to diminish the British control of trade with the Caribbean and North American colonies, which opened up the possibility of direct Swedish trade with the West Indies.

At the same time, Sweden avoided being connected too much with France. For example, when the French minister Vergennes, in the winter 1778–79, proposed to the Swedish envoy in Paris, Gustaf Philip Creutz, the opening of French West Indian trade to the Swedes, Creutz declined. The Swedish authorities were well aware of the risky character of this generous suggestion. The major purpose, of course, was to supply the French West Indies under cover of the neutral Swedish flag; a strategy frequently employed by the French but not accepted by the British.

In spring 1779, the envoy Creutz obtained another flattering but risky proposal. The Marquis de Lafayette, who had recently returned from America and was currently preparing a new naval expedition against the British West Indies, proposed to purchase or charter four Swedish vessels for the expedition, and to hand over in exchange an island which the French were supposed to conquer from the British.[19] Such a proposal was even more hazardous for Swedish neutrality than supplying the French West Indies with provisions.

Parallel to the ongoing struggle, the Swedes investigated the prospects for a Swedish colony in North America. Count Axel von Fersen, a well-known

---

[18] Engerman 2000, p. 247.
[19] Hildebrand 1951, p. 4; Essén 1928, p. 230.

Swedish aristocrat, prepared himself to take part in the French campaign in America. There were, indeed, many Swedish officers who participated. In addition to von Fersen, there were about a hundred Swedes in the French forces, and another hundred-and-thirty in the Dutch forces and in continental navies.[20] But, the motives of most of the Swedes were not political. They were career officers, and the American war was only another opportunity in their military careers.

During his stay at America von Fersen was supposed to investigate—albeit very cautiously—whether there were any part of North America, or perhaps an island, that the American colonies would in future be prepared to hand over to Sweden. After his arrival in Philadelphia, von Fersen seems to have pursued this issue in cooperation with the French envoy, but nothing happened.[21]

The years 1779–82 were marked by cautious Swedish diplomatic activity in Paris, North America and Stockholm. The envoy Creutz had put out a few of feelers to see how seriously France would consider Swedish mediation in the war. At the beginning of the war, Gustav III in person was proposed as a mediator between Great Britain and France. And the envoy investigated whether the French were really prepared to support Sweden on the issue of a colony. There were new discussions about the islands of Dominique and Grenada as possible Swedish colonies. Nevertheless, the favourite subject of these discussions was again the old Swedish dream—Tobago: a large island, with the capacity to develop into a substantial centre of sugar production.[22] However, there was a problem; Tobago was British. The Swedish reasoning followed this line: when France took over Tobago and concluded peace with Britain, the island might be handed over to Sweden without annoying the British.

The Swedes were forced to maintain a delicate balance between the country's official neutrality and the de facto alliance with France. Thus, for example, Sweden's neutrality caused bitterness in Bourbon Spain, the closest ally of France. As we saw in the consular reports from Cadiz, Spanish privateers seriously threatened Swedish neutrality shipping through Gibraltar. They captured about thirty Swedish ships in the winter of 1779–80 alone, claiming that the Swedes were working for the British (part 4.6.2).

Swedish hopes for a West Indian colony rose and declined, depending on the news from the battlefield. When France was successful, Swedish hopes for a colony surged, and when the British took the initiative the Swedish demands declined. In the winter of 1781–82, the French position in the West Indies deteriorated. Paradoxically, it was a consequence of the success of the American rebels. The British recognized that they had lost on the American continent and they concentrated their entire endeavour in the Caribbean. In April 1782, the British navy crushed the French squadron near Dominique and, after this British victory, the French concentrated on maintaining the status quo. In Jan-

---

[20] Barton 1966; Barton 1975, pp. 24–25; Elovson 1929; Sundström 2000.
[21] Barton 1975, p. 25.
[22] Hildebrand 1951, pp. 8–10.

uary 1783, the peace treaty between France and Britain was signed. One of the consequences of the treaty, and one of the few French rewards, was the French possession of Tobago. All other islands occupied by the French during the war were returned to the British. But the French now lost interest in discussing Tobago with Gustav III.[23]

It took another year before the subject was again raised in Paris. In 1783–84, the Swedish king was on his *grand tour* through Europe, shaping Sweden's new foreign policy and looking for new allies. France was at that time in international isolation and was eager to keep its old ally Sweden close at hand. In this situation, France was prepared to remunerate Gustav III with a colony—but not Tobago. In spring 1784, France proposed Sweden's takeover of the tiny island of St. Barthélemy, in exchange for staple rights in Sweden's second seaport of Gothenburg. Gustav III accepted, and the treaty for St. Barthélemy's transition from France to Sweden was signed during the king's visit to Paris on 1 July 1784.[24] The following year the first Swedish Governor, Gustaf Thomas von Rajalin, took possession of St. Barthélemy, and Sweden became a colonial power in the West Indies.

What kind of island did France give to Sweden? From the French point of view, St. Barthélemy was of very limited strategic and economic importance. It was far from the other French islands and was very poor. According to an old saying, the island was so poor that even pirates paid the inhabitants for their goods.[25] The island covered 21 square-kilometres, with no space for the production of colonial goods, and even a shortage of fresh water. Around 1780, the colony had some 750 inhabitants, about half of them slaves.[26]

There was also no possibility in developing St. Barthélemy along the lines of the sugar-producing colonies that France and Britain possessed, but this did not mean that St. Barthélemy was a worthless asset. In fact, at least some Swedish politicians saw quite clearly that the island could be exploited in the same way as were some Dutch and Danish West Indian islands. A good example of this approach was the economist and politician Johan Liljecrantz, Gustav III's minister of finance.[27] Two years after the colony's acquisition, Liljecrantz wrote a report on St. Barthélemy's economic development. His report also illustrates the economic logic of Sweden's commercial policy in the late eighteenth century, the same logic that determined the policy of Swedish neutrality shipping in southern European waters. Notably, Liljecrantz as minister of finance had a very large influence on the shape of Gustavian trade and shipping policy. In the report, Liljecrantz deemed the island unsuitable for agricultural production and too poor and sparsely populated to provide any sizeable market for Swedish products. Therefore the trade monopoly practices of the great colonial powers, such

---

[23] Hildebrand 1951, p. 23.
[24] Hildebrand 1951, p. 39.
[25] Hildebrand 1951, p. 59.
[26] Tingbrand 2002, p. 67.
[27] Kumlien 1980–81.

as Britain, France or Spain, were not to be recommended. Instead, Sweden should follow the examples of the Dutch and Danish West Indian colonies and open up St. Barthélemy for transit trade. Liljecrantz proposed to declare St. Barthélemy a free port and to invite foreign merchants to settle there. Religious freedom as well as a free haven for debtors should be guaranteed, to promote such settlement.

In fact, the governor proclaimed St. Barthélemy's harbour, Gustavia, a free harbour as early as April 1785. He had to do so; the island could not survive without necessities imported from the surrounding islands. Officially, Gustav III issued the decree making St. Barthélemy's harbour a free port on 7 September 1785.[28] The declaration was translated into French and English, and widely circulated throughout the West Indies, to make all prospective immigrants aware of the grand business opportunities to be found there.[29]

From this point of view, Liljecrantz might be seen as a promoter of a free trade policy. However, the same man proposed organizing Sweden's direct trade with St. Barthélemy and the West Indies in company form. It must be pointed out that the projected chartered company was not a typical monopoly company; Swedes other than shareholders in the company were to be allowed to participate in the transatlantic trade. Liljecrantz' major argument for a Swedish West India Company was the shortage of resources for transatlantic trade in Sweden. Swedish merchants were financially too weak to carry out the transatlantic trade on the basis of private merchant enterprises.[30]

In this case too, Liljecrantz's project was realized. The Swedish West India trade was regulated by a decree issued on 31 October 1786, and the same decree established the Swedish West India Company. The document highlighted the fact that until that time Sweden had had no significant trade with the West Indies, and asserted that the trade treaty with the United States and the acquisition of St. Barthélemy were the first steps toward remedying this deficit. The decree regulated both the administration of the Swedish colony and the conditions of the West India Company. We will focus below on the conditions of the Company trade.

The government awarded the company the right to trade with St. Barthélemy, other West Indian islands and North America for fifteen years, with the exception of those colonial possessions where trade with foreigners was prohibited. In a legal sense, the company had the same status as the Swedish East India Company. It was a joint stock company with a limited charter. The company was allowed to engage in the slave trade on the African coast and to import slaves. As regards West Indian production, the Company received the right of establishing factories for refining West Indian products, both on St. Barthélemy and in Sweden, and it was permitted to keep warehouses and offices on St. Barthélemy or in other places in the West Indies.

---

[28] Essén 1928, p. 242.
[29] Tingbrand 2002, p. 67.
[30] Essén 1928, p. 244.

As previously mentioned, its privileged position did not give the company monopoly trading rights. Any Swede or foreigner was allowed to carry on trade with St. Barthélemy. Nevertheless, in comparison with private enterprises, the company paid lower duties. The company also had a very important role in the administration of the colony. It salaried the administration and it was responsible for keeping the harbour and shipping yard in operation.[31]

In spite of all the plans for the company and for the development of West Indian trade, it was apparent that the major business of the Swedish island would be transit trade within the West Indies, and between the West Indian islands and the United States. In particular, Americans were interested in making use the Swedish colony. For example, the Swedish representative in Madrid, Carl August Ehrensvärd, received a number of American proposals after 1784 concerning the transit trade with the Spanish and French islands. According to one of these proposals, the Americans should carry products forbidden, but highly desirable, in the French colonies to St. Barthélemy. As the French were allowed to visit the Swedish colony, they could buy the products there and transport them to their islands. The other favoured subject of these discussions was the smuggling traffic with the Spanish colonies, especially on the northern coast of South America.

Yet the transit traffic to the Spanish islands had never played a significant role for St. Barthélemy. In reality, a much more important part of St. Barthélemy's transit trade concerned the prohibited exchange between the British West Indian islands and the young American republic.[32] By the 1770s, the British settlements in the Caribbean and North America formed a well-integrated economic unit. The American colonies supplied the Caribbean with agricultural products (fish, flour, etc.) in exchange for sugar, molasses and rum. For the British North American colonies, the British West Indies were their major trading partner. But the American War of Independence abruptly ended this exchange, with disastrous consequences for both sides, and the peace of 1783, in spite of the hopes surrounding it, did not result in the revival of the trade. The British West Indian islands stayed closed to American ships and to some important products (fish and salt meat). Notwithstanding the pressure of the West Indian lobby, the London government did not change its mind. Consequently, both the colonies and the republic went through a period of deep recession in 1782–89, which not only cost wealth, especially in the southern US states and the West Indies, but also many slaves' lives due to the shortage of provisions.[33]

The necessity of finding transit channels between the two markets made St. Barthélemy a meeting place where many Americans and Britons (from the British West Indies) settled. American commodities were exchanged for colonial products and then redistributed to the British islands. This transport traffic appeared rapidly to expand. According to an official Swedish letter of 1786, no

---

[31] Hildebrand 1951, pp. 118–119.
[32] Hildebrand 1951, pp. 122–123.
[33] McCusker 1985, pp. 368–376.

less than 979 foreign vessels called at Gustavia, about half of them with American cargoes.[34]

For the following year (March-December 1787), there are more detailed statistics on the traffic in Gustavia harbour. According to the shipping lists, the number of incoming vessels was 1,033, with a total tonnage of 22,194 lasts, and the number of outgoing vessels was 1,082, with a tonnage 22,934 lasts.[35] With an average tonnage of just 22 lasts, the majority of these vessels were rather small, and busied themselves principally with traffic between the islands. Yet the overall figures testify to an impressive volume of traffic. At the same time, the overall carrying capacity of the Swedish merchant marine was 60–70,000 lasts (table 5.5).

A detailed analysis of one month shows that the traffic was completely dominated by vessels from the British islands. In June 1787, 78 of 159 incoming vessels arrived from the British West Indian islands, 26 vessels arrived from the United States, and 21 came from St. Eustatius. The remaining ships arrived from the French and Danish islands. Only three vessels came directly from Sweden, two of them from Gothenburg and one from Åbo (Turku). One of the Gothenburg vessels continued with ballast to the United States, while the remaining two loaded their return cargoes at Gustavia. No other vessels arrived directly from Europe.[36]

The rapid expansion of the transit exchange on St. Barthélemy was also mirrored in the increasing population, which reached about 1,600 in 1787, considerably more than during the French period.[37]

However, these signs of success did not mean much for Sweden, because the trade was almost exclusively confined to transit within the West Indies. Due to the fact that Gustavia was a free harbour, Sweden did not receive much income from duties. It seems that Swedish officials, aiming to increase the transit trade as much as possible, allowed passage to vessels with even lower duties than stipulated, despite the official rates already being low.[38]

On the one hand, the plan for making St. Barthélemy a transit entrepôt between different parts of the West Indies and the United States was rather successful. On the other hand, the original plan to make St. Barthélemy a centre of Swedish trade with the Americas was a partial failure. Direct Swedish trade with the Caribbean and North America continued to be of minor importance even after 1784.

---

[34] Hildebrand 1951, p. 131.
[35] Hildebrand 1951, p. 163. Data on shipping lists of Carl Fredrik Bagge and Samuel Fahlberg, partly in tons partly in lasts. Hildebrand calculated into lasts with 1 last=2 tons.
[36] Hildebrand 1951, p. 164.
[37] Hildebrand 1951, p. 171.
[38] Hildebrand 1951, p. 163.

6.4 The trade treaty with the United States

As previously mentioned, the American War of Independence opened up new opportunities for Swedish commercial activities, and the acquisition of the colony of St. Barthélemy was one important step in this direction. In the long-term perspective, however, the early establishment of diplomatic relations with the United States was even more important. And alongside the issue of a West Indian colony, the question of diplomatic relations with the American republic had already been brought to the fore during the war.

On the one hand, the Swedish authorities hoped for a share in the lucrative transit trade between Europe, North America and the West Indies; here the acquisition of a colony in the West Indies was the most important issue. On the other hand, an independent American republic, no longer subject to British protection policy, was seen as a prospective market for Swedish iron and manufactures. Discussions about potential trade between North America and Sweden were carried on as early as the 1770s. For example, the Swedish priest Johan Wiksell, who served in Delaware in a Swedish Church Congregation, informed Gustav III of the commercial potential of North America.[39]

A more ambitious attempt to acquire useful information was made after 1780, when the official of the Swedish Board of Mines, Samuel Gustaf Hermelin, was sent to the United States to investigate commercial opportunities, especially for Sweden's major export—iron. Hermelin stayed in America for two years, between 1782 and 1784. In detailed letters, he informed Sweden both of the political situation in the young republic and the commercial opportunities there. His reports are the first Swedish traveller's account of the development of the United States.[40] Nevertheless, the journey had no direct effect on the development of Swedish-American commercial exchange.

The third aspect in establishing links between Sweden and the United States was the old Swedish dream of making Sweden a major gateway in the Baltic trade and a staple place for Baltic products. This was one of the ambitions of the aforementioned Johan Liljecrantz, the strong man of Gustavian economic policy. By connecting Sweden and the United States as early as possible, Swedish politicians hoped to encourage the Americans to enter the Baltic trade via Sweden. This was one of the reasons why the Swedes were so eager to sign a trade treaty with the US as soon as possible after the treaty of Paris (1783), i.e. before other countries. Moreover, in contrast to other neutral European states, Sweden allowed American vessels to visit Sweden during the war years.[41]

Thus the arguments for establishing diplomatic contacts with the prospective new republic were strong, and already in March 1782 the Swedish envoy in

---

[39] Stellan Dahlgren's lecture on the Swedes in Delaware during the eighteenth century (spring 2002, Dep. of History, Uppsala University).
[40] Hermelin 1894.
[41] Essén 1928, p. 184.

Paris, Creutz, obtained instructions to contact Benjamin Franklin and start negotiations concerning the American-Swedish trade treaty. At the same time, Creutz was asked to keep the negotiations secret, first because of the British reaction, but also because of that of Russia. Russia was the major import market in the Baltic and Sweden's most important rival in the export trade.

The Swedish text of the treaty appeared finished by late 1782, and it broadly followed the French-American treaty of 1778. The treaty was also concerned with the conditions of neutrality shipping. Creutz was instructed to extend the negotiations as long as the war continued; however, Franklin accepted the final version of the treaty as early as February 1783. The official date of the signature of the treaty was 3 April 1783, and thus Sweden became the first neutral state to sign a trade treaty with the United States.[42]

The treaty also included the right of appointing Swedish consuls to the US, and the reciprocal right of appointing US consuls to Sweden. And as early as September 1783, Gustav III appointed the first two consuls. Richard Söderström was appointed for Boston, whereas Carl Hellstedt was appointed for Philadelphia. In January 1784, the king appointed another consul, Adolf Schough, for Charleston.[43]

In summary, in the course of the American War of Independence and directly after it, Sweden carried on an ambitious and clearly articulated policy, with the aim of taking a share in the immensely profitable West Indian trade and channelling American trade with the Baltic to Sweden. The trade treaty with the US and the appointment of consuls was one dimension of this policy. The acquisition of St. Barthélemy, in the process turning Gustavia harbour into a free port, and the establishment of the Swedish West India Company, was another part. This, over the course of four years, created a new institutional framework for the Swedish transatlantic trade. Due to the changed international environment, and Britain's weakened position in the Atlantic, Swedish policy was more practical than the colonial dreams of the previous decades. In addition to the more favourable international environment, Sweden had substantial shipping capacity. It also had experience in long-distance shipping, and there were masters and seamen accustomed to sailing to the West Indies on chartered voyages. How far did Sweden fulfil its ambitions? The question will be answered in the next section primarily via the reports of the Swedish consuls to the United States and through the data on trade.

6.5 Swedish trade with the West Indies

There was no direct commodity trade between 'the West Indies' (in Swedish trade statistics, a term inclusive of both the West Indian islands and the Amer-

---

[42] Essén 1928, pp. 186–195; Hildebrand 1951, p. 26.
[43] Almqvist 1912–15, pp. 347–348.

icas) and Sweden until the war years of 1776–83.[44] In 1782, imports first reached the noteworthy value of 11,000 rixdollars, and they increased to over 100,000 rixdollars in the following two years, 1783 and 1784. Yet after 1784 they declined again, and the level did not develop greatly during the remaining years of the century. As regards exports, there were already noticeable volumes during the 1770s. In parallel with imports, the greatest numbers were attained in the later wartime years of 1782 and 1783, with export values accounting for 73,000 and 153,000 rixdollars. After the war, decline and stagnation followed. However, even in the best years, export and import values hovering about 100,000 rixdollars represented about 2 per cent of Sweden's total imports during the wartime boom (about 5 million rixdollars). Thus, even in its best years in the 1780s, the exchange between the West Indies and Sweden represented a negligible share of Sweden's total foreign trade, and even this meagre trade stagnated after 1784.

Swedish imports from the West Indies consisted primarily of tobacco, coffee, and sugar. On the export side we find no iron. Instead, the most important export commodity was herring, from Sweden's west coast. Some cargoes of herring, about four to five thousand barrels in all, may already be traced in the course of the 1760s and 1770s, and herring completely dominated Swedish exports to the region until 1782. Most probably the Swedish herring was used as food for slaves on Caribbean sugar plantations, as well as the herring from New England and Newfoundland. North Atlantic herring was one of the most important commodities in the triangular Atlantic trade, and the west-Swedish herring had a small share in this market.

Yet from 1782, the Swedish East India Company's re-exports became much more important than herring. This trade, consisting mostly of Chinese tea, had a few very good years during the war years of 1776 to 1783. Then, when the Dutch, French and British were engaged in war, the Danish and Swedish East India Companies were left as the only non-belligerent tea-traders. Especially after 1780, the Swedish East India Company re-exports surged to over two million rixdollars annually; and part of the Company's tea also went to the West Indies.[45]

The re-export boom disappeared promptly after 1783, when the British changed their East India trade policy. In the so-called Commutation Act (1784), they reduced import duties on tea and, at the same time, increased imports.[46] Subsequently, the European market for Swedish re-exports disappeared. However, it seems that the West Indies continued to be one of the places where the Swedish East India re-exports found buyers, even after 1784.

---

[44] The following picture of the exchange between Sweden and the West Indies is based on Hildebrand's analysis of the trade statistics of the Board of Trade, see Hildebrand 1951, pp. 315–318, tables 1–5, see also, pp. 41–43. For the figure of Sweden's total imports, see Essén 1928, p. 175. It is worth mentioning that the data on the total Swedish foreign trade in 1780–83 were exceptional high.

[45] Nyström 1883, table 4; Müller 2003, p. 37

[46] Mui 1984, p. 13.

Table 6.1: *Swedish trade with 'the West Indies' in rixdollars (including the Caribbean, St. Barthélemy, and North America)*

Year	Import	Export	Herring export	East India Company's re-exports
1777	42	8,107	7,967	2,278
1778		12,241	11,848	32
1779	1,844	12,161	11,426	
1780		2,925	2,664	
1781		2,540	2,525	
1782	11,270	73,412	13,226	45,377
1783	119,456	153,005	17,136	110,568
1784	133,083	67,485	2,800	153,456
1785	85,706	60,965	6,811	24,594
1786	90,225	36,714	9,507	27,426
1787	46,518	48,294	9,104	7,526
1788	139,088	30,715	0	39,589
1789				
1790	27,609	17,040		
1791	37,102	25,335		
1792	86,462	24,964		14,200
1793	43,340	40,622		99,142
1794	67,677	100,750		7,742
1795	109,318	89,445		60,221

Source: Hildebrand 1951, table 1–5, pp. 315–318, For the East India Company's re-exports, see Nyström 1883, table 4.
Note: In some years (1777, 1788, 1793) the East India Company's re-exports to the West Indies exceed Sweden's total exports to the area. This is most probably a consequence of the late entry of the re-exports in the trade statistics of the Board of Trade.

Nevertheless, in parallel with overall Swedish foreign trade, the West Indies' share in Swedish East India Company re-exports was marginal.

This pattern of trade, of course, was not at all in accordance with the grand policy outlined above. In the course of the 1780s, Swedish trade did not increase as planned. Further, instead of iron, Swedish exports consisted mainly of herring and East India re-exports. There were some limited iron exports, which, in conjunction with the Swedish West Indian trade in general, reached their peak in 1784, to decline in the following years.[47]

One of the reasons why the Swedish West Indian trade was so limited was the fact that so few merchants were engaged in it. Besides the West India Company—focusing primarily on trade with St. Barthélemy, and first active after 1786—the most closely-involved individuals appear to have been the Gothenburg brothers Carl and Richard Söderström, the latter being the first Swedish merchant and consul in the United States. Carl Söderström was a partner of the leading Gothenburg merchant, Christian Arfwidsson (Arfwedson), himself from an established merchant family. We have already encountered one of the family members, Arvid Arfwedson, in his capacity as the Lisbon consul.

[47] Adamson 1969, pp. 60–61 (table 1).

Christian Arfwidsson was one of Gothenburg's biggest shipowners and heavily engaged in neutrality shipping in the 1776–83 war years. His speciality seemed to be risky affairs. For example, during wartime, he proposed to France's government the importing of African slaves to the French West Indies on his own account.[48] Carl Söderström and Arfwidsson also appeared to collaborate in their West Indian business. In particular, this began to develop after Richard Söderström settled in the United States, in 1780. According to a letter of Axel von Fersen, Mr. Söderström, who must be Richard Söderström, was already in Boston in 1780.[49]

According to Söderström's own information, he organised two slave expeditions to Africa between 1780 and 1784, both of them very profitable. It is not clear if there was any connection between Arfwidsson's proposals to the French government and Richard Söderström's expeditions, but clearly the three men were interested in this kind of trade. The East India re-exports were another profitable trade they were engaged in. For example, Richard Söderström proposed to the Swedish authorities to organise direct Swedish trade between the East and West Indies, and by-pass the Swedish East India Company.[50] Thus, it is very probable that the two brothers organised the Swedish East India re-exports destined for the West Indies. It is worth mentioning, in this context, that Gothenburg was the seat of the Swedish East Indian Company and the place where public sales of East India cargoes were carried out, and the Arfwidsson/Arfwedson family was deeply engaged in this business.[51]

The relationship between Christian Arfwidsson and Carl Söderström ended in 1786, when Söderström illegally sold a cargo of pawned iron and disappeared, leaving his companion with debts. This was also a period of decline in the Swedish exchange with the West Indies, but it is difficult to say if the trade declined because of Carl Söderström's failure. More probably, the decline represented an adjustment to peace conditions, in which Swedish neutrality was no advantage.

The limited exchange between Sweden and the West Indies in the 1780s does not mean that American merchants were not interested in northern-European trade. In fact, US trade and shipping with this region expanded substantially, only not with Sweden. After 1783, the first American contacts were made with the Dutch and German merchants who had already been engaged in North American trade during the colonial period. The American merchants established their contacts with northern Europe through the Dutch, German and Danish commercial networks in the West Indies.[52] With the help of these networks they also soon found their way to the Baltic Sea. Copenhagen and St.

---

[48] Hallendorff 1920, pp. 172–173.
[49] Barton 1975, p. 24.
[50] Hildebrand 1951, p. 246.
[51] Rosman 1945, pp. 308 ff.
[52] Rabuzzi 1998, p. 180; on the Dutch-American trade, see Klooster 1995; Postma 1998; Enthoven and Postma 2003.

Petersburg then became their favourite destinations. According to the Sound Toll Register, in the 1783–1807 period over 1,200 American ships entered the Baltic Sea, 499 of which were destined for Copenhagen and 603 for St. Petersburg. Yet only two vessels gave Stockholm as their destination.[53]

Nevertheless, the situation was not as critical as the Sound Toll Register figures indicate. The register does not record the arrival of American vessels at Gothenburg, which thus conceals Gothenburg's important role in direct Swedish-American trade. As previously mentioned, both the key personnel and the more commercially attractive commodities (herring and teas) for this trade were to be found in Gothenburg.

Nevertheless, the post-1784 exchange with the West Indies far from realised Sweden's ambitions of becoming a gateway for American trade in the Baltic. In fact, Sweden's most dangerous trading rival, Russia, became a leading trade partner of the young republic in the Baltic. The important positions of Copenhagen and St. Petersburg in the American trade with the Baltic must be attributed to their roles as re-distribution centres of colonial commodities. Neither Stockholm nor Gothenburg had such a role. American vessels entered the Baltic Sea with cargoes of colonial products (sugar, tobacco, etc.), and they returned with cargoes of naval stores and iron, also typical Swedish commodities. But due to the position of St. Petersburg as a redistribution centre for colonial goods, the Americans acquired their return cargoes there, and partly also in Denmark. A comparison of Russian (from St. Petersburg) and Swedish (from Gothenburg) iron exports to the US shows that Russian iron dominated this trade until the beginning of the Continental System.[54]

In the early 1780s, Sweden pursued an ambitious foreign trade policy in the West Indies and, during the American War of Independence, all these aims appeared achievable. Sweden was supposed to take part in the lucrative West Indian trade in the same manner as did the other smaller states. The Dutch and Danish trading outposts in the West Indies formed a model for the Swedish colony of St. Barthélemy. The independent American republic was seen as a potential market for Swedish commodities, especially iron, and in addition Sweden, due to its early establishment of diplomatic contacts with the United States, would be a gateway for American trade into the Baltic Sea.

However, it soon became clear that these ambitious aims would not be accomplished. Direct Swedish trade and shipping with the West Indies remained quite insignificant. The ambition of turning St. Barthélemy into a transit entrepôt succeeded, especially as regards the exchange between the United States and the British West Indies. But the transit traffic circumvented Swedish trade *per se*, and neither the Swedish colonial administration nor the Swedish merchants could properly engage in or exploit it. In the Baltic, the American vessels preferred to go to Copenhagen and St. Petersburg.

---

[53] Rasch 1965, pp. 36–37.
[54] Adamson 1969, p. 61.

6.6 The first Swedish consul to the United States

Compared to Swedish ambitions, Swedish trade with the West Indies was not satisfactory. But an exclusive focus on the direct commodity exchange fails to give due weight to the role of the triangular trade and shipping between southern Europe, the Caribbean islands and North America, in which Swedish tramp shipping played a certain role. It is also apparent that after 1793, when another conflict between Britain and France—now a revolutionary Republic—broke out, the Swedish vessels were also prepared to exploit their neutrality on these new routes. This development is difficult to discern in trade statistics or in the Sound Toll Register. Consular reports from the United States, however, provide a more complex view. The focus of the concluding part of this chapter will be on this source. Of the three consuls appointed in 1783–84, only Richard Söderström has left reports. Nevertheless, neither is his extant correspondence complete.

Richard Söderström's appointment as the consul to the United States was primarily motivated by his expertise in American trade. In 1783, Söderström had already been in the United States for three years. As mentioned earlier, he settled there in 1780 and, in partnership with his brother Carl, carried on trade between Gothenburg and the West Indies, the latter including, in this context, the US. He made contact with Swedish officers in the French service and one of them, Per Ulric Lillienhorn, recommended him for the consular service.[55] Söderström was appointed consul in Boston. According to Samuel Hermelin's letters, the increase in American-Swedish trade in 1782 was associated with Richard Söderström.[56]

Carl Hellstedt, the other Swedish consul, was appointed to Philadelphia. At the time of his appointment, Hellstedt had a firm (Hellstedt and Minor) in London; but it is not clear if this business involved commercial exchange with the West Indies. Hellstedt moved to Philadelphia and established a trading firm there, but his business did not develop well. In 1792, Söderström reported that Hellstedt was deeply indebted and incapable of conducting his consular duties. In parallel with the overall consular service, Swedish consuls to the United States were not salaried. They had to make their living from trade and consular fees.[57] In 1793, Hellstedt retired and returned to Sweden. Adolf Schough, the consul appointed to Charleston a couple of months after Söderström and Hellstedt had taken up their positions, never left Sweden, and the Charleston consulate was abandoned after a year-long vacancy.[58]

For an account of the Swedish consular service in the United States we have to rely on Richard Söderström's reports. Only a few of his reports preserved

---

[55] Hildebrand 1951, pp. 244–246; Elovson 1928, p. 318.
[56] Hildebrand 1951, p. 43.
[57] Söderström to BoT, 20 December 1792, Richard Söderström's reports 1786–1799, Americana vol. 1, SNA.
[58] Almqvist 1912–15, p. 606.

from the 1780s, but for the 1790s the situation is better. Söderström was appointed a consul to Boston but he did not stay there. His reports are dated first from New York (1786–90) and then from Philadelphia (1792–99).[59] Usually, his reports concerned the Swedish trade interests in the United States, but, to a surprising extent, he informed the Board of Trade about the political situation in the country. Söderström was no unbiased observer. He saw American political, commercial and shipping developments through the eyes of the Swedish interest.

Söderström's letters from New York, from the late 1780s, almost exclusively concerned the political situation. For example, he reported on the conflicts between the states of the union, and on the election of George Washington as the President of the United States. He forwarded to Stockholm copies of all important laws and decrees issued by the Congress. He even paid attention to economic development. In 1790, Söderström wrote that the American states had become less and less dependent on European commodities during the 1780s. There were very few comments on Swedish shipping and trade to the United States. The few notes on these issues almost exclusively concerned escaping Swedish seamen. Apparently this was not only a problem for Swedish shipping within the Mediterranean. High American wages tempted Swedish seamen to change flag. Yet in 1790, another reason for Swedish seamen to leave Swedish ships seems to have been the Russo-Swedish War.[60] The problem with these seamen bears witness to the fact that Swedish-flagged ships were travelling between European (non-Swedish) ports and the US.

In December 1792, Söderström applied for the extension of his consular district to the whole United States—not merely Boston—and he also asked for the right to appoint vice-consuls. He argued as to how important it was for him, as a Swedish representative, to reside in the same place where the Congress met. In the same letter he also informed the Board of Trade that he bought a landed estate. This might be indirect evidence that his trading firm had not done well in the late 1780s.[61]

The application, in fact, was a request to promote his Boston consulate into the general consulate for the whole United States. The letter was forwarded to the Stockholm Merchant Association, which expressed its disapproval. The Stockholm merchants' answer is worth presenting in detail. It is very enlightening in terms of the situation of Swedish-American trade by 1790. First, the Association commented on the economic situation of both consuls, Hellstedt and Söderström. Apparently neither of them, according to the Stockholm merchants, could carry out their consular duties. Söderström was living on his farm, as he openly admitted, and Hellstedt was out of business. According to the Stockholm merchants, Söderström's farming activities were not a proper

[59] Richard Söderström's reports preserved mainly in the collection Diplomatica Americana SNA, 1790, and partly in the Consular Reports, BoT SNA
[60] Söderström's reports 1786–90, dated at New York, Americana vol. 1, SNA.
[61] Söderström to BoT, 20 December 1792, Americana vol. 1, SNA.

occupation for a Swedish consul to the United States.[62] The merchants concluded that Swedish trade with the United States was so limited that no consuls could live on commissions from the Swedish-American trade and that, at the end of the day, Swedish consuls in the United States were superfluous. In addition, the merchants pointed out that both Söderström and Hellstedt had been appointed consuls without their approval and that they were unknown to them. Söderström's application to promote his consulate to the status of general consulate was declined.

It is worth looking at the case in detail, because the Association's unenthusiastic view of the Swedish consular service in the US and of Swedish-American trade has a more complicated background. The Stockholm elite most probably saw Söderström and his business associates as competitors. This perhaps explains their statement that Richard Söderström was an unknown person to them—which was very strange, considering his long career and contacts with the Arfwedson family. The Stockholm merchants had at least two strong interests of their own in the question. Many representatives of the Stockholm Merchant Association were shareholders in the Swedish West India Company, and the Association lent a substantial sum of money to the company (20,000 rixdollars). The West India Company competed with private Swedish transatlantic trade, as well as with people like Söderström and his business friends. The company trade did not develop very well, so the shareholders were almost certainly prepared to undermine the competition.[63] The incident mirrors in a sense the differing interests of the Gothenburg (connected to Richard Söderström) and Stockholm (connected to the West India Company) mercantile groups.

During the following years Söderström's situation improved. In March 1793, he was appointed Danish consul to the United States, which at the least doubled his potential commissions and consular duties. From 1793, when war between Britain and France again broke out, Sweden could exploit its neutrality anew, and the deteriorating relations between the United States and Britain had similar consequences for the Swedes. Swedish shipping capacity was in demand, as was the consul's assistance. When Söderström again applied for an extended consular district, in 1794, the Board of Trade approved his application, despite another critical statement on the matter by the Stockholm Merchant Association.[64]

In a lengthy letter of October 1793, Söderström characterises the improving conditions of Swedish shipping to the United States in detail. He mentions the ongoing war in Europe as the most important reason for the improvement.

---

[62] Stockholm Merchant Association to BoT, received 6 August 1793, Consular Reports, Boston EVI aa 54, BoT SNA.
[63] Hildebrand 1951, p. 246. For details on the Association's loan to the Company, see Hildebrand 1951, p. 300.
[64] Söderstöm to BoT, 5 September 1795, Philadelphia, Americana vol. 1, SNA. The letter confirms the extension of his district and the right of appointing vice-consuls.

Söderström even inserted a notice in American newspapers, informing the American merchants of Sweden's neutrality. As usual, even this form of neutrality shipping was connected with risks. French privateers were taking neutrals sailing between the Caribbean and the mainland, as two Swedish-flagged vessels found to their cost.

Söderström's data on the Swedish traffic in American ports in 1793–94 provide a view of the growth in shipping between the Mediterranean and the United States. In 1793, prior to October, two Swedish vessels arrived in Boston from Sicily with cargoes of salt, wine and brandy, and returned with fish, sugar and coffee. Another vessel arrived in New York from Livorno, with a cargo of wine and olive oil. There was also dynamic traffic involving Swedish-flagged vessels from St. Barthélemy. St. Barthélemy-registered Swedes unloaded their cargoes of sugar, coffee and rum at different ports of the US, and returned with American products. Between October 1793 and May 1794, at least another twenty Swedish vessels arrived from the Mediterranean.[65]

This shipping exclusively involved tramp shipping between the United States, the Mediterranean and St. Barthélemy. Regarding direct trade between the United States and Sweden, Söderström mentioned in his letter that his American business friends had asked him why American exporters had to pay much higher duties in Sweden than the Swedes, and why the trade with Sweden was not as liberal as that with Denmark. According to their complaints, for example, the Swedish duties on tobacco imports were as much as 50 per cent of the commodity value.

Another issue in the correspondence was that of free staple rights in Gothenburg. In 1794, Gothenburg received general liberty of entrepôt for foreign merchandise (*nederlagsrätten*). The same year, Marstrand, a small harbour on Sweden's west coast, which had been proclaimed a free port (*porto franco*) in 1775, lost its rights.[66] Marstrand was too small to promote transit trade with Sweden. Instead Copenhagen, with its free staple rights, functioned as a transit entrepôt, and many American vessels obtained their return cargoes there, cargoes consisting among other things of Swedish iron.

Giving free staple rights to Gothenburg was very much in accordance with the free trade policy of Johan Liljecrantz. The opening of Gothenburg for the transit trade has to be seen as an important precondition for the town's role during the wars of 1793–1815, and especially in the period 1806–15.

The years 1793 and 1794 were also very good years for Swedish neutrality shipping to the United States. Söderström described the changed situation in his letter of 3 May 1794 in the following words:

> I can say that this and the previous year are the only years in which something of importance has happened [meaning in terms of Swedish business].[67]

---

[65] Söderstöm to BoT, 2 October 1793, Philadelphia, Americana vol. 1, SNA; see also Hildebrand 1951, p. 249.
[66] Essén 1928; af Malmborg 2001, p. 78.

In February 1794 alone, three Swedish and five Danish ships arrived in American ports, all from the Mediterranean and all subsequently loaded in the United States with return cargoes of grain and flour. For example, one of the Swedish ships was chartered, on a Spanish account, from Cadiz to Virginia and back for a freight of £650, which Söderström considered a low price.[68] In letter after letter, he accused the Swedish shipowners of being bad businessmen, as they were losing vast amounts of money on contracts made in Spain and Portugal. Instead, he suggested, they should charter their ships in the United States.

As an example of how profitable Swedish shipping could be, if shipowners would simply follow his advice, Söderström referred to a freight contact which he had made with the house of Küsel and Hebbe (most probably concerning the ship *Grefven af Haga*, of 192 lasts). He chartered the ship for a voyage from Baltimore to Spanish Hispaniola and Hamburg for £3,300. In addition, the shipowner was paid the freight from Lisbon to Baltimore (£480). Thus the total revenue for this contract was £3,780. The same vessel was chartered in Portugal for the voyage Lisbon-Baltimore-Lisbon for £980. According to Söderström, all Swedish vessels could obtain such advantageous contracts if they were chartered in American ports and not in Europe.[69]

The consul repeatedly expressed his concern that American shipping would ultimately elbow out the tramp shipping of small European states, the Danes and Swedes in particular.

> My thought is that it is in all the European powers' interest to exclude the Americans from the Mediterranean as long as possible and to increase the cost of such permission [for them] as much as possible, hence if they will be allowed [to enter the Mediterranean] all freights that other nations' vessels have always had will be taken over by them.[70]

In this perspective, it is understandable why so much of Söderström's attention was drawn to the conditions of American tramp shipping. In these years two issues were especially in focus: the problems with the Algiers corsairs and the crisis of British-American relations in 1793–94.

In numerous letters from winter 1793–94 and spring 1794, Söderström reported on the American war with Algiers and the conditions of shipping between the Mediterranean and the United States. He referred in detail to the American discussions on this issue, referring both to the issue of the payment of ransoms/gifts on the part of the Swedes, Danes and Dutch, and the issue of building an American convoy fleet of frigates. During the spring of 1794, Congress already seemed prepared to follow the small states' example in North Africa and pay. But until 1795 the United States had no peace treaty with

---

[67] Söderström to BoT, 3 May 1794, Philadelphia, Americana vol. 1, SNA.
[68] Söderstöm to BoT, 28 February 1794, Philadelphia, Americana vol. 1, SNA.
[69] Söderstöm to BoT, 24 May 1794, Philadelphia, Americana vol. 1, SNA.
[70] Söderström to BoT, 10 January 1794, Philadelphia, Americana vol. 1, SNA.

Algiers, and corsairs were capturing American ships. Swedish ships, on the other hand, moved safely both inside and outside the Mediterranean. Therefore Swedish-flagged ships had a good reputation among American merchants.

The second issue was the crisis in British-American relations, which was one of the consequences of the outbreak of the European war. American shipping suffered terribly from British raids. According to Söderström, up until the end of March 1794 the British had taken about 200 American vessels in the Caribbean, loaded both with cargoes from the United States to the French West Indian islands and with return cargoes. The American authorities considered confiscating all neutral ships in American seaports. Söderström communicated this information to his contacts in the American seaports, to warn Swedish and Danish shipmasters, and, heeding his warnings, the majority of the Nordic vessels left the US by the end of March 1794.[71]

On 27 March 1794, the American authorities declared the Embargo Law. The law was implemented for 30 days with a possibility of extension to 60 or 90 days.[72] Shipping in the American ports was paralysed, and war between the United States and Britain seemed unavoidable. The Embargo Law affected four Swedish vessels, all destined for Portugal with grain and flour. On the other hand, the consul also mentioned two Swedish vessels, which left the ports of Petersburg (Virginia) and Philadelphia even during the embargo.

By the end of May the situation had stabilised. The United States sent a mission to Britain led by John Jay, the US chief justice and envoy extraordinary, with the aim of settling British-American relations. By the end of the year, 19 November 1794, the so-called Jay treaty was concluded. However, it took another year before Congress ratified it. The treaty settled American–British relations in many problematic areas, one of them being tramp shipping and the trade with the West Indies. For Americans, the most important outcome of the treaty was that the US retained—for the time being—unbroken neutrality in the European wars. Americans became major sea carriers in the troubled years of the French Revolutionary and Napoleonic Wars.

From Söderström's point of view, of course, the peaceful settlement of the crisis was not good news. The war between the US and Britain that he had hoped for did not arrive, and the Swedes and Danes lost a profitable shipping opportunity. Söderström's letters from autumn 1794 and spring 1795 are sadly missing. He would surely have referred in detail to the negotiations and the Jay treaty. The next preserved letter, dated June 1795, primarily concerned this treaty's consequences for American commerce.[73] In his evaluation, Söderström disagreed completely with the American public, who had interpreted the Jay treaty as a surrender to the British, and whose bitterness was great when Congress accepted it. In contrast, the Swedish consul saw the Jay treaty as being very advantageous for the Americans. He mentioned specifically the opening of

---

[71] Söderström to BoT, 25 March 1794, Philadelphia, Americana vol. 1, SNA.
[72] Söderström to BoT, 28 March and 17 April 1794, Philadelphia, Americana vol. 1, SNA.
[73] Söderström to BoT, 27 June 1795, Philadelphia, Americana vol. 1, SNA.

direct American trade with the East Indies—apparently a trade that concerned him very much. As regards the conditions of Swedish shipping, the freight rates for voyages to the Mediterranean were still quite profitable in June 1795. However, few Swedish vessels arrived in the United States that year.

During the following three years Söderström's correspondence is again sparse. It is difficult to say whether letters are missing from the archives, or whether he simply did not report. A number of letters of 1798 again give a picture of risky shipping conditions, especially for American vessels. In 1798, however, the American problems related to French privateers. But even Spanish and British were seizing American shipping. Söderström's May reports described American shipmasters that did not have the courage to leave their ports, and French privateers waiting along the coast and capturing Americans. He mentioned seizures of vessels engaged in European trade, and also some richly laden East Indiamen.

In direct trade with Europe, the Americans could commonly use the English convoying, but in the West Indies the situation was worse. With the aim of increasing the safety of their shipping, the Americans launched an ambitious program for building a convoy fleet of about twenty frigates. The consul followed the progress of this program in detail, and in June he could report on the first incidents in which American frigates had freed American vessels and even taken a French privateer.[74]

As in the earlier years, Söderström saw these unstable conditions as a profitable opportunity for Swedish shipping. In May there were about forty Swedish and Danish ships waiting in the American seaports, and their masters were asking Söderström for advice. The consul recommended that Swedish masters should offer their ships for charter for European voyages. In Söderström's opinion, the French privateers could not treat the Danes and Swedes in the same way as they treated the Americans. However, the Swedish masters were less enthusiastic, as they knew that neither Swedish nor Danish vessels invariably avoided being taken by French privateers. For example, the ship *Neptunus*, based in Gävle, first sailed from Baltimore to St. Barthélemy with a cargo of sawn timber, and this voyage ended well. But it was taken on the way from St. Barthélemy to Haiti and forced to go to Guadeloupe.[75]

In spring 1798, Söderström appointed new Swedish vice-consuls. Joseph Winthrop became the vice-consul in Charleston, South Carolina. Jonathan Swift was appointed the Swedish vice-consul in Alexandria (for the district of Virginia and Maryland). Christian U. Grill was appointed for Baltimore (Maryland) and Henrik Gahn for New York (district of New York and Connecticut). Gahn and Grill were the only Swedes among the appointed vice-consuls, and were both members of known merchant families. In New Hampshire and

---

[74] Söderström to BoT, 12 April and 10 May 1798 Philadelphia, On liberation of the captured ships see 2 June 1798, Philadelphia, Americana vol. 1, SNA.

[75] Söderström to BoT, 10 May 1798, Philadelphia, Americana vol. 1, SNA.

Massachusetts, Swedish interests were represented by Ch. F. Degen. All Söderström's vice-consuls gave assistance to both Swedish and Danish ships.[76]

Other letters also reveal an increasing American interest in direct trade with Sweden. The foremost reason for the interest was the news of the French capture of Bremen and Hamburg, which had, as earlier mentioned, a key position in the American redistribution network in northern Europe. American merchants were looking for alternative destinations, safe from the French, and Sweden was one such destination. Söderström wrote that perhaps as early as the summer of 1798, American vessels could unload their cargoes in Gothenburg. He was receiving queries from American seaports regarding import rules and duties in Gothenburg.[77] We cannot evaluate the importance of Söderström's information for the transformation of the Swedish-American trade pattern; it would take another eight years before Gothenburg began to play such a role. But the original notion of Gothenburg's new prominence was clearly already in evidence in the summer of 1798.

The West Indies and American foreign policy, once again, received much attention in the following year's correspondence. Söderström reported on the secret mission of Dr. Heyens, a brother of Alexander Hamilton, who was sent to Haiti to sign a trade treaty with general Toussaint l'Ouverture, the leader of Haiti's rebels. Heyens was favourably received on Haiti and, as a result of the negotiations, the Haitian leader, Toussaint, received American military support. It is clear that American mercantile circles expected large advantages to accrue from this mission.

We have already mentioned that Haiti was France's most important colony. Before the French Revolution, the island was the biggest producer of sugar and coffee in the Caribbean. In fact, according to the estimated plantation output for 1770, Haiti alone was producing more colonial goods than all the British West Indies.[78] Söderström wrote that if the trade treaty was concluded it might result in '[…] an endless traffic from this island to America and England […]', and he was hoping that Sweden could obtain a share in this trade.[79] These grand expectations were not fulfilled; the coming years of political unrest destroyed completely Haiti's plantation economy. In 1804, Haiti became the second independent state in the Americas.

Once again, the topic of the balance between the legal and illicit forms of neutral shipping consumed much of the consul's time. On the one hand, privateering against Danish and Swedish shipping continued, and Söderström was engaged in legal proceedings concerning the captured vessels. He was frequently having to travel between Baltimore and New York to take part in court proceedings. On the other hand, he made an effort to limit the illegal use of the Swedish flag. For example, in autumn 1799, the case of the ship *Continencen*

---

[76] Söderström to BoT, 12 April 1798, Philadelphia, Americana vol. 1, SNA.
[77] Söderström to BoT, 2 June 1798, Philadelphia, Americana vol. 1, SNA.
[78] For the data see Engerman 2000, especially, pp. 246–247, table 9.3.
[79] Söderström to BoT, 28 February and 16 May 1799, Philadelphia, Americana vol. 1, SNA.

consumed much of his attention. The ship arrived in Boston from St. Thomas in the West Indies with a Swedish Algerian passport as the only document supporting its Swedish nationality. Söderström ordered the ship into custody to avoid suspicion. Nevertheless, it became clear—most probably due to the testimony of Swedish shipmasters—that *Continencen* really was a Swedish vessel, based at Gamla Karleby, and that it had sailed to the West Indies with a chartered Mediterranean cargo—as had so many other Swedish vessels.[80]

American vessels taken by privateers off St. Barthélemy's coast were another recurrent theme affecting Söderström's consular duties. A letter from the American consul on St. Barthélemy, Job Wall, sheds light on the character of the problem.[81] The French privateers used to take their American prizes into Gustavia, and the Swedish Governor there did nothing to stop them. At least in one case, in 1799, a French privateer also sold its prize in Gustavia. According to the documents concerning the American schooner *Reliance*, taken into Gustavia, the American master asked the Swedish Governor to have his vessel restored but was refused. Instead the schooner was sold in the town, which of course annoyed the local American merchants.[82]

As regards Swedish and Danish shipping, freight rates paid for voyages to Europe were very high. Söderström reported (December 1799) on freight rates from £6 to 7 and 10 shillings per ton. The Danes seemed to exploit the situation well, but there were only a few Swedish vessels in US ports.[83] Unfortunately, Söderström does not give us any statistical data on the volume of Swedish trade or traffic in America. He was apparently more concerned with news about American political life and the international situation than about shipping lists, in spite of the fact that he was no admirer of republican government. In a letter of 1799 he wrote:

> I have now followed their Republican Government for fourteen years but it does not suit me at all and I hope never to be forced to take an oath as a citizen of a Republic.[84]

Looking at the whole period of Söderström's stay in the United States, the situation of 1798–1800 was clearly much better than the years directly after the American War of Independence. From the beginning of the French Revolutionary Wars, Swedish shipping could again employ a neutrality strategy. In America, however, the use of neutrality was to a high degree dependent on the political situation of the young republic, and not least on the competition with American shipping.

---

[80] Söderström to BoT, 10 October 1799 Philadelphia, Americana vol. 1, SNA.

[81] Job Wall was an Amercian merchant who settled in St. Barthélemy in 1793. He married a Swedish woman and he applied for service as American consul in the colony. After initial decline, he was appointed in 1799. Already in 1793 Wall was engaged in a similar case, when the French took into Gustavia an American vessel and sold it. Hildebrand 1951, pp. 286–288.

[82] Söderström to BoT, 10 October 1799, Philadelphia, Americana vol. 1, SNA.

[83] Söderström to BoT, 30 December 1799, Philadelphia, Americana vol. 1, SNA.

[84] Söderström to BoT, 13 August 1798, Consular Reports, Philadelphia EVI aa 374, BoT SNA.

Americans had employed the same neutrality strategy as Sweden and Denmark—though much more successfully. The years 1793–1807 were a period of unprecedented growth for the US merchant fleet, which became the leading carrier of the world and in many ways replaced the British. From 290,000 tons before the war (1792) US shipping tonnage increased to almost 1.3 million tons in 1807. The latter figure represented about 60 per cent of British shipping capacity.[85]

In comparison, the Danish and Swedish overseas merchant fleets at that moment together had an estimated tonnage of about half a million tons.[86] Hence, the Nordic carrying capacity was considerably lower, but even the Danes and Swedes were leading neutral carriers and the path of development of their shipping in the war years was comparable with that of the Americans. The three countries, despite many other differences, had similar preconditions for employing the neutrality strategy. One precondition was sufficient shipping capacity and expertise in long-distance shipping. Another precondition was their rather peripheral location, from the perspective of the French-British struggle. Nevertheless, 'peripheral' was a relative term, as the Danes were to find in 1801 and 1807.

6.7 Conclusions

Sweden entered the field of transatlantic trade and shipping with grand ambitions in the early 1780s. First, Sweden aimed to take part in the profitable West Indian trade. The acquisition of St. Barthélemy and the transformation of Gustavia harbour into a free port confirmed that the Swedish authorities were seeking to follow the Danish and Dutch model in the West Indian trade. Second, the new independence of the British North American colonies seemed to open up a new market for Swedish products, especially iron. Third, the Swedes hoped to make Sweden a gateway for American exchange with the Baltic. Two preconditions for this trade were the rapid diplomatic recognition of, and a trade treaty with, the United States.

After a decade, the results of the policy were not very satisfying. Swedish exports to the West Indies (including the US) were rather limited. Gothenburg did not become an American gateway to the Baltic. The rapidly expanding direct American trade with northern Europe went via the large redistribution entrepôts such as Bremen and Hamburg, and Copenhagen and St. Petersburg in the Baltic.

The colonial endeavour in the Caribbean appeared to be more successful. St. Barthélemy became an important transit location in the American trade with the West Indian islands, in particular those of Britain. But the Swedish share in

---

[85] Crouzet 2000, p. 305
[86] Lindvall 1917, p. 422 and table 5.5 in this book. For the French estimate of Danish tonnage (1786), see e.g. Unger 1992, p. 261, and Johansen 1992, p. 484.

this transit trade was insignificant, and the Swedish West India Company, established to promote Swedish trade with the West Indies, was not a success.

The situation improved after the outbreak of the French Revolutionary Wars. Sweden, once again, made use of its neutrality. Richard Söderström's reports from the 1790s (especially 1793, 1794, 1798 and 1799) testify to the rising numbers of Swedish vessels that arrived in American ports. Due to the tense relations between the United States and Britain before the Jay treaty, and the American war with the French of 1798–1800, there also was a profitable market for Swedish shipping. Nevertheless, this shipping almost exclusively concerned the traffic between the Mediterranean, the large northern European ports, the West Indies, and the United States. Swedish vessels were employed in tramp shipping between Europe, the United States and the West Indies. This was not the kind of trade that the policy of the early 1780s was intended to promote.

The wartime boom also made St. Barthélemy an important transit site. Cargoes of belligerent nations were converted into neutral cargoes; vessels obtained new owners, flags and passports. Vessels making such a metamorphosis were called 'new-made Swedes'. The key role of St. Barthélemy in this kind of semi-illicit trade is apparent in Söderström's reports. Yet the thriving transit business in St. Barthélemy did not give anything to Sweden, and there were no Swedish merchants who participated in it.

Transatlantic connection: from neutrality shipping to iron trade

The English fleet during the French and Napoleonic Wars effectively reduced the supply of world shipping to such a degree as to leave the American merchant marine almost the sole source of supply. In consequence, freight rates, except for the brief interval of the Peace of Amiens, more than doubled and American shipping earnings played a strategic role in the development of the American economy during this period.

Douglass C. North [1]

7.1 Introduction

American shipping and trade went through a dramatic process of development in the period of the French Revolutionary and Napoleonic Wars. US shipping capacity increased by some 300 per cent, at the same time as the freight rates doubled in comparison with the previous peace period. Despite the many risks involved, shipping became a highly profitable business for the republic. Unquestionably, the boom was connected with the war, and these profitable opportunities disappeared with the Congress of Vienna. But by 1815, European wars had been continuing for 22 years. As with the cases of Swedish or Danish neutrality shipping, it is very difficult to evaluate the importance of the wartime shipping boom in a long-term perspective. Nevertheless, the wealth accumulated did not disappear in 1815. As Douglass C. North indicated, the money earned in shipping played a strategic role in the economic development of the United States during the period.

The American shipping boom was possible because of Britain's naval mastery. The British navy effectively eliminated the shipping capacity of its continental foes and so opened a vast market for sea transport to its former colony. At the same time, the British did not have enough vessels to fill the capacity gap. The Royal Navy left its enemies with privateering as the only effective means of disturbing British control of the seas, which affected British carrying

[1] North 1968, pp. 219–220.

business substantially. Insurance premiums surged and wages in British merchant shipping increased in parallel with the navy's demand for men.[2]

In contradistinction to Danish and Swedish neutrality shipping, which was based on hiring out shipping capacity to foreigners, the American vessels carried their own North-American products together with West Indian re-exports. The American transatlantic trade was based on exports, which meant that American shipowners had problems finding suitable return cargoes. Soon, American shipmasters found that Swedish iron was a perfect return cargo. It was heavy, and thus useful as ballast, as the Dutch also discovered, and it easily found a market in the United States. Iron-exporting Gothenburg was not far from Hamburg, Bremen or Copenhagen, and so it became a favourite stopover point on American vessels' home voyages.

There had been some mercantile contacts between the United States and Gothenburg since the early 1780s, but international trade conditions had not been favourable to Gothenburg until the endorsement of the Continental System. Then, for a couple of years, Gothenburg became a very important place in the transit trade between Britain and the United States on the one hand, and the continental countries on the other. American participation in this trade was very important, as we will see. When the transit exchange of the Continental System boom period disappeared after 1815, as rapidly as it had originally appeared, the pattern of loading return cargoes of Swedish iron in Gothenburg survived. For three decades, the United States became Sweden's most important iron market.

This chapter focuses, in the first instance, on the establishment of this direct connection between Sweden and the United States. However, it will also seek to reveal any links between the pattern of the direct Swedish-American trade in iron and Sweden's ambitious policy of the early 1780s. The direct trade between Sweden and the United States will be explored from two perspectives: first, we will look at Gothenburg's role in the establishment of this direct trade; second, we will analyse the development of this trade from the perspective of Swedish consuls to the US. The chronological narrative will be complemented by data on trade exchange and shipping.

7.2 American shipping and trade in Sweden under the Continental System

Sweden's neutrality has been highlighted here as the major factor in the development of Swedish shipping in the late eighteenth century, but neutrality primarily concerned tramp shipping between foreign ports. Swedish harbours did not see any direct neutrality boom. In 1806 the situation changed. Due to the enforcement of Napoleon's Continental System, and the consequent British blockade, Sweden became one of the few countries accessible for British and

---

[2] Kennedy 1976, p. 131.

Table 7.1: *British exports to Sweden and some other countries of northern Europe 1802–12 (£ '000s)*

Year	Sweden	Russia	Denmark and Norway	Prussia	Germany including Helgoland	Total British exports
1802	91	1,282	427	818	8,005	41,412
1803	82	1,260	1,684	1,544	5,111	31,439
1804	125	1,200	3,776	3,941	1,335	34,451
1805	124	1,508	4,360	5,017	1,652	34,309
1806	175	1,692	1,438	462	5,608	36,527
1807	653	1,700	4,898	153	351	34,567
1808	2,358	395	21	70	1,532	34,554
1809	3,524	879	258	595	5,953	50,287
1810	4,871	877	236	2,597	2,153	45,870
1811	523	731	726	57	61	32,410
1812	2,308	1,807	757	84	199	43,242

Source: Crouzet 1958, p. 883, table 1.

American vessels. This time, the only other neutral actor left was the United States, because the two other important neutrals of the previous century, the Dutch Republic and Denmark, were eliminated—the former due to occupation, the latter due to the British capture of the Danish fleet and the subsequent Danish alliance with Napoleon.[3]

In the course of 1807, many British merchants previously settled in Tönningen (in Danish territory) and in Hamburg left these seaports and moved to Helgoland or Sweden.[4] Gothenburg became a major entrepôt of British trade in northern Europe. The British trade statistics reveal Sweden's sudden rise in import levels at the other countries' expense. In 1806, Sweden imported British commodities valued at £175,000. The next year the import value increased to £653,000, and in 1810 it reached almost £5 million.[5] Thus, in the course of four years British exports to Sweden increased thirty-fold. On the other hand, Swedish exports to Britain only doubled.[6] This shift, of course, reduced the damage caused by the Continental System.

The American trade followed the same pattern but its increase was even more spectacular. American exports to Sweden were valued at a tiny $90,000 in 1807. In 1808 the US trade with Europe was paralysed because of Jefferson's Embargo Law (December 1807–March 1809). But the next year, 1809, American exports to Sweden reached a value of $5.44 million, and in 1810 a value of $5.86 million. In 1811, the export value fell back to $630,000. These exports consisted of typical American products (tobacco and cotton) and re-ex-

---

[3] On the Denmark's situation after the failure of the Armed Neutrality of 1800, and capture of the Danish navy in 1807, see Feldbaek 1980, pp. 202–208.
[4] On the role of Helgoland, see e.g. Heckscher 1918, p. 124.
[5] Crouzet 1958, pp. 265–266, p. 883 (table 1).
[6] Adamson 1969, pp. 65–66.

Table 7.2: *Colonial and American products stored in Gothenburg (tons), and the value of US exports ($ million) to Sweden 1807–16*

Year	Cotton	Coffee	Sugar	Rice	Tobacco	Value of US exports to Sweden
1807	–	484.1	946.7	137.1	7.6	0.09
1808	11.7	571.0	1,226.8	22.8	127.9	–
1809	301.5	1,244.9	3,184.2	315.6	497.2	5.44
1810	555.0	1,953.3	6,160.7	297.4	413.5	5.86
1811	108.4	73.8	21.1	605.9	305.2	0.63
1812		1,688.6	1,454.6			
1813		2,454.7	2,207.4			
1814		1,669.0	1,448.6			
1815		223.3	54.4			
1816		29.0	5.9			

Source: Tiselius 1935, pp. 22 and 365; Adamson 1969, p. 66

ports of colonial products (sugar and coffee). Table 7.2 provides an overview of the rapid development of the colonial import trade into Gothenburg.

The volume of the American shipping engaged in this trade confirms the earlier picture of a boom. Before 1809 about fifteen American vessels called at Gothenburg annually, mainly to pick up ballast. They usually arrived only to load up a cargo of bar-iron for their return voyage. The total number of American ships entering Gothenburg in 1809 was as much as 169. Many came directly from the United States.[7] The same year the total number of incoming ships in Gothenburg was 1,392—the best year of the of the Continental System period.

Because of the complicated political situation and the vast amount of illicit activities, the registered data are not fully reliable. A substantial share of the transit trade simply by-passed the Swedish authorities, at the same time as vessels and cargoes were changing nationality. It was usual that commodities were stored outside the city; the herring fisheries along the coast had been stagnating for some years, and so they provided storage facilities for transit cargoes.[8]

The employment of Gothenburg and western Sweden as a kind of depot for American and West Indian commodities left considerable free capacity for outward shipping. This capacity was partly filled with sawn timber destined for Britain, partly with iron destined for the United States. In 1809, twenty-five of the seventy American vessels registered as loading cargoes in Gothenburg took on iron, while the remaining vessels loaded sawn timber for Britain. In 1810 the shipping to Britain declined and even higher share of shipping capacity went directly to the United States. Consequently, Swedish iron exports to North America soared to 16,395 metric tons in 1810. This volume then repre-

[7] Tiselius 1935, p. 26.
[8] Adamson 1969, p. 70.

sented about two-thirds of American iron production.[9]

The establishment of the trade link between Sweden and the United States after 1807 also had diplomatic aspects; both the states simply became more important for each other. More senior diplomatic representatives than consuls were appointed, and the trade treaty was renewed. The United States was one of the few states in which Sweden had diplomatic representation during the wars. In August 1812, Johan Albert Kantzow Sr., the Lisbon consul since 1782 and the first Swedish representative to Brazil, was appointed Swedish envoy (*ministerresident*) to the United States. However, Kantzow's voyage to Washington took too long. He went to the US via London, where he was supposed to mediate between the Americans and the British in the conflict concerning American shipping and British naval interests. When war between the US and Britain broke out, he still was in London. In October 1813, he finally arrived at Washington. The American mission in Stockholm, however, was opened even later, in April 1814, due to political opposition at home.[10] Kantzow's diplomatic missions on the other side of Atlantic certainly had an important influence on his son Johan Albert Kantzow Jr's engagement in the transatlantic trade. His firm Kantzow and Biel belonged was among the most active in both the trade with North America and Brazil.

The extreme changes in Gothenburg's transit trade in these years depended on developments outside the control of the Gothenburg merchants: warfare on the continent and the violent changes in Swedish foreign policy. Therefore an outline of Sweden's political situation between 1806 and 1815 is necessary in order to make these developments comprehensible. Paradoxically, the same policy which provided the Gothenburg merchants with the opportunity of making enormous profits also draw Sweden into a catastrophic war against Russia, entailed the loss of Finland, and brought on a constitutional revolution. The Russo-Swedish war of 1808–09 was a minor part of the Napoleonic Wars, but, for Sweden, it was a true national trauma.

The conflict with Russia was a consequence of the Swedish King Gustav IV Adolf's uncompromising policy against Napoleon. With the treaty of Tilsit of 1807, the Russian Emperor Alexander I made a complete turnabout in Russia's foreign policy, becoming a Napoleonic ally. The two Emperors divided Europe into spheres of influence with disastrous consequences for Sweden. The Swedish king refused to adapt to the new situation and Sweden's relations with Russia deteriorated rapidly. In February 1808, Russia declared war, and was soon joined by Denmark, a reluctant ally of France and Russia after the disastrous war of 1807 with Britain. Danish participation in the war, however, was not particularly visible. The only notable signs were the activities of the Swedish and Danish privateers.[11]

---

[9] Adamson 1969, pp. 68–70; Hildebrand 1957, p. 96
[10] Tunberg 1935, pp. 357–358; Jansson 1964, pp. 51–52
[11] On the Danish privateering activities and the British navy's convoy protection, see Tiselius 1935, pp. 125–146.

The war developed into a Swedish catastrophe on the eastern front. Finland was occupied and even northern and western Sweden were endangered. Under the looming shadow of civil war, Gustav IV Adolf was removed in a bloodless constitutional revolution on 13 March 1809, and a new regime soon signed a peace treaty with Russia (September 1809).[12]

The bloodless revolution also entailed the re-orientation of Swedish policy toward France, and, from January 1810, Sweden formally entered the Continental System. In spite of this foreign policy shift, Swedish-British relations remained relatively good, and the flow of colonial commodities continued to arrive in Gothenburg. In fact, the opportunity for illicit trade with the continent even increased. As part of the settlement with France, Swedish Pomerania again came under Swedish rule, which opened a new, convenient smuggling avenue to the continent. The British, who controlled the waters between Denmark and Sweden, agreed that they would not seize Swedish vessels travelling between Swedish ports, which also included vessels travelling between Gothenburg, Scania and Swedish Pomerania. The smuggling traffic from Gothenburg to the continent was, in fact, carried on under British protection.[13] Hence, in spite of Sweden's formal participation in the Continental System, 1810 became the best year in this Swedish-British wartime trade.

The French were, of course, aware of the smuggling traffic between Sweden and Britain, and late in 1810 (November) they forced the new Swedish government to declare war on Britain. Thus, under pressure of a French ultimatum, on 17 November 1810, Sweden declared war. On both sides, the declaration was seen as a formality, forced on Sweden by the French; nevertheless Anglo-Swedish trade declined. In 1811, British exports to Sweden reached only one-tenth of the previous year's value (table 7.1).[14] As early as summer 1812, Sweden left the Continental System and the peculiar 'war' with Britain was ended.

The two opposite sides of the Swedish experience in the turmoil of 1807–12 are worth mentioning. On the one hand, these years proved that Sweden, in spite of its peripheral location, was not safe from the continental wars. In the extreme post-1807 situation, traditional neutrality policy did not work. On the other hand, the escalation of the British-French conflict at least made Sweden's west coast a huge marketplace for illicit transit traffic, and provided the Swedish merchants with immensely profitable opportunities. It is difficult, if not impossible, to assess the actual impact of these years on Gothenburg's, or even on Sweden's, future economic development. However, at least in terms of the shift of the iron trade away from Britain and to the US, the years of the Continental System were crucial.

There is a striking similarity between the Danish and Swedish experiences of these years, in spite of the fact that Denmark became strongly connected to the

---

[12] Barton 1986, pp. 275–293
[13] Crouzet 1958, p. 427; Tiselius 1935, p. 224.
[14] Crouzet 1958, p. 600.

continental powers. Like Sweden in 1808, Denmark too was confronted with an impossible choice—in the Danish case between Britain and France. Due to a conflict concerning Danish neutrality shipping, Denmark was propelled into war with Britain and forced into the French camp. The consequences were disastrous. First, Copenhagen was bombarded and the Danish fleet seized; second, Denmark proper lost contact with Norway, Iceland and its other colonies because of the British blockade. The loss of Norway to Sweden, in 1814, was one of the consequences of this development.

In conclusion, until the maelstrom of 1806/7, both the Nordic kingdoms employed their neutrality strategy rather successfully. However, the escalation of the war between France and Great Britain no longer left any space for the peripheral smaller powers. In the extreme post-1806 conditions their neutrality strategy did not work. As the historian of the Danish neutrality policy, Ole Feldbæk, has pointed out, in the course of the French Revolutionary and Napoleonic Wars the small powers became relatively weaker and the great powers relatively stronger: the room for an independent international policy shrank. An escalation of the wars also entailed the great powers becoming less concerned with the interests of the small powers, and the legitimate opportunity for neutrality that shaped so much eighteenth-century Danish and Swedish policy disappeared.[15] The successes and failures of eighteenth-century Scandinavian neutrality of course invite to a comparison with the region's twentieth-century neutrality, which also seemed to work rather well until 1939, but did not function so successfully in the extremes of the Second World War and the Cold War.

Unsurprisingly, the Gothenburg merchants had no opportunity to affect developments at international level. But they could exploit the opportunities that the wartime boom provided them with. The rapid adjustment of the economy in western Sweden is visible in the establishment of new processing industries, and in the rise of a new entrepreneurial group in the city. Between 1806 and 1815, three new sugar refineries were established in Gothenburg. The sugar industry, based on imports, became the city's dominant industry, even more important than textiles. The tobacco processing industry also expanded.[16] The rapid expansion of these industries would have been unthinkable without the huge transit trade. In addition, the Gothenburg shipping industry expanded. Whereas, in the 1780s and 1790s, the total tonnage of Gothenburg's merchant fleet increased from about 8,700 lasts to 10,300 lasts, it expanded to over 16,000 lasts in the period 1811–15.[17] Certainly, a significant part of the growth might be explained by changes of flag, as the number of American vessels that 'became' Swedish indicates.

The number of merchants with burgher rights followed the same path. By 1806, there were about 200 merchants in Gothenburg. After a minor increase in 1807–09, the merchant community doubled; by 1813–14 there were about

---

[15] Feldbaek 1980, p. 202.
[16] Andersson 1977b, p. 5.
[17] Andersson 1977a, p. 30.

440 merchants. After the wars, the number of merchants declined, yet stabilised at over 300 merchants in the early 1820s.[18]

The influx of new merchants also changed the character of the Gothenburg merchant community. In addition to the group established by the end of the eighteenth century, a group of new entrepreneurial talents entered the merchant elite after 1800. Many of these men were of foreign origin and for many of them trade contacts with the Americans played a very important role. Alexander Barclay, Joseph and Olof Hall, Olof Wijk and James Dickson belonged to this group.[19]

In particular, Olof Wijk is representative of these men. As we saw in the introduction to chapter 6, he had very good contacts with the American merchants, who used his business as cover during the 1812–14 war. He obtained his burgher rights in 1808, after taking over a firm belonging to James Christie, in which he started his career. An analysis of his firm's accounts from the period reveals remarkable profitability, as well as a very rapid increase in the firm's turnover and accumulation of wealth. In 1808, his business had a turnover of 36,000 *kronor*.[20] In 1809, the turnover of his firm increased to 85,000, and in 1810 to 129,000 *kronor*. After stagnation in 1811 (122,000), it continued to expand, reaching 354,000 *kronor* in 1814. Hence, in a six-year period, the turnover of Wijk's firm increased tenfold. The business was also hugely profitable. The profits were highest in the first two years, with a profitability of 103.4 per cent in 1808, and 84.2 per cent in 1809 (annual profit on his own capital). The profits appear to have been made in the privateering business. In period 1808–09, during the Swedish war with Russia and Denmark, Wijk was engaged in privateering.[21]

The firm's profitability also reached a more than satisfactory 30 per cent in the years 1810–14. In this period, Wijk's business concerned shipping and trade, partly based on American investments. Wijk became a registered shipowner of at least two previously American vessels. During the post-war crisis, the firm's turnover declined, but not by very much, and the firm had begun to rise again by 1818. In 1825, after ten peaceful years, the Wijk enterprise's turnover was about half a million *kronor*. This short summary does not testify only to the extremely profitable years of the Continental System boom, Gothenburg's 'golden age'; it also proves Wijk's capacity to exploit the wartime boom, as well as underlining his skill in adapting to the very different conditions obtaining after the war.[22]

Olof Wijk, in contrast to many other merchants, survived the crisis of 1816–20. One of the reasons why Wijk avoided the bankruptcy that befell so many of his colleagues was his early focus on the American iron trade. Swedish iron

---

[18] Andersson 1977b, pp. 18, 25.
[19] Andersson 1977b, p. 55
[20] Andersson 1977b, p. 60 Andersson's calculation is made in *kronor*. The contemporary accounting currency was however rixdollars.
[21] Clemensson 1978, p. XIV; Tiselius 1935, p. 131.
[22] Andersson 1977b, p. 57.

exports to North America can partly be connected to the 1808–14 boom; as previously noted, iron was the perfect return cargo for vessels arriving with American products.

Alex Barclay is another representative of the group. Barclay was of Scottish origin, but lived in Hamburg for at least five years at the beginning of the century. He left Hamburg after the establishment of the Continental System and settled in Gothenburg. In 1807 he applied for Swedish burgher rights. Due to his international contact network he rapidly built up a large merchant house, specialised in imports of colonial commodities (tobacco, cotton, and sugar). Like Olof Wijk, Barclay managed to survive the post-1815 decline. However, his short-term decline after the 'golden age' was rapid. In the period 1810–12, Barclay was among the highest-taxed merchants in the city, and he declared high annual income rates. In 1816–20 he declared no income at all. But in the beginning of the 1820s, his situation again improved—mainly due to his iron trade—and during the 1820s and 1830s he was among Gothenburg's leading iron merchants.[23]

The pattern of shipping in which the American vessels took cargoes of Swedish bar-iron on their home voyages was already established during the 1790s, long before the Continental System boom. However, no Swedish ships took part in this trade. Boston seems to have been the major destination for these cargoes. Price quotations on 'Swedes iron' from Boston are dated as early as 1792.[24] By 1800 a couple of American ships had already been returning regularly to Gothenburg year after year. The first American merchants with this kind of business with Gothenburg were the Parsons from Boston. Their ship *Peregrine* returned to Gothenburg every year between 1792 and 1807.[25] On the Swedish side, the houses of Martin Holtermans Söner, and Low and Smith were the first suppliers. Both Swedish firms were among the group of old and well-established iron traders. As it became more and more difficult to sell iron on the British market, due to the introduction of Cort's technology, and due to the high British duties, other Swedish merchants also found the American market attractive.

Nevertheless, the export figures for the period before the expansion of 1807 show that the American market was in fact quite insignificant, usually less than 1,000 metric tons per annum. (By the late eighteenth century, Sweden was exporting about 40–50,000 metric tons overall.[26]) The situation changed very quickly after the introduction of the Continental System. As previously mentioned, in 1810 the iron exports from Sweden to the US increased to over 16,000 tons. A comparison between Stockholm and Gothenburg also shows, however, that the North America destination was something especially typical for Gothenburg, and that it resulted from Gothenburg's special situation.

---

[23] Andersson 1977a, pp. 54–55.
[24] Adamson 1969, p. 63.
[25] Adamson 1969, p. 64 (note 13).
[26] Eklund 2001, p. 52; Hildebrand 1957, p. 96.

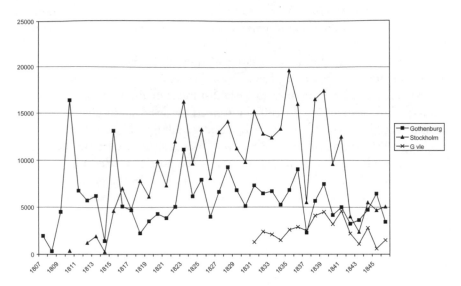

Figure 7.1: Iron exports to the United States, from Gothenburg, Stockholm, and Gävle, 1807–46 (in metric tons)
Source: Adamson 1969, pp. 69, 77–80, and 87 (Appendix G)

Stockholm's share in the iron exports to the US was quite small, and increased only later, as figure 7.1 shows.

It is clear that the development of iron exports to North America differed from the pattern of the Continental System boom. We have seen above that Gothenburg lost its staple market function for American products as soon as the Continental System was abolished. The iron trade declined too, but not at all to the same degree, and it later began to increase again. In the post-1815 period, Stockholm iron exports to North America became much more important than during the Continental System boom. This reorganization in Sweden's iron trade would not have been so easy, and perhaps not even possible, without the channels and networks established during the wars and especially in the 'golden age' of the Continental System boom.

Tables 7.1 and 7.2 provide a clear picture of Gothenburg's and Sweden's inward and outward commodity flows. However, they do not say anything about the complicated interplay between American and Swedish actors. The adaptations to rapid political changes, and often the employment of illegal or semi-illegal practices, would not have been possible without mutual trust and close co-operation. The examples of the American vessels that changed 'owner' and flag after July 1812 testify to this trust and co-operation. Olof Wijk, who became the registered owner of several such vessels, undertook the transaction in partnership with three New England merchants.

The firm of Joseph and Olof Hall provides an even more enlightening example. The brothers established their firm in June 1813, in the middle of the

208

Anglo-American War. American merchants immediately placed the huge sum of £20,000 at the firm's disposal. Such an investment strategy presupposed, of course, that the war would continue for some time.[27] With the help of the American money, the Hall family firm's trade rapidly expanded. In 1815, it was among the biggest Gothenburg iron exporters.

However, the American investment in the Hall firm was made possible by the extensive relations with Americans that the Hall family was busily building up long before the firm of Joseph and Olof Hall was established. Joseph Hall travelled to North America as early as 1807, and he became a supercargo on American ships sailing between the USA, the West Indies and Europe. In 1812, he was working as the Gothenburg agent of William Gray, a leading Boston merchant. Gray's business did not only concern the Swedish-American trade. In 1812 Gray even attempted, with the help of Joseph Hall, to charter a Swedish vessel for a voyage to Argentina to purchase a cargo of hides.[28] Despite the influx of American money, the Hall firm did not manage to adapt to the economic decline after 1815. In 1816 it suffered a spectacular bankruptcy, one of the bigger in the history of Gothenburg.

The Hall firm's debts show how closely it was linked to its British and American partners. About half of the firm's debts were placed in Britain, particularly at the firm of Bainbridge and Brown in London, and one-sixth (94,700 of 650,800 rixdollars) was owed to William Gray in Boston.[29]

The number of bankruptcies in the 1816–20 period indicates the depth of the post-1815 crisis. In only five years (1816–20), 551 firms went bankrupt. This figure represented one-half of all bankruptcies between 1751 and 1820 (1,133 in total).[30] This is, of course, very good evidence for the fragility of the economy during the Continental System period.

Even if Gothenburg's role as a gateway for colonial and American products to the continent between 1807 and 1815 period was short-lived, the bubble economy of the Continental System left some lasting impressions. From the Swedish-American point of view, the most important consequence was the establishment of the Swedish iron market in the US. American shipmasters learned to load a cargo of iron on their return voyages, and consumers on the other side of the Atlantic became accustomed to the varieties of Swedish bar-iron. This exchange would not have been possible without the establishment of Swedish-American business networks. And these transatlantic networks continued to play an important role in Swedish-American trade relations long after 1815, and even after the decline of the Swedish iron trade with the United States by 1840.

---

[27] Adamson 1969, p. 72.
[28] Adamson 1969, pp. 71–72; Andersson 1996, p. 254; see also *SBL* vol. 17, p. 782 Joseph Hall Junior (1787–1845).
[29] Andersson 1996, pp. 253–254; see also Adamson 1966.
[30] Andersson 1996, p. 251.

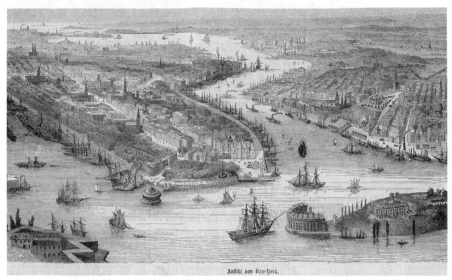

15. A view of New York (undated, beginning of the nineteenth century) (UUL)

7.3 Swedish consuls to the United States, 1800–15

The spectacular growth in Swedish-American trade after 1806 was partly a consequence of Sweden's peripheral location, partly a result of Gustav IV's anti-French policy, as described above. However, the ambitious trade policy of the early 1780s, described in chapter 6, played no significant role in the development. This is among the reasons why it has left relatively few traces in the reports of Swedish consuls to the United States. This section will look at these reports in the post-1800 period. In particular, we have reports from two consuls, Richard Söderström from Philadelphia and Henrik Gahn from New York. Unfortunately, there are no reports preserved from Boston, the second most important US destination. Between 1799 and 1809, there is an inexplicable gap in the reporting of both consuls. This might be a consequence of the insecurity of the Atlantic traffic. The reports frequently mention that every letter was sent to Stockholm in a number of copies via different routes, to make its delivery as secure as possible—the best evidence of the insecurity in the traffic between the US and Sweden. (For example, Söderström sent his letters via Portugal.) Another reason for the reporting lapse might, however, be lack of interest. Indeed, Gahn mentioned the lack of interest on the Swedish side in his reports of 1809.

Richard Söderström, the pioneer of Swedish-American trade since the early 1780s, also continued to carry out his consular duties until his death in 1815. His 1810–14 reports confirm, more or less, the established pattern of Swedish-flagged tramp shipping in the southern parts of the United States. There were few 'proper' (i.e. other than St. Barthélemy-registered) Swedish vessels arriving in southern US ports. And the Swedish-flagged vessels frequently changed flag. As Söderström admitted:

> [...] the vessels that arrived today under the Swedish trading flag show the American flag tomorrow [...] [they] go from here under the American flag, and in 5 or 6 weeks arrive once again from some port under the Swedish flag.[31]

In 1813 there were some 'proper' Swedish vessels calling at Charleston. But these vessels were also employed in tramp shipping, chartered for voyages between foreign ports. For example, on 24 January 1813, the brig *Anna* arrived in Charleston from Cadiz with a cargo of Spanish salt; in March 1813, the ship *Providentia* arrived in Charleston carrying ballast from London.[32] However, the Swedish shipping in the area was much more limited than that on the northern US coast. As Södertröm mentions, this was partly due to the British blockade of the southern coast. The northern ports, Boston and New York, were on the other hand free, and provided opportunities for profitable tramp shipping.

There are only a few of Söderström's reports from the time of the Anglo-American war. It appears that he was too weak to continue in his duties. The first Swedish consul to the United States, and one of the first merchants to open commercial contacts between the new republic and Sweden, died in April 1815 in Philadelphia, after a thirty-five year long career in America.

If Söderström's reports from the war years are rather scarce, another Swedish consul, Henrik Gahn, left a rich and detailed collection of reports for the years after 1809. Gahn settled in New York as early as 1792, establishing the firm Gahn and Mumford, as his application for the consulate there informs us.[33] Six years later, he was appointed Swedish vice-consul to New York, and in 1799 he applied to the Board of Trade for a consulate in New York.[34] Formally, his appointment in November 1799 also established Sweden's consulate in New York. However, Gahn's first New York reports, preserved in the archives of the Board of Trade, are from 1809.

His letters of 1809 mainly deal with the conditions of US foreign trade. He noted the worsening of relations between the United States and Great Britain, a consequence of the Non-Intercourse Law, which prohibited American trade with belligerent countries. The law made Swedish carrying capacity and commodities desirable in the American ports. In particular, St. Barthélemy benefited, as the American vessels were allowed to unload their cargoes there.[35]

In a letter of May 1810, Gahn wrote about the abolition of the Non-Intercourse and Embargo Laws, and indicated what consequences the new situation might have for Swedish trade, and for Sweden.

---

[31] Söderström to BoT, 28 April 1810, Consular Reports, Philadelphia EVI aa 374, BoT SNA.
[32] Söderstöm to BoT, 5 April 1813, Consular Reports, Philadelphia EVI aa 374, BoT SNA.
[33] Runeby 1969, pp. 76–79.
[34] Gahn to BoT, Undated application (the date of the arrival to BoT, 20 July 1799) Consular Reports, New York, E VI aa 352, BoT SNA. See also Runeby 1969, p. 76.
[35] Gahn to BoT, 25 November 1809, Consular Reports, New York, E VI aa 352, BoT SNA.

The [American] trade should be strong with Great Britain and its dependent countries, but I have reason to hope that Gothenburg and other Swedish ports shall enjoy an important if not the most important advantage in this American transit trade with the European Continent; hence, because of the latest news from other than the Swedish, Russian, and Prussian areas of the same Continent, people here are not very inclined to send any expeditions to Europe, without first calling at some Swedish port for intelligence. It is seen as dangerous to arrive, according to previous habit, at an English port with ships and cargoes destined for the continent, because at present this is reason enough for being declared a prize. People here doubt Sweden's capacity to keep her independence in the transit trade for a longer period than the other countries closer to France, but this is still the case.[36]

Gahn's picture confirms the view that 'proper' Swedish vessels had little to offer in direct Swedish-American traffic. Instead he hoped that Americans would exploit Sweden's peripheral location and neutrality in the transit trade with the continent, which is exactly what happened. Moreover, there was the opportunity to employ St. Barthélemy for shipping between the West Indies and the US. In his capacity as the Swedish consul, Gahn issued documents for the vessels purchased by Swedish subjects and, due to the war, the years 1812 and 1813 were especially dynamic. Between July and October 1812 alone, the consul issued Swedish documents for at least ten vessels, all but one acquired by the 'Swedes' from St. Barthélemy.[37]

Another consequence of the Anglo-American conflict was the rising number of proper Swedish vessels in American ports. In August 1812, the Swedish ship *Prudentia* arrived in New York. Gahn noted that this was the first 'proper' Swedish craft to arrive in New York for many years. The purpose of the voyage was a charter to Europe. The ship had arrived in ballast and it was consigned to the house of George and John Laurie, which offered it for charter to Europe. However, instead of being chartered, *Prudentia* was sold to a St. Barthélemy merchant, R. Hansenstere, in September 1812. [38]

In 1813, in the first three months alone, nine Swedish vessels arrived in New York. Not surprisingly, six of them were registered at Gothenburg. The majority of the vessels obtained cargo for St. Barthélemy or for Portugal (Lisbon and Porto). Only one of the nine mentioned vessels, *Gustaf Adolph* from Norrköping, was bound for Stockholm, with tobacco and colonial products.

The British were not unaware of the fact that St. Barthélemy had no production of its own, and thus all St. Barthélemy cargoes were re-exports from surrounding islands. And all the islands around the Swedish colony were at that moment under British control.[39] After the peace treaty between the United States and Britain (December 1814), many Swedish shipowners saw their opportunity in North America. Gahn's records mentioned at least thirty Swedish-

---

[36] Gahn to BoT, 7 May 1810, Consular Reports, New York, E VI aa 352, BoT SNA.
[37] Gahn to BoT, 26 August 1812, Consular Reports, New York, E VI aa 352, BoT SNA.
[38] Gahn to BoT, 26 August 1812, Consular Reports, New York, E VI aa 352, BoT SNA.
[39] Gahn to BoT, 8 March 1813, Consular Reports, New York, E VI aa 352, BoT SNA.

flagged vessels, which arrived in New York in 1815; six of them were still from St. Barthélemy, and nine arrived directly from the Iberian Peninsula, typically with non-Swedish cargoes (salt). But there were also six vessels loaded with iron, direct from Gothenburg, Stockholm, and Gävle. The number of vessels loaded with iron might have been even higher, as Gahn's data only covered some vessels. On the other hand, it should be noted that, in 1815, the total number of vessels was highly exceptional (Appendix H).

In addition to the activities of the Swedish arrivals in New York, Gahn's reports also included some data from other ports on the east coast. Not surprisingly, Boston appears to have been the second most frequented harbour, with eleven arrivals. *Redligheten*, based in Gävle, shipowner Per Brandström, arrived with 250 American prisoners of war on board. Vice-consul Kimball from Savannah reported on five arrivals of Swedish-flagged vessels. One of them, the schooner *Hannibal*, was sailing to St. Barthélemy 'with flour and slaves'. This cargo shows that in 1815 Sweden was still indirectly participating in the slave trade. But in 1814, as an element of the Vienna treaties, Sweden had in fact signed an international treaty forbidding this kind of trade.[40]

The year 1815 was also a high point for Swedish shipping in the period. The decline after the wars was rapid. As early as October 1815 Gahn expressed worries about the difficulty in finding proper return cargoes. Between January and September 1816, only five Swedish vessels called at New York; there were none between September 1816 and January 1817, and only two in the first half of 1817.[41] The situation was the same in the other American ports. It is evident that the disappearance of Swedish shipping after 1815 was just another aspect of the 1816–20 crisis in Sweden. Gahn's later reports, dated 1818 and 1819, did not concern themselves much with business conditions; perhaps there was not much to report. Instead, his focus was on the yellow fever in New York, in September and October 1819.

Gahn's correspondence shows that the number of Swedish vessels calling at New York in 1815 was exceptionally high. Nevertheless, the account of the shipping in that year, indicates two clearly discernible patterns. On the one hand, there was the traditional pattern, established by the late eighteenth century, with Swedish vessels chartered for the triangular trade between the Iberian Peninsula (Lisbon, Cadiz), the West Indies (mainly St. Barthélemy) and the American coast. In 1815, this pattern still appears to have been dominant. In parallel, we may trace a new pattern of direct trade and shipping of iron between Sweden and the United States, with iron as the major commodity— marking out the future of Swedish-American trade.

---

[40] The declaration concerning the slave trade's abolition was signed on 30 May 1814, by the powers represented at the Congress of Vienna. *Sveriges och Norges traktater*, vol. 10, 1815–1845, pp. 1–3.

[41] Gahn to BoT, 8 January 1817, 11 and 18 June 1817, Consular Reports, New York, E VI aa 352, BoT SNA.

7.4 A postscript: Swedish-American trade in the 1815–40 period

The picture presented here of Swedish-American trade in the period 1800–15 reveals a discrepancy between Swedish-flagged tramp shipping on the one hand, and the pattern of the iron trade with the US on the other. Swedish tramp shipping was mainly built on the traditional triangular trade, with vessels travelling between the Mediterranean and the large western European ports, the West Indies (St. Barthélemy), and the US. This business exploited Swedish neutrality shipping in a satisfying and fruitful way. The trade in Swedish iron destined for the US markets had its origins in the American trade with the continent in the Continental System period. This trade was conducted through direct contacts between Sweden's west coast and the US, and the iron was carried on American bottoms.

Whereas tramp shipping declined in the post-1815 period, iron exports to the United States survived and soon began to grow again. In the 1820s and 1830s, they reached between 10,000 and 20,000 metric tons annually, which made Sweden the United States' leading iron supplier; whereas Russia, which had dominated the iron trade before 1807, only accounted for between one-third and one-fourth of the Swedish volumes. In two decades, the United States replaced Great Britain as Sweden's most important trading partner.

The Swedish historian Rolf Adamson has investigated which firms participated in this trade. His data for Gothenburg indicate that, in the post-1815 period, the major part of the trade with North America was managed by three or four houses. These were Alex Barclay, James Dickson and Co., A.P. Fröding's Widow and Co., and Olof Wijk. All of them established their American contacts as early as the Continental System boom era, or even before, and the iron trade with the United States was their core business.

In the 1820s and 1830s, many Swedish dealers in iron visited the US and strengthened their personal contacts with American partners. (These Swedes included Christian Ungewitter, J.P. Fröding, L.G. Morsing, Olof Wijk.)[42]. Of course, they also travelled and observed developments in the American iron industry and trade. Olof Wijk has left a detailed diary of his US journey from the years 1829–30, which reveals the density of the social contacts between the Swedish, American and British merchant families. On his journey, Wijk met many Americans whom he knew from the Continental System period. Yet the diary also testifies to Wijk's interest in the American iron industry.[43]

In 1832, another representative of the Swedish merchant elite visited North America. Carl David Arfwedson, a member of the influential Arfwedson family, represented the leading Stockholm iron firm of Tottie and Arfwedson in the US, the grandam of the Swedish iron trade which had dominated the business

---

[42] *Swedish Passenger Arrivals*, 1995.
[43] Clemensson 1978. The diary is frequently referring to relationships with the people Olof Wijk met. See also Runeby 1969, p. 67.

since the mid-eighteenth century.[44] Arfwedson also left a detailed account of his travels in the US and Canada, which he published after his return to Sweden. Moreover, Arfwedson married a daughter to an American partner, and after his return to Stockholm he was appointed the US consul there, on the recommendation of his many friends and relatives in America.[45] This connection shows the importance of the American market for the firm of Tottie and Arfwedson. However, despite these important American contacts, the major part of Tottie and Arfwedson's iron was still destined for Britain.[46]

The other large iron firm in Stockholm, Kantzow and Biel, was even more dependent on the American market. This firm invested heavily in transatlantic trade, and not only in the iron trade with the United States. After 1800, the firm was also one of the first to be engaged in trade with South America and the East Indies. The position of Johan Albert Kantzow, the Lisbon consul in the 1780s and 1790s, the first Swedish diplomatic representative to Brazil, and, after 1812, the first Swedish envoy to the US, certainly played an important role in Kantzow and Biel's geographical orientation.[47] Perhaps Kantzow and Biel's dependency on the American markets was also the reason for the firm's bankruptcy in 1847, when Swedish iron exports to North America declined.[48]

Shipping on American bottoms continued to dominate the Swedish-American exchange in the 1820s. A high proportion of iron cargoes was also purchased directly by American shipowners, which reminds one of the custom of taking iron as ballast. In the early 1830s, the pattern of shipping changed. The volume of iron carried on Swedish ships increased almost tenfold, from 452 metric tons to 4,211 metric tons between 1830 and 1833.[49] The change of the trade pattern in the early 1830s is also apparent when we look more closely at the relations between Stockholm's Kantzow and Biel, and the New York firm of Boorman, Johnson and Co., the most important dealers in Swedish iron in the city. In the 1820s, the New York firm was still chartering American ships for iron transports and shipping was undetaken at the firm's risk. But during the 1830s, cargoes of iron were sent to New York in the Swedish supplier's vessels and at Swedish risk. In the 1840s, Boorman, Johnson and Co. effectively monopolised Swedish iron exports to America.[50]

The picture of Swedish-American trade relations in the 1820s and 1830s, as described above, is largely confirmed in the consular reports from the United States. The following account is based on the New York reports, which re-

---

[44] In 1800–20, Tottie and Arfwedson exported between 6,000 and 7,000 metric tons annually and by the late 1830s as much as 10,000 metric tons, about one fourth of all Stockholm iron, see Adamson 1966, Appendix, p. 5 (table C); Attman 1958, p. 71.
[45] Runeby 1969, pp. 69–75; Arfwedson 1834 (1969).
[46] Adamson 1969, p. 77.
[47] Adamson 1969, p. 77; Adamson 1966, Appendix, p. 5.
[48] *SBL* vol. 20, pp. 612–613, The entry on Kantzow mentions the bankruptcy of the London house Lysaght, Smith and Co., as the reason of Kantzow's bankrupty.
[49] Adamson 1969, p. 83.
[50] Adamson 1969, pp. 92–93.

mained high in terms of both frequency and quality, in comparison with other Swedish consulates in the US.

In the 1820s, as has been pointed out, the major part of the Swedish iron to reach North America arrived on American vessels. Therefore there was not much to report in terms of Swedish-flagged shipping. In New York, Swedish-flagged vessels seldom appeared, and the situation was not different in other districts.[51] Yet there were some Swedish vessels regularly returning to New York. One of them was *Commercen* from Stockholm. It is mentioned in September 1819, and once again in July 1823, this time with a specified cargo of 2,250 ship pounds of iron, the consignee being the New York firm of Boorman and Johnson. *Commercen* arrived in New York once again in July 1824.[52]

The majority of Swedish vessels appear to have come directly from Sweden with cargoes of iron (vessels from Gävle, Stockholm, Norrköping and Gothenburg). Some of them returned to Sweden, some others were chartered for voyages to European ports, and even to Latin America. For example, the brig *Johan Albert* arrived in 1825 with a cargo of iron, and continued on to Brazil. The same vessel also returned regularly. It was back in January 1827, left in March 1827, and promptly returned again in October of the same year. It called in America once again in July 1828.[53] The owners of *Johan Albert* were the house of Kantzow and Biel; the vessel was surely named after Johan Albert Kantzow Sr. The shipping lists of the Swedish consul in Rio de Janeiro bear witness to the extensive Swedish traffic in Brazil.[54]

Sweden's rising interest in the new republics in South America is also exemplified by the affair of two Swedish warships, ship-of-the-line *Tapperheten* and the frigate *Af Chapman*, that took up much consular attention in 1826 and 1827.[55] Colombia and Mexico negotiated with Sweden regarding the purchase of five warships, which were intended to be used in the struggle with Spain. The affair became a major political issue, especially in the relationship with Russia, which supported Spain. Under Russian threat, the negotiations with the new republics were stopped and three of the ships were returned to the navy. But *Tapperheten* and *Af Chapman* were already in Colombia when the purchase was terminated. The affair was managed, on the Swedish side, by the

---

[51] There are some preserved shipping lists (1821 and 1823) made by Severin Lorich, Swedish consul in Philadelphia 1818–1834, for other American ports Philadelphia, Boston Baltimore. But the number of ships mentioned does not challenge the picture provided in Gahn's much more detailed and exact reports for New York. Consular shipping lists, vols. 1817, 1821–23, BoT (*Kammarkontoret*), SNA. On Lorich see Almqvist 1912–13, p. 348.

[52] Gahn to BoT, 7 September 1819, 31 July 1823, 31 July 1824, Consular Reports, New York, E VI aa 352, BoT SNA.

[53] Gahn to BoT, 8 November 1825, 16 March 1827, 1 October 1827, 24 July 1828, Consular Reports, New York, E VI aa 352, BoT SNA.

[54] Consular shipping lists from Rio de Janeiro, by the Swedish consul Westin, vols. 1809–19, 1820, 1821, BoT (Kammarkontoret), SNA.

[55] On the affair see Swärd 1949; Hildebrand 1950, pp. 407–421; *Amiralitetskollegiets historia* 1977, pp. 67–72; Glete 1993a, pp. 225–226.

Stockholm house of Michaelson and Benedics, who are also mentioned as the shipowners in Gahn's reports.

In March 1726, the vessels left Cartagena in Colombia, and it was decided to send them to New York. However, the shipowners Michaelson and Benedics failed—according to the consul—to find any acceptable proposals as to the vessels and their crews. When the vessels anchored in New York, the issue was simply handed over to the Swedish consul. The stay at New York caused considerable outlays for the vessels and their crews, and as the shipowners did not show any interest in the vessels, the District Court in New York decided to sell them publicly and to cover the outlays from the proceeds. In September 1826, *Tapperheten* and *Af Chapman* were sold at public auction, the former for $30,500 and latter for $33,500.[56]

In summary, Gahn's reports show that the number of Swedish ships calling at New York in the 1820s was negligible. The Swedes were almost excluded from the direct trade between Sweden and the United States, but the Swedish situation was not exceptional. To illustrate the American dominance in shipping, we may quote the data on the total number of clearings in the harbour of New York, which Gahn sent to Stockholm. In all there were 1,429 vessels cleared in New York in 1825; 1,325 of them (93 per cent) were American. There were 61 British vessels. Other nations cleared were: Dutch 10 vessels, Colombians 8, Bremen 7, Danes 5, Swedes 5, French 4, and Hamburg 4.[57]

The American dominance in shipping to and from North America reflected American protectionist policy, a frequent subject of the consul's reports. For example, in December 1824, Gahn noted that American vessels had a more privileged position in Sweden than Swedish ones in the US.[58] In January 1826, he reported on the Congress negotiations that dealt with import rules and which, as Gahn stated, were beneficial to the American vessels.[59] Yet the new trade treaties between Sweden-Norway and the United States, the first from 1816 and the second from 1827, had agreed on reciprocity in the direct Swedish-American trade.[60] Consequently, American protectionism primarily concerned import duties, not shipping.

In the early 1830s, the situation of Swedish shipping notably changed. In 1829, Gahn still noted only 11 Swedish-flagged vessels calling in New York[61]; in 1830, there were 10, one of them, *Gustavia*, from St. Barthélemy[62]; and the reports from 1831 mentioned 13 Swedish ships calling in New York.[63] In 1832,

---

[56] Gahn to BoT, 16 and 24 August, 8 and 26 September 1826, Consular Reports, New York, E VI aa 352, BoT SNA.

[57] Gahn to BoT, an undated cutting in the letter of 31 January 1826,. Consular Reports, New York, E VI aa 352, BoT SNA.

[58] Gahn to BoT, 11 December 1824, Consular Reports, New York, E VI aa 352, BoT SNA.

[59] Gahn to BoT, 16 January 1826 Consular Reports, New York, E VI aa 352, BoT SNA.

[60] Friendship and Trade Treaty with the United States, 4 September 1816, Stockholm, and Trade and Shipping Treaty with the United States, 4 July 1827, Stockholm, *Sveriges och Norges traktater med främmande magter.* vol. 10, 1896, pp. 107–115, 350–360. See Fredrickson 1956, pp. 112–113.

[61] Gahn to BoT, 29 March 1830, Consular Reports, New York, E VI aa 353, BoT SNA.

the number of Swedish clearings jumped to 22. The increasing activity of Swedish ships also entailed two shipwrecks: *Amphitrite* and *Christine Louise*.[64]

In 1833, the number of Swedish vessels almost doubled. In his summary of the year 1833's shipping activities, Gahn noted that 39 Swedish-flagged vessels cleared in New York, and as many as 28 of them came directly from Sweden with cargoes of iron, only 11 arriving via foreign ports.[65] In the years 1829–33, the number of Swedish vessels arriving in New York quadrupled. But this time, there was no neutrality boom; instead, the Swedish iron exporters were carrying their iron at their own risk.

The organization of the iron trade changed. Swedish suppliers sent iron to a very limited number of American dealers, and the iron was carried on the consignors' (meaning Swedish) vessels. Suitably, the Swedish iron merchants were also big shipowners. On the American side, the trade in iron accumulated in the hands of a few firms. The aforementioned case of Boorman and Johnson is illuminating. In the 1830s and 1840s, the firm reached a near monopoly on sales of Swedish iron in New York.[66]

In his reports, naturally, Gahn paid a good deal of his attention to iron. He noted and commented on any important changes in prices, as well as developments in the American market.[67] He also reported on the development of the American iron industry and the political debates concerning the industry's protection and duties on iron imports. For example, in August 1830 he sent a report on conditions in the American iron industry to the Board of Trade.[68]

The West Indian shipping, so important before 1815, more or less disappeared from the correspondence. Instead, Gahn frequently reported on US relations with the new South-American republics and their former mother country, Spain.[69] Another issue which his reports frequently commented on was the health situation. It is apparent that knowledge of contagious diseases or unhealthy conditions in ports might well have affected shipowners' decisions regarding destinations. Gahn might also be seen as the first intermediary of the scientific exchange between the USA and Sweden. For example, as early as 1825, he helped established contact between one Professor Silliman of New

[62] Gahn to BoT, 8 December 1829–16 December 1830, Consular Reports, New York, E VI aa 353, BoT SNA.

[63] Gahn to BoT, letters 8 January 1831–1 January 1832, Consular Reports, New York, E VI aa 353, BoT SNA.

[64] Gahn to BoT, 1 January, 1832–8 December, 1832, Consular Reports, New York, E VI aa 353, BoT SNA.

[65] Gahn to BoT, 1 January 1834, Consular Reports, New York, E VI aa 353, BoT SNA.

[66] Adamson 1969, p. 92.

[67] Gahn to BoT, 16 August 1827, 8 February 1831, Consular Reports, New York, E VI aa 353, BoT SNA.

[68] Gahn to BoT, 9 August 1830, on the duties 16 February 1833, 1 February 1830, Consular Reports, New York, E VI aa 353, BoT SNA.

[69] See e.g. his report on US relations with Mexico and new South-American republics. Gahn to BoT, 1 September 1825, Consular Reports, New York, E VI aa 353, BoT SNA.

16. New-York Price-Current, December 9, 1809 (Henrik Gahn's reports, BoT SNA)

Haven and Jacob Berzelius, renowned Swedish chemist and Secretary of the Swedish Academy of Sciences.[70]

Gahn's reports also included numerous newspaper cuttings, price notices, copies of US laws and duty regulations, trade statistics, and similar documents. Clearly, the volume of business information that reached Sweden in this way was impressive, but it is difficult to ascertain if and how it was employed. In spite of the fact that Gahn does not appear to have actively participated in the Swedish-American trade, his reports give us a detail-rich picture of the changing conditions in this trade.

Gahn's correspondence clearly shows that, after 1815, the period of Swedish neutrality shipping was over. The Swedish-flagged traffic from St. Barthélemy disappeared, as well as the Swedish tramp shipping between Europe, the West Indies, and North America. On the other hand, the Swedish iron exports to the

---

[70] In May 1833, Gahn reported on the exchange of scientific articles between the Swedish Academy of Sciences and Philadelphia, Boston and New Haven, see Gahn to BoT, 19 March 1825, 19 May 1830, and 10 May 1832, Consular Reports, New York, E VI aa 353, BoT SNA.

US adjusted to the new situation in the post-1815 period. This trade was primarily based on free American capacity on return routes; the Swedes had no advantage of neutrality in this business. However, by 1830 the situation had changed again and the number of Swedish vessels engaged in direct Swedish-American trade increased. Hence in the mid-1830s, another shift in the shipping pattern between the US and Sweden was completed. At that time, according to contemporary estimates, the Swedish tonnage clearing in New York alone reached 9,800 tons: 4,200 from Gothenburg, 3,300 from Stockholm, and as much as 2,300 from Gävle. Boston, the second American port, cleared 6,100 tons of Swedish tonnage: 4,900 from Gothenburg and 1,200 from Stockholm.[71] The United States also became, not only an important buyer of Swedish iron, but also a significant destination for Swedish tonnage. The Swedish vessels returning to Europe often went to non-Swedish destinations.

The shift in the shipping pattern had a number of reasons. Mainly, it reflected technological changes in the English and American iron industries. English rolled iron became cheaper and its exports to the US rapidly expanded.[72] In addition, by the late 1830s, the British puddling and rolling technology had been introduced in the US and, accordingly, the market for ordinary Swedish bar-iron diminished.

Swedish iron merchants were very much aware of the worsening situation. To evaluate it and perhaps to find ways to retain the American market, the Swedish Association of Ironmasters (*Jernkontoret*) sent the metallurgist E.G. Danielsson to the United States. His report published in Sweden, in 1845, provides a fascinating picture of the United States, especially compared to the first Swedish report on the United States by Samuel Hermelin 60 years before. He presents the United States as a country going through the process of industrialisation, and so transforming from a primarily coast-bound, export-dependent, and maritime economy into a continental economy with a vast domestic market, and a very different transport situation. According to Danielsson, Swedish iron exports to the United States were fated to meet same end as the exports to Great Britain four decades earlier.[73]

In fact, the decline of Swedish iron exports to the United States was not so dramatic as Danielsson predicted. The United States continued, even in the 1850s and 1860s, to import quantities of Swedish iron, but an increasing share of Swedish iron went once again to Britain. The exceptional position that the United States had had in the Swedish iron trade in the 1820s and 1830s was gone.[74] The transformation among Gothenburg's leading iron exporters illuminates the depth of the change. Olof Wijk more or less left the American market and, after 1842, focused his interest on the trade with the East Indies. Alex Barclay and Co. moved from iron to cotton spinning. James Dickson moved to

[71] Adamson 1969, p. 86.
[72] Adamson 1969, p. 95.
[73] Danielsson 1845.
[74] Adamson 1969, pp. 102–113; see also Attman 1958, p. 158.

17. United States' Shipping List and Prices Current, October 16, 1812 (Henrik Gahn's reports, New York, BoT SNA)

timber exports and sawmills. David Carnegie, the fourth of the large Gothenburg iron merchants, diversified into the sugar-refining and brewing industries.[75] Typical for all of them was their continuing interest in the Atlantic economy: either they based their business on imports of typical colonial products (sugar, tobacco, cotton), or went into the expanding timber trade with Britain.

7.5 Conclusions

In 1800–31, the total numbers of Algerian passports issued for Swedish and Norwegian ships varied between 400 and 500 annually (see figure 5.2). The number of registered Swedish ships in international shipping hovered around a thousand (see table 5.5). If we consider these numbers as representative for Swedish long-distance shipping, we have to conclude that the volume employed in the shipping to North America was rather insignificant. With the exception of the year 1815 the annual numbers of Swedish ships in the US seldom exceeded ten.

The situation improved remarkably in the early 1830s, when Swedish iron merchants had to adapt to new conditions in the American iron trade and carry their iron on their own ships. Yet the increase in Swedish shipping to the US in the early 1830s was an adjustment to the new conditions of Swedish iron exports to the US. It had nothing to do with Sweden's protection of shipping or with Sweden's neutrality. In fact, Sweden's protectionist policy had been abolished in a series of trade treaties after 1815. The treaties, as for example the Swedish-American treaties of 1816 and 1827, mutually guaranteed the same rights to foreign and domestic ships, which in practice nullified the Navigation Act.[76]

But, with the decline of the British market by 1800, the transatlantic connection established in the years 1807–15 had a crucial role for the survival and adaptation of the Swedish iron industry. The United States was also important as a market for iron.

Chapter 6 has highlighted the Swedish engagement in the West Indies and North America—a result of a conscious and ambitious policy that, in fact, rested on Sweden's previous experience of neutrality. For example, the plans for turning St. Barthélemy into a neutral entrepôt followed this reasoning very clearly. And, after 1793, the strategy also worked as planned; there was an increasing volume of Swedish shipping, and St. Barthélemy became a free staple point for merchants from belligerent countries. Nevertheless, Sweden itself never became a major player in this trade.

Instead, the main neutrality profits were made in Sweden proper. After

---

[75] Adamson 1969, p. 102.
[76] Heckscher 1940, p. 21.

1807, Sweden became the only neutral country outside the Continental System, and Gothenburg, a port with access to the Atlantic, became a significant loophole in the Continental System. Vast volumes of colonial and American products were channelled to the continent via Sweden. However, there is a significant difference between Sweden's employment of neutrality in the late eighteenth century (1756–63, 1776–83, and 1793–1800) and the employment of neutrality after 1807. In the late eighteenth century, Sweden employed its neutrality primarily in tramp shipping, especially in southern Europe, and between Europe and North America. This was the pattern of shipping revealed so clearly in the Algerian passport data. The employment of neutrality in the years 1807–15 was based on Sweden's peripheral location, i.e. on the fact that western Sweden could be used for illicit transit trade to the continent. But in the extreme situation of the Napoleonic Wars, the opportunity for exploiting neutrality became rather limited. Small powers (such as Denmark, Sweden, and the Dutch Republic), that had successfully managed to exploit their neutrality in the late eighteenth century, found their freedom of action more and more circumscribed. The escalation of the wars left almost no space for neutrals—with the exception of the United States. The French Revolutionary and Napoleonic Wars strengthened the trend in which small powers became smaller, with more and more limited opportunities to act freely, whereas the great powers became greater. The deteriorating international situation of Denmark and Sweden was marked by their territorial losses.

The post-1815 world was very different. In the late eighteenth century, the economy of Swedish shipping rested very much on the advantages of Sweden's low protection costs (protectionist policy, treaties with the Barbary states, consular service, convoying system, and neutrality). These factors lost much of their importance on the seas dominated by the *Pax Britannica*, and in a world in which the conflict-frequency between the great powers declined and changed character. The Danish and Swedish shipowners had to adjust to new conditions. They became less interested in southern Europe, but more interested in the Baltic, transatlantic shipping, and trade with Britain. The growth of Swedish shipping to the US, in the early 1830s, is a good example of this adjustment.[77]

---

[77] On the Danish post-Napoleonic experience, see Johansen 1990, pp. 25–26.

CHAPTER 8
Conclusion

As this ongoing war creates favourable conditions for neutral Nations' flags, it does not harm our shipping and trade, and it is desirable to profit from it as much as possible.

Hans Jacob Gahn to the Swedish Board of Trade, Cadiz 17 February 1779 [1]

The purpose of this book was to study the role of the consular service in eighteenth-century Swedish trade and shipping. The Swedish consular service has been perceived as a typical tool in Sweden's active economic policy of that period, and—from the neo-institutional perspective—as an example of institutional modernisation. The consular service reduced, in one way or another, the transaction costs of Swedish actors.

First, consuls acquired information on business and political conditions in their districts, and they forwarded this information to the Board of Trade in Stockholm, thus reducing information costs for Swedish economic actors. This aspect of the consular service has not received much attention in this study, partly, due to the difficulty of evaluating the use of the available information, but is is clear that the volume and quality of the information that reached Stockholm was significant.

Second, consuls often acted as commission agents of Swedish merchants, and even as their legal representatives in local courts. In this way, they diminished the costs of making and enforcement contracts and of defending the actors' property rights. It is clear that this, in particular, was an important function in the Mediterranean and the Iberian Peninsula—distant areas in which Swedish actors lacked established social networks. The function was less important for Swedish consulates in Britain, the Dutch Republic, and the Baltic area, where Swedish trade followed early-established patterns.

Thirdly, the consular service reduced the protection costs of Swedish actors.

---

[1] Gahn to BoT, 17 February 1779, Cadiz, Consular Reports, Cadiz 1719–1802, E VI aa:67, BoT SNA.

In particular, this function was important in areas where such costs were relatively high, such as in southern Europe. The Swedish consular service in North Africa was established for exactly this task.

It is clear that the consular service had an effect on Sweden's overall transaction costs in trade, but it is very difficult to measure that effect. In addition, the service itself was not free; on the one hand, it reduced some direct transaction costs, on the other hand, it also caused new, indirect costs. Merchants and shipowners had to pay *consulade* fees and duties to the Convoy Office, which ultimately financed the convoying and consular services in North Africa. Sweden's policy relating to shipping (including the Navigation Act) had, in the course of the whole century, been a frequent subject of criticism and disapproval. Nevertheless, the major institutions of the policy survived until the beginning of the nineteenth century, which may be seen as some proof of their efficiency.

The concept of transaction costs is rather abstract; therefore the major focus in this study was on one specific component of transaction costs, namely the protection costs of Swedish shipping in southern Europe. A starting point of the analysis of shipping was the hypothesis that the protection costs of Swedish shipping were *comparatively* lower than the protection costs of other shipping nations, and that this was a major factor in the growth of Swedish shipping in southern Europe. In contrast to the established view, the present writer has highlighted the significance of Swedish tramp shipping in the Mediterranean. This was as important, perhaps even more important, as a factor in the growth of shipping than the demand for Swedish staple commodities in southern Europe and salt imports to Sweden. However, it is always difficult to estimate the importance of tramp shipping for an economy: in contrast to foreign trade, there are no reliable statistics on freight incomes or tramp shipping in general.

The attention paid by the consuls to the conditions of tramp shipping, however, indicates its importance for Swedish actors. Moreover, there is indirect quantitative evidence. The annual numbers of Algerian passports issued reveal that the Mediterranean and the Iberian Peninsula became very important destinations for Swedish shipping. Lists of Swedish vessels calling at Marseilles, Cadiz, and Livorno also show Sweden as one of the leading shipping nations there. The strong correlation between the numbers of Algerian passports issued and war and peace periods indicates that Swedish shipping closely followed the development of the international demand for neutral shipping. In spite of the fact that the protection of national shipping was a typical feature of eighteenth-century mercantilist policy, there was an international market for shipping, and especially for neutral shipping in wartime. And in this market, small neutral powers, such as Denmark, Sweden, the Dutch Republic, and in the post-1783 period the United States, played an important role. In economic terms, neutrality entailed lower protection costs for neutrals as against belligerents, and so was a competitive advantage.

The analysis of the Algerian passport registers (chapter 5) showed that the increase in Swedish shipping in southern Europe primarily concerned the later part of the eighteenth century, and its boom-and-bust curves closely followed wartime and peacetime periods. However, in spite of the decline in peace periods, Swedish shipping still continued to grow in a long-time perspective. The most plausible explanation for the long-term growth was a combination of the comparatively high productivity and low overall costs in Swedish shipping. The high labour productivity in Swedish shipping is connected to the composition of Swedish foreign trade, which included many bulky commodities. Swedish vessels in southern Europe were larger, and they had higher tons-per-man ratios and lower wage costs than their competitors—factors which were relevant even in peacetime.

On the other hand, small crews and high tons-per-man ratios might also be related to the relative safety of Swedish vessels. Due to the treaties with the Barbary states, and the consular service in North Africa, Swedish vessels were safer from corsairs, which fact implied fewer guns, smaller crews, and not least lower insurance premiums.

In summary, three factors have highlighted as preconditions for Swedish shipping in southern Europe. The first one was the state's protection policy, including the institutions of the Convoy Office, the consular service in southern Europe, and the peace treaties with the Barbary states. But the Navigation Act should also be included in this institutional package. The system was created in the 1720s and 1730s. The protection system entailed the reduction of protection costs of shipping on enterprise level, but at the same time, it implied new costs for the state and for economic actors. The accounts of the Convoy Office indicate very clearly the substantial level of 'public' protection costs. Sweden's neutrality was the second factor. It was connected to relative safety and so to comparatively lower protection costs for Swedish-flagged shipping. It became an especially important factor between 1756 and 1800. The Algerian passports issued in the period indicate a very close correlation between Sweden's neutrality and her shipping booms in wartime (see especially table 5.7). It appears that neutrality was the most important factor in the growth of Swedish shipping in the late eighteenth century.

These two 'protection cost' factors were linked to the consular service, as consuls played an important role in giving information about shipping safety and about respect for neutral flags—and, of course, as they represented Swedish shipowners and the state in their relations with the Barbary states, as well as in the prize courts of southern Europe. Some economic historians have pointed to declining protection costs as one of the major factors of productivity growth in shipping in the late eighteenth century. The Swedish experience of shipping to and in southern Europe appears to fit in well with this explanatory model.

The third factor concerns overall costs and productivity in Swedish long-distance shipping. Chapter 5 includes a case study of labour productivity in Swedish shipping in southern Europe, which indicates that the productivity was high (at least for vessels employed in tramp shipping within the Mediterranean). The Swedish tons-per-man ratios appear being higher compared to other merchant marines. However, the market for southern-European tramp shipping was very fragmented; a high labour productivity on board of a large timber carrier was no comparative advantage, if a small rapid craft was in demand. The large variety of Swedish-flagged vessels confirms this fragmentation. Nevertheless, the high labour productivity, high average capacity of vessels, and low wage costs, were no general disadvantages for Swedish shipowners. When the effects of volatility of neutrality's booms and busts are reduced, this factor explains the Swedish shipping expansion in a long-term perspective. This rather high productivity was also a precondition of survival of the Swedish, but also Norwegian, shipping industries in the post-1815 years.

The second part of the book (chapters 6 and 7) focused on the establishment of Swedish trade and consular service in North America. The purpose was to examine if there was any connection between the early establishment of the Swedish-American diplomatic and trading contacts and the shift of Swedish iron exports from Great Britain to the United States after 1800. In the early 1780s, Sweden had very ambitious policy as regards the 'West Indies' (then including even North America). The American independence and the Sweden's acquisition of own colony in the West Indies, St. Barthélemy, are seen as the first steps in the Swedish participation in the triangular trade, the richest trade of the late eighteenth century. It is significant that employment of neutrality played an important role even here. But Sweden's attempt to take part in the rich triangular trade was no success. It is true that the neutrality shipping based in St. Barthélemy thrived, but the vessels involved were no Swedish proper and Sweden had very limited use of its colony. The consular service in the United States could not do much to promote this trade.

The breakthrough for the Swedish-American trade came after 1807, but it did not concern the triangular trade in the West Indies. Instead, American neutral shipping used Gothenburg as a loophole in the Continental System. American vessels unloaded in Gothenburg cargoes of colonial and American products and returned home with cargoes of Swedish bar-iron. The iron trade survived the post-1815 crisis and almost a half of Swedish iron went to North America. Noticeably, until the 1830s there were very few Swedish vessels participating in this direct exchange. Thus, even if the policy employed for the 'West Indies' after 1780 reminded the ambitious policy for southern Europe from the 1720s and 1730s, the results were very different.

During the French Revolutionary and Napoleonic Wars, there were three merchant marines using their neutrality as a competitive advantage: Sweden, Denmark, and the United States. For all of them neutrality implied lower protection costs. All of them also could employ their rather peripheral situation, from a perspective of continental powers. Yet it is important to stress that neutrality shipping was possible due to the increased safety of the seas in general, and due to a kind of acceptance from Britain's part. The escalation of the

Napoleonic wars significantly reduced freedom of action of small neutral states and neutrality shipping lost its ground.

After 1815, the situation changed radically and neutrality was no longer a competitive advantage. Scandinavian states, especially Norway, continued to be important carriers in international shipping—in 1870, Sweden and Norway had together the world's third merchant fleet.[2] But the factors beyond the successful shipping industries of the Scandinavian states were not longer neutrality and low protection costs. In the nineteenth century, the shift from sail to steam and from wood to iron became the major factor of development in long-distance shipping.

---

[2] Kaukiainen 1993, p. 89.

Appendices

Appendix A
Swedish consulates 1700–1905

Aalborg 1819
Åbo (Turku) 1814
Adelaide 1855
Aden 1875
Akyab 1857
Alexandria 1821
Algiers 1730
Alicante 1738
Amsterdam 1714
Ancona 1816
Antigua 1903
Antwerp 1815
Archangel 1839
Athens 1832
Bagdad 1905
Bahia 1827
Baku 1897
Baltimore 1816
Bangkok 1866
Barcelona 1795
Batavia 1844
Bayonne 1769
Belize 1862
Berlin 1831
Bilbao 1845
Bombay 1863
Bordeaux 1709
Boston 1793
Bremen 1823
Breslau 1877
Bridgetown 1867
Brisbane 1882
Brussels 1858
Budapest 1873
Buenos Aires 1835
Cadiz 1719
Cagliari 1744

Cairo 1821
Calais 1780
Calcutta 1846
Canton 1852
Cape Town 1841
Caracas 1840
Cartagena 1770
Cette and Montpellier 1748
Christchurch 1874
Civita Vechia 1804
Cologne 1904
Colombo 1859
Copenhagen 1788
Corfu 1825
Curacao 1878
Danzig 1724
Dresden 1842
Dschiddah (Jidda) 1876
Dunkirk 1754
Düsseldorf 1878
Elsinore 1706
Fiume 1885
Flensburg 1816
Fort de France 1905
Frankfurt am Main 1827
Freetown 1895
Fremantle 1904
Galatz 1860
Geneva 1867
Genoa 1748
Georgetown 1878
Gibraltar 1798
Greifswald 1827
Guaiaquil 1853
Guatemala 1882
Hamburg 1730
Hamilton 1866

Hannover 1883
Havana 1835
Havre 1774
Helsingfors (Helsinki) 1859
Hongkong 1859
Honolulu 1854
Jamestown 1844
Johannesburg 1898
Karlsruhe 1884
Kiel 1817
Kingstown 1852
Kobe 1901
Köningsberg 1800
Kristiania 1787
La Guayara 1853
La Paz 1905
La Valetta 1822
Larnaca 1880
Le Croisic 1769
Leipzig 1858
Leith 1808
Levuka 1882
Libau 1797
Lima 1854
Lisbon 1694
Liverpool 1854
Livorno 1725
London 1730
Lorient 1778
Lourenco-Marques 1883
Lübeck 1721
Madeira 1807
Madras 1865
Madrid 1883
Malaga 1738
Manila 1840
Marseilles 1732

Melbourne 1853
Memel 1804
Messina 1824
Mexico City 1886
Monaco 1877
Monrovia 1872
Montevideo 1836
Moscow 1652
München 1888
Nagasaki 1888
Nantes 1752
Naples 1750
New Providence 1879
New York 1799
Newcastle on Tyne 1874
Nuremberg 1874
Odessa 1819
Ostend 1804
Palermo 1819
Panama 1848
Pappeetee 1850
Paris 1796
Pernambuco 1834
Philadelphia 1798
Piraeus 1878
Ponte a Pitre 1876
Port Louis 1814

Port of Spain 1883
Port Stanley 1877
Quebeck 1851
Rangoon 1862
Reval 1817
Riga 1777
Rio de Janeiro 1804
Rochefort 1852
Rochelle & St Martin 1742
Rome 1788
Rönne 1834
Rostock 1794
Rotterdam 1798
Rouen 1731
San Domingo 1880
San Francisco 1850
San Juan 1854
San Salvador 1904
Santa Fé de Bogota 1875
Shanghai 1864
Singapore 1845
Smyrna 1736
St Georges 1866
St Johns 1883
St Petersburg 1758
St Pierre 1875
St Thomas 1854

Setubal 1800
Stettin 1801
Stralsund 1816
Stuttgart 1885
Surabaya 1904
Suva 1901
Sydney 1852
Tamatave 1876
Tangier 1768
Teheran 1905
Tokio 1893
Trapani 1764
Trieste 1781
Tripoli 1741
Tunis 1737
Valparaiso 1848
Venice 1739
Vera Cruz 1876
Viborg 1782
Victoria (Br Colombia) 1876
Victoria (Hong Kong) 1855
Vienna 1762
Warsaw 1875
Washington 1858
Wellington 1879
Yokohama 1879

Source: Register of reports received from Swedish consuls abroad. The dates differ from appointment dates of consuls (table 2.1). The dates indicate established contact between BoT and consulate. (Skrivelser från konsuler, E VI a, BoT SNA)

Appendix B

Swedish ships passing the Sound from the west, according to place of departure, 1700–83

Year	All Swedish ships passing from the west	France	Portugal	Spain	Italy	Other Mediter-ranean	Total southern Europe
1700	107	13	25	0	0	0	38
1705	293	54	35	1	0	0	90
1710	1	0	0	0	0	0	0
1715	0	0	0	0	0	0	0
1720	23	0	0	0	0	0	0
1725	224	23	17	0	0	0	40
1730	514	17	30	0	0	0	40
1735	334	45	34	8	5	0	92
1740	179	27	18	4	9	0	58
1745	186	28	16	5	5	1	55
1750	228	34	32	15	25	1	107
1755	436	35	33	12	18	1	99
1760	383	33	37	2	9	0	81
1765	422	41	42	9	18	0	110
1770	366	41	26	7	33	1	108
1775	491	54	15	29	56	0	154
1780	724	33	47	18	24	1	123
1783	1,101	47	119	24	50	0	240

Swedish ships passing the Sound from the east, according to destination, 1700–83

Year	All Swedish ships passing from the east	France	Portugal	Spain	Italy	Other Mediter-ranean	Total southern Europe
1700	no data						
1705	no data						
1710	17	0	0	0	0	0	0
1715	no data						
1720	16	0	0	0	0	0	0
1725	191	9	12	2	0	0	23
1730	285	14	22	3	0	0	39
1735	281	35	35	1	1	8	80
1740	210	25	28	3	1	11	68
1745	230	12	25	4	13	8	62
1750	225	39	43	11	5	13	111
1755	381	44	24	17	11	6	102
1760	452	11	33	10	14	5	73
1765	415	23	49	12	5	8	97
1770	404	50	31	6	7	31	125
1775	473	81	39	14	15	3	152
1780	821	59	67	14	44	1	185
1783	1,030	56	66	30	55	30	237

Source: Bang and Korst 1930

Appendix C

Arrivals of northern-European vessels in Marseilles harbour, 1732–92

Year	English	Dutch	Swedish	Danish	Other	Total
1709			1			1
1710		2	4	1		7
1711			1			1
1732	64	20	2	0		86
1733	113	32	1	0		146
1734	84	30	5	0		119
1735	87	39	10	0		136
1736	92	27	7	0		126
1737	75	29	2	0		106
1738	92	27	3	0		122
1739	55	21	7	0		83
1740	6	34	8	0	1	49
1741	10	42	8	1	4	65
1742	15	54	6	0	3	78
1743	12	82	13	1	10	118
1744	4	58	18	2	8	90
1745	1	95	16	0	9	121
1746	0	97	22	1	9	129
1747	1	81	16	8	3	109
1748	43	39	20	14		116
1749	206	103	22	19		350
1750	187	91	24	8		310
1751	125	77	14	2		218
1752	105	61	15	2		184
1753	81	62	19	9		171
1754	56	72	16	9		153
1755	63	30	30	16		139
1756	0	60	61	42		163
1757	0	40	37	26		103
1758	1	34	12	16		63
1759	0	72	13	19		105
1760	0	71	13	15		99
1761	2	98	15	36		151
1762	3	87	7	25		122
1763	27	65	21	33		146
1764	64	135	24	24		247
1765	42	45	22	12		121
1766	44	84	27	19		174
1767	45	72	26	20		163
1768	41	52	25	15		133
1769	53	77	42	4		176
1770	68	69	30	1		168
1771	67	95	43	2		207
1772	57	64	32	10		163
1773	56	67	39	15		177
1774	67	78	45	18		208

Year	English	Dutch	Swedish	Danish	Other	Total
1775	59	44	31	15		149
1776	38	36	28	12		114
1777	38	49	44	25		156
1778	7	87	42	33		169
1779	1	93	30	48		172
1780	1	54	22	34		111
1781	0	23	42	60	2	127
1782	0	1	52	68	1	122
1783	14	10	51	95		170
1784	13	19	38	61		131
1785	27	16	55	112	1	211
1786	34	30	65	100		229
1787	47	27	58	69		201
1788	50	37	27	49		163
1789	74	44	1	47		166
1790	39	42	5	62		148
1791	37	39	22	59		157
1792	56	44	15	60		175
Total 1732–92	2,749	3,363	1,466	1,453		9,084

Source: Carrière 1973, p. 1061.
Note: There were no Swedish ships registered between 1712 and 1731.

Appendix D

The numbers of Algerian passports issued, 1739–1831

1739	136		1786	289
1740	136		1787	321
1741	134		1788	163
1742	114		1789	3
1743	126		1790	115
1744	167		1791	354
1745	176		1792	257
1746	163		1793	398
1747	173		1794	408
1748	135		1795	394
1749	159		1796	362
1750	160		1797	425
1751	151		1798	467
1752	183		1799	516
1753	145		1800	624
1754	112		1801	369
1755	132		1802	545
1756	156		1803	677
1757	141		1804	717
1758	177		1805	586
1759	132		1806	259
1760	174		1807	366
1761	187		1808	306
1762	203		1809	400
1763	212		1810	552
1764	225		1811	352
1765	201		1812	310
1766	169		1813	696
1767	172		1814	782
1768	180		1815	1,012
1769	176		1816	583
1770	198		1817	530
1771	246		1818	511
1772	270		1819	473
1773	267		1820	431
1774	278		1821	466
1775	222		1822	389
1776	236		1823	478
1777	253		1824	523
1778	287		1825	482
1779	282		1826	463
1780	320		1827	493
1781	373		1828	501
1782	441		1829	448
1783	339		1830	506
1784	370		1831	466
1785	389			

Total passports issued: 30,546.
Source: Algerian passport registers, 1739–1768, C II b. BoT SNA.

Appendix E

The outlays of the Swedish Convoy Office 1726–1809

(1726–1776 in d.s.m., 1777–1809 in new rixdollars)

1726/27	2,599		1777	64,633
1727/28	18,826		1778	58,277
1728/29	232,301		1779	57,789
1729/30	32,477		1780	198,245
1730/31	41,533		1781	53,510
1731/32/	80,915		1782	50,676
1732/33	20,673		1783	64,491
1733/34	22,398		1784	43,589
1734/35	51,848		1785	56,554
1735/36	65,645		1786	50,682
1736/37	53,366		1787	72,364
1737/38	68,012		1788	35,215
1738/39	35,957		1789	41,732
1739	45,181		1790	50,826
1740	52,670		1791–92	30,164
1741	55,696		1793	215,733
1742	36,169		1794	102,671
1743	60,854		1795	64,030
1744	63,685		1796	607,097
1745	95,656		1797	17,712 rdr bko
1746	148,270			42,089 rdr rgs
1747	125,475		1798	86,870 rdr bko
1748	169,675			91,748 rdr rgs
1749	102,336		1799	108,431 rdr bko
1750	100,404			75,643 rdr rgs
1751	79,487		1800	10,536 rdr bko
1752	74,454			131,663 rdr rgs
1753	128,099		1801	24,139 rdr bko
1754	68,194			241,612 rdr rgs
1755	407,480		1802	56,986 rdr bko
1756	208,522			132,695 rdr rgs
1757	148,528		1803	287,775 rdr bko
1758	270,521			113,738 rdr rgs
1759	459,001		1804	784,660
1760	321,650		1805	340,263
1761	319,749		1806	82,324
1762	209,514		1807	377,216
1763	438,140		1808	92,445
1764	668,229		1809	238,317
1765	1,259,744			
1766	286,342			
1767	1,335,957			
1768	307,678			
1769	243,220			
1770	224,226			
1771	528,336			
1772	458,521			
1773	408,283			
1774	275,362			
1775	546,310			
1776	519,827			

Source: Åmark 1961, pp.762–775.
rdr bko   *riksdaler banko*
rdr rgs   *riksdaler riksgäld*

Appendix F

The calculation of estimated value of ships (see table 5.11)

The calculation of the capital stock employed in the Swedish shipping beyond Cape Finisterre is based on the estimated shipping capacity employed and its value according to estimated value per last.

Whereas the estimate of the employed shipping capacity (B) is rather representative, the estimated capital stock employed (C) is a very rough estimate. The reason is the difficulty in forming a coherent evaluation of ships over such long period. The estimate employed is based on the following data:

According to Claes Grill's treatise on Sweden's shipping and shipbuilding (1749), the estimated building cost of a new ship (280 lasts), to be employed in long-distance shipping, was 305 d.s.m. per last (914 d.c.m.). The insurance policies (from 1761) of the seven ships owned by the firm of Carlos and Claes Grill show considerable variance of ship value per last. (*Catharina Sofia* 327 d.s.m., *Experientia* 171 d.s.m., *Vigilantia* 437 d.s.m., *Levant Fregatt* 373 d.s.m., *Resolution* 269 d.s.m., *Lovisa Ulrica* 194 d.s.m., *Stor Ammiralen* 194 d.s.m.)* An average value per last of Grill's ships is 284 d.s.m. Grill's firm was among the most active in the shipping beyond Cape Finisterre, thus the estimate appears reasonably representative. In addition, the estimates based on insurance policies should be more representative than data from inventories, which frequently underestimated ships' real values. Yet the number of cases is very limited.

Jari Ojala, on the basis of inventories from the Finnish seaport of Gamla Karleby (Kokkola), estimated an average value per last of 152 d.s.m. (455 d.c.m.). The period covered is 1760–1810, and the number of cases is 82. Accounting books of the house of Donner and Falander (1779–1800), from Wasa, show an average value of 237 d.s.m. (710 d.c.m.) per last, yet the number of cases is only 11 and the variation is considerable. Armas Luukko argues that the ship value per last (based on ships from the seaport of Wasa) was about 210 d.s.m. (630 d.c.m.) by the late eighteenth century. The number of Finnish cases is substantially larger than for Grill's example. On the other hand the Finnish cases also included ships engaged in coastal and Baltic shipping. The values of these ships were (we may tentatively suppose) somewhat lower than the values of ships employed in long-distance shipping.**

With the calculated values per last from the above, the present writer estimates that the value per last varied between 150 and 300 d.s.m. It is worth noting that the estimate does not consider shipping capital's depreciation by age. This estimate is used as a basis for the calculation of the total capital stock employed in Swedish shipping beyond Cape Finisterre.

*(Müller 1998, p. 205, table 6.9 insurance policies, and Börjeson 1932, pp. 315–340, data on the tonnage of Grill's ships).
** (for the data on Finnish ships, see Ojala 1999, pp. 88–102; Ojala 1996, pp. 252–270. I thank Jari Ojala for help in finding the data.)

Appendix G

Swedish iron exports to the United States 1807–46 (in metric tons)

Year	Gothenburg	Stockholm	Gävle
1807	1,945		
1808	333		
1809	4,500		
1810	16,395	364	
1811	6,802		
1812	5,755	1,211	
1813	6,238	1,924	
1814	1,423	256	
1815	13,196	4,624	
1816	5,104	7,038	
1817	4,695	4,762	
1818	2,236	7,827	
1819	3,519	6,150	
1820	4,299	9,904	
1821	3,848	7,336	
1822	5,045	12,034	
1823	11,178	16,324	
1824	6,167	9,669	
1825	7,947	13,325	
1826	3,979	8,102	
1827	6,632	13,021	
1828	9,279	14,157	
1829	6,814	11,275	
1830	5,113	9,818	
1831	7,323	15,240	1,300
1832	6,474	12,847	2,400
1833	6,702	12,417	2,100
1834	5,258	13,365	1,500
1835	6,825	19,660	2,600
1836	9,056	16,028	2,900
1837	2,301	5,519	2,500
1838	5,670	16,551	4,100
1839	7,485	17,443	4,500
1840	4,167	9,607	3,200
1841	5,010	12,520	4,600
1842	3,251	4,016	2,200
1843	3,638	2,378	1,100
1844	4,729	5,522	2,800
1845	6,453	4,682	600
1846	3,443	5,070	1,500

Source: Adamson 1969, pp. 69, 77–80, 87.

Appendix H

Swedish-flagged ships arriving at New York (March–December 1815)

Name	Date of arrival	Home port	Shipowner	From, with cargo	Consignee	To, with cargo
Amphitrion	1/7	Gävle	Dan Elfstrand	Lisbon, salt		Lisbon, corn flour
Aurora	23/5	Gothenburg	Ekman and Co	Cadiz	Bayard and McEvers	Richmond, Virginia, ballast
Betty	12/8	Gävle	Per Bransträm and Co	Gävle, iron		
Carl	14/6	St. Bart		St. Bart		
Carl Johan	1/9	Stockholm				
Carlshamn	8/5	St. Bart	Johan Bernhad Elbers	Port au Prince, Haiti, dyes	Kleine	Guadaloupe
Concordia	3/7	Gothenburg		Cadiz		
Continuation	18/11	Stockholm	J Holtström	Lisbon, salt		
Couriren	27/11	Gothenburg	Olof Wijk	Lisbon, salt, sulphur, raisins	Mr A A Duff	
Dahlkarlen	27/3	Gothenburg	Johan F Elgren	Halifax (after 9 months of confiscation)	Bond and Beson	
Drottning Christina	4/12	Stockholm	Kantzow and Biel	Stockholm, iron	Jacob Mark	
Eliza	28/6	St. Bart		St. Bart, sugar, coffee, cotton, china, and campech tree		
Guadaloupe	15/8	Gothenburg	Alex Barclay	Gothenburg, iron		
Henrietta Elisa	22/11	Sw Pommern				
Little Bill	19/4	St. Bart	William Israel	St. Bart	Kleine	St. Bart, with provisions and other necessities
Maria Carolina	17/8	Stockholm				
Maria Christina	6/6	Kungälv	Hindrich Dercks	Plymouth, with American prisoners of war		
Matrosen	5/8	Gothenburg	J and B Hull and Dickson	Gothenburg, iron		
Minerva	24/7	Uddevalla		Tenerife, wine		
Minerva	25/12	Gothenburg	Low, Smith and Co	Gothenburg, iron and steel		Gothenburg
Neptunus	27/3	Helsingborg	Carl M Flygborg	Lisbon	Robert Dickey	Charleston, S Carolina
Oscar	27/6	Gothenburg	A D Otterdahl and Son	Cadiz	Bond and Pearson	
Prins Oscar	23/11	Stockholm		Lisbon, salt	Vasques and Meuron	
Segerktrantsen	17/7	Stockholm		Lisbon		Porto
Siren	1/8	Stockholm	Nils Flodman	Lisbon		

Name	Date of arrival	Home port	Shipowner	From, with cargo	Consignee	To, with cargo
Sophia	27/5	Gothenburg	Johan Aron Andren	Liverpool		Gothenburg
Sophia Albertina	27/3	St. Bart	William Henry Morton	St. Bart		
Stockholm	10/8	Stockholm		Stockholm, iron		
Thetis	6/6	Stockholm	Carl Magnus Fris' Widow	Bristol	J and T Meyer for sale	
Trio	14/3	St. Bart	William Henry Morton			

Source: Henrik Gahn to the Board of Trade, 1815 Consular Reports, New York, E VI aa 352, BoT SNA.

241

Note on volume and weight units, measurement of shipping capacity, and money

ship pound (*skeppund stapelstadsvikt*), a weight unit, used in metal exports, 1 ship pound=136 kg (*Historisk statistik för Sverige*, 1972, p. 64)

barrel (*tunna, öltunna*), a volume unit used in trade with tar, pitch and salt, 1 barrel=125.6 litre (*Historisk statistik för Sverige*, 1972, p. 64)

Measurement of shipping capacity

The measurement of early modern shipping capacity is a complex problem, especially if we aim to compare capacity between different countries. In general, there are two tonnage measurement units: the last employed in German–Dutch and Scandinavian shipping, and the ton especially employed in western Europe. In eighteenth-century Sweden after 1726, standard measurement procedures were employed: the unit used was the heavy last (*svår läst*), equal to a ship's carrying capacity of 18 ship pounds of iron in weight (1 heavy last=18 ship pounds=2.448 metric ton) (Andersson 1945–1946, pp. 94–95). Thus the registered Swedish capacity is roughly equal to modern deadweight tonnage. The traditional ton burden, employed in the measurement of early modern English shipping, and used in comparative research, is equal to 2,200 English pounds, which is almost exactly 1 metric ton. Therefore, in comparisons, I have only converted Swedish registered tonnage from lasts into metric tons. The Swedish data here refers to registered tonnage in lasts (or metric tons), which makes the data comparable, at least roughly, to established estimates of eighteenth-century tonnage in tons burden (e.g. Lucassen and Unger 2000).

Moreover, there are large differences between the registered tonnages, measured tonnages, and actual carrying capacity of vessels. On measurement procedures and differences between the 'registered' and 'measured' capacity in eighteenth-century Atlantic shipping see McCusker 1997. It has to be stressed that any calculations based on early modern tonnages are very rough estimates, and should be understood as such.

For a comprehensive discussion on the measurement of early modern tonnages, see Lane 1964; French 1973; Unger 1992, p. 250; Glete 1993b, pp. 67–70, 332 (note); Lucassen and Unger 2000, p. 128. For Swedish measurement of tonnage see Andersson 1945–1946 and Owen Jansson 1945–1946.

Money

In the eighteenth century, Sweden's monetary system included three units: rix-dollars (*riksdaler specie*), dollar-silver-money (*daler silvermynt*) [d.s.m.], and dollar-copper-money (*daler kopparmynt*) [d.c.m.]. Between 1723 and 1776, the exchange rate between d.s.m. and d.c.m. was stable, 1 d.s.m.=3.d.c.m. On the other hand, the rate between rixdollar and d.s.m. varied: thus in 1723, 1 rixdollar=3 d.s.m.=9 d.c.m.. In the 1776 monetary reform, d.s.m. and d.c.m. were abandoned for a single monetary unit, rixdollars, at an exchange rate 1 rixdollar=6.d.s.m.=18 d.c.m. This exchange rate was used for the conversion of new rixdollars to d.s.m. in the post-1776 period (e.g. table 5.11).

In the 1790s, monetary problems gave rise to a difference between two bank note systems, *riksdaler riksgälds* [rdr rgs], issued by *Riksgäldskontoret*, and *riksdaler banco* [rdr bco], issued by *Riksbank* and equal to the silver *riksdaler specie*. In 1803, *riksdaler riksgälds* was incorporated into the rixdollar system, at an exchange rate of 1 rdr rgs= 2/3 rdr bco.

In the 1873 monetary reform, a new unit, the *krona* replaced the *riksdaler*. (rixdollar) (*Historisk statistik för Sverige*, 1972, p. 662–663.)

Bibliography

Unpublished Sources

Riksarkivet (Swedish national archives)
Kommerskollegium, Huvudarkivet (Archives of the Board of Trade)
  Ansökningar om konsulattjänsten (Applications of consuls), E XVII g.
  Skrivelser från Ostindiska Kompaniet, Levantiska kompaniet 1741–54 (Consular reports from Smyrna), E XVII aa.
  Skrivelser från konsuler och ministrar (Consular Reports): Lissabon, Cadiz, Marseilles, Livorno, New York, Philadelphia, Boston, Tangier, Tripoli, Tunis, Algiers, E VI aa.
  Sjöpassdiarier (Algerian passport registers) 1739–1831, C II b.
  Särskilda utredningar och berättelser 1744–1752, Om handelen på Cadix, Om handelen på Lissabon, R Angerstein (R. Angerstein's report), F IV:85.

Kommerskollegium, Kammarkontoret
  Konsulernas skeppslistor (Consular shipping lists), 1817–1823

Diplomatica: Americana (Richard Söderström's reports).

Secondary Works and Published Sources

Åberg, Martin, *Svensk handelskapitalism–Ett dynamiskt element i frihetstidens samhälle? En fallstudie av delägarna i Ostindiska kompaniets 3:e oktroj 1766–1786.* (licentiate's dissertation, Department of History, Gothenburg University), 1988.
Adamson, Rolf, 'Swedish Iron Exports to the United States, 1783–1860', in *Scandinavian Economic History Review*, 1969, pp. 58–114.
Adamson, Rolf, *Järnavsättning och bruksfinansiering 1800–1860.* Göteborg 1966.
Ahlberger, Christer and Mörner, Magnus, 'Betydelsen av några latinamerikanska produkter för Sverige före 1810'. in *Historisk tidskrift* (Swedish), 1993, pp. 80–104.
Alanen, Aulis J., *Der Aussenhandel und die Schiffahrt Finnlands im 18. Jahrhundert.* Helsinki 1957.
Almqvist, Johan Axel, *Kommerskollegium och riksens ständers manufakturkontor samt konsulsstaten. Administrativa och biografiska anteckningar.* Stockholm 1912–15.
Åmark, Karl, *Sveriges statsfinanser 1719–1809.* Stockholm 1961.
Amiralitetskollegiets historia. 3 vols, Malmö 1977.

245

Andersen, Dan H. and Voth, Hans-Joachim, 'The Grapes of War: Neutrality and Mediterranean Shipping under Danish Flag, 1747–1807', in *Scandinavian Economic History Review,* 2000/1, pp. 5–27.

Andersen, Dan H., 'Danske handelsforsøg på Levanten 1752–65', in *Erhvervshistorisk årbog. Meddelelser fra erhvervsarkivet* 42. 1992, pp. 132–182.

Andersen, Dan H., 'Denmark-Norway, Africa, and the Caribbean 1660–1917: modernisation financed by slaves and sugar?', in Pieter Emmer and Olivier Petré-Grenouilleau (eds.), *A Deus ex Machina Revisited. Atlantic Colonial Trade and European Economic Development XVIIth–XIXth Centuries,* (forthcoming 2004).

Andersen, Dan H., 'Matroslønninger i den danske handelsflåde 1750–1807', in Erik Gøbel (ed.), *Hilsen fra søens folk. Feskrift til Anders Monrad Møller. 2. maj 2002.* København 2002, pp. 25–31.

Andersen, Dan H., *The Danish Flag in the Mediterranean. Shipping and Trade, 1747–1807.* 2 vols, (PhD Dissertation) University of Copenhagen 2000.

Andersson, Anders, 'Om svensk skeppsmätning i äldre tid', in *Sjöhistorisk Årsbok,* 1945–1946, pp. 49–140.

Andersson, Bertil, *Göteborgs handlande borgerskap. Ekonomiska förhållanden för handelsgrupperna i Göteborg 1806–1825.* Göteborg 1977 (1977b).

Andersson, Bertil, *Göteborgs historia, Näringsliv och samhällsutveckling. Från fästningsstad till handelsstad 1619–1820.* Stockholm 1996.

Andersson, Bertil, *Handel och hantverk i Göteborg. Två företagargruppers ekonomiska utveckling 1806–1825.* Göteborg 1977 (1977a).

Angerstein, Reinhold, *Dagbok öfver resan genom Provence, Laguedoc, samt en del af Spanien och Portugal åren 1751 och 1752.* utgivna av Jernkontoret, Stockholm (1996a).

Angerstein, Reinhold, *Om handeln på Cadix, Om handeln på Lissabon, Om handeln på Senegalia och Ancona, 1752.* utgivna av Jernkontoret, Stockholm (1996b).

Arfwedson, Carl David, *The United States and Canada in 1832, 1833, and 1834.* (reprint) New York 1969.

Åström, S.-E., 'The English Navigation Laws and the Baltic Trade, 1660–1700', in *Scandinavian Economic History Review,* 1960, pp. 3–18.

Attman, Artur, *Fagerstabrukets historia. Adertonhundratalet.* Uppsala 1958.

Bang, Nina Ellinger and Korst, Knud, *Tabeller over skibsfart och varetransport gennem Øresund 1661–1783.* København 1930.

Barbour, Violet, 'Dutch and English Merchant Shipping in the Seventeenth Century', (reprint) in Pieter Emmer and Femme Gaastra (eds.), *The Organization of Interoceanic Trade in European expansion 1450–1800,* vol. 13, An Expanding World The European Impact on World History 1450–1800. Aldershot 1996, pp. 103–130.

Barker, T., 'Consular Reports: A Rich but Neglected Historical Source', in *Business History,* 1981/3, pp. 265–266.

Barton, H. Arnold, 'Sweden and the War of American Independence', in *The William and Mary Quarterly,* July 1966/3, pp. 408–430.

Barton, H. Arnold, *Count Hans Axel von Fersen. Aristocrat in an Age of Revolution.* Boston 1975.

Barton, H. Arnold, *Scandinavia in the Revolutionary Era, 1760–1815.* Minneapolis 1986.

Bellman, Carl Michael, *Fredmans sånger* (1791). Stockholm 1997.

Betänkande 1857, Underdånigt betänkande angående svenska och norska consul-väsendet jemte förslag till förnyad consulstadga af dertill i nåder förordnade comiterade afgifvet den 20 maj 1856. Stockholm 1857.

Betänkande 1876, Underdånigt betänkande angående svenska och norska konsultväsendet... avgifvet den 4 November 1876 av den enligt nådigt beslut den 12 febr. 1875 förordnade svensk-norska komité. Stockholm 1876.

Bjurling, Oscar, 'Stockholms förbindelser med utlandet under 1670-talets växlingar', in *Forum Navale,* No. 10, 1951, pp. 3–37.

Bjurling, Oscar, 'Stockholms och Sveriges sjöfart åren 1680–1692', in *Forum Navale,* No. 27, 1972, pp. 42–59.

Boberg, Stig, 'Realitet och politisk argumentering i konsulatfrågan 1890–1891', in *Scandia,* 1968, pp. 24–65.

Boëthius, Bertil and Heckscher, Eli F., *Svensk handelsstatistik 1637–1737.* Stockholm 1938.

Bonney, Richard (ed.), *Economic Systems and State Finance.* Oxford 1995.

Borg, Eskil, *Svenska konsuler och slavar i Barbareskkaparnas Tripoli. En studie i makt, girighet, våld och förtryck.* Kristianstad 1987.

Börjeson, D.Hj.T., *Stockholms segelsjöfart. Anteckningar om huvudstadens kofferdiflotta och dess män med en översikt av stadens och rikets sjöfartsförhållanden från äldsta tid intill våra dagar.* Stockholm 1932.

Bruijn, Jaap R., 'Productivity, profitability and costs of private and corporate Dutch ship owning in the seventeenth and eighteenth centuries', in James D. Tracy (ed.), *The Rise of merchant empires. Long-distance trade in the early modern trade, 1350–1750.* Cambridge 1990, pp. 174–194.

Carlén, Stefan, 'An institutional analysis of the Swedish salt market, 1720–1862', in *Scandinavian Economic History Review,* 1994, pp. 3–28.

Carlén, Stefan, *Staten som marknadens salt. En studie i institutionsbildning, kollektivt handlande och tidig välfärdspolitik på en strategisk varumarknad i övergången mellan merkantilism och liberalism 1720–1862.* Stockholm 1997.

Carlson, Bengt, 'Sverige handel och sjöfart på Medelhavet 1797–1803', in Åke Holmberg (ed.), *Handel och sjöfart under gustaviansk tid.* Meddelanden från historiska institutionen i Göteborg, nr 4. Göteborg 1971, pp. 1–25.

Carlsson, A.W., *Med mått mätt. Svenska och utländska mått genom tiderna.* Stockholm 1997.

Carrière, Charles, *Négociants marseillais au XVIIIe siècle.* Marseilles 1973.

Chydenius, Anders, *Källan till Rikets Wan-magt,* Stockholm 1765.

Clemensson, Per (ed.), *Två göteborgare på resa i Nya och Gamla Werlden. Olof Wijk dä:s resejournal 1828–1830. Hilda Wijks resedagbok 1832–1833.* Göteborg 1978.

Colley, Linda, *Captives. Britain, Empire and the World 1600–1850.* London 2002.

Crouzet, François, 'America and the crisis of the British imperial economy, 1803–1807', in John J. McCusker and Kenneth Morgan (eds.), *The Early Modern Atlantic Economy.* Cambridge 2000, pp. 278–318.

Crouzet, François, *L'Economie britannique et le blocus continental (1806–1813).* Paris 1958.

Dahlgren, Stellan and Norman, Hans, *The Rise and Fall of New Sweden. Governor Johan Risingh's Journal 1654–1655 in Its Historical Context.* Uppsala 1988.

Danielsson, E.G., *Anteckningar om Norra Amerikas Fri-staters Jerntillverkning samt handel med Jern- och Stålvaror.* Stockholm 1845.

Davis, Ralph, *The Rise of the English Shipping Industry. In the Seventeenth and Eighteenth Centuries.* London 1962.

Desfeuilles, Paul, 'Scandinaves et Barbaresques à la fin de l'Ancien Régime', in *Cahiers de Tunisie,* 1956, no 15, pp. 327–349.

Droste, Heiko, 'Johan Adler Salvius i Hamburg. Ett nätverksbygge i 1600-talets Sverige', in Kerstin Abukhanfusa (ed.), *Mare Nostrum. Om Westfaliska freden och Östersjön som ett svenskt maktcenturm.* Skrifter utgivna av Riksarkivet 13. Stockholm 1999, pp. 243–255.

Ekegård, Einar, *Studier i svensk handelspolitik under den tidigare frihetstiden.* Uppsala 1924.

Eklund, Åsa, *Iron production, iron trade and iron markets. Swedish iron on the British market in the first half of the eighteenth century.* (licentiate diss., Dep. of Economic History, Uppsala University), 2001.

Eliaeson, Sven and Björk, Ragnar, *Union & secession.* Stockholm 2000.

Elovson, Harald, 'De svenska officerarna i nordamerikanska frihetskriget', in *Scandia,* 1928, pp. 314–327.

Emmer, Pieter, 'The Myth of Early Globalization. The Atlantic Economy, 1500–1800', in *European Review,* February 2003, pp. 37–48.

Engels, Marie-Christine, *Merchants, Interlopers, Seamen and Corsairs. The 'Flemish' Community in Livorno and Genoa (1615–1635).* Hilversum 1997.

Engerman, Stanley L., 'France, Britain and the economic growth of colonial North America', in John J. McCusker and Kenneth Morgan (eds.), *The Early Modern Atlantic Economy.* Cambridge 2000, pp. 227–249.

Enthoven, Victor and Postma, Johannes (eds.), *Riches from Atlantic commerce. Dutch transatlantic trade and shipping, 1585–1817.* Boston 2003.

Ericsson, Birgitta, 'Stockholms storborgerskap och intressespelet kring produktplakatet', in *Studier i äldre historia, tillägnade Herman Schück 5/4 1985.* Stockholm 1985, pp. 301–312.

Essén, Åke W., *Johan Liljecrantz som handelspolitiker. Studier i Sveriges yttre handelspolitik 1773–1786.* Lund 1928.

Evans, Chris, Jackson, Owen and Rydén, Göran, 'Baltic iron and the British iron industry in the eighteenth century', in *Economic History Review,* 2002/4, pp. 642–665.

Everaert, John, 'Willem Bolts: India Regained and Lost: Indiamen, Imperial Factories and Country-Trade (1775–1785)' in Kuzhippalli Skaria Mathew (ed.), *Mariners, Merchants and Oceans. Studies in Maritime History.* New Delhi 1995, pp. 61–67.

Feldbæk, Ole, 'Eighteenth-Century Danish Neutrality. Its Diplomacy, Economics and Law', in *Scandinavian Journal of History,* 1983, pp. 3–21.

Feldbæk, Ole, 'The Anglo-Danish Convoy Conflict of 1800. A Study of Small Power Policy and Neutrality', in *Scandinavian Journal of History,* 1977, pp. 161–182.

Feldbæk, Ole, *Dansk søfarts historie, Storhandelens tid 1720–1814,* vol. 3. København 1997.

Feldbæk, Ole, *Denmark and the Armed Neutrality 1800–1801. Small Power Policy in a World War.* Copenhagen 1980.

Ferguson, Niall, *The Cash Nexus, Money and Power in the Modern World, 1700–2000.* London 2001.

Florén, Anders and Karlsson, Åsa (eds.), *Främlingar—ett historiskt perspektiv.* Uppsala 1998.

Florén, Anders and Rydén, Göran, 'A Journey into the Market Society. A Swedish Pre-industrial Spy in the Middle of the Eighteenth Century', in Ragnar Björk and Karl Molin (eds.), Societies made up of history. Stockholm 1996, pp. 259–301.

Florén, Anders and Rydén, Göran, 'Sketches of Spain: The Journey of Reinald Rücker Angerstein 1752', in Ken Benson, Magnus Mörner and Ingmar Söhrman (eds.), *Spanish–Swedish Relations from the mid seventeenth century to the early nineteenth century.* Göteborg 2002.

Fredrickson, William, 'American shipping in the trade with Northern Europe 1783–1860', in *Scandinavian Economic History Review,* 1956/2, pp. 109–125.

French, Christopher J., 'Eighteenth–Century Shipping Tonnage Measurements', in *The Journal of Economic History,* 1973/2, pp. 434–443.

French, Christopher, J., 'Productivity in the Atlantic shipping industry: A Quantitative Study', in *Journal of Interdisciplinary History,* 1987, pp. 613–638.

Furber, Holden, 'In the footsteps of a German 'nabob': William Bolts in the Swedish Archives', in Rosane Rocher (ed.), *Private Fortunes and Company Profits in the India trade in the 18th century.* Aldershot 1997, pp. 7–18.

Gasslander, Olle, 'The Convoy Affair of 1798', in *Scandinavian Economic History Review*, 1954/1, pp. 22–30.

Gerentz, Sven, *Kommerskollegium och näringslivet*. Stockholm 1951.

Gerste, Ronald D., *Schweden und die Amerikanische Revolution. Der Einfluss des Amerikanischen Unabhängigkeitskrieges auf Amerikabild, Revolutionsverständnis und Politik Schwedens*. Düsseldorf 1994.

Glete, Jan, 'Beredskap och vidmakthållande. Varvet och linjeflottan 1772–1866', in Erik Norberg, (ed.), *Karlskronavarvets historia*. vol. 1, 1680–1866, Karlskrona 1993 (1993a), pp. 145–247.

Glete, Jan, 'De statliga örlogsflottornas expansion. Kapprustningen till sjöss i Väst- och Nordeuropa 1650–1680', in *Studier i äldre historia, tillägnade Herman Schück 5/4 1985*. Stockholm 1985, pp. 257–271.

Glete, Jan, *Navies and nations: Warships, navies and state building in Europe and America 1500–1860*, 2 vols, Stockholm 1993 (1993b).

Glete, Jan, *War and the state in early modern Europe. Spain, the Dutch Republic and Sweden as fiscal-military states, 1500–1600*. London 2002.

Glete, Jan, *Warfare at Sea 1500–1650. Maritime conflicts and the transformation of Europe*. London 2000.

Gøbel, Erik, 'Danish Trade to the West Indies and Guinea, 1671–1754', in *Scandinavian Economic History Review*, 1983. pp. 21–48.

Gøbel, Erik, 'De algeriske søpasprotokoller. En kilde til langfarten 1747–1840', in *Arkiv. Tidskrift for arkivforskningn*. 1982–83/2–3, pp. 65–108.

Gonzalez, Guadaloupe Carrasco, 'Cádiz y el Báltico. Casa comerciales suecas en Cádiz (1780–1800)', in Alberto Ramos Santana (ed.), *Comercion y navigación entre España y Suecia (siglos X–XX)*, Cadiz 2000, pp. 317–346.

Grill, Claes, *Tal om Sjö-fartens nytta och förmån för riket, i synnerhet då han drifves med hembyggde och utur egne Hamnar utrustade Skepp, hållit för Kongl. Vetenskaps Academien af Claes Grill... den 4 Febr 1749*. Stockholm 1749.

Hahr, Gösta, *Hinrich Hahr, en handelsman från frihetstidens Stockholm*. Stockholm 1966.

Håkansson, Stefan, *Konsulerna och exporten 1905–1921. Ett 'Government failure'*. Lund 1989.

Hallendorff, C., 'Arfwidsson, Christian', in *SBL*, vol. 2, Stockholm 1920.

Hancock, David, *Citizens of the World. London Merchants and the Integration of the British Atlantic Community, 1735–1785*. Cambridge 1997.

Harley, C. Knick, 'Ocean Freight Rates and Productivity 1740–1913. The primacy of Mechanical Invention Reaffirmed', in *The Journal of Economic History*, 1988/4, pp. 851–876.

Hattendorf, John B. and others (eds.), *British naval documents 1204–1960*, published by Scholar Press for the Navy Records Society 1993.

Haugard, Joel, *Gustaf Kierrman. Ett fantastiskt levnadsöde under Frihetstiden*. Stockholm 1947.

Heckscher, Eli F., *Ekonomi och historia*. Stockholm 1922.

Heckscher, Eli F., *Den svenska handelssjöfartens ekonomiska historia sedan Gustaf Vasa. Sjöhistoriska samfundets skrifter*, no 1, Uppsala 1940.

Heckscher, Eli F., *Kontinentalsystemet. Den stora handelsspärrningen för hundra år sedan*. Stockholm 1918.

Heckscher, Eli F., *Sveriges ekonomiska historia från Gustav Vasa*. 2 vols, Stockholm 1935–49.

Helgason, Thorsteinn, 'Historical Narrative as Collective Therapy: the Case of the Turkish Raid in Iceland', in *Scandinavian Journal of History*, 1997, pp. 275–289.

Herlitz, Lars, 'Nordercrantz, Anders', in *SBL*, vol. 27, Stockholm 1990–91.

Hermelin, Sam. Gust., *Berättelse om Nordamerikas förenta stater 1784. Bref till Kansli-presidenten.* Stockholm 1894.

Hildebrand, Ingegerd, *Den svenska kolonin S:t Barthélemy och Västindiska kompaniet fram till 1796.* Lund 1951.

Hildebrand, Karl-Gustaf, 'Latinamerika, Sverige och skeppshandeln 1825', in *Historisk tidskrift* (Swedish), 1950, pp. 392–421.

Hildebrand, Karl-Gustaf, *Fagerstabrukens historia. Sexton- och sjuttonhundratalen.* Uppsala 1957.

Historisk statistik för Sverige. Utrikeshandeln 1732–1970. vol. 3, Stockholm 1972.

Högberg, Staffan, 'Consular Reports to the Swedish Board of Trade', in *Business History,* 1981/3, pp. 294–297.

Högberg, Staffan, 'Svensk medelhavsfart och Sveriges handel med Portugal under Napoleontiden', in *Forum navale,* No. 19–20, 1964, pp. 16–42.

Högberg, Staffan, *Utrikeshandel och sjöfart på 1700-talet. Stapelvaror i svensk export och import 1738–1808.* Stockholm 1969.

Isacson, Maths and Magnusson, Lars, *Proto-industrialisation in Scandinavia. Craft Skills in the Industrial Revolution.* Leamington Spa 1987.

Israel, Jonathan I., *Dutch Primacy in World Trade, 1585–1740.* Oxford 1989.

Jägerskiöld, Olof, *Den svenska utrikespolitikens historia,* vol. II:2, Stockholm 1957.

Jansson, Alfred E., 'v. Kantzow. En adlig köpmannasläkt', in *Forum navale,* No. 19–20, 1964, pp. –43–59.

Johansen, Hans Chr., 'Danish Shipping Service as a Link Between the Mediterranean and the Baltic 1750–1850', in Lewis R. Fisher and Helge W. Nordvik (eds.), *Shipping and Trade (1750–1959), Proceedings Tenth International Economic History Congress Leuven 1990.* Leuven 1990, pp.18–27.

Johansen, Hans Chr., 'Scandinavian shipping in the late eighteenth century in a European perspective', in *Economic History Review,* 1992/3, pp. 479–493.

Johansen, Hans Chr., *Shipping and Trade between the Baltic Area and Western Europe 1784–95.* Odense 1983.

Johnson, Seved, 'Neutralitetsförbundet 1800 i sitt storpolitiska sammanhang', in *Historisk tidskrift* (Swedish), 1953, pp. 313–327.

Johnson, Seved, *Sverige och stormakterna 1800–1804. Studier i svensk handels- och utrikespolitik.* Lund 1957.

Jörberg, Lennart, *Growth and fluctuations of Swedish industry 1869–1912. Studies in the process of industrialisation.* Stockholm 1961.

Karlsson, Åsa, 'Den kända och okända Orienten. Svenska resenärer i Osmanska riket under 1700-talet', in Hanna Hodacs and Åsa Karlsson (eds.), *Från Karakorum till Siljan.* Lund 2000, pp.197–225.

Kaukiainen, Yrjö, *Sailing into twilight. Finnish shipping in an age of transport revolution, 1860–1914.* Helsinki 1991.

Kaukiainen, Yrjö, *History of Finnish Shipping.* London and New York 1993.

Kennedy, Paul M., 'The Costs and Benefits of British Imperialism 1846–1914', in *Past and Present,* 1989, pp. 186–192.

Kennedy, Paul M., *The Rise and Fall of British Naval Mastery.* London 1976.

Klooster, Willem Wubbo, *Illicit Riches. The Dutch trade in the Caribbean, 1648–1795,* (PhD dissertation) Leiden 1995.

Koerner, Lisbet, *Linnaeus. Nature and Nation.* Cambridge (Mass.) 1999.

Koninckx, Christian, *The First and Second Charters of the Swedish East India Company (1731–1766).* Kortrijk 1980.

Krantz, Olle, *Utrikeshandel, ekonomisk tillväxt och strukturförändring efter 1850.* Malmö 1987.

Krëuger, Johan Henrik. *Sveriges förhållanden till Barbareskstaterna i Afrika.* Stockholm 1856.

Kumlien, Kjell, 'Johan Liljecrants, Liljecrantz (Westerman)', in *SBL*, vol. 23, Stockholm 1980–81.

Lane, Frederic C., 'Economic Consequences of Organized Violence', in *The Journal of Economic History*, 1958, pp. 401–417.

Lane, Frederic C., 'Oceanic Expansion: Force and Enterprise in the Creation of Oceanic Commerce', in *The Journal of Economic History*, 1950, pp. 19–31.

Lane, Frederic C., 'Tonnages, Medieval and Modern. Economic History Review', 1964, pp. 213–233.

Larsson, Jan, *Diplomati och industriellt genombrott. Svenska exportsträvanden på Kina, 1906–1916.* Uppsala 1977.

Lindmark, Daniel, 'Swedish Lutherans Encountering Religious Diversity in Colonial America: From American mission studies to American religious history', in Daniel Lindmark (ed.), *Swedishness Reconsidered. Three centuries of Swedish-American identities.* Umeå 1999, pp. 13–45.

Lindvall, Axel, 'Bidrag til oplysning om Danmark-Norges Handel og Skibfart 1800–1807', in *Historisk tidskrift* (Danish), 1917, pp. 387–478.

Linné, Carl von, *Anmärkningar om thée och thée-drickandet.* Stockholm (first printed 1745), 1963.

Lucassen, Jan and Unger, Richard W., 'Labour productivity in Ocean shipping, 1450–1875', in *International Journal of Maritime History*, 2000/2, pp. 127–141.

Magnusson, Lars and Nyberg, Klas, *Konsumtion och industrialisering i Sverige 1820–1914. Ett ekonomisk-historiskt forskningsprogram*, Uppsala Papers in Economic History, No 38, Uppsala 1995.

Magnusson, Lars, *Korruption och borgerlig ordning. Naturrätt och ekonomisk diskurs i Sverige under Frihetstiden*, Uppsala Papers in Economic History, No 20, Uppsala 1989.

Magnusson, Lars, *Mercantilism. The shaping of an economic language.* London and New York 1994.

Magnusson, Lars, *Sveriges ekonomiska historia.* Stockholm 1996.

Malmborg, Mikael af, *Neutrality and State-Building in Sweden.* Basingstoke 2001.

Marzagalli, Silvia, 'A Vital Link in Wartime. The Organization of a Trade and Shipping Network between the United States and Bordeaux, 1793–1815', in Olaf Uwe Janzen (ed.), *Merchant Organization and Maritime Trade in the North Atlantic, 1660–1815. Research in Maritime History* No 15. St. John's, Newfoundland 1998, pp. 199–219.

McCusker, John J. and Morgan, Kenneth (eds.), *The Early Modern Atlantic economy*, Cambridge 2000.

McCusker, John J. and Menard, Russell, *The Economy of British America, 1607–1789.* Chapel Hill 1985.

McCusker, John J., 'The Tonnage of Ships Engaged in British Colonial Trade During the Eighteenth Century', in John J. McCusker, *Essays in the Economic History of the Atlantic World.* London and New York 1997, pp. 43–75.

McCusker, John J., *Essays in the Economic History of the Atlantic World.* London and New York 1997

Mellander, Karl, 'Svensk-portugisiska förbindelser under Sveriges stormaktstid', in *Historisk tidskrift* (Swedish), 1926, pp. 109–139, and 1927, pp. 337–405.

Menard, Russell R., 'Transport Costs and long-range trade, 1300–1800. Was there a European 'transport revolution' in the early modern era?', in James D. Tracy (ed.), *The political economy of merchant empires.* Cambridge 1991.

Mitchell, B.R., (ed.), *International Historical Statistics – Europe 1750–1993.* London 1998.

Mui, Hoh-cheung, and Mui, Lorna H., *The Management of Monopoly. A Study of the East India Company's Conduct of its Tea Trade, 1784–1833.* Vancouver 1984.

251

Müller, Leos and Ojala, Jari, 'Consular Services of the Nordic Countries during the Eighteenth and Nineteenth Centuries: Did they really work?' in Gordon Boyce and Richard Gorski (eds.), *Resources and Infrastructures in the Maritime Economy, 1500–2000, Research in Maritime History,* No. 22, St. John's, Newfoundland 2002, pp. 23–41.

Müller, Leos, 'The Swedish East India Trade and International Markets: Re-exports of teas, 1731–1813', in *Scandinavian Economic History Review,* 2003/3, pp. 28–44.

Müller, Leos, 'Sjömakten och den civila sjöfarten i Sverige 1650–1809', in Hans Norman (ed.), *Skärgårdsflottan. Uppbyggnad, militär användning och förankring i det svenska samhället 1700–1824.* Lund 2000, pp. 342–352.

Müller, Leos, 'Swedish-American Trade and the Swedish Consular Service, 1780–1840', in *International Journal of Maritime History,* 2002/1, pp. 1–16.

Müller, Leos, *The Merchant Houses of Stockholm, c. 1640–1800. A Comparative Study of Early–Modern Entrepreneurial Behaviour.* Uppsala 1998.

Nelson, Philip K., *Carl Bernhard Wadström. Mannen bakom myterna.* Norrköping 1998.

Nilsson, Torbjörn, 'Striden om konsulerna: unionspolitik och modernisering 1870–1905. Om konsulsutnämningar i den svensk-norska unionen', in Kent Zetterberg and Gunnar Åselius (eds.), *Historia, krig och statskonst.* Stockholm 2000, pp. 261–288.

Nilzén, Göran, 'Anders Nordencrantz som konsul i Portugal. En studie över bitterhetens ideologiska och politiska följder', in *Personhistorisk tidskrift,* 1987, pp. 38–49.

North, Douglass C. 'Ocean Freight Rates and Economic Development 1750–1913', in *Industrial Revolutions. Commercial and Financial Services.* vol. 11 [reprint, 1958], Oxford–Cambridge 1994, pp. 215–233

North, Douglass C., 'Sources of Productivity Change in Ocean Shipping, 1600–1850', in *The Journal of Political Economy,* 1968/5, pp. 953–970.

North, Douglass C., and Thomas, Robert Paul, *The Rise of the Western World. A New Economic History.* Cambridge 1979.

North, Douglass C., *Institutions, Institutional Change and Economic Performance.* Cambridge (Mass.) 1990.

Nyström, Johan Fredrik, *De svenska ostindiska kompanierna: historisk-statistisk framställning.* Göteborg 1883.

Nyström, Per, *Stadsindustriens arbetare före 1800-talet.* Stockholm 1955.

O'Rourke, Kevin H. and Williamson, Jeffrey G., 'After Columbus: Explaining Europe's Overseas Trade Boom, 1500–1800', in *The Journal Economic History,* 2002/2, (2002b), pp. 417–456.

O'Rourke, Kevin H. and Williamson, Jeffrey G., 'When did globalisation begin?', in *European Review of Economic History,* 2002, (2002a), pp. 23–50.

O'Rourke, Kevin H. and Williamson, Jeffrey G., *Globalization and History. The Evolution of a Nineteenth-Century Atlantic Economy.* Cambridge (Mass.) 1999.

O'Brien, Patrick, 'European Economic Development: The Contribution of the Periphery', in *The Economic History Review,* 1982/1, pp. 1–18.

Ödell, Anders Svensson, *Svensk agent ved Sundet: Toldkommissær og agent i Helsingør Anders Svenssons depecher til Gustav II Adolf og Axel Oxenstierna 1621–1626.* Leo Tandrup, (ed.), Aarhus 1971.

Ojala, Jari, 'Approaching Europe: The merchant networks between Finland and Europe during the eighteenth and nineteenth centuries', in *European Review of Economic History,* 1997/1 (1997a), pp. 323–352.

Ojala, Jari, 'Productivity and Technological Change in Eighteenth and Nineteenth-Century Sea Transport. A Case Study of Sailing Ship Efficiency in Kokkola, Finland 1721–1913', in *International Journal of Maritime History,* 1997/1, pp. 93–123.

Ojala, Jari, *Tehokasta Liiketoimintaa Pohjanmaan Pikku-Kaupungeissa. Purjemerenkulun kannattavuus ja tuottavuus 1700–1800-luvulla.* Helsinki 1999.

Ojala, Jari, *Tuhannen purjelaivan kaupunki. Kokkolan purjemerenkulun historia.* Kokkola 1996.

Olán, Eskil, *Sjörövarna på Medelhavet och Levantiska compagniet. Historien om Sveriges gamla handel med Orienten.* Stockholm 1921.

Owen Jansson, Sam, 'Om last och lästetal', in *Sjöhistorisk Årsbok*, 1945–46, pp. 27–48.

Padfield, Peter, *Maritime Supremacy & The Opening of the Western Mind. Naval Campaigns that Shaped the Modern World 1588–1782.* London 1999.

Platt, Desmond C.M., 'The Role of the British Consular Service in Overseas Trade 1825–1914', in *The Economic History Review*, 1963/3, pp. 494–512.

Platt, Desmond C.M., *The Cinderella Service. British Consuls since 1825.* Hamden (Conn.) 1971.

Pomeranz, Kenneth, *The Great Divergence. China, Europe, and the Making of the Modern World Economy*, Princeton 2000.

Postma, Johannes, 'Breaching the Mercantile Barriers of the Dutch Colonial Empire: North American Trade with Surinam during the Eighteenth Century', in Olaf Uwe Janzen (ed.), *Merchant Organization and Maritime Trade in the North Atlantic, 1660–1815. Research in Maritime History*, No 15. St. John's, Newfoundland 1998, pp. 107–131.

Rabuzzi, Daniel A., 'Cutting Out The Middleman? American Trade In Northern Europe, 1783–1815', in Olaf Uwe Janzen (ed.), *Merchant Organization and Maritime Trade in the North Atlantic, 1660–1815. Research in Maritime History*, No 15. St. John's, Newfoundland 1998, pp. 175–197.

Rålamb, Claes, *Diarium under resa till Konstantinopel 1657–1658.* Stockholm 1963.

Rasch, Aage, 'American trade in the Baltic, 1783–1807', in *Scandinavian Economic History Review*, 1965, pp. 31–64.

Rimborg, Bertil, *Magnus Durell och Danmark.* Göteborg 1997.

Rosman, Holger and Munthe, Arne, *Släkten Arfwedson. Bilder ur Stockholms handelshistoria under tre århundraden.* Stockholm 1945.

Runblom, Harald, *Svenska företag i Latinamerika. Etableringsmönster och förhandlingstaktik 1900–1940.* Uppsala 1971.

Runeby, Nils, *Den nya världen och den gamla. Amerikabild och emigrationsuppfattning i Sverige 1820–1860.* Uppsala 1969.

Salvo, Carmen, 'Il ruolo instituzionale e la composizione sociale del Consolato del Mare di Messina tra Medio Evo ed Età Moderna', in Carmel Vassallo (ed.), *Consolati di Mare and Chambers of Commerce.* Malta 2000, pp. 17–27.

Samuelsson, Kurt, *De stora köpmanshusen i Stockholm 1730–1815. En studie i den svenska handelskapitalismens historia.* Stockholm 1951.

Schön, Lennart, 'Internal and external factors in Swedish industrialization', in *Scandinavian Economic History Review*, 1997, pp. 209–223.

Schön, Lennart, *En modern svensk ekonomisk historia. Tillväxt och omvandling under två sekel.* Stockholm 2000.

Scott, James Brown (ed.), *The Armed Neutralities of 1780 and 1800. A Collection of Official Documents Preceded by the View of Representative Publicists.* New York 1918.

Shepherd, James F. and Walton, Gary M., *Shipping Maritime Trade, and the Economic Development of Colonial North America.* Cambridge 1972.

Sicking, Louis, *Zeemacht en onmacht. Maritieme politiek in de Nederlanden, 1488–1558.* Amsterdam 1998.

Simonsson, Ivar, 'Arfwedson', in *SBL*, vol. 2, Stockholm 1920.

Simonsson, Ivar, 'Bellman', in *SBL*, vol. 3, Stockholm 1922.

Sprinchorn, Carl, 'Madagaskar och dess sjöröfvare i Karl XII:s historia', in *Karolinska förbundets årsbok*, 1921, pp. 241–260

Sprinchorn, Carl, 'Sjuttonhundratalets planer och förslag till Svensk kolonisation i främmande världsdelar', in *Historisk tidskrift* (Swedish), 1923, pp. 109–162.

Steensgaard, Niels, 'Consuls and Nations in the Levant from 1570–1650', in *Scandinavian Economic History Review,* 1967, pp. 13–55.

Sundström, Ulf, 'En gustaviansk sjöofficer. Johan Herman Schutzercrantz 1762–1821', in Hans Norman (ed.), *Skärgårdsflottan. Uppbyggnad, militär användning och förankring i det svenska samhället 1700–1824.* Lund 2000, pp. 279–290.

Svenskt Biografiskt Lexikon, (*SBL*), Stockholm 1918–.

Svenson, Sven G., *Gattjina traktaten 1799. Studier i Gustaf IV Adolfs utrikespolitik 1796–1800.* Uppsala 1952.

Svensson, Artur S. (ed.), *Svenska flottans historia.* Malmö 1943.

Sveriges och Norges traktater med främmande magter, 1815–1845, vol. 10, Stockholm 1896.

Sveriges traktater med främmande magter. 1632–1645, vol. 5, Stockholm 1909.

Sveriges traktater med främmande magter. 1723–1771. vol. 8, Stockholm 1922.

Swärd, Sven Ola, *Latinamerika i svensk politik under 1810- och 1820-talen.* Uppsala 1949.

Swedish Passenger Arrivals in the United States 1820–1850, Nils William Olsson and Erik Wikén (eds.), Stockholm 1995.

The Statistical History of the United States. From Colonial Times to the Present, New York 1976.

Tingbrand, Per, 'A Swedish Interlude in the Caribbean', in *Forum navale,* No. 57, 2002, pp. 64–92.

Tiselius, Carl A., *Göteborg under kontinentaltiden. Perioden 1808–1810.* Göteborg 1935.

Trulsson, Sven G., *British and Swedish policies and strategies in the Baltic after the Peace of Tilsit in 1807. A Study of Decision-Making.* Lund 1976.

Tunberg, Sven and others, *Den svenska utrikesförvaltningens historia.* Uppsala 1935.

Unger, Richard W., 'The Tonnage of Europe's Merchant Fleets, 1300–1800', in *American Neptune,* 1992/4, pp. 247–261.

Vallerö, Rolf, 'von Hökerstedt, Jacob Olofsson', *SBL,* vol. 19, Stockholm 1971–73.

Vallerö, Rolf, *Svensk handels- och sjöfartsstatistik 1637–1813. En tillkomsthistorisk undersökning.* Stockholm 1969.

Vassallo, Carmel, 'The Consular Network of XVIII-Century Malta', in *Proceedings of History Week 1994,* (The Malta Historical Society) Malta 1996, pp. 51–62.

Vella, Sebastian, 'The bureaucracy of the Consolato del Mare in Malta (1697–1724)', in Carmel Vassallo (ed.), *Consolati di Mare and Chambers of Commerce.* Malta 2000, pp. 69–80.

Ventegodt, Ole, *Redere, rejser og regnskaber. Et par flensborgske partrederiregnskaber 1783–1812.* Flensborg 1989.

Ville, Simon, 'Total Factor Productivity in the English shipping Industry. The Northeast Coal Trade, 1700–1850', in *Economic History Review,* 1986/3, pp. 355–370.

Virrankoski, Pentti, 'Anders Chydenius and the government of Gustavus III of Sweden in the 1770s', in *Scandinavian Journal of History,* 1988, pp. 107–119.

Virrankoski, Pentti, *Anders Chydenius. Demokratisk politiker in upplysningens tid.* Stockholm 1995.

Vries, Jan de and Woude, Ad van der, *The First Modern Economy. Success, Failure, and Perseverance of the Dutch Economy, 1500–1815.* Cambridge 1997.

Wadström, Carl Bernhard, *An Essay on Colonization. Particularly Applied to the Western Coast of Africa with Some Free Thoughts on Cultivation and Commerce* [1794], New York 1968.

Wahlström, Lydia, *Sverige och England under revolutionskrigens början.* Stockholm 1917.

Wallerstein, Immanuel, *The modern world-system.* 3 vols, New York 1974–89.

Walton, Gary M., 'Sources of Productivity Change in American Colonial Shipping, 1675–1775', in *The Economic History Review*, 1967/1, pp. 67–78.

Wandel, C.F, *Danmark og Barbareskerne 1746–1845*. København 1919.

Weibull, Jörgen, *Inför unionsupplösningen 1905. Konsulatfrågan*. Stockholm 1962.

Windler, Christian, 'Tributes and presents in Franco-Tunisian diplomacy', in *Journal of Early Modern History*, 2000/4, pp. 168–199.

Index

Acta Universitatis Upsaliensis
STUDIA HISTORICA UPSALIENSIA

Department of History, University of Uppsala,
S:t Larsgatan 2, SE-753 10 Uppsala, Sweden

1. *Gustaf Jonasson:* Karl XII och hans rådgivare. Den utrikespolitiska maktkampen i Sverige 1697–1702. 1960.
2. *Sven Lundkvist:* Gustav Vasa och Europa. Svensk handels- och utrikespolitik 1534–1557. 1960.
3. *Tage Linder:* Biskop Olof Wallquists politiska verksamhet till och med riksdagen 1789. 1960.
4. *Carl Göran Andræ:* Kyrka och frälse i Sverige under äldre medeltid. 1960.
5. *Bengt Henningsson:* Geijer som historiker. 1961.
6. *Nils Runeby:* Monarchia mixta. Maktfördelningsdebatt i Sverige under den tidigare stormaktstiden. 1962.
7. *Åke Hermansson:* Karl IX och ständerna. Tronfrågan och författningsutvecklingen 1598–1611. 1962.
8. Hundra års historisk diskussion. Historiska föreningen i Upsala 1862–1962. 1962.
9. *Sten Carlsson:* Byråkrati och borgarstånd under frihetstiden. 1963.
10. *Gunnar Christie Wasberg:* Forsvarstanke og suverenitetsprinsipp. Kretsen om Aftenposten i den unionspolitiske debatt 1890–mars 1905. 1963.
11. *Kurt Ågren:* Adelns bönder och kronans. Skatter och besvär i Uppland 1650–1680. 1964.
12. *Michael Nordberg:* Les ducs et la royauté. Etudes sur la rivalité des ducs d'Orléans et de Bourgogne 1392–1407. 1964.
13. *Stig Hadenius:* Fosterländsk unionspolitik. Majoritetspartiet, regeringen och unionsfrågan 1888–1899. 1964.
14. *Stellan Dahlgren:* Karl X Gustav och reduktionen. 1964.
15. *Rolf Torstendahl:* Källkritik och vetenskapssyn i svensk historisk forskning 1820–1920. 1964.
16. *Stefan Björklund:* Oppositionen vid 1823 års riksdag. Jordbrukskris och borgerlig liberalism. 1964.
17. *Håkan Berggren & Göran B. Nilsson:* Liberal socialpolitik 1853–1884. Två studier. 1965.
18. *Torsten Burgman:* Svensk opinion och diplomati under rysk-japanska kriget 1904–1905. 1965.
19. *Erik Wärenstam:* Sveriges Nationella Ungdomsförbund och högern 1928–1934. 1965.
20. *Torgny Nevéus:* Ett betryggande försvar. Värnplikten och arméorganisationen i svensk politik 1880–1885. 1965.
21. *Staffan Runestam:* Förstakammarhögern och rösträttsfrågan 1900–1907. 1966.
22. *Stig Ekman:* Slutstriden om representationsreformen. 1966.
23. *Gunnar Herrström:* 1927 års skolreform. En Studie i svensk skolpolitik 1918–1927. 1966.
24. *Sune Åkerman:* Skattereformen 1810. Ett experiment med progressiv inkomstskatt. 1967.
25. *Göran B. Nilsson:* Självstyrelsens problematik. Undersökningar i svensk landstingshistoria 1839–1928. 1967.
26. *Klaus-Richard Böhme:* Bremisch-verdische Staatsfinanzen 1645–1676. Die schwedische Krone als deutsche Landesherrin. 1967.
27. *Gustaf Jonasson:* Karl XII:s polska politik 1702–1703. 1968.
28. *Hans Landberg:* Statsfinans och kungamakt. Karl X Gustav inför polska kriget. 1969.
29. *Rolf Torstendahl:* Mellan nykonservatism och liberalism. Idébrytningar inom högern och bondepartierna 1918–1934. 1969.
30. *Nils Runeby:* Den nya världen och den gamla. Amerikabild och emigrationsuppfattning i Sverige 1820–1860. 1969.
31. *Fred Nilsson:* Emigrationen från Stockholm till Nordamerika 1880–1893. En studie i urban utvandring. 1970.
32. *Curt Johanson:* Lantarbetarna i Uppland 1918–1930. En studie i facklig taktik och organisation. 1970.
33. *Arndt Öberg:* De yngre mössorna och deras utländska bundsförvanter 1765–1769. Med särskild hänsyn till de kommersiella och politiska förbindelserna med Storbritannien, Danmark och Preussen. 1970.
34. *Torgny Börjeson:* Metall 20 – Fackföreningen och människan. 1971.
35. *Harald Runblom:* Svenska företag i Latinamerika. Etableringsmönster och förhandlingstaktik 1900–1940. 1971.
36. *Hans Landberg, Lars Ekholm, Roland Nordlund & Sven A. Nilsson:* Det kontinentala krigets ekonomi. Studier i krigsfinansiering under svensk stormaktstid. 1971.
37. *Sture Lindmark:* Swedish America 1914–1932. Studies in Ethnicity with Emphasis on Illinois and Minnesota. 1971.
38. *Ulf Beijbom:* Swedes in Chicago. A Demographic and Social Study of the 1846–1880 Immigration. 1971.
39. *Staffan Smedberg:* Frälsebonderörelser i Halland och Skåne 1772–76. 1972.
40. *Björn Rondahl:* Emigration, folkomflyttning och säsongarbete i ett sågverksdistrikt i södra Häl-

singland 1865–1910. Söderala kommun med särskild hänsyn till Ljusne industrisamhälle. 1972.

41. *Ann-Sofie Kälvemark:* Reaktionen mot utvandringen. Emigrationsfrågan i svensk debatt och politik 1901–1904. 1972.

42. *Lars-Göran Tedebrand:* Västernorrland och Nordamerika 1875–1913. Utvandring och återinvandring. 1972.

43. *Ann-Marie Petersson:* Nyköping under frihetstiden. Borgare och byråkrater i den lokala politiken. 1972.

44. *Göran Andolf:* Historien på gymnasiet. Undervisning och läroböcker 1820–1965. 1972.

45. *Jan Sundin:* Främmande studenter vid Uppsala universitet före andra väldskriget. En studie i studentmigration. 1973.

46. *Christer Öhman:* Nyköping och hertigdömet 1568–1622. 1973. (Ej i bokhandeln)

47. *Sune Åkerman, Ingrid Eriksson, David Gaunt, Anders Norberg, John Rogers & Kurt Ågren:* Aristocrats, Farmers and Proletarians. Essays in Swedish Demographic History. 1973.

48. *Uno Westerlund:* Borgarsamhällets upplösning och självstyrelsens utveckling i Nyköping 1810–1880. 1973. (Ej i bokhandeln)

49. *Sven Hedenskog:* Folkrörelserna i Nyköping 1880–1915. Uppkomst, social struktur och politisk aktivitet. 1973. (Ej i bokhandeln)

50. *Berit Brattne:* Bröderna Larsson. En studie i svensk emigrantagentverksamhet under 1880-talet. 1973.

51. *Anders Kullberg:* Johan Gabriel Stenbock och reduktionen. Godspolitik och ekonomiförvaltning 1675–1705. 1973.

52. *Gunilla Ingmar:* Monopol på nyheter. Ekonomiska och politiska aspekter på svenska och internationella nyhetsbyråers verksamhet. 1870–1919. 1973.

53. *Sven Lundkvist:* Politik, nykterhet och reformer. En studie i folkrörelsernas politiska verksamhet 1900–1920. 1974.

54. *Kari Tarkiainen:* "Vår gamble Arffiende Ryssen". Synen på Ryssland i Sverige 1595–1621 och andra studier kring den svenska Rysslandsbilden från tidigare stormaktstid. 1974.

55. *Bo Öhngren:* Folk i rörelse. Samhällsutveckling, flyttningsmönster och folkrörelser i Eskilstuna 1870–1900. 1974.

56. *Lars Ekholm:* Svensk krigsfinansiering 1630–1631. 1974.

57. *Roland Nordlund:* Krig på avveckling. Sverige och tyska kriget 1633. 1974.

58. *Clara Nevéus:* Trälarna i landskapslagarnas samhälle. Danmark och Sverige. 1974.

59. *Bertil Johansson:* Social differentiering och kommunalpolitik. Enköping 1863–1919. 1974.

60. *Jan Lindroth:* Idrottens väg till folkrörelse. Studier i svensk idrottsrörelse till 1915. 1974.

61. *Richard B. Lucas:* Charles August Lindbergh, Sr. A Case Study of Congressional Insurgency, 1906–1912. 1974.

62. *Hans Norman:* Från Bergslagen till Nordamerika. Studier i migrationsmönster, social rörlighet och demografisk struktur med utgångspunkt från Örebro län 1851–1915. 1974.

63. *David Gaunt:* Utbildning till statens tjänst. En kollektivbiografi av stormaktstidens hovrättsauskultanter. 1975.

64. *Eibert Ernby:* Adeln och bondejorden. En studie rörande skattefrälset i Oppunda härad under 1600-talet. 1975.

65. *Bo Kronborg & Thomas Nilsson:* Stadsflyttare. Industrialisering, migration och social mobilitet med utgångspunkt från Halmstad, 1870–1910. 1975.

66. *Rolf Torstendahl:* Teknologins nytta. Motiveringar för det svenska tekniska utbildningsväsendets framväxt framförda av riksdagsmän och utbildningsadministratörer 1810–1870. 1975.

67. *Allan Ranehök:* Centralmakt och domsmakt. Studier kring den högsta rättskipningen i kung Magnus Erikssons länder 1319–1355. 1975.

68. *James Cavallie:* Från fred till krig. De finansiella problemen kring krigsutbrottet år 1700. 1975.

69. *Ingrid Åberg:* Förening och politik. Folkrörelsernas politiska aktivitet i Gävle under 1880-talet. 1975.

70. *Margareta Revera:* Gods och gård 1650–1680. Magnus Gabriel De la Gardies godsbildning och godsdrift i Västergötland. I. 1975.

71. *Aleksander Loit:* Kampen om feodalräntan. Reduktionen och domänpolitiken i Estland 1655–1710. I. 1975.

72. *Torgny Lindgren:* Banko- och riksgäldsrevisionerna 1782–1807. "De redliga män, som bevakade ständers rätt". 1975.

73. *Rolf Torstendahl:* Dispersion of Engineers in a Transitional Society. Swedish Technicians 1860–1940. 1975.

74. From Sweden to America. A History of Migration. Red. Harald Runblom & Hans Norman. 1976.

75. *Svante Jakobsson:* Från fädernejorden till förfäders land. Estlandssvenskt bondfolks rymningar till Stockholm 1811–1834; motiv, frekvens, personliga konsekvenser. 1976.

76. *Lars Åkerblom:* Sir Samuel Hoare och Etiopienkonflikten 1935. 1976.

77. *Gustaf Jonasson:* Per Edvin Sköld 1946–1951. 1976.

78. *Sören Winge:* Die Wirtschaftliche Aufbau-Vereinigung (WAV) 1945–53. Entwicklung und Politik einer ,,undoktrinären" politischen Partei in der Bundesrepublik in der ersten Nachkriegszeit. 1976.

79. *Klaus Misgeld:* Die ,,Internationale Gruppe demokratischer Sozialisten" in Stockholm 1942–1945. Zur sozialistischen Friedensdiskussion während des Zweiten Weltkrieges. 1976.

80. *Roland Karlman:* Evidencing Historical Classifications in British and American Historiography 1930–1970. 1976.

81. *Berndt Fredriksson:* Försvarets finansiering. Svensk krigsekonomi under skånska kriget 1675–79. 1976.

82. *Karl Englund:* Arbetarförsäkringsfrågan i svensk politik 1884–1901. 1976.

83. *Nils Runeby:* Teknikerna, vetenskapen och kulturen. Ingenjörsundervisning och ingenjörsorganisationer i 1870-talets Sverige. 1976.

84. *Erland F. Josephson:* SKP och Komintern 1921–1924. Motsättningarna inom Sveriges Kommunistiska Parti och dess relationer till den Kommunistiska Internationalen. 1976.

85. *Sven Lundkvist:* Folkrörelserna i det svenska samhället 1850–1920. 1977.

86. *Bo Öhngren:* GEOKOD. En kodlista för den administrativa indelningen i Sverige 1862–1951. 1977.

87. *Mike L. Samson:* Population Mobility in the Netherlands 1880–1910. A Case Study of Wisch in the Achterhoek. 1977.

88. *Ugbana Okpu:* Ethnic Minority Problems in Nigerian Politics: 1960–1965. 1977.

89. *Gunnar Carlsson:* Enköping under frihetstiden. Social struktur och lokal politik. 1977.

90. *Sten Carlsson:* Fröknar, mamseller, jungfrur och pigor. Ogifta kvinnor i det svenska ståndssamhället. 1977.

91. *Rolf Pålbrant:* Arbetarrörelsen och idrotten 1919–1939. 1977.

92. *Viveca Halldin Norberg:* Swedes in Haile Selassie's Ethiopia 1924–1952. A Study in Early Development Co-operation. 1977.

93. *Holger Wester:* Innovationer i befolkningsrörligheten. En studie av spridningsförlopp i befolkningsrörligheten utgående från Petalax socken i Österbotten. 1977.

94. *Jan Larsson:* Diplomati och industriellt genombrott. Svenska exportsträvanden på Kina 1906–1916. 1977.

95. *Rolf Nygren:* Disciplin, kritikrätt och rättssäkerhet. Studier kring militieombudsmannaämbetets (MO) doktrin- och tillkomsthistoria 1901–1915. 1977.

96. *Kenneth Awebro:* Gustav III:s räfst med ämbetsmännen 1772–1799 – aktionerna mot landshövdingarna och Göta hovrätt. 1977.

97. *Eric De Geer:* Migration och influensfält. Studier av emigration och intern migration i Finland och Sverige 1816–1972. 1977.

98. *Sigbrit Plaenge Jacobson:* 1766-års allmänna fiskestadga. Dess uppkomst och innebörd med hänsyn till Bottenhavsfiskets rättsfrågor. 1978.

99. *Ingvar Flink:* Strejkbryteriet och arbetets frihet. En studie av svensk arbetsmarknad fram till 1938. 1978.

100. *Ingrid Eriksson & John Rogers:* Rural Labor and Population Change. Social and Demographic Developments in East-Central Sweden during the Nineteenth Century. 1978.

101. *Kerstin Moberg:* Från tjänstehjon till hembiträde. En kvinnlig låglönegrupp i den fackliga kampen 1903–1946. 1978.

102. *Mezri Bdira:* Relations internationales et sousdéveloppement. La Tunisie 1857–1864. 1978.

103. *Ingrid Hammarström, Väinö Helgesson, Barbro Hedvall, Christer Knuthammar & Bodil Wallin:* Ideologi och socialpolitik i 1800-talets Sverige. Fyra studier. 1978.

104. *Gunnar Sundberg:* Partipolitik och regionala intressen 1755–1766. Studier kring det bottniska handelstvångets hävande. 1978.

105. *Kekke Stadin:* Småstäder, småborgare och stora samhällsförändringar. Borgarnas sociala struktur i Arboga, Enköping och Västervik under perioden efter 1680. 1979.

106. *Åke Lindström:* Bruksarbetarfackföreningar. Metalls avdelningar vid bruken i östra Västmanlands län före 1911. 1979.

107. *Mats Rolén:* Skogsbygd i omvandling. Studier kring befolkningsutveckling, omflyttning och social rörlighet i Revsunds tingslag 1820–1977. 1979.

108. *János Perényi:* Revolutionsuppfattningens anatomi. 1848 års revolutioner i svensk debatt. 1979.

109. *Kent Sivesand:* Skifte och befolkning. Skiftenas inverkan på byar och befolkning i Mälarregionen. 1979.

110. *Thomas Lindkvist:* Landborna i Norden under äldre medeltid. 1979.

111. *Björn M. Edsman:* Lawyers in Gold Coast Politics c. 1900–1945. From Mensah Sarbah to J.B. Danquah. 1979.

112. *Svante Jakobsson:* Osilia–Maritima 1227–1346. Studier kring tillkomsten av svenska bosättningar i Balticum, i synnerhet inom biskopsstiftet Ösel-Wiek. 1980.

113. *Jan Stattin:* Hushållningssällskapen och agrarsamhällets förändring – utveckling och verksamhet under 1800-talets första hälft. 1980.

114. *Bertil Lundvik:* Solidaritet och partitaktik. Den svenska arbetarrörelsen och spanska inbördeskriget 1936–1939. 1980.

115. *Ann-Sofie Kälvemark:* More children of better quality? Aspects on Swedish population policy in the 1930's. 1980.

116. *Anders Norberg:* Sågarnas ö. Alnö och industrialiseringen 1860–1910. 1980.

117. *Jan Lindegren:* Utskrivning och utsugning. Produktion och reproduktion i Bygdeå 1620–1640. 1980.

118. *Gustaf Jonasson:* I väntan på uppbrott? Bondeförbundet/Centerpartiet i regeringskoalitionens slutskede 1956–1957. 1981.

119. *Erland Jansson:* India, Pakistan or Pakhtunistan? The Nationalist Movements in the North-West Frontier Province, 1937–47. 1981.

120. *Ulla-Britt Lithell:* Breast-feeding and Reproduction. Studies in marital fertility and infant mortality in 19th century Finland and Sweden. 1981.

121. *Svenbjörn Kilander:* Censur och propaganda. Svensk informationspolitik under 1900-talets första decennier. 1981.

122. *Håkan Holmberg:* Folkmakt, folkfront, folkdemokrati. De svenska kommunisterna och demokratifrågan 1943–1977. 1982.

123. *Britt-Marie Lundbäck:* En industri kommer till stan. Hudiksvall och trävaruindustrin 1855–1880. 1982.

124. *Torkel Jansson:* Samhällsförändring och sammanslutningsformer. Det frivilliga föreningsväsendets uppkomst och spridning i Husby-Rekarne från omkring 1850 till 1930. 1982.

125. *Per Jansson:* Kalmar under 1600-talet. Omland, handel och krediter. 1982.

126. *Svante Jakobsson:* Fattighushjonets värld i 1800-talets Stockholm. 1982.

127. *Runo Nilsson:* Rallareliv. Arbete, familjemönster och levnadsförhållanden för järnvägsarbetare på

banbyggena i Jämtland–Härjedalen 1912–1928. 1982.

128. *J. Alvar Schilén:* Det västallierade bombkriget mot de tyska storstäderna under andra väldskriget och civilbefolkningens reaktioner i de drabbade städerna. 1983.

129. *Bodil Nävdal-Larsen:* Erik XIV, Ivan Groznyj og Katarina Jagellonica. 1983.

130. *Birgitta Olai:* Storskiftet i Ekebyborna. Svensk jordbruksutveckling avspeglad i en östgötasocken. 1983.

131. *Ann Hörsell:* Borgare, smeder och änkor. Ekonomi och befolkning i Eskilstuna gamla stad och Fristad 1750–1850. 1983.

132. *Ragnar Björk:* Den historiska argumenteringen. Konstruktion, narration och kolligation – förklaringsresonemang hos Nils Ahnlund och Erik Lönnroth. 1983.

133. *Björn Asker:* Officerarna och det svenska samhället 1650–1700. 1983.

134. *Erik Tiberg;* Zur Vorgeschichte des Livländischen Krieges. Die Beziehungen zwischen Moskau und Litauen 1549–1562. 1984.

135. *Bertel Tingström:* Sveriges plåtmynt 1644–1776. En undersökning av plåtmyntens roll som betalningsmedel. 1984.

136. *Curt Ekholm:* Balt- och tyskutlämningen 1945–1946. Omständigheter kring interneringen i läger i Sverige och utlämningen till Sovjetunionen av f d tyska krigsdeltagare. Del 1: Ankomsten och interneringen. 1984. Andra upplagan 1995.

137. *Curt Ekholm:* Balt- och tyskutlämningen 1945–1946. Omständigheter kring interneringen i läger i Sverige och utlämningen till Sovjetunionen av f d tyska krigsdeltagare. Del 2: Utlämningen och efterspelet. 1984. Andra upplagan 1995.

138. *Sven H. Carlson:* Trade and dependency. Studies in the expansion of Europe. 1984.

139. *Torkel Jansson:* Adertonhundratalets associationer. Forskning och problem kring ett sprängfullt tomrum eller sammanslutningsprinciper och föreningsformer mellan två samhällsformationer, c:a 1800–1870. 1985.

140. *Bernt Douhan:* Arbete, kapital och migration. Valloninvandringen till Sverige under 1600-talet. 1985.

141. *Göran Rydeberg:* Skatteköpen i Örebro län 1701–1809. 1985.

142. *Habib Ben Abdallah:* De l'iqta' étatique à l'iqta' militaire. Transition économique et changements sociaux à Baghdad, 247–447 de l'Hégire/861–1055 ap. J. 1986.

143. *Margot Höjfors Hong:* Ölänningar över haven. Utvandringen från Öland 1840–1930 – bakgrund, förlopp, effekter. 1986.

144. *Carl Johan Gardell:* Handelskompani och bondearistokrati. En studie i den sociala strukturen på Gotland omkring 1620. 1986.

145. *Birgitta Olai:* "... till vinnande af ett redigt Storskifte ...". En komparativ studie av storskiftet i fem härader. 1987.

146. *Torkel Jansson:* Agrarsamhällets förändring och landskommunal organisation. En konturteckning av 1800-talets Norden. 1987.

147. *Anders Florén:* Disciplinering och konflikt. Den sociala organiseringen av arbetet: Jäders bruk 1640–1750. 1987.

148. *Tekeste Negash:* Italian Colonialism in Eritrea 1882–1941: Policies, Praxis and Impact. 1988.

149. *Lotta Gröning:* Vägen till makten. SAP:s organisation och dess betydelse för den politiska verksamheten 1900–1933. 1988.

150. *Ove Pettersson:* Byråkratisering eller avbyråkratisering. Administrativ och samhällsorganisatorisk strukturomvandling inom svenskt vägväsende 1885–1985. 1988.

151. *Knut Ohlsson:* Grosshandlare, bönder, småfolk. Trönös skogsnäringar från och med det industriella genombrottet. 1988.

152. *Eva Österberg & Dag Lindström:* Crime and Social Control in Medieval and Early Modern Swedish Towns. 1988.

153. *Marie C. Nelson:* Bitter Bread. The Famine in Norrbotten 1867–1868. 1988.

154. *Gísli Ágúst Gunnlaugsson:* Family and Household in Iceland 1801–1930. Studies in the relationship between demographic and socioeconomic development, social legislation and family and household structures. 1988.

155. *Elsa Lunander:* Borgaren blir företagare. Studier kring ekonomiska, sociala och politiska förhållanden i förändringens Örebro under 1800-talet. 1988.

156. *Ulla-Britt Lithell:* Kvinnoarbete och barntillsyn i 1700- och 1800-talets Österbotten. 1988.

157. *Annette Thörnquist:* Lönearbete eller egen jord? Den svenska lantarbetarrörelsen och jordfrågan 1908–1936. 1989.

158. *Stefán F. Hjartarson:* Kampen om fackföreningsrörelsen. Ideologi och politisk aktivitet på Island 1920–1938. 1989.

159. *György Nováky:* Handelskompanier och kompanihandel. Svenska Afrikakompaniet 1649–1663. En studie i feodal handel. 1990.

160. *Margareta Åman:* Spanska sjukan. Den svenska epidemin 1918–1920 och dess internationella bakgrund. 1990.

161. *Sven A. Nilsson:* De stora krigens tid. Om Sverige som militärstat och bondesamhälle. 1990.

162. *Birgitta Larsson:* Conversion to Greater Freedom? Women, Church and Social Change in Northwestern Tanzania under Colonial Rule. 1991.

163. *Dag Lindström:* Skrå, stad och stat. Stockholm, Malmö och Bergen ca 1350–1622. 1991.

164. *Svenbjörn Kilander:* Den nya staten och den gamla. En studie i ideologisk förändring. 1991.

165. *Christer Öhman:* Den historiska romanen och sanningen. Historiesyn, värdestruktur och empiri i Georg Starbäcks historiska författarskap. 1991.

166. *Maria Ågren:* Jord och gäld. Social skiktning och rättslig konflikt i södra Dalarna ca 1650–1850. 1992.

167. *Stina Nicklasson:* Högerns kvinnor. Problem och resurs för Allmänna valmansförbundet perioden 1900–1936/1937. 1992.

168. *Lars Petterson:* Frihet, jämlikhet, egendom och Bentham. Utvecklingslinjer i svensk folkundervisning mellan feodalism och kapitalism, 1809–1860. 1992.

169. *Alberto Tiscornia:* Statens, godsens eller böndernas socknar? Den sockenkommunala självstyrelsens utveckling i Västerfärnebo, Stora Malm och Jäder 1800–1880. 1992.

170. *Iréne Artæus:* Kvinnorna som blev över. Ensamstående stadskvinnor under 1800-talets första hälft – fallet Västerås. 1992.

171. *Anders Fröjmark:* Mirakler och helgonkult. Linköpings biskopsdöme under senmedeltiden. 1992.

172. *Hernán Horna:* Transport Modernization and Entrepreneurship in Nineteenth Century Colombia. Cisneros & Friends. 1992.

173. *Janne Backlund:* Rusthållarna i Fellingsbro 1684–1748. Indelningsverket och den sociala differentieringen av det svenska agrarsamhället. 1993.

174. *Agneta Breisch:* Frid och fredlöshet. Sociala band och utanförskap på Island under äldre medeltid. 1994.

175. *Åsa Karlsson:* Den jämlike undersåten. Karl XII:s förmögenhetsbeskattning 1713. 1994.

176. *Elisabeth Elgán:* Genus och politik. En jämförelse mellan svensk och fransk abort- och preventivmedelspolitik från sekelskiftet till andra världskriget. 1994.

177. *Lennart Thorslund:* Humanism mot rationalism. Mora 1890–1970: Om två förhållningssätt och deras betydelse i småstadens planeringshistoria. 1995.

178. *Paul A. Levine:* From Indifference to Activism. Swedish Diplomacy and the Holocaust; 1938–1944. 1996. (2nd revised and enlarged edition, with a new postscript by the author. 1998.)

179. *Bengt Nilsson:* Kvinnor i statens tjänst – från biträden till tjänstemän. En aktörsinriktad undersökning av kvinnliga statstjänstemäns organisering, strategier och kamp under 1900-talets första hälft. 1996.

180. *Tsegaye Tegenu:* The Evolution of Ethiopian Absolutism. The Genesis and the Making of the Fiscal Military State, 1696–1913. 1996.

181. *Sören Klingnéus:* Bönder blir vapensmeder. Protoindustriell tillverkning i Närke under 1600- och 1700-talen. 1997.

182. *Dag Blanck:* Becoming Swedish-American. The Construction of an Ethnic Identity in the Augustana Synod, 1860–1917. 1997.

183. *Helene Carlbäck-Isotalo:* Att byta erkännande mot handel. Svensk-ryska förhandlingar 1921–1924. 1997.

184. *Martin Melkersson:* Staten, ordningen och friheten. En studie av den styrande elitens syn på statens roll mellan stormaktstiden och 1800-talet. 1997.

185. *Henrik Ågren:* Tidigmodern tid. Den sociala tidens roll i fyra lokalsamhällen 1650–1730. 1998.

186. *Peter Reinholdsson:* Uppror eller resningar? Samhällsorganisation och konflikt i senmedeltidens Sverige. 1998.

187. *Gudrun Andersson:* Tingets kvinnor och män. Genus som norm och strategi under 1600- och 1700-tal. 1998.

188. *Leos Müller:* The Merchant Houses of Stockholm, c. 1640–1800, A Comparative Study of Early-Modern Entrepreneurial Behaviour. 1998.

189. *Ylva Hasselberg:* Den sociala ekonomin. Familjen Clason och Furudals bruk 1804–1856. 1998.

190. *Marie Lennersand:* Rättvisans och allmogens beskyddare. Den absoluta staten, kommissionerna och tjänstemännen, ca 1680–1730. 1999.

191. *Örjan Simonson.* Den lokala scenen. Torstuna härad som lokalsamhälle under 1600-talet. 1999.

192. *Cecilia Trenter:* Granskningens retorik och historisk vetenskap. Kongnitiv identitet i recensioner i dansk historisk tidskrift, norsk historisk tidsskrift och svensk historisk tidskrift 1965–1990. 1999.

193. *Stefan Johansson:* En omskriven historia. Svensk historisk roman och novell före 1867. 2000.

194. *Martin Linde:* Statsmakt och bondemotstånd. Allmoge och överhet under stora nordiska kriget. 2000.

195. *Lars Båtefalk:* Staten, samhället och superiet. Samhällsorganisatoriska principer och organisatorisk praktik kring dryckenskapsproblemet och nykterhetssträvandena i stat, borgerlig offentlighet och associationsväsende ca 1700–1900. 2000.

196. *Lena Milton:* Folkhemmets barnmorskor. Den svenska barnmorskekårens professionalisering under mellan- och efterkrigstid. 2001.

197. *Maj-Britt Nergård:* Mellan krona och marknad. Utländska och svenska entreprenörer inom svensk järnhantering från ca 1580 till 1700. 2001.

198. *Silke Neunsinger:* Die Arbeit der Frauen – die Krise der Männer. Die Erwerbstätigkeit verheirateter Frauen in Deutschland und Schweden 1919–1939. 2001.

199. *Lars Geschwind:* Stökiga studenter. Social kontroll och identifikation vid universiteten i Uppsala, Dorpat och Åbo under 1600-talet. 2001.

200. *Samuel Edquist:* Nyktra svenskar. Godtemplarrörelsen och den nationella identiteten 1879–1918. 2001.

201. *Torbjörn Eng:* Det svenska väldet. Ett konglomerat av uttrycksformer och begrepp från Vasa till Bernadotte. 2001.

202. *Peter Ericsson:* Stora nordiska kriget förklarat. Karl XII och det ideologiska tilltalet. 2001.

203. *Rosemarie Fiebranz:* Jord, linne eller träkol? Genusordning och hushållsstrategier, Bjuråker 1750–1850. 2002.

204. *Håkan Gunneriusson:* Det historiska fältet. Svensk historievetenskap från 1920-tal till 1957. 2002.

205. *Karin Hassan Jansson:* Kvinnofrid. Synen på våldtäkt och konstruktionen av kön i Sverige 1600–1800. 2002.

206. *Johan Sjöberg:* Makt och vanmakt i fadersväldet. Studentpolitik i Uppsala 1770–1850. 2002.

207. *Hanna Hodacs:* Converging World Views. The European Expansion and Early-Nineteenth-Century Anglo-Swedish Contacts. 2003.

208. *Louise Berglund:* Guds stat och maktens villkor. Politiska ideal i Vadstena kloster, ca 1370–1470. 2003.

209. *Kristina Tegler Jerselius:* Den stora häxdansen. Vidskepelse, väckelse och vetande i Gagnef 1858. 2003.

210. *David Ludvigsson:* The Historian-Filmmaker's Dilemma. Historical Documentaries in Sweden in the Era of Häger and Villius. 2003.

211. *Börje Henningsson:* Det röda Dalarna. Socialdemokrater, anarkosyndikalister och kommunister inom Dalarnas Arbetarrörelse 1906–1937. 2004.

212. *Sofia Ling:* Kärringmedicin och vetenskap. Läkare och kvacksalverianklagade i Sverige omkring 1770–1870. 2004.